Adobe Photoshop
Flash & Dreamweaver CS6
Web Design Portfolio

AGAINST THE CLOCK
mastering graphic technology

Managing Editor: Ellenn Behoriam
Cover & Interior Design: Erika Kendra
Copy Editor: Angelina Kendra

The fonts utilized in these training materials are the property of Against The Clock, Inc., and are supplied to the
legitimate buyers of the Against The Clock training materials solely for use with the exercises and projects provided
in the body of the materials. They may not be used for any other purpose, and under no circumstances may they be
transferred to another individual, nor copied or distributed by any means whatsoever.

A portion of the images supplied in this book are copyright © PhotoDisc, Inc., 201 Fourth Ave., Seattle, WA 98121,
or copyright ©PhotoSpin, 4030 Palos Verdes Dr. N., Suite 200, Rollings Hills Estates, CA. These images are the sole
property of PhotoDisc or PhotoSpin and are used by Against The Clock with the permission of the owners. They may
not be distributed, copied, transferred, or reproduced by any means whatsoever, other than for the completion of the
exercises and projects contained in this Against The Clock training material.

Against The Clock and the Against The Clock logo are trademarks of Against The Clock, Inc., registered in the
United States and elsewhere. References to and instructional materials provided for any particular application program,
operating system, hardware platform, or other commercially available product or products do not represent
an endorsement of such product or products by Against The Clock, Inc.

Photoshop, Acrobat, Illustrator, InDesign, PageMaker, Flash, Dreamweaver, Premiere, and PostScript are trademarks
of Adobe Systems Incorporated. Macintosh is a trademark of Apple Computer, Inc. QuarkXPress is a registered
trademark of Quark, Inc. Word, Excel, Office, Microsoft, and Windows are either registered trademarks or trademarks
of Microsoft Corporation.

Other product and company names mentioned herein may be the trademarks of their respective owners.

10   9   8   7   6   5   4   3   2   1

Print book: 978-1-936201-21-1
Ebook book: 978-1-936201-22-8

4710 28th Street North, Saint Petersburg, FL 33714
800-256-4ATC • www.againsttheclock.com

Acknowledgements

ABOUT AGAINST THE CLOCK

Against The Clock, long recognized as one of the nation's leaders in courseware development, has been publishing high-quality educational materials for the graphic and computer arts industries since 1990. The company has developed a solid and widely-respected approach to teaching people how to effectively utilize graphics applications, while maintaining a disciplined approach to real-world problems.

Having developed the *Against The Clock* and the *Essentials for Design* series with Prentice Hall/Pearson Education, ATC drew from years of professional experience and instructor feedback to develop *The Professional Portfolio Series*, focusing on the Adobe Creative Suite. These books feature step-by-step explanations, detailed foundational information, and advice and tips from industry professionals that offer practical solutions to technical issues.

Against The Clock works closely with all major software developers to create learning solutions that fulfill both the requirements of instructors and the needs of students. Thousands of graphic arts professionals — designers, illustrators, imaging specialists, prepress experts, and production managers — began their educations with Against The Clock training books. These professionals studied at Baker College, Nossi College of Art, Virginia Tech, Appalachian State University, Keiser College, University of South Carolina, Gress Graphic Arts Institute, Hagerstown Community College, Kean University, Southern Polytechnic State University, Brenau University, and many other educational institutions.

ABOUT THE AUTHOR

Erika Kendra holds a BA in History and a BA in English from the University of Pittsburgh. She began her career in the graphic communications industry as an editor at Graphic Arts Technical Foundation before moving to Los Angeles in 2000. Erika is the author or co-author of more than twenty books about Adobe graphic design software. She has also written several books about graphic design concepts such as color reproduction and preflighting, and dozens of articles for online and print journals in the graphics industry. Working with Against The Clock for more than ten years, Erika was a key partner in developing *The Professional Portfolio Series* of software training books.

CONTRIBUTING AUTHORS, ARTISTS, AND EDITORS

A big thank you to the people whose artwork, comments, and expertise contributed to the success of these books:

- **Steve Bird,** Adobe Certified Expert
- **Colleen Bredahl,** United Tribes Technical College
- **John Craft,** Appalachian State University
- **Debbie Davidson,** Against The Clock, Inc
- **Charlie Essers,** photographer, Lancaster, Calif.
- **Chris Hadfield,** Doane College
- **Jennifer Hair,** Shawnee Mission East High School
- **Kelly McCormack,** Adobe Certified Instructor
- **Pam Harris,** University of North Texas at Dallas
- **Brian McDaniel,** Central Georgia Technical College
- **Samantha Schmitz,** Double D Cupcakes, Lancaster, Calif.
- **Richard Schrand,** International Academy of Design & Technology, Nashville, TN
- **Jay Tarby,** John Carroll University
- **Michael Watkins,** Baker College of Flint

Finally, thanks also to **Angelina Kendra**, editor, for making sure that we all said what we meant to say.

Project Goals

Each project begins with a clear description of the overall concepts that are explained in the project; these goals closely match the different "stages" of the project workflow.

The Project Meeting

Each project includes the client's initial comments, which provide valuable information about the job. The Project Art Director, a vital part of any design workflow, also provides fundamental advice and production requirements.

Project Objectives

Each Project Meeting includes a summary of the specific skills required to complete the project.

Real-World Workflow

Projects are broken into logical lessons or "stages" of the workflow. Brief introductions at the beginning of each stage provide vital foundational material required to complete the task.

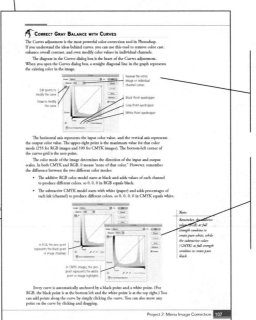

Step-By-Step Exercises

Every stage of the workflow is broken into multiple hands-on, step-by-step exercises.

Visual Explanations

Wherever possible, screen shots are annotated so you can quickly identify important information.

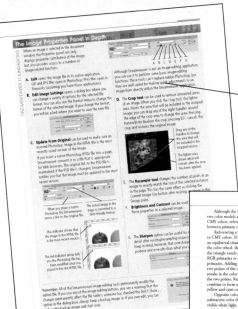

Web Design Foundations

Additional functionality, related tools, and underlying graphic design concepts are included throughout the book.

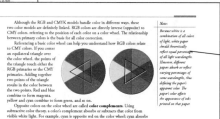

Advice and Warnings

Where appropriate, sidebars provide shortcuts, warnings, or tips about the topic at hand.

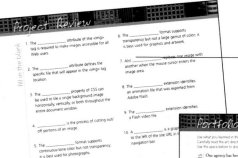

Project Review

After completing each project, you can complete these fill-in-the-blank and short-answer questions to test your understanding of the concepts in the project.

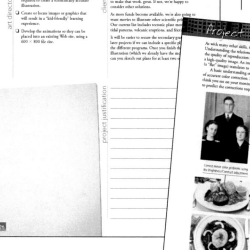

Portfolio Builder Projects

Each step-by-step project is accompanied by a freeform project, allowing you to practice skills and creativity, resulting in an extensive and diverse portfolio of work.

Visual Summary

Using an annotated version of the finished project, you can quickly identify the skills used to complete different aspects of the job.

Projects at a Glance

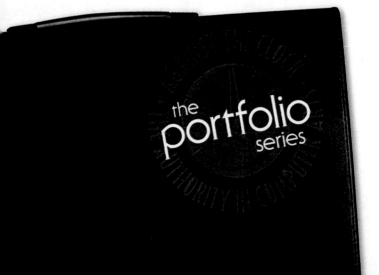

the portfolio series

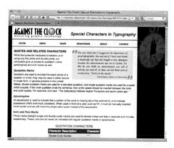

The Against The Clock *Portfolio Series* teaches graphic design software tools and techniques entirely within the framework of real-world projects; we introduce and explain skills where they would naturally fall into a real project workflow.

The project-based approach in *The Professional Portfolio Series* allows you to get in depth with the software beginning in Project 1 — you don't have to read several chapters of introductory material before you can start creating finished artwork.

Our approach also prevents "topic tedium" — in other words, we don't require you to read pages and pages of information about text (for example); instead, we explain text tools and options as part of a larger project (in this case, as part of a book cover).

Clear, easy-to-read, step-by-step instructions walk you through every phase of each job, from creating a new file to saving the finished piece. Wherever logical, we also offer practical advice and tips about underlying concepts and graphic design practices that will benefit students as they enter the job market.

The projects in this book reflect a range of different types of Web design jobs, from correcting menu images to building a complete Web page with CSS. When you finish the projects in this book (and the accompanying Portfolio Builder exercises), you will have a substantial body of work that should impress any potential employer.

The nine CS6 projects are described briefly here; more detail is provided in the full table of contents (beginning on Page viii).

Contents

Project 2   MENU IMAGE CORRECTION   81

Contents

Contents

Contents

PREREQUISITES

The Professional Portfolio Series is based on the assumption that you have a basic understanding of how to use your computer. You should know how to use your mouse to point and click, as well as how to drag items around the screen. You should be able to resize and arrange windows on your desktop to maximize your available space. You should know how to access drop-down menus, and understand how check boxes and radio buttons work. It also doesn't hurt to have a good understanding of how your operating system organizes files and folders, and how to navigate your way around them. If you're familiar with these fundamental skills, then you know all that's necessary to use *The Professional Portfolio Series*.

RESOURCE FILES

All of the files you need to complete the projects in this book — except, of course, the Adobe application files — are on the Student Files Web page at www.againsttheclock.com. See the inside back cover of this book for access information.

Each archive (ZIP) file is named according to the related project (e.g., **WC6_RF_Project1.zip**). At the beginning of each project, you must download the archive file for that project and expand that archive to access the resource files that you need to complete the exercises. Detailed instructions for this process are included in the Interface chapter.

Files required for the related Portfolio Builder exercises at the end of each project are also available on the Student Files page; these archives are also named by project (e.g., **WC6_PB_Project1.zip**).

SYSTEM REQUIREMENTS

The Professional Portfolio Series was designed to work on both Macintosh or Windows computers; where differences exist from one platform to another, we include specific instructions relative to each platform. One issue that remains different from Macintosh to Windows is the use of different modifier keys (Control, Shift, etc.) to accomplish the same task. When we present key commands, we follow the Macintosh/Windows format — Macintosh keys are listed first, then a slash, followed by the Windows key command.

WEB HOSTING

To make Web files accessible to the browsing public, you need to have access to some type of server. On the inside back cover of this book, you have a code that you need to gain access to the required resource files. The same code also provides access to a six-month, free trial Web hosting account at Pair Networks (www.pair.com).

If you don't already have access to an online server, go to **www.pair.com/atc/** to sign up for your hosting account. You must enter your contact information, and the code from the inside back cover of your book. You should then define a user name in the last field; this will become part of the server name for your hosting account.

After clicking Continue in this screen, the resulting message warns that the setup process can take up to one business day (although it is usually about an hour). When the setup process is complete, you will receive an acknowledgement that your request is being processed. You will receive a confirmation email (sent to the email you defined in the Signup Form) with your username and password information. Once you receive the confirmation email, you are ready to complete the final stage of this project.

Adobe Photoshop is the industry-standard application for working with pixels — both manipulating existing ones and creating new ones. Many Photoshop experts specialize in certain types of work. Photo retouching, artistic painting, image compositing, and color correction are only a few types of work you can create with Photoshop. Our goal in this book is to teach you how to use the available tools to succeed with different types of jobs that you might encounter in your professional career.

Although not intended as a layout-design application, you can use Photoshop to combine type, graphics, and images into a finished design; many people create advertisements, book covers, and other projects entirely in Photoshop. Others argue that Photoshop should never be used for layout design; Adobe InDesign is the preferred page-layout application. We do not advocate doing *all* or even *most* layout composite work in Photoshop, but because many people use the application to create composite designs, we feel the projects in this book portray a realistic workflow.

The simple exercises in this introduction are designed to let you explore the Photoshop user interface. Whether you are new to the application or upgrading from a previous version, we highly recommend following these steps to click around and become familiar with the basic workspace. When you begin Project 1, you will be better prepared to jump right in and start pushing pixels.

EXPLORE THE PHOTOSHOP INTERFACE

The first time you launch Photoshop, you will see the default user interface (UI) settings as defined by Adobe. When you relaunch after you or another user has quit, the workspace defaults to the last-used settings — including open panels and the position of those panels on your screen. We designed the following exercise so you can explore different ways of controlling panels in the Photoshop user interface.

1. **Create a new empty folder named WIP (Work in Progress) on any writable disk (where you plan to save your work).**

2. **Download the WC6_RF_InterfacePS.zip archive from the Student Files Web page.**

3. **Macintosh users: Place the ZIP archive in your WIP folder, then double-click the file icon to expand it.**

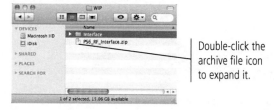

Double-click the archive file icon to expand it.

Windows users: Double-click the ZIP archive file to open it. Click the folder inside the archive and drag it into your primary WIP folder.

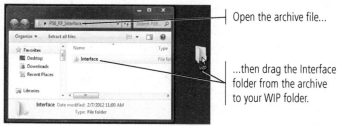

Open the archive file...

...then drag the Interface folder from the archive to your WIP folder.

The resulting **Interface_PS** folder contains all the files you need to complete the exercises in this introduction.

4. **Macintosh users: While pressing Command-Option-Shift, start Photoshop. Click Yes when asked if you want to delete Settings files.**

Windows users: Choose Adobe Photoshop CS6 in the Start menu, and then immediately press Control-Alt-Shift. Click Yes when asked if you want to delete the Settings files.

This step resets Photoshop to the preference settings that are defined by Adobe as the application defaults. This helps to ensure that your application functions in the same way as what we show in our screen shots.

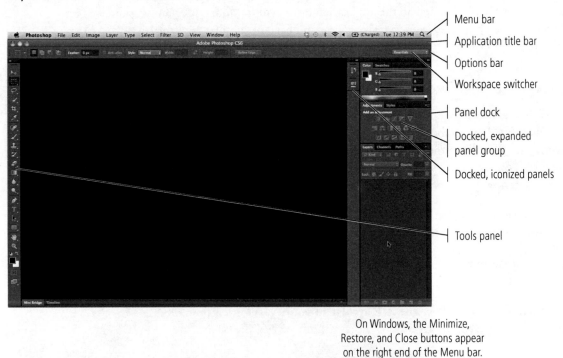

Menu bar
Application title bar
Options bar
Workspace switcher
Panel dock
Docked, expanded panel group
Docked, iconized panels
Tools panel

On Windows, the Minimize, Restore, and Close buttons appear on the right end of the Menu bar.

Menu bar
Options bar

In general, the Macintosh and Windows workspaces are virtually identical, with a few primary exceptions:

- On Macintosh, the application's title bar appears below the Menu bar; the Close, Minimize, and Restore buttons appear on the left side of the title bar, and the Menu bar is not part of the Application frame.
- On Windows, the Close, Minimize, and Restore buttons appear at the right end of the Menu bar, which is part of the overall Application frame.

Also, Macintosh users have two extra menus (consistent with the Macintosh operating system structure). The Apple menu provides access to system-specific commands. The Photoshop menu follows the Macintosh system-standard format for all applications; this menu controls basic application operations such as About, Hide, Preferences, and Quit.

Finally, remember that on Macintosh systems, the Preferences dialog box is accessed in the Photoshop menu; Windows users access the Preferences dialog box from the Edit menu.

Note:

*Many menu commands and options in Photoshop are **toggles**, which means they are either on or off; when an option is checked, it is toggled on (visible or active). You can toggle an active option off by choosing the checked menu command, or toggle an inactive option on by choosing the unchecked menu command.*

Understanding the Application Frame

On Windows, each running application is contained within its own frame; all elements of the application — including the Menu bar, panels, tools, and open documents — are contained within the Application frame.

Adobe also offers the Application frame to Macintosh users as an option for controlling the workspace. When the Application frame is active, the entire workspace exists in a self-contained area that can be moved around the screen. All elements of the workspace (excluding the Menu bar) move when you move the Application frame.

The Application frame is active by default, but you can toggle it off by choosing Window>Application Frame. If the menu option is checked, the Application frame is active; if the menu option is not checked, it is inactive.

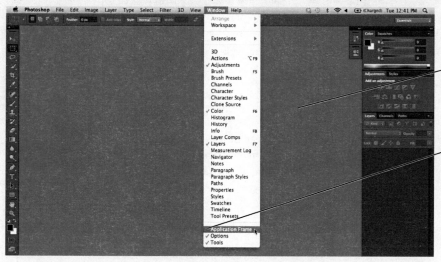

When the Application frame is not active, the desktop is visible behind the workspace elements.

When the Application frame is not active, the option is unchecked in the Window menu.

5. Macintosh users: Choose Photoshop>Preferences>Interface.
Windows users: Choose Edit>Preferences>Interface.

Preferences customize the way many of the program's tools and options function. When you open the Preferences dialog box, the active pane is the one you choose in the Preferences submenu. Once open, however, you can access any of the Preference categories by clicking a different option in the left pane; the right side of the dialog box displays options related to the active category.

If you have used a previous version of Photoshop, you might have already noticed the rather dark appearance of the panels and interface background. In CS6, the application uses a darker "theme" as the default. You can change this color in the Interface pane of the Preferences dialog box.

Note:

*As you work your way through this book, you will learn not only what you can do with these different collections of Preferences, but also **why** and **when** you might want to adjust them.*

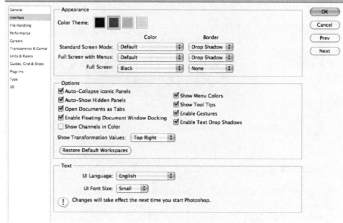

6. Click OK to dismiss the Preferences dialog box, then continue to the next exercise.

EXPLORE THE ARRANGEMENT OF PHOTOSHOP PANELS

As you gain experience and familiarity with Photoshop, you will develop personal artistic and working styles. You will also find that different types of jobs often require different but specific sets of tools. Adobe recognizes this wide range of needs and preferences among users; Photoshop includes a number of options for arranging and managing the numerous panels so you can customize and personalize the workspace to suit your specific needs.

We designed the following exercise to give you an opportunity to explore different ways of controlling Photoshop panels. Because workspace preferences are largely a matter of personal taste, the projects in this book instruct you to use certain tools and panels, but where you place those elements within the interface is up to you.

1. **With Photoshop open, Control/right-click the title bar above the left column of docked panel icons. Choose Auto-Collapse Iconic Panels in the contextual menu to toggle on that option.**

   As we explained in the Getting Started section, when commands are different for the Macintosh and Windows operating systems, we include the different commands in the Macintosh/Windows format. In this case, Macintosh users who do not have right-click mouse capability can press the Control key and click to access the contextual menu. You do not have to press Control *and* right-click to access the menus.

   (If you're using a Macintosh and don't have a mouse with right-click capability, we highly recommend that you purchase one.)

   Control/right-clicking a dock title bar opens the dock contextual menu, where you can change the default panel behavior. If you toggle on the Auto-Collapse Iconic Panels option (which is inactive by default), a panel will collapse as soon as you click away from it.

   Dock title bar ⊢

   This option should be checked (active) after you select it. ⊢

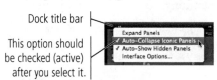

2. **In the left column of the panel dock, hover your mouse cursor over the top button until you see the name of the related panel ("History") in a tool tip.**

3. **Click the History button to expand that panel.**

   The expanded panel is still referred to as a **panel group** even though the History panel is the only panel in the group.

   Panel group drop zone ⊢

   Clicking a panel button expands that panel to the left of the button. ⊢

   Click here to manually collapse the panel back into the dock. ⊢

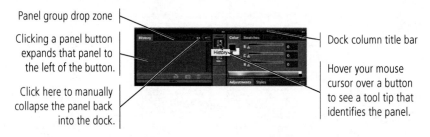

   ⊢ Dock column title bar

   ⊢ Hover your mouse cursor over a button to see a tool tip that identifies the panel.

4. **Click away from the expanded panel, anywhere in the workspace.**

   Because the Auto-Collapse Iconic Panels option is toggled on (from Step 1), the History panel collapses as soon as you click away from the panel.

Note:

All panels can be toggled on and off using the Window menu.

If you choose a panel that is open but iconized, the panel expands to the left of its icon.

If you choose a panel that is open in an expanded group, that panel comes to the front of the group.

If you choose a panel that isn't currently open, it opens in the same position as when it was last closed.

Note:

*Collapsed panels are referred to as **iconized** or **iconic**.*

Note:

The Auto-Collapse Iconic Panels option is also available in the User Interface pane of the Preferences dialog box, which you can open directly from the dock contextual menu.

Note:

When you expand an iconized panel that is part of a group, the entire group expands; the button you clicked is the active panel in the expanded group.

5. **Click the History panel button to re-expand the panel. Control/right-click the expanded panel group's drop zone and choose Close from the contextual menu.**

Note:

The panel group's contextual menu is the only way to close a docked panel. You can choose Close to close only the active panel, or close an entire panel group by choosing Close Tab Group from the contextual menu.

You can create multiple columns of panels in the dock. Each column, technically considered a separate dock, can be expanded or collapsed independently of other columns.

Control/right-click the panel group drop zone to access that panel group's contextual menu.

6. **Repeat Step 5 to close the Properties panel.**

Closing the remaining group removes the entire second dock column.

7. **In the remaining dock column, Control/right-click the drop zone of the Color panel group and choose Close Tab Group from the contextual menu.**

When you close a docked group, other panel groups in the same column expand to fill the available space.

The remaining groups in the dock column expand to fill the available space.

8. **Click the Layers panel tab and drag left, away from the panel dock.**

A panel that is not docked is called a **floating panel**. You can iconize floating panels (or panel groups) by double-clicking the title bar of the floating panel group.

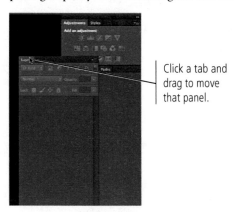

Click a tab and drag to move that panel.

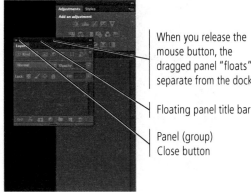

When you release the mouse button, the dragged panel "floats" separate from the dock.

Floating panel title bar

Panel (group) Close button

9. **Click the Layers panel tab (in the floating panel group). Drag between the two existing docked panel groups until a blue line appears, then release the mouse button.**

To move a single panel to a new location, click the panel tab and drag. To move an entire panel group, click the panel group drop zone and drag. If you are moving panels to another position in the dock, the blue highlight indicates where the panel (group) will be placed when you release the mouse button.

The blue highlight shows where the panel will be placed if you release the mouse button.

When you release the mouse button, the Layers panel becomes part of a separate panel group.

10. **Control/right-click the drop zone behind the Adjustments/Styles panel group, and choose Minimize from the contextual menu.**

When a group is minimized, only the panel tabs are visible. Clicking a tab in a collapsed panel group expands that group and makes the selected panel active.

Note:

To add a panel to an existing group, drag the panel to the target group's drop zone. A blue highlight will surround the group where the moved panel will be added.

Minimizing a panel group collapses it to show only the panel tabs.

11. **Move the cursor over the line between the Layers and Channels/Paths panel groups. When the cursor becomes a double-headed arrow, click and drag down until the Layers panel occupies approximately half of the available dock column space.**

You can drag the bottom edge of a docked panel group to vertically expand or shrink the panel; other panels in the same column expand or contract to fit the available space.

Note:

You can also double-click a panel tab to minimize the panel group. If a panel group is already minimized, double-clicking a panel tab expands the minimized group.

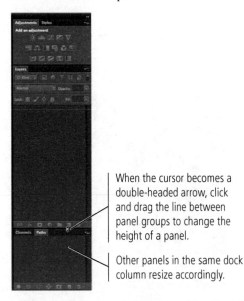

When the cursor becomes a double-headed arrow, click and drag the line between panel groups to change the height of a panel.

Other panels in the same dock column resize accordingly.

Note:

To create a new dock column, drag a panel or panel group until a pop-out "drawer" outlines the edge where the new column will be added.

12. Double-click the title bar above the column of docked panels to collapse those panels to icons.

Double-clicking the dock title bar collapses an expanded column (or vice versa).

Buttons that are grouped together in the dock represent a panel group.

13. Move the cursor over the left edge of the dock column. When the cursor becomes a double-headed arrow, click and drag right.

If you only see the icons, you can also drag the dock edge to the left to reveal the panel names. This can be particularly useful until you are more familiar with the application and the icons used to symbolize the different panels.

Click here and drag right to hide the panel names.

14. On the left side of the workspace, double-click the Tools panel title bar.

The Tools panel can't be expanded, but it can be displayed as either one or two columns; double-clicking the Tools panel title bar toggles between the two modes.

The one- or two-column format is a purely personal choice. The one-column layout takes up less horizontal space on the screen, which can be useful if you have a small monitor. The two-column format fits in a smaller vertical space, which can be especially useful if you have a widescreen monitor.

Double-click the Tools panel title bar to toggle between the one-column and two-column layouts.

15. Continue to the next exercise.

Note:

Dragging the left edge of a dock column changes the width of all panels in that dock column. This works for both iconized and expanded columns.

Note:

Throughout this book, our screen shots show the Tools panel in the one-column format. Feel free to work with the panel in two columns if you prefer.

Note:

The Tools panel can also be floated by clicking its title bar and dragging away from the edge of the screen. To re-dock the floating Tools panel, simply click the title bar and drag back to the left edge of the screen; when the blue line highlights the edge of the workspace, releasing the mouse button puts the Tools panel back into the dock.

PHOTOSHOP FOUNDATIONS

In the Tools panel, tools with a small white mark in the lower-right corner have **nested tools**.

This arrow means the tool has other nested tools.

A tool tip shows the name of the tool.

If you hover your mouse over a tool, a **tool tip** shows the name of the tool, as well as the associated keyboard shortcut for that tool if one exists. (If you don't see tool tips, check the Show Tool Tips option in the General pane of the Preferences dialog box.)

You can access nested tools by clicking the primary tool and holding down the mouse button, or by Control/right-clicking the primary tool to open the menu of nested options.

If a tool has a defined shortcut, pressing that key activates the associated tool. Most nested tools have the same shortcut as the default tool. By default, you have to press Shift plus the shortcut key to access the nested variations; for example, press Shift-M to toggle between the Rectangular and Elliptical Marquee tools. You can change this behavior in the General pane of the Preferences dialog box by unchecking the Use Shift Key for Tool Switch option. When this option is off, you can simply press the shortcut key multiple times to cycle through the variations.

Not all nested tools can be accessed with a shortcut. In the marquee tools, for example, the shortcut toggles only between the rectangular and elliptical variations.

Finally, if you press and hold a tool's keyboard shortcut, you can temporarily call the appropriate tool (called **spring-loaded keys**); after releasing the shortcut key, you return to the tool you were using previously. For example, you might use this technique to switch temporarily from the Brush tool to the Eraser tool while painting.

The following chart offers a quick reference of nested tools, as well as the shortcut for each tool (if any). Nested tools are shown indented and in italics.

Move tool (V)

Rectangular Marquee tool (M)
  Elliptical Marquee tool (M)
  Single Row Marquee tool
  Single Column Marquee tool

Lasso tool (L)
  Polygonal Lasso tool (L)
  Magnetic Lasso tool (L)

Quick Selection tool (W)
  Magic Wand tool (W)

Crop tool (C)
  Perspective Crop tool (C)
  Slice tool (C)
  Slice Select tool (C)

Eyedropper tool (I)
  3D Material Eyedropper tool (I)
  Color Sampler tool (I)
  Ruler tool (I)
  Note tool (I)
  Count tool (I)

Spot Healing Brush tool (J)
  Healing Brush tool (J)
  Patch tool (J)
  Content Aware Move tool (J)
  Red Eye tool (J)

Brush tool (B)
  Pencil tool (B)
  Color Replacement tool (B)
  Mixer Brush tool (B)

Clone Stamp tool (S)
  Pattern Stamp tool (S)

History Brush tool (Y)
  Art History Brush tool (Y)

Eraser tool (E)
  Background Eraser tool (E)
  Magic Eraser tool (E)

Gradient tool (G)
  Paint Bucket tool (G)
  3D Material Drop tool (G)

Blur tool
  Sharpen tool
  Smudge tool

Dodge tool (O)
  Burn tool (O)
  Sponge tool (O)

Pen tool (P)
  Freeform Pen tool (P)
  Add Anchor Point tool
  Delete Anchor Point tool
  Convert Point tool

Horizontal Type tool (T)
  Vertical Type tool (T)
  Horizontal Type Mask tool (T)
  Vertical Type Mask tool (T)

Path Selection tool (A)
  Direct Selection tool (A)

Rectangle tool (U)
  Rounded Rectangle tool (U)
  Ellipse tool (U)
  Polygon tool (U)
  Line tool (U)
  Custom Shape tool (U)

Hand tool (H)
  Rotate View tool (R)

Zoom tool (Z)

CREATE A SAVED WORKSPACE

You have extensive control over the appearance of your Photoshop workspace — you can choose what panels are visible, where they appear, and even the size of individual panels or panel groups. Over time you will develop personal preferences — the Layers panel always appears at the top, for example — based on your work habits and project needs. Rather than re-establishing every workspace element each time you return to Photoshop, you can save your custom workspace settings so they can be recalled with a single click.

1. **Click the Workspace switcher in the Options bar and choose New Workspace.**

   The Workspace switcher is labeled Essentials (the default workspace) by default.

   The Workspace switcher includes options for saving and managing workspaces.

2. **In the New Workspace dialog box, type `Portfolio` and then click Save.**

   You didn't define custom keyboard shortcuts or menus, so those two options are not relevant in this exercise.

   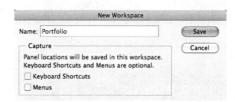

3. **Open the Window menu and choose Workspace>Essentials (Default).**

   Saved workspaces can be accessed in the Window>Workspace submenu as well as the Workspace switcher on the Options bar.

   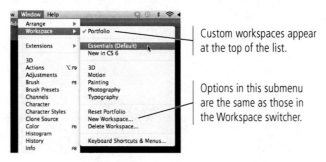

   Custom workspaces appear at the top of the list.

   Options in this submenu are the same as those in the Workspace switcher.

   Calling a saved workspace restores the last-used state of the workspace. You made a number of changes since calling the Essentials workspace at the beginning of the previous exercise, so calling the Essentials workspace restores the last state of that workspace — in essence, nothing changes from the saved Portfolio workspace.

   The only apparent difference is the active workspace name.

Note:

Because workspace preferences are largely a matter of personal taste, the projects in this book instruct you regarding which panels to use, but not where to place those elements within the interface.

Note:

If a menu option is greyed out, it is not available for the active selection.

Note:

The Delete Workspace option opens a dialog box where you can choose a specific user-defined workspace to delete. You can't delete the default workspaces that come with the application.

4. **Open the Workspace switcher and choose Reset Essentials (or choose Window>Workspace>Reset Essentials).**

Remember, saved workspaces remember the last-used state; calling a workspace again restores the panels exactly as they were the last time you used that workspace. For example, if you close a panel that is part of a saved workspace, the closed panel will not be reopened the next time you call the same workspace. To restore the saved state of the workspace, including opening closed panels or repositioning moved ones, you have to use the Reset option.

Note:

If you change anything and quit the application, those changes are remembered even when Photoshop is relaunched.

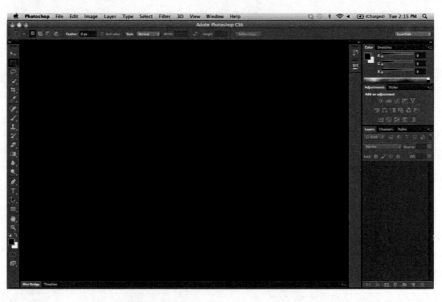

5. **Continue to the next exercise.**

Customizing Keyboard Shortcuts and Menus

PHOTOSHOP FOUNDATIONS

People use Photoshop for many different reasons; some use only a limited set of tools to complete specific projects. Photoshop allows you to define the available menu options and the keyboard shortcuts that are associated with menu commands, panel menus, and tools.

At the bottom of the Edit menu, two options (Keyboard Shortcuts and Menus) open different tabs of the same dialog box. (If you don't see the Keyboard Shortcuts or Menus options in the Edit menu, choose Show all Menu Items to reveal the hidden commands.) Once you have defined custom menus or shortcuts, you can save your choices as a set so you can access the same custom choices again without having to redo the work.

Click here to access existing saved sets. Save the changes to the current set. Save the changes as a new set. Delete the selected set.

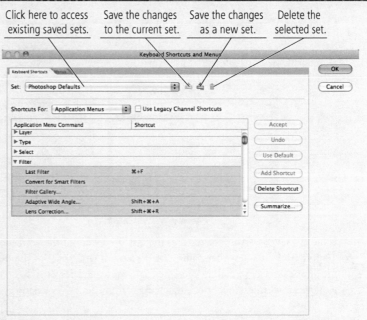

EXPLORE THE PHOTOSHOP DOCUMENT VIEWS

There is much more to using Photoshop than arranging the workspace. What you do with those panels — and even which panels you need — depends on the type of work you are doing in a particular file. In this exercise, you open a Photoshop file and explore interface elements that will be important as you begin creating digital artwork.

1. **In Photoshop, choose File>Open.**

2. **Navigate to your WIP>Interface_PS folder and select bryce2.jpg in the list of available files.**

   The Open dialog box is a system-standard navigation dialog. This is one area of significant difference between Macintosh and Windows users.

3. **Press Shift, and then click bryce3.jpg in the list of files.**

   Pressing Shift allows you to select multiple contiguous (consecutive) files in the list.

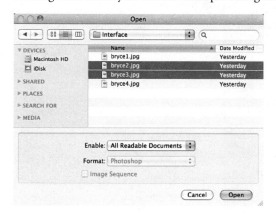

Note:

Press Command/ Control-O to access the Open dialog box.

4. Click Open.

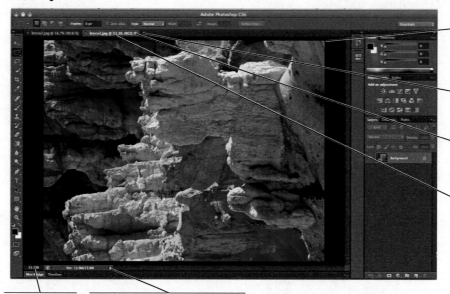

Photoshop files appear in a **document window**.

Each open document is represented by a separate tab.

The active file tab is lighter than other tabs.

The **document tabs** show the file name, view percentage, color space, and current viewing mode.

View Percentage field

Use this menu to show different document information, such as file size (default), profile, dimensions, etc.

5. Click the bryce2.jpg tab to make that document active.

6. Highlight the current value in the View Percentage field (in the bottom-left corner of the document window) and type 40.

Different people prefer larger or smaller view percentages, depending on a number of factors (eyesight, monitor size, and so on). As you complete the projects in this book, you will see our screen shots zoom in or out as necessary to show you the most relevant part of a particular file. In most cases we do not tell you what specific view percentage to use for a particular exercise, unless it is specifically required for the work being done.

Note:

Macintosh users: If you turn off the Application frame, opening multiple files creates a document window that has a separate title bar showing the name of the active file.

Click the tab to activate a specific file in the document window.

Changing the view percentage of the file does not affect the size of the document window.

7. Choose View>Fit On Screen.

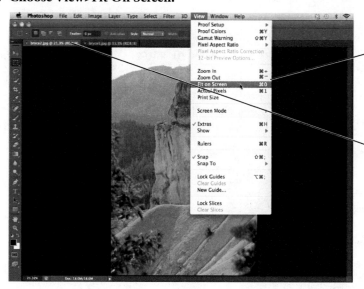

These five options affect the view percentage of a file.

The Fit On Screen command automatically calculates view percentage based on the size of the document window.

8. Click the Zoom tool in the Tools panel. In the Options bar, click the Actual Pixels button.

The Options bar appears by default at the top of the workspace below the Menu bar. It is context sensitive, which means it provides different options depending on which tool is active.

When the Zoom tool is active, the Actual Pixels button (the same as the Actual Pixels command in the View menu) changes the image view to 100%.

Note:

You can toggle the Options bar on or off by choosing Window>Options.

Note:

Dragging with the Zoom tool enlarges the selected area to fill the document window.

If Resize Windows to Fit is checked, zooming in a floating window affects the size of the actual document window.

If Zoom All Windows is checked, zooming in one window affects the view percentage of all open files.

Scrubby Zoom enables dynamic image zooming depending on the direction you drag in the document window.

The Options bar shows options related to the active tool.

Zoom tool

9. **Press Option/Alt, and then click anywhere in the document window.**

One final reminder: we list differing commands in the Macintosh/Windows format. On Macintosh, you need to press the Option key; on Windows, press the Alt key. (We will not repeat this explanation every time different commands are required for the different operating systems.)

Clicking with the Zoom tool enlarges the view percentage in specific, predefined percentage steps. Pressing Option/Alt while clicking with the Zoom tool reduces the view percentage in the reverse sequence of the same percentages.

Note:

You can zoom a document between approximately 0.098% and 3200%. We say approximately because the actual smallest size is dependent on the original image size; you can zoom out far enough to "show" the image as a single tiny square, regardless of what percentage of the image that represents.

Option/Alt-clicking with the Zoom tool reduces the view percent in the predefined sequence of percentages.

When the Zoom tool is active, pressing Option/Alt changes the cursor to the Zoom Out icon.

10. **Click the Hand tool (near the bottom of the Tools panel). Click in the document window, hold down the mouse button, and drag around.**

The Hand tool is a very easy and convenient option for changing the area of an image that is currently visible in the document window.

If Scroll All Windows is checked, dragging in one window affects the visible area of all open files.

These four buttons duplicate the same options in the View menu.

Note:

You can press the Spacebar to access the Hand tool when another tool is active.

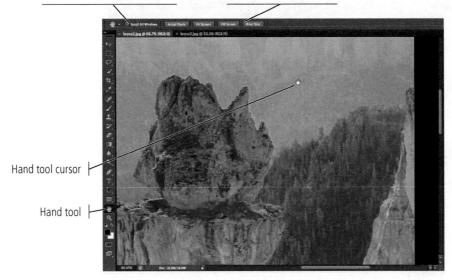

Hand tool cursor

Hand tool

11. **Click the bryce3.jpg tab to make that document active.**

12. **In the Tools panel, choose the Rotate View tool (nested under the Hand tool). Click in the document window and drag right to turn the document clockwise.**

The Rotate View tool turns an image without permanently altering the orientation of the file; the actual image data remains unchanged. This tool allows you to more easily work on objects or elements that are not oriented horizontally (for example, working with text that appears on an angle in the final image).

If you are unable to rotate the image view, your graphics processor does not support OpenGL — a hardware/software combination that makes it possible to work with complex graphics operations. If your computer does not support OpenGL, you will not be able to use a number of Photoshop CS6 features (including the Rotate View tool).

Type a specific angle in this field to rotate the image view.　Click and drag around this icon to rotate the image view.　Clicking Reset View restores the original image orientation.　If Rotate All Windows is checked, dragging in one window affects the view angle of all open files.

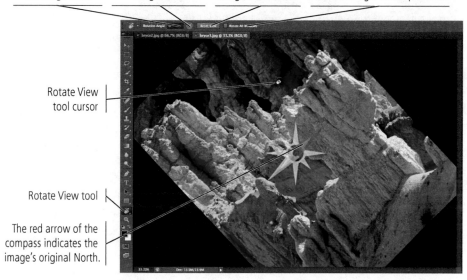

Rotate View tool cursor

Rotate View tool

The red arrow of the compass indicates the image's original North.

13. **In the Options bar, click the Reset View button.**

As we said, the Rotate View tool is **non-destructive** (i.e., it does not permanently affect the pixels in the image). You can easily use the tool's options to define a specific view angle or to restore an image to its original orientation.

Resetting the view restores the image's original orientation.

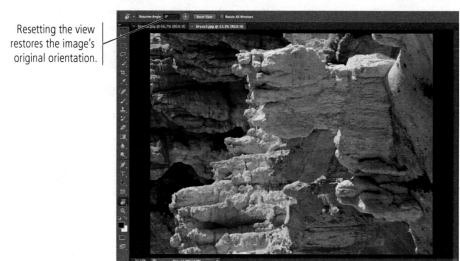

14. **Continue to the next exercise.**

EXPLORE THE ARRANGEMENT OF MULTIPLE DOCUMENTS

You will often need to work with more than one Photoshop file at once. Photoshop incorporates a number of options for arranging multiple documents. We designed the following simple exercise so you can explore these options.

1. **With bryce2.jpg and bryce3.jpg open, choose File>Open.**

   The Open dialog box defaults to the last-used location, so you should not have to navigate back to the WIP>Interface_PS folder.

2. **Click bryce1.jpg in the list to select that file.**

3. **Press Command/Control and click bryce4.jpg to add that file to the active selection.**

   Pressing Command/Control allows you to select and open non-contiguous files.

Note:

All open files are listed at the bottom of the Window menu.

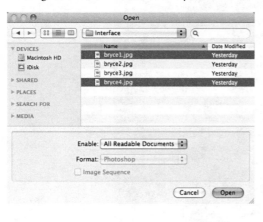 

4. **Click Open to open both selected files.**

5. **With bryce4.jpg active, choose Window>Arrange>Float in Window.**

   You can also separate all open files by choosing Window>Arrange>Float All In Windows.

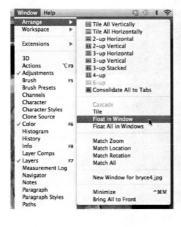 

Floating a document separates the file into its own document window.

The title bar of the separate document window shows the same information that was in the document tab.

6. Choose Window>Arrange>4-up.

The defined arrangements provide a number of options for tiling multiple open files within the available workspace. These arrangements manage all open files, including those in floating windows.

The options' icons suggest the result of each command. The active file remains active; this is indicated by the brighter text in the active document's tab.

7. Choose Window>Arrange>Consolidate All to Tabs.

This command restores all documents — floating or not— into a single tabbed document window.

8. At the bottom of the Tools panel, click the Change Screen Mode button.

Photoshop has three different **screen modes**, which change the way the document window displays on the screen. The default mode, which you saw when you opened these three files, is called Standard Screen mode.

9. **Choose Full Screen Mode with Menu Bar from the Change Screen Mode menu.**

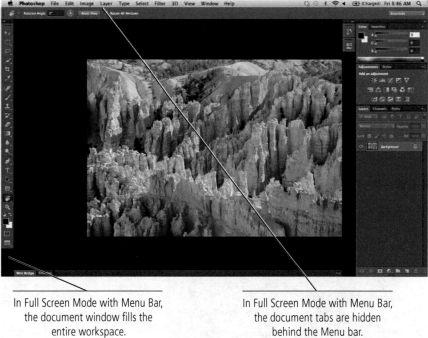

In Full Screen Mode with Menu Bar, the document window fills the entire workspace.

In Full Screen Mode with Menu Bar, the document tabs are hidden behind the Menu bar.

10. **Click the Change Screen Mode button in the Tools panel and choose Full Screen Mode. Read the resulting warning dialog box, and then click Full Screen.**

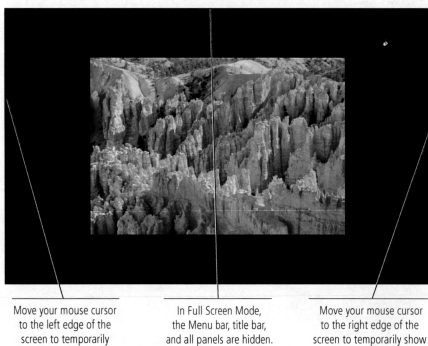

Move your mouse cursor to the left edge of the screen to temporarily show the Tools panel.

In Full Screen Mode, the Menu bar, title bar, and all panels are hidden.

Move your mouse cursor to the right edge of the screen to temporarily show docked panels.

Summing Up the Photoshop View Options

Most Photoshop projects require some amount of zooming in and out to various view percentages, as well as navigating around the document within its window. As we show you how to complete different stages of the workflow, we usually won't tell you when to change your view percentage because that's largely a matter of personal preference. However, you should understand the different options for navigating around a Photoshop file so you can easily and efficiently get to what you want, when you want to get there.

View Percentage Field

You can type a specific percentage in the View Percentage field in the bottom-left corner of the document window.

View Menu

The View menu also provides options for changing the view percentage, including the associated keyboard shortcuts. (The Zoom In and Zoom Out options step through the same predefined view percentages that the Zoom tool uses.)

Zoom In	Command/Control-plus (+)
Zoom Out	Command/Control-minus (-)
Fit On Screen	Command/Control-0 (zero)
Actual Pixels (100%)	Command/Control-1

Zoom Tool

You can click with the **Zoom tool** to increase the view percentage in specific, predefined intervals. Pressing Option/Alt with the Zoom tool allows you to zoom out in the same predefined percentages. If you drag a marquee with the Zoom tool, you can zoom into a specific location; the area surrounded by the marquee fills the available space in the document window.

When the Zoom tool is active, you can also activate the Scrubby Zoom option in the Options bar. This allows you to click and drag left to reduce the view percentage, or drag right to increase the view percentage; in this case, the tool does not follow predefined stepped percentages.

Hand Tool

Whatever your view percentage, you can use the **Hand tool** to drag the file around in the document window. The Hand tool changes only what is visible in the window; it has no effect on the actual pixels in the image.

Mouse Scroll Wheel

If your mouse has a scroll wheel, rolling the scroll wheel up or down moves the image up or down within the document window. If you press Command/Control and scroll the wheel, you can move the image left (scroll up) or right (scroll down) within the document window. You can also press Option/Alt and scroll the wheel up to zoom in or scroll the wheel down to zoom out.

(In the General pane of the Preferences dialog box, the Zoom with Scroll Wheel option is unchecked by default. If you check this option, scrolling up or down with no modifier key zooms in or out and does not move the image within the document window.)

Navigator Panel

The **Navigator panel** is another method of adjusting how close your viewpoint is and what part of the page you're currently viewing (if you're zoomed in close enough so you can see only a portion of the page). The Navigator panel shows a thumbnail of the active file; a red rectangle represents exactly how much of the document shows in the document window.

The red rectangle shows the area of the file that is visible in the document window.

Drag the red rectangle to change the visible portion of the file.

Use the slider and field at the bottom of the panel to change the view percentage.

11. Press the Escape key to return to Standard Screen mode.

12. Click the Close button on the bryce4.jpg tab.

When multiple files are open, clicking the Close button on a document tab closes only that file.

13. **Macintosh: Click the Close button in the top-left corner of the Application frame.**

Closing the Macintosh Application frame closes all open files, but does *not* quit the application.

On Macintosh, closing the Application frame closes all files open in that frame.

Windows: Click the Close button on each document tab to close the files.

Clicking the Close button on the Windows Menu bar closes all open files *and* quits the application. To close open files *without* quitting, you have to manually close each file.

Click the Close buttons on each document tab to close the open files.

Clicking the Menu bar Close button closes all open files, and also quits the application.

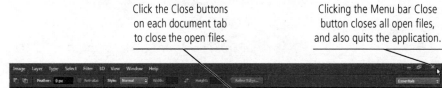

The Undo command (Edit>Undo or Command/Control-Z) only steps back to the last one action you completed; after you use the Undo command, it toggles to Redo. You can also use the Step Backward command (Edit>Step Backward or Command-Option-Z/Control-Alt-Z) to move back in the history one step at a time, or use the History panel (Window>History) to navigate back to earlier stages of your work.

Every action you take is recorded as a state in the History panel. You can click any state to return to that particular point in the document progression. You can also delete specific states or create a new document from a particular state using the buttons at the bottom of the panel.

By default, the History panel stores the last 20 states; older states are automatically deleted. You can change that setting in the Performance pane of the Preferences dialog box. Keep in mind, however, that storing a larger number of states will increase the memory that is required to work with a specific file.

Keep the following in mind when using the History panel:

- The default snapshot shows the image state when it was first opened.

- The oldest state is at the top of the list; the most recent state appears at the bottom.

- The History State slider identifies the active state.

- You can save any particular state as a snapshot to prevent it from being deleted when that state is no longer within the number of states that can be stored.

- The history is only stored as long as the file is open; when you close a file, the history (including snapshots) is not saved.

- When you select a specific state, the states below it are dimmed so you can see which changes will be discarded if you go back to a particular history state.

- Selecting a state and then changing the image eliminates all states that come after it.

- Deleting a state deletes that state and those that came after it. If you choose Allow Non-Linear History in the History Options dialog box (accessed in the History panel Options menu), deleting a state deletes only that state.

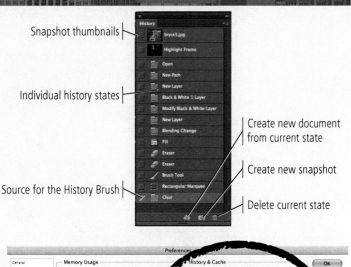

Snapshot thumbnails

Individual history states

Create new document from current state

Create new snapshot

Source for the History Brush

Delete current state

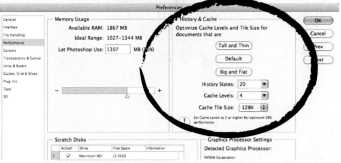

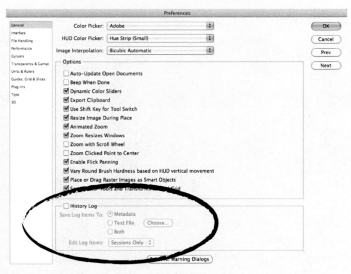

If you need to keep a record of a file's history even after you close the file, you can activate the History Log option in the General pane of the Preferences dialog box. When this option is checked, you can save the history log as metadata, in a text file, or both. You can also determine the level of detail that will be recorded in the history log.

- Sessions Only records each time you launch or quit and each time you open and close individual files.

- Concise adds the text that appears in the History panel to the Sessions information.

- Detailed gives you a complete history of all changes made to files.

Composite Movie Ad

Tantamount Studios, one of the largest film production companies in Hollywood, is developing a new movie called "Aftermath." You have been hired to develop an advertisement that will be used to announce the movie in several different trade magazines.

This project incorporates the following skills:

❏ Creating a single composite ad from multiple supplied images

❏ Compositing multiple photographs, using various techniques to silhouette the focal object in each image

❏ Incorporating vector graphics as rasterized layers and Smart Object layers

❏ Scaling and aligning different objects in relation to the page and to each other

❏ Managing individual layout elements using layers and layer groups

❏ Saving multiple versions of a file to meet different output requirements

client comments

Here's a basic synopsis of the movie:

A massive hurricane, unlike anything ever seen on the West Coast of the United States, takes aim at San Francisco. The category 6 hurricane sparks tidal waves, fires, floods — the resulting destruction dwarfs even the earthquake and fire of 1906. The movie follows the storm survivors through the process of rebuilding, both personally and politically.

This movie is going to be one of our summer blockbusters, and we're throwing a lot of resources behind it. We'll be putting the same ad in multiple magazines, and they all use different software to create the magazine layouts. We need the ad to work for all of our placements, regardless of what software is being used by the magazine publishers.

art director comments

The client loved the initial concept sketch I submitted last week, so we're ready to start building the files. I've had the photographer prepare the images we need, and the client has provided the studio and rating logo files. They also sent me the first two magazines' specs:

Magazine 1

- Bleed size: 8.75 × 11.25″

- Trim size: 8.5 × 11″

- Live area: 8 × 10.5″

- Files should be submitted as native layout files or layered TIFF

Magazine 2

- Sizes are the same as Magazine 1

- Files should be submitted as flattened TIFF or PDF

project objectives

To complete this project, you will:

❑ Resize a raster image to change resolution

❑ Composite multiple images into a single background file

❑ Incorporate both raster and vector elements into the same design

❑ Transform and arrange individual layers to create a cohesive design

❑ Create layer groups to easily manage related layer content

❑ Use selection techniques to isolate images from their backgrounds

❑ Save two different types of TIFF files for different ad requirements

Stage 1 **Compositing Images and Artwork**

Technically speaking, **compositing** is the process of combining any two or more objects (images, text, illustrations, etc.) into an overall design. When we talk about compositing in Photoshop, we're typically referring to the process of combining multiple images into a single cohesive image. Image compositing might be as simple as placing two images into different areas of a background file; or it could be as complex as placing a person into a group photo, carefully clipping out the individual's background, and adjusting the shadows to match the lighting in the group.

Types of Images

There are two primary types of digital artwork: vector graphics and raster images.

Vector graphics are composed of mathematical descriptions of a series of lines and shapes. Vector graphics are **resolution independent**; they can be freely enlarged or reduced, and they are automatically output at the resolution of the output device. The shapes that you create in Adobe InDesign, or in drawing applications such as Adobe Illustrator, are vector graphics.

Raster images, such as photographs or files created in Adobe Photoshop, are made up of a grid of independent pixels (rasters or bits) in rows and columns (called a **bitmap**). Raster files are **resolution dependent** — their resolution is fixed, determined when you scan, photograph, or otherwise create the file. You can typically reduce raster images, but you cannot enlarge them without losing image quality.

Line art is a type of raster image that is made up entirely of 100% solid areas; the pixels in a line-art image have only two options: they can be all black or all white. Examples of line art are UPC bar codes or pen-and-ink drawings.

Screen Ruling

The ad that you will be building in this project is intended to be placed in print magazines, so you have to build the new file with the appropriate settings for commercial printing. When reproducing a photograph on a printing press, the image must be converted into a set of printable dots that fool the eye into believing it sees continuous tones. Prior to image-editing software, pictures that were being prepared for printing on a press were photographed through a screen to create a grid of halftone dots. The result of this conversion is a halftone image; the dots used to simulate continuous tone are called **halftone dots**. Light tones in a photograph are represented as small halftone dots; dark tones become large halftone dots.

The screens used to create the halftone images had a finite number of available dots in a horizontal or vertical inch. That number was the **screen ruling**, or **lines per inch (lpi)** of the halftone. A screen ruling of 133 lpi means that in a square inch there are 133 × 133 (17,689) possible locations for a halftone dot. If the screen ruling is decreased, there are fewer total halftone dots, producing a grainier image; if the screen ruling is increased, there are more halftone dots, producing a clearer image.

Line screen is a finite number based on a combination of the intended output device and paper. You can't randomly select a line screen. Ask your printer what line screen will be used before you begin creating your images.

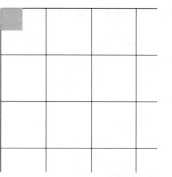
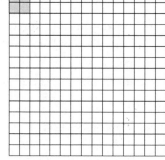

72 ppi   300 ppi

Each white square represents a pixel. The highlighted area shows the pixel information used to generate a halftone dot. If an image only has 72 pixels per inch, the output device has to generate four halftone dots per pixel, resulting in poor printed quality.

If you can't find out ahead of time, or if you're unsure, follow these general guidelines:

- Newspaper or newsprint: 85–100 lpi

- Magazine or general commercial printing: 133–150 lpi

- Premium-quality-paper jobs (such as art books or annual reports): 150–175 lpi; some specialty jobs might use 200 lpi or more

Image Resolution

When a printer creates halftone dots, it calculates the average value of a group of pixels in the raster image and generates a spot of appropriate size. A raster image's resolution — measured in **pixels per inch (ppi)** — determines the quantity of pixel data the printer can read. Regardless of their source — camera, scanner, or files created in Photoshop — images need to have sufficient resolution so the output device can generate enough halftone dots to create the appearance of continuous tone. In the images to the right, the same raster image is reproduced at 300 ppi (top) and 72 ppi (bottom); notice the obvious degradation in quality in the 72-ppi version.

Ideally, the printer will have four pixels for each halftone dot created. The relationship between pixels and halftone dots defines the rule of resolution for raster-based images — the resolution of a raster image (ppi) should be two times the screen ruling (lpi) that will be used for printing.

For line art, the general rule is to scan the image at the same resolution as the output device. Many laser printers and digital presses image at 600–1200 dots per inch (dpi); imagesetters used to make printing plates for a commercial press typically output at much higher resolution, possibly 2400 dpi or more.

OPEN A FILE FROM ADOBE BRIDGE

Adobe Bridge is a stand-alone application that ships and installs along with Photoshop. This asset-management tool enables you to navigate, browse, and manage files anywhere on your system. If you have the entire Adobe Creative Suite, Bridge can also help streamline the workflow as you flip from one application to another to complete a project.

1. **Download WC6_RF_Project1.zip from the Student Files Web page.**

2. **Expand the ZIP archive in your WIP folder (Macintosh) or copy the archive contents into your WIP folder (Windows).**

   This results in a folder named **Movie**, which contains all of the files you need for this project. You should also use this folder to save the files you create in this project.

   If necessary, refer to Page 1 of the Interface chapter for specific information on expanding or accessing the required resource files.

3. **In Photoshop, open the Mini Bridge panel.**

   If you are working from the default Essentials workspace, the Mini Bridge panel is docked at the bottom of the document window (grouped with the Timeline panel).

   If the Mini Bridge panel is not currently visible, you can open it by choosing Window>Extensions>Mini Bridge.

Note:

Adobe Bridge is a complete stand-alone application. However, this is a book about Photoshop, not Bridge. We're simply introducing you to the Bridge interface and showing you how to use Bridge to navigate and access files. We encourage you to read the Bridge documentation (accessed in the Help menu when you are in the Bridge application).

4. **If you see a Launch Bridge or Reconnect button in the panel, click it to launch the separate Bridge application.**

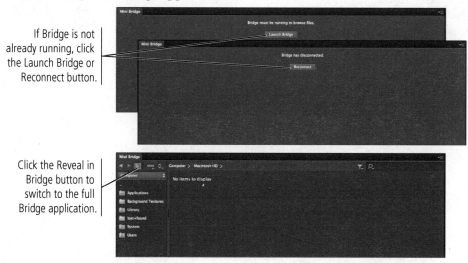

If Bridge is not already running, click the Launch Bridge or Reconnect button.

Click the Reveal in Bridge button to switch to the full Bridge application.

5. **Click the Reveal in Bridge button below the Mini Bridge panel tab.**

6. **In Bridge, use the Folders panel to navigate to your WIP>Movie folder.**

   Bridge is primarily a file manager, so you can think of it as a media browser. If some panels aren't visible, you can access them in the Bridge Window menu.

7. **Click the bricks.jpg thumbnail in the Content panel to select it.**

8. **If you don't see the Metadata panel, choose Window>Metadata. Review the File Properties of the selected image.**

   The most important information in File Properties is the resolution and color mode. This image was photographed at 72 ppi in the RGB color mode. (We explain more about color modes in Project 2: Menu Image Correction.)

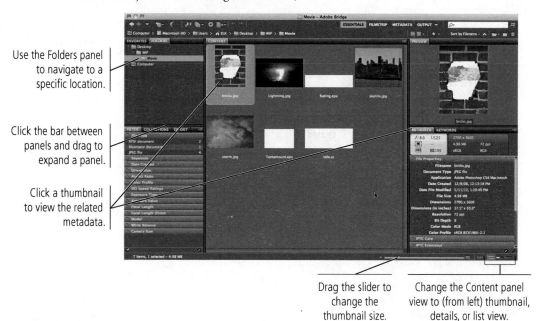

Use the Folders panel to navigate to a specific location.

Click the bar between panels and drag to expand a panel.

Click a thumbnail to view the related metadata.

Drag the slider to change the thumbnail size.

Change the Content panel view to (from left) thumbnail, details, or list view.

9. **Double-click the `bricks.jpg` thumbnail to open that file in Photoshop.**

   In this case, Bridge is an alternative to the File>Open method for opening files in Photoshop. The Bridge method can be useful because it provides more information than Photoshop's Open dialog box.

10. **If the rulers are not visible on the top and left edges, choose View>Rulers.**

    As you can see in the rulers, this image has a very large physical size. As you saw in the image metadata (in Bridge), however, the current image is only 72 ppi; for commercial printing, you need at least 300 ppi. You can use the principle of **effective resolution** to change the file to a high enough resolution for printing.

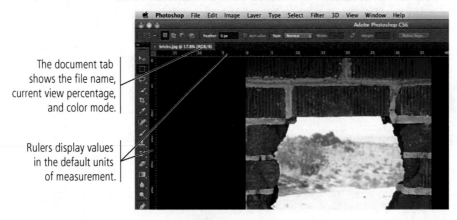

The document tab shows the file name, current view percentage, and color mode.

Rulers display values in the default units of measurement.

Note:

Although designers trained in traditional (non-digital) methods are sometimes comfortable talking about picas or ciceros, most people use inches as the standard unit of measurement in the U.S.

You can change the default unit of measurement in the Units & Rulers pane of the Preferences dialog box. Double-clicking either ruler opens the appropriate pane of the Preferences dialog box.

11. **Choose File>Save As. If necessary, navigate to your WIP>Movie folder as the target location. Change the file name (in the Save As field) to `aftermath`.**

    Since this is a basic image file with only one layer (so far), most of the other options in the Save As dialog box are grayed out (not available).

12. **Choose Photoshop in the Format menu and then click Save.**

    You can save a Photoshop file in a number of different formats, all of which have specific capabilities, limitations, and purposes. While you are still working on a file, it's best to keep it as a native Photoshop (PSD) file. When you choose a different format, the correct extension is automatically added to the file name.

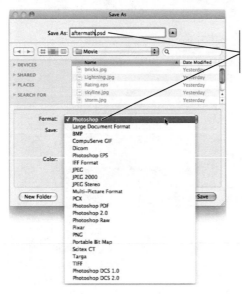

Files saved in the native Photoshop format display a ".psd" extension.

Note:

Also called "native", the PSD format is the most flexible format to use while building files in Photoshop.

13. **Continue to the next exercise.**

Understanding File Saving Preferences

You can control a number of options related to saving files in the File Handling pane of the Preferences dialog box.

Image Previews. You can use this menu to always or never include image thumbnails in the saved file. If you choose Ask When Saving in this menu, the Save As dialog box includes an option to include the image preview/thumbnail.

On Macintosh, you have two additional options: Icon and Windows Thumbnail. You can check the Icon option to show the image thumbnail in the Open dialog box and Finder (instead of the default Photoshop file icon). Although Macintosh can almost always read Windows information, Windows sometimes has trouble with certain Macintosh data — specifically, file thumbnails; you can check the Windows Thumbnail option to include a thumbnail that will be visible in the Windows Open dialog box.

Append File Extension. On Macintosh, you can use this menu to always or never include the file extension in the saved file. If the Ask When Saving option is selected in this menu, the Save As dialog box includes options to append the file extension (in lower case or not). On Windows, file extensions are always added to saved files; this preference menu has only two options: Use Upper Case and Use Lower Case.

Save As to Original Folder. When this option is checked, choosing File>Save As automatically defaults to the location where the original file is located.

Save in Background. In Photoshop CS6, the Save process occurs by default in the background — in other words, you can continue working even while a file is being saved. In previous versions, you could not interact with the application while a file was being saved. Especially when you work with large files, this can be a significant time saver because you don't have to sit and wait the several minutes it might take to save a very large file. (The only thing you can't do while a file is being saved is use the Save As command; if you try, you will see a warning advising you to wait until the background save is complete.)

Automatically Save Recovery Information Every... This new feature in Photoshop CS6 means that your work is being saved in a temporary file, every 10 minutes by default; if something happens — an application crash or power outage, for example — you will be able to restore your work back to the last auto-saved version. In other words, the most you will lose is 10 minutes' work!

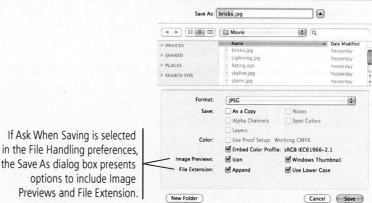

Macintosh

Windows

If Ask When Saving is selected in the File Handling preferences, the Save As dialog box presents options to include Image Previews and File Extension.

When a file is being saved in the background, the completed percentage appears in the document tab.

Every raster image has a defined, specific resolution that is established when the image is created. If you scan an image to be 3″ high by 3″ wide at 150 ppi, that image has 450 pixels in each vertical column and 450 pixels in each horizontal row. Simply resizing the image stretches or compresses those pixels into a different physical space, but does not add or remove pixel information. If you resize the 3 × 3″ image to 6 × 6″ (200% of the original), the 450 pixels in each column or row are forced to extend across 6″ instead of 3″, causing a marked loss of quality.

The **effective resolution** of an image is the resolution calculated after any scaling is taken into account. This number is equally important as the original image resolution — and perhaps moreso. The effective resolution can be calculated with a fairly simple equation:

Original resolution ÷ (% magnification ÷ 100) = Effective resolution

If a 300-ppi image is magnified 150%, the effective resolution is:

300 ppi ÷ 1.5 = 200 ppi

In other words, the more you enlarge a raster image, the lower its effective resolution becomes. In general, you can make an image 10% or 15% larger without significant adverse effects; the more you enlarge an image, however, the worse the results. Even Photoshop, which offers very sophisticated formulas (called "algorithms") for sizing images, cannot guarantee perfect results.

Effective resolution can be a very important consideration when working with client-supplied images, especially those that come from consumer-level digital cameras. Many of those devices capture images with a specific number of pixels rather than a number of pixels per inch (ppi). In this exercise, you will explore the effective resolution of an image to see if it can be used for a full-page printed magazine ad.

1. **With aftermath.psd open, choose Image>Image Size.**

   The Image Size dialog box shows the number of pixels in the image, as well as the image dimensions and current resolution. You can change any value in this dialog box, but you should understand what those changes mean before you do so.

   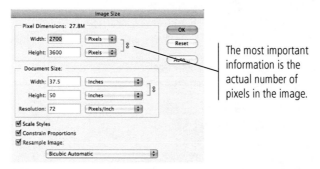

   The most important information is the actual number of pixels in the image.

2. **Check the Resample Image option at the bottom of the dialog box.**

   The options in this dialog box remember the last-used choices. The Resample option might already be checked in your dialog box.

   Resampling means maintaining the existing resolution in the new image dimensions; in other words, you are either adding or deleting pixels to the existing image. When this option is turned on, you can change the dimensions of an image without affecting the resolution, or you can change the resolution of an image (useful for removing excess resolution or **downsampling**) without affecting the image size.

3. **Change the Resolution field to 300 pixels/inch.**

When you change the resolution with resampling turned on, you do not change the file's physical size. To achieve 300-ppi resolution at the new size, Photoshop needs to add a huge number of pixels to the image. You can see at the top of the dialog box that this change would increase the total number of pixels from 2700 × 3600 to 11250 × 15000.

You can also see that changing the resolution of an image without affecting its physical dimensions would have a significant impact on the file size. Changing the resolution to 300 ppi at the current size would increase the file size to nearly 483 megabytes.

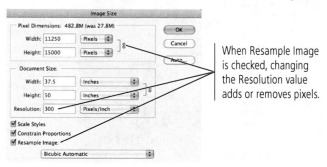

When Resample Image is checked, changing the Resolution value adds or removes pixels.

4. **Press Option/Alt and click the Reset button to restore the original image dimensions in the dialog box.**

In many Photoshop dialog boxes, pressing the Option/Alt key changes the Cancel button to Reset. You can click the Reset button to restore the original values that existed when you opened the dialog box.

Pressing Option/Alt changes the Cancel button to Reset.

5. **Uncheck the Resample Image option at the bottom of the dialog box.**

6. **Change the Resolution field to 300 pixels/inch.**

Resizing *without* resampling basically means distributing the same number of pixels over a different amount of physical space. When you resize an image without resampling, you do not change the number of pixels in the image. (In fact, those fields in the dialog box become simple text; the fields are unavailable and you cannot change the number of pixels in the image.)

You can see how changing one of the linked fields (Resolution) directly affects the other linked fields (Width and Height). By resizing the image to be 300 ppi — enough for commercial print quality — you now have an image that is 9″ × 12″.

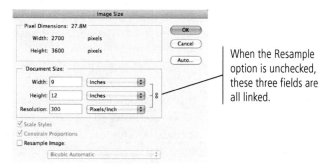

When the Resample option is unchecked, these three fields are all linked.

7. **Click OK to apply the change and return to the document window.**

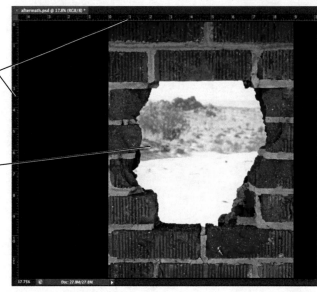

The rulers change to reflect the new dimensions of the file.

Because you did not resample the image, the screen display does not change.

8. **Save the file and continue to the next exercise.**

Because you have already saved this working file with a new name, you can simply choose File>Save, or press Command/Control-S to save without opening a dialog box. If you want to change the file name, you can always choose File>Save As.

More on Resolution and Resampling

PHOTOSHOP FOUNDATIONS

Discarding Pixels

Higher resolution means larger file sizes, which translates to longer processing time for printing or longer download time over the Internet. When you scale an image to a smaller size, simply resizing can produce files with far greater effective resolution than you need. Resampling allows you to reduce the physical size of an image without increasing the resolution, resulting in a smaller file size.

The caveat here is that once you discard (delete) pixels, they are gone. If you later try to re-enlarge the smaller image, you will not achieve the same quality as the original (before it was reduced). You should always save reduced images as copies instead of overwriting the originals.

Resampling

In general, you should always scan images to the size you will use in your final job. If you absolutely must resize a digital image, you can use resampling to achieve better results than simply changing the image size. Photoshop offers five types of resampling algorithms to generate extra pixel data (when increasing the image size) or to determine which pixels to discard (when reducing the image size).

☑ Constrain Proportions
☑ Resample Image:

✓ Nearest Neighbor (preserve hard edges)
  Bilinear
  Bicubic (best for smooth gradients)
  Bicubic Smoother (best for enlargement)
  Bicubic Sharper (best for reduction)
  Bicubic Automatic

- **Nearest Neighbor** is a low-quality but quick method. Nearest neighbor interpolates new pixel information based on only one of the squares in the grid of pixels, usually resulting in an image with a blocky appearance.

- **Bilinear** is a medium-quality resampling method. Bilinear resampling averages adjacent pixels to create new information.

- **Bicubic** creates the most accurate pixel information for continuous-tone images; it also takes the longest

to process and produces a softer image. To understand how this option works, think of a square bisected both horizontally and vertically — bicubic resampling averages the value of all four of those squares (pixels) to interpolate the new information.

- **Bicubic Smoother** is useful for enlarging images with smoother results than basic bicubic resampling.

- **Bicubic Sharper** is useful for reducing the size of an image and maintaining sharp detail.

The final step in preparing the workspace is defining the live area of the page. **Trim size** is the actual size of a page once it has been cut out of the press sheet. According to your client, the magazine has a trim size of 8.5″ × 11″.

Any elements that print right to the edge of a page (called **bleeding**) must actually extend beyond the defined trim size. The **bleed allowance** is the amount of extra space that should be included for these bleed objects; most applications require at least 1/8″ bleed allowance on any bleed edge.

Because of inherent variation in the mechanical printing and trimming processes, most magazines also define a safe or **live area**; all important design elements (especially text) should stay within this live area. The live area for this project is 8 × 10.5″.

1. **With aftermath.psd open, choose the Crop tool in the Tools panel.**

   When you choose the Crop tool, a crop marquee appears around the edges of the image. The marquee has eight handles, which you can drag to change the size of the cropped area.

Set Additional Crop Options

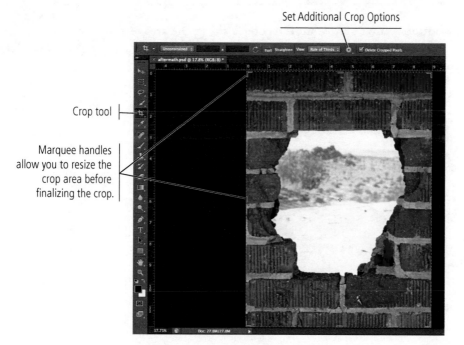

Crop tool

Marquee handles allow you to resize the crop area before finalizing the crop.

2. **In the Options bar, make sure Unconstrained is selected in the left menu, and check the Delete Cropped Pixels option.**

   The menu on the left end of the Options bar can be used to define a specific aspect ratio for the cropped area (see Page 35).

   If the Delete Cropped Pixels option is checked, areas outside the cropped areas are permanently removed from all layers in the file. If this option is not checked, cropped pixels remain in the file, but exist outside the edges of the file canvas. The Background layer, if one exists, is converted to a regular layer (you'll learn more about Background layers later in this project).

   This is an important distinction — by maintaining cropped pixels, you can later transform or reposition layers to reveal different parts of the layer within the newly cropped canvas size.

3. **Click the right-center handle of the crop marquee and drag left until the cursor feedback shows W: 8.750 in.**

Note:

If rulers are not still visible, choose View>Rulers or press Command/Control-R.

When you drag certain elements in the document window, live cursor feedback (also called "heads-up display") shows information about the tranformation. When dragging a side crop marquee handle, for example, the feedback shows the new width of the area.

You might need to zoom into at least 66.7% view percentage to achieve the exact dimensions needed for this project.

Click and drag the marquee handle to resize the marquee area.

Use the cursor feedback to find the appropriate measurement.

4. **Repeat Step 3 with the bottom-center handle until feedback shows the area of H: 11.250 in.**

Remember, the defined trim size for this ad is 8.5″ × 11″. Anything that runs to the page edge has to incorporate a 0.125″ bleed allowance, so the actual canvas size must be large enough to accommodate the bleed allowance on all edges:

[Width]   8.5″ + 0.125″ + 0.125″ = 8.75

[Height]   11″ + 0.125″ + 0.125″ = 11.25

The Crop Tools in Depth

When the Crop tool is selected, the Options bar can be used to define a number of settings related to the cropped area.

The left menu includes a number of common aspect ratios as presets. If you choose one of these options, the crop marquee is constrained to the aspect ratio defined in the preset. It's important to note that these presets do not define the actual size of the resulting crop, only the aspect ratio.

You can also choose the **Size and Resolution** option to define custom settings for the result of a crop. For example, if you define the width and height of a crop area as 9″ × 9″ at 300 ppi, when you click and drag to draw, the crop area will be restricted to the same proportions defined in the Width and Height fields (in this example, 1:1).

When you finalize the crop, the resulting image will be resized to be 9″ × 9″, regardless of the actual size of the crop marquee. This presents a problem if you remember the principles of resolution.

Enlarging a 3″ × 3″ area (for example) to 9″ × 9″ means the application needs to create enough pixels to fill in the 6 extra inches — at 300 ppi, Photoshop needs to create ("interpolate") more than 1800 pixels per linear inch. Although Photoshop can slightly enlarge images with reasonable success, such a significant amount of new data will not result in good quality. As a general rule, you should avoid enlarging raster images, and certainly no more than about 10%.

The crop area is constrained to the aspect ratio of the defined width and height.

The resulting cropped image is the actual size defined in the Crop Image Size & Resolution dialog box.

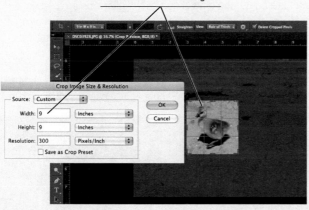

You can use the **View menu** to show a variety of overlays within the crop area; these follow basic design principles, such as the Rule of Thirds and the Golden Spiral.

You can also use the commands in this menu to turn the overlay on or off. If you choose Auto Show Overlay, the selected overlay only appears when you drag the marquee handles or click inside the marquee area to move the image inside the crop area.

You can also click the **Set Additional Crop Options** button to access a variety of crop-related choices.

- If you check the **Use Classic Mode** option, the crop marquee reverts to the same appearance and behavior as in previous versions of Photoshop.

- When **Auto Center Preview** is checked, the crop area will always be centered inthe document window; the image dynamically moves in the document window as you resize the crop area.

- When **Show Cropped Area** is checked, the area outside the crop marquee remains visible in the document window until you finalize the crop.

- When **Enable Crop Shield** is checked, areas outside the crop marquee are partially obscured by a semi-transparent solid color. You can use the related options to change the color and opacity of the shielded area.

When the Crop tool is selected, you can click the **Straighten** button in the Options bar and then draw a line in the image to define what should be a straight line in the resulting image. The image behind the crop marquee rotates to show what will remain in the cropped canvas; the line you drew is adjusted to be perfectly horizontal or vertical.

Click the Straighten button, then draw a line representing what you want to be "straight" in the cropped image.

The image is rotated behind the crop marquee to be "straight" based on the line you drew.

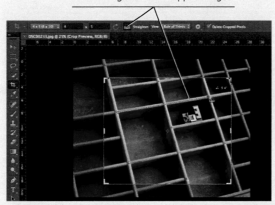
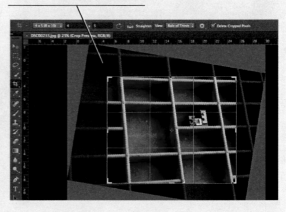

The **Perspective Crop tool** (nested under the Crop tool) can be used to draw a non-rectangular crop area. To define the area you want to keep, simply click to place the four corners of the area, then drag the corners in any direction as necessary. When you finalize the crop, the image inside the crop area is straightened to a front-on viewing angle. You should use this option with care, however, because it can badly distort an image.

In this first example, we used the actual lines in the photograph to draw the perspective crop marquee. After finalizing the crop, the type case appears to be perfectly straight rather than the original viewing angle at which it was photographed.

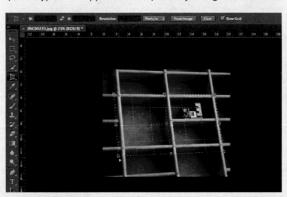
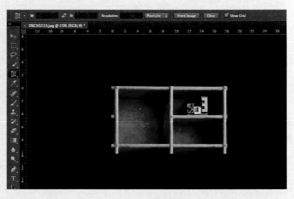

In this second example, we used the Perspective Crop tool to try to adjust the photograph of an historic hop kiln. You can see the obvious distortion in the resulting image.

5. **Click inside the crop area and drag to reposition the image so it is approximately centered in the crop area.**

   When you change the size of the marquee, the area outside the marquee is "shielded" by a darkened overlay so you can get an idea of what will remain after you finalize the crop.

   You can drag the image inside the crop area to change the portion that will remain in the cropped image. By default, the crop area remains centered in the document window; instead, the image moves behind the crop area.

Note:

You can also use the Arrow keys on your keyboard to "nudge" the image in a specific direction.

You can click inside the crop area to drag the area without changing its size.

By default, the crop marquee remains centered in the document window.

Areas outside the crop marquee are darkened.

The image moves behind the marquee to show which section will be inside the cropped area.

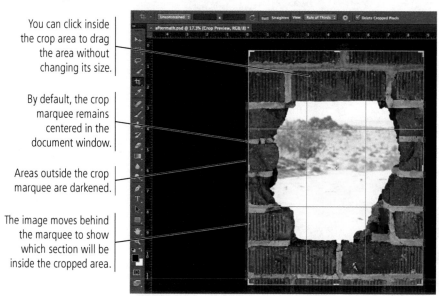

Note:

It might be helpful to toggle off the Snap feature (View>Snap), which causes certain file elements to act as magnets when you move a marquee or drag a selection.

6. **Press Return/Enter to finalize the crop.**

7. **Choose the Move tool, and then open the Info panel (Window>Info).**

   As we explained in the Interface chapter, the panels you see depend on what was done the last time you (or someone else) used the Photoshop application. Because workspace arrangement is such a personal preference, we tell you what panels you need to use but we don't tell you where to put them.

Note:

Remember: panels can always be accessed in the Window menu.

8. **Click the horizontal page ruler at the top of the page and drag down to create a guide positioned at the 1/8″ (0.125″) mark.**

   If you watch the vertical ruler, you can see a marker indicating the position of the cursor. In addition to the live cursor feedback, the Info panel also shows the precise numeric position of the guide you are dragging.

   Here again, it helps to zoom in to a higher view percentage if you want to precisely place guides. We found it necessary to use at least 66.7% view before the Info panel reflected exactly the 0.125″ position. If you zoom in, you can press the Spacebar to temporarily access the Hand tool to reposition the image so you can see the top-left corner.

Note:

If rulers are not visble, choose View>Rulers or press Command/Control-R.

Note:

The X coordinate refers to an object's horizontal position and Y refers to the vertical position.

Click and drag from the horizontal ruler to add a horizontal guide.

The blue line indicates the location of the guide you're dragging.

Watch the ruler or cursor feedback to see the location of the guide you're dragging.

The Info panel shows the exact Y location of the guide you're dragging.

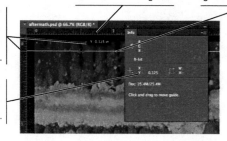

9. **Click the vertical ruler at the left and drag right to place a guide at the 0.125" mark.**

Watch the marker on the horizontal ruler to judge the guide's position.

Drag from the vertical ruler to add a vertical guide.

The cursor feedback and Info panel show the exact X location of the guide you're dragging.

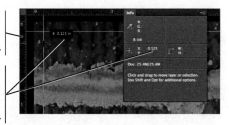

Note:

Use the Move tool to reposition placed guides. Remove individual guides by dragging them back onto the ruler.

If you try to reposition a guide and can't, choose View>Lock Guides. If this option is checked, guides are locked; you can't move them until you toggle this option off.

10. **Choose View>New Guide. In the resulting dialog box, choose the Vertical option and type 8.625 in the field and click OK.**

You don't need to type the unit of measurement because the default unit for this file is already inches. Photoshop automatically assumes the value you type is in the default unit of measurement.

11. **Choose View>New Guide again. Choose the Horizontal option and type 11.125 in the field. Click OK.**

At this point you should have four guides – two vertical and two horizontal, each 1/8" from the file edges. These mark the trim size of your final 8.5 × 11" file.

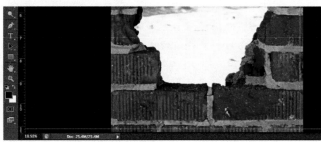

Note:

Press Option/Alt and click a guide to change it from vertical to horizontal (or vice versa). The guide rotates around the point where you click, which can be useful if you need to find a corner based on the position of an existing guide.

12. **In the top-left corner of the document window, click the zero-point crosshairs and drag to the top-left intersection of the guides.**

You can reposition the zero point to the top-left corner of the bleed allowance by double-clicking the zero-point crosshairs.

Zero-point crosshairs

Drag to here to change the 0/0 point of the rulers. This new zero point will be the origin for measurements you make in this file.

13. **Drag new guides 0.25" inside each trim guide to mark the live area of the page.**

These guides mark the defined live area of the ad (8 × 10.5″). This is how we determined where to put these guides:

[Width]   8.5″ − 8.0″ = 0.5 ÷ 2 = 0.25″

[Height]   11″ − 10.5″ = 0.5″ ÷ 2 = 0.25″

Notice that this step says "drag new guides". It is important to realize that the View>New Guide dialog box always positions guides from the original document zero-point (top-left corner); If you use that method, you would have to place the guides 0.375″ from each edge of the file — 0.125″ for the existing bleed guide plus 0.25″ for the live area.

The live cursor feedback is also subject to this limitation. When you drag guides, the feedback always shows measurements based on the original zero point. The Info panel, however, correctly shows measurements based on the repositioned zero point.

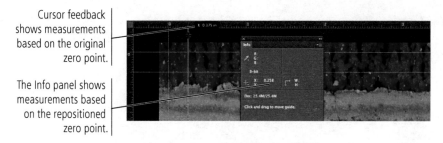

Cursor feedback shows measurements based on the original zero point.

The Info panel shows measurements based on the repositioned zero point.

14. **Click the View menu and make sure a checkmark appears to the left of Lock Guides. If no checkmark is there, choose Lock Guides to toggle on that option.**

After you carefully position specific guides, it's a good idea to lock them so you don't accidentally move or delete them later. If you need to move a guide at any point, simply choose View>Lock Guides to toggle off the option temporarily.

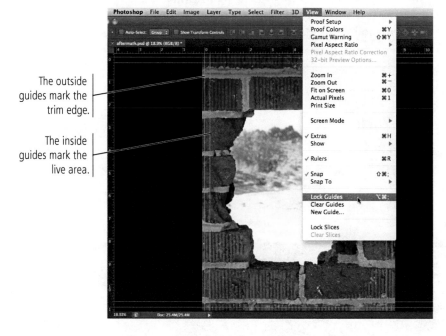

The outside guides mark the trim edge.

The inside guides mark the live area.

Note:

You can press Command/Control-; to toggle the visibility of page guides.

15. **Save the file and continue to the next exercise.**

DRAG A FILE TO COMPOSITE IMAGES

Compositing multiple images in Photoshop is a fairly simple process — or at least, it starts out that way. There are, of course, a number of technical and aesthetic issues that you must resolve when you combine multiple images in a single design.

1. **With aftermath.psd open, use the Mini Bridge panel to navigate back to the Bridge application.**

2. **Click the storm.jpg thumbnail, then review the metadata for that file.**

   This image is only 180 ppi, but it has a physical size much larger than the defined ad size. The principle of effective resolution might make this image usable in the composite ad.

The storm.jpg image is 180 ppi.

3. **Double-click the storm.jpg thumbnail to open that file in Photoshop.**

4. **Open the Window>Arrange menu and choose 2-up (Vertical) to show both open files at one time.**

   As you saw in the Interface chapter, these options are useful for arranging and viewing multiple open files within your workspace.

5. **Choose the Move tool in the Tools panel.**

6. **Click in the storm.jpg image window and drag into the aftermath.psd image window, then release the mouse button.**

   Basic compositing can be as simple as dragging a selection from one file to another. If no active selection appears in the source document, this action moves the entire active layer from the source document.

> **Note:**
>
> *When you created the background file for this project, you created a raster image that contains pixels. Digital photographs and scans are also pixel-based, which is why you use Photoshop to edit and manipulate those types of files.*

> **Note:**
>
> *On Windows, the cursor shows a plus sign to indicate that you are adding the image as a new layer in the document to which you dragged.*

Move tool

The outline shows the shape of the layer you're dragging from one document to another.

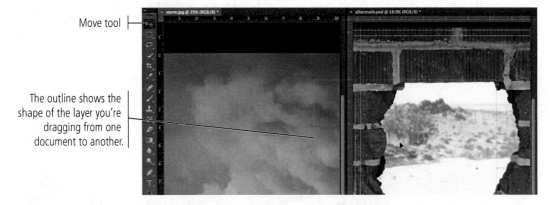

7. **Click the Close button on the storm.jpg document tab to close that file.**

   After closing the storm file, the aftermath.psd document window expands to fill the available space.

   If you remember from the Bridge metadata, the storm image was 17.1″ × 11.4″ at 180 ppi. Photoshop cannot maintain multiple resolutions in a single file. When you move the image content into the aftermath file, it adopts the resolution of the target file (in this case, 300 ppi). The concept of effective resolution transforms the storm image/layer to approximately 10.25″ × 6.825″ at 300 ppi.

8. **Open the Layers panel (Window>Layers).**

   The original aftermath.psd file had only one layer — Background. Before editing, every scan and digital photograph has this characteristic. When you copy or drag content from one file into another, it is automatically placed on a new layer with the default name "Layer *n*", where "n" is a sequential number.

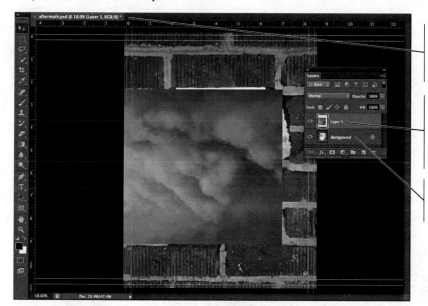

When a file contains more than one layer, the document tab shows the name of the active layer.

A new layer (Layer 1) is automatically added to contain the contents that you dragged from the storm.jpg file.

The Background layer contains the original bricks file content.

9. **Choose File>Save, and read the resulting message.**

   Because this is the first time you have saved the file after adding new layers, you should see the Photoshop Format Options dialog box, with the Maximize Compatibility check box already activated. It's a good idea to leave this check box selected so your files will be compatible with other CS6 applications and other versions of Photoshop.

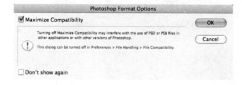

Note:

If you don't see this warning, check the File Handling pane of the Preferences dialog box. You can set the Maximize PSD and PSB File Compatibility menu to Always, Never, or Ask.

10. **Make sure the Maximize Compatibility check box is selected and click OK.**

11. **Continue to the next exercise.**

OPEN FILES WITH MINI BRIDGE

Mini Bridge provides access to certain file-management operations of the full Bridge application, from a panel directly within Photoshop.

1. **With aftermath.psd open, choose View>Fit on Screen to show the entire image centered in the document window.**

2. **If necessary, open the Mini Bridge panel.**

3. **In the Mini Bridge panel, click the arrow to the right of Computer to open the list of available folders. Use these arrows to navigate to the location of your WIP>Movie folder.**

   Once you find the Movie folder, the images in the folder appear in the primary area of the panel.

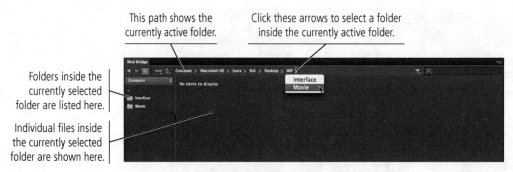

This path shows the currently active folder.

Click these arrows to select a folder inside the currently active folder.

Folders inside the currently selected folder are listed here.

Individual files inside the currently selected folder are shown here.

4. **Scroll through the thumbnails (if necessary), and double-click the skyline.jpg image thumbnail to open that file.**

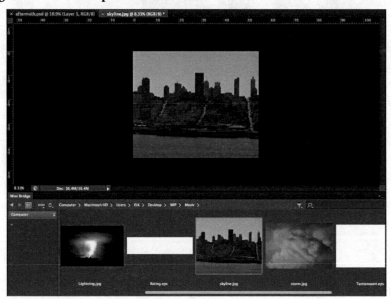

Note:

As in the full Bridge application, double-clicking a file in the Mini Bridge panel opens that file in a separate document window.

5. **Open the Image Size dialog box (Image>Image Size). Make sure the Resample Image option is not checked and change the Resolution field to 300 ppi. Click OK to return to the document window.**

6. **Choose the Rectangular Marquee tool in the Tools panel and review the options in the Options bar.**

By default, dragging with a marquee tool creates a new selection. You can use the buttons on the left end of the Options bar to add to the current selection, subtract from the current selection, or intersect with the current selection.

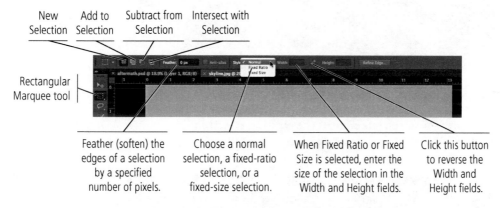

7. **Choose the New Selection option in the Options bar. Click outside of the top-left corner, drag down past the bottom edge of the image, and drag right to create a selection area that is 8.5″ wide.**

You can't select an area larger than the current canvas, so the top, left, and bottom edges of the selection snap to the canvas edges. The live cursor feedback, as well as the mark on the horizontal ruler, help to determine the selection area's width.

Note:

The edges of this image will be hidden by the bricks, so you don't need the full 8.75″ width of the overall ad.

Note:

Press Shift while dragging a new marquee to constrain the selection to a square (using the Rectangular Marquee tool) or circle (using the Elliptical Marquee tool).

8. **Click inside the selection marquee and drag it to the approximate center of the image.**

You can move a selection marquee by clicking inside the selected area with the Marquee tool and dragging to the desired area of the image.

The live cursor feedback shows how far you have moved the area.

The Marquee tool is still active.

"Marching ants" identify the selected area.

Click inside the selection marquee and drag to reposition it.

Note:

If you want to move a marquee, make sure the Marquee tool is still selected. If the Move tool is active, clicking inside the marquee and dragging will actually move the contents within the selection area.

9. **In the Options bar, choose the Subtract from Selection option.**

10. **Click near the waterline at the left edge of the existing selection, drag down past the bottom edge of the image, and right past the right edge of the existing selection.**

Note:

Press Shift to add to the current selection or press Option/Alt to subtract from the current selection.

Subtract from Selection is active.

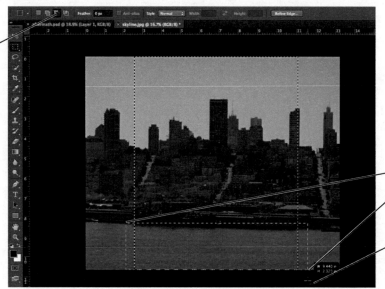

Click here...

...and drag to here.

The cursor shows a minus sign because you are subtracting from the existing selection.

You only want the city to appear in the ad, so you don't need the water area of this image. When you release the mouse button, the selection is the area of the first marquee, minus the area of the second marquee. (This two-step process isn't particularly necessary in this case, but you should know how to add to and subtract from selections.)

11. **Choose Edit>Copy.**

The standard Cut, Copy, and Paste options are available in Photoshop, just as they are in most applications. Whatever you have selected will be copied to the Clipboard, and whatever is in the Clipboard will be pasted.

12. **Click the Close button on the skyline.jpg document tab to close the file. When asked, click Don't Save.**

Although the city would have adopted the resolution of the composite file, you manually resized the image so you could see the appropriate measurements for making your selection. You don't need to save this change.

13. **With the aftermath.psd file active, choose Edit>Paste.**

The copied selection is pasted in the center of the document window. Because you used the Fit on Screen option at the beginning of this exercise, the pasted image is centered in the document. Another new layer is automatically created to store the pasted content.

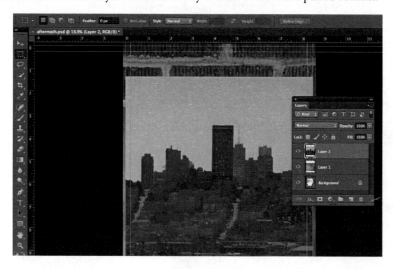

14. **Save the file and continue to the next exercise.**

PLACE A FILE FROM MINI BRIDGE

In addition to opening new files, you can also use the Mini Bridge panel to place content directly into an open file. This removes a few steps from the process of compositing multiple images.

1. **With aftermath.psd open, choose View>Fit on Screen.**

2. **In the Mini Bridge panel, navigate to the WIP>Movie folder if necessary.**

3. **Click the Lightning.jpg thumbnail in the panel and drag it to the aftermath.psd document window.**

   The placed file appears with bounding box handles and crossed diagonal lines. The placement isn't final until you press Return/Enter; if you press the Escape key, the file will not be placed.

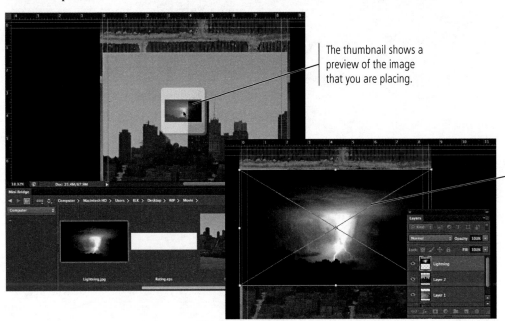

The thumbnail shows a preview of the image that you are placing.

Crossed diagonal lines and bounding box handles indicate that the placement is not yet final.

4. **Press Return/Enter to finalize the placement.**

   After you finalize the placement, the bounding box handles and crossed diagonal lines disappear. In the Layers panel, the placed file has its own layer (just as the copied layers do). This layer, however, is automatically named, based on the name of the placed file.

   The layer's thumbnail indicates that this layer is a **Smart Object** — it is linked to the file that you placed. Changes in the original file will also be reflected in the file where the original is placed.

Note:

You can place either raster or vector files as Smart Objects. If you place a raster file as a Smart Object, double-clicking the thumbnail opens the placed raster file in another Photoshop window.

The layer adopts the name of the placed file.

This icon identifies a Smart Object layer.

5. **Control/right-click the Smart Object layer name and choose Rasterize Layer.**

You don't need to maintain a link to the original file, so this step converts the Smart Object layer to a regular layer.

Control/right-click the layer name to access the contextual menu for that layer.

The Lightning layer is now a regular layer.

6. **Save the file and continue to the next exercise.**

 ## RASTERIZE A VECTOR FILE

As you learned earlier, vector graphics are based on a series of mathematical descriptions that tell the computer processor where to draw lines. Logos and title treatments — such as the ones you will use in this project — are commonly created as vector graphics. Although Photoshop is typically a "paint" (pixel-based) application, you can also open and work with vector graphics created in illustration programs like Adobe Illustrator.

1. **With aftermath.psd open, choose File>Open and navigate to your WIP>Movie folder.**

2. **Select title.ai in the list of files and then click Open.**

This is an Adobe Illustrator file of the movie title text treatment. The Format menu defaults to Photoshop PDF because Illustrator uses PDF as its underlying file structure.

When you open a vector file (Illustrator, EPS, or PDF) in Photoshop, it is rasterized (converted to a raster graphic). The Import PDF dialog box allows you to determine exactly what and how to rasterize the file. The default values in this box are defined by the contents of the file you're opening.

The Crop To options determine the size of the opened file. Depending on how the file was created, some of these values might be the same as others:

- **Bounding Box** is the outermost edges of the artwork in the file.
- **Media Box** is the size of the paper as defined in the file.
- **Crop Box** is the size of the page including printer's marks.
- **Bleed Box** is the trim size plus any defined bleed allowance.
- **Trim Box** is the trim size as defined in the file.
- **Art Box** is the area of the page as defined in the file.

Note:

If you double-clicked title.ai in Adobe Bridge, it would default to open in Adobe Illustrator — its native application, or the application in which it was created. You could, however, Control/right-click the thumbnail in Bridge and choose Open With>Adobe Photoshop CS6 from the contextual menu.

Note:

The Image Size fields default to the settings of the bounding box you select. You can change the size, resolution, color mode, and bit depth by entering new values.

3. **Highlight the Width field and type 8, and make sure the Resolution field is set to 300 pixels/inch.**

You know the live area of the ad you're building is 8″ wide, so you can import this file at a size small enough to fit into that space. Because the Constrain Proportions option is checked by default, the height changes proportionally to match the new width.

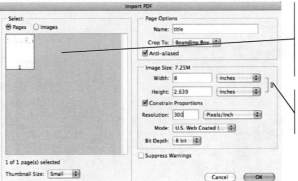

If you're opening a multi-page PDF or an Illustrator file with more than one artboard, this window shows previews of each "page" in the file.

When this chain icon appears, the width and height are constrained.

4. **Click OK.**

The title treatment file opens in Photoshop. The checkered area behind the text indicates that the background is transparent. If you look at the Layers panel, you will see that Layer 1 isn't locked; because it's transparent, it is not considered a background layer.

5. **Choose Select>All.**

This command creates a marquee for the entire canvas.

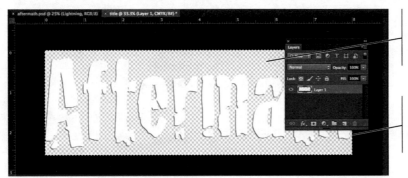

The gray-and-white checked pattern identifies areas of transparency in the layer content.

Using the Select>All command surrounds the entire canvas in a selection marquee.

6. **Choose Edit>Copy, then click the Close button on the title document tab to close that file. Click Don't Save when asked.**

7. **With the aftermath.psd file active, choose Edit>Paste.**

Note:

Command/Control-clicking a layer thumbnail results in a selection around the contents of that layer.

8. **Save aftermath.psd and continue to the next exercise.**

PLACE MULTIPLE EPS GRAPHICS

Vector graphics offer several advantages over raster images, including sharper edges and free scaling without deteriorating image quality. To take advantage of these benefits, you might want to maintain vector files as vector objects instead of rasterizing them. Photoshop CS6 gives you the option to do exactly that — maintaining vector information and raster information in the same file.

1. **With aftermath.psd open, open the Mini Bridge panel (Window> Extensions>Mini Bridge) if the panel is not already open.**

2. **Click the Rating.eps thumbnail to select it.**

3. **Press Command/Control and then click the Tantamount.eps file to add it to the active selection.**

   These vector graphics were created in Adobe Illustrator and saved as EPS files. (The EPS format supports both raster and vector information, however, so don't assume that an EPS file always contains only vector information.

4. **Click either of the selected thumbnails and drag into the aftermath.psd image window to place both files.**

   Unlike opening or placing a native Illustrator file, there are no further options when you place an EPS file.

Note:

If you place a native Illustrator file from the Mini Bridge panel, you can define the Crop To area for the placement, but you can't access any of the other options that are available when you open an Illustrator file.

The cursor icon shows how many files are being placed.

Press Command/Control to select non-contiguous files in the panel.

After releasing the mouse button, the first selected file appears with crossed diagonal lines (not yet finalized).

5. **Press Return/Enter to finalize the placement of the first file.**

After finalizing, the first file no longer shows the bounding box handles.

The second file automatically appears, ready to be finalized.

Note:

If you have the entire Adobe Creative Suite, Smart Objects provide extremely tight integration between Adobe Photoshop and Adobe Illustrator. You can take advantage of the sophisticated vector-editing features in Adobe Illustrator, and then place those files into Photoshop without losing the ability to edit the vector information.

6. **Press Return/Enter again to finalize the placement of the second file.**

The two placed files are stored on layers named based on the placed file names.

The placed files are Smart Object layers.

7. **Save the file and continue to the next stage of the project.**

Right now, you have a fairly incomprehensible mess of four raster images and three vector objects all piled on top of one another. You will start to make sense of these files in the next stage.

Stage 2 Managing Layers

Your ad file now has most of the necessary pieces, but it's still not an actual design — just a pile of images. When you composite images into a cohesive design, you almost certainly need to manipulate and transform some of the layers to make all of the pieces work together.

Photoshop includes a number of options for managing layers: naming layers for easier recognition, creating layer groups so multiple layers can be manipulated at once, moving layers around on the canvas, transforming layers both destructively and non-destructively, controlling individual layer visibility, and arranging the top-to-bottom stacking order of layers to determine exactly what is visible. You will use all of these options in this stage of the project.

NAME LAYERS AND LAYER GROUPS

It's always a good idea to name your layers because it makes managing the file much easier — especially when you work with files that include dozens of layers. Even with only four unnamed layers in this file (counting the Background layer), it would be tedious to have to toggle each layer on to find the one you want.

1. **With aftermath.psd open, review the Layers panel.**

2. Click the eye icons to hide all but Layer 1.

Toggling layer visibility is an easy way to see only what you want to see at any given stage in a project.

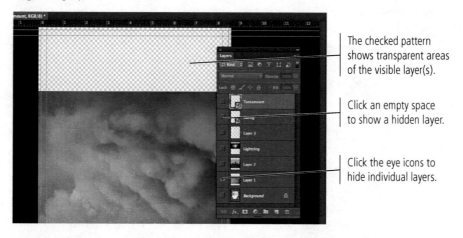

The checked pattern shows transparent areas of the visible layer(s).

Click an empty space to show a hidden layer.

Click the eye icons to hide individual layers.

Note:

To show or hide a series of contiguous layers, click the visibility icon (or empty space) for the first layer you want to affect, hold down the mouse button, and drag down to the last layer you want to show or hide.

3. Double-click the Layer 1 layer name, and then type Storm.

You can rename any layer by simply double-clicking the name and typing.

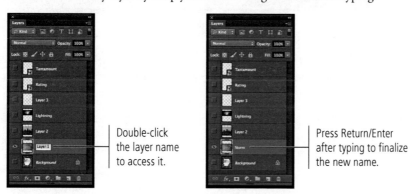

Double-click the layer name to access it.

Press Return/Enter after typing to finalize the new name.

Note:

You can Option/Alt-click a layer's visibility icon to hide all other layers in the file.

4. Click the eye icon to hide the renamed Storm layer, and then click the empty space to the left of Layer 2 to show only that layer.

5. Double-click the Layer 2 name and then type Skyline to rename the layer.

6. Repeat Steps 4–5 to rename Layer 3 as Title.

7. Click the spaces on the left side of the Layers panel (where the eye icons were) to show all hidden layers.

8. In the Layers panel, click the Tantamount layer to select it.

9. Press Shift and click the Rating layer to select that layer as well.

Since the Tantamount layer was already selected, the Rating layer should now be a second selected (highlighted) layer.

Note:

Press Shift and click to select contiguous layers in the Layers panel.

Press Command/Control and click to select non-contiguous layers in the Layers panel.

10. **Click the button in the top-right corner of the panel to open the Layers panel Options menu. Choose New Group from Layers.**

This option creates a group that automatically contains the selected layers. You can also create an empty group by choosing New Group (this option is available even when no layer is selected) or by clicking the New Group button at the bottom of the panel.

Click here to open the panel Options menu.

Two layers are selected.

New Group button

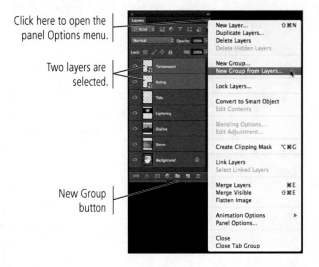

Note:

You can create a group from selected layers by dragging the selected layers onto the New Group button at the bottom of the panel. In this case, the new group is automatically named "Group N" (N is a placeholder for a sequential number); of course, you can rename a layer group just as easily as you can rename a layer.

11. **In the New Group from Layers dialog box, type Logos in the Name field and click OK.**

As with any other layer, you should name groups based on what they contain so you can easily identify them later.

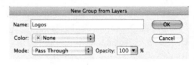

Note:

You can create up to ten levels of nested layer groups, or groups inside of other groups.

12. **Click the arrow to the left of the Logos group name to expand the layer group.**

You have to expand the layer group to be able to access and edit individual layers in the group. If you select the entire layer group, you can move all layers within the group at the same time. Layers in the group maintain their position relative to one another.

Note:

You can click the eye icon for a layer folder to hide the entire layer group (and all layers inside the folder).

13. **Save the file and continue to the next exercise.**

MOVE AND TRANSFORM SMART OBJECT LAYERS

Photoshop makes scaling, rotating, and other transformations fairly easy to implement, but it is important to realize the potential impact of your transformations.

1. **With aftermath.psd open, click the Tantamount layer (in the Logos folder) in the Layers panel to select only that layer.**

2. **Choose the Move tool in the Tools panel.**

   As the name suggests, the Move tool is used to move a selection around on the canvas. You can select a specific area, and then click and drag to move only the selection on the active layer. If there is no active selection area, you can click and drag to move the contents of the entire active layer.

3. **In the Options bar, make sure the Auto-Select option is not checked.**

   When Auto-Select is checked, you can click in the image window and drag to move the contents of the layer containing the pixels where you click; you do not need to first select the layer in the Layers panel before moving the layer content. This is very useful in some cases, as you will see later in this project. However, the Auto-Select option is *not* very useful when the contents of multiple layers are stacked on top of each other (as is the case in your file as it exists now).

   > *Note:*
   >
   > *Deselect all layers by clicking in the empty area at the bottom of the Layers panel.*

4. **Click in the image window and drag until the Tantamount layer content snaps to the bottom-right live-area guides.**

   If you toggled off the Snap feature when you used the Crop tool, you should turn it back on now by choosing View>Snap.

This option should not be checked.

Move tool

With no marching ants in the image window, select the layer you want to move, then click and drag in the document window to move the layer's contents.

5. **Click the Rating layer in the Layers panel to select that layer.**

6. **Click in the image window and drag until the Rating layer content snaps to the bottom-left live-area guides.**

7. **With the Rating layer still active, choose Edit>Free Transform.**

   When you use the transform options, bounding box handles surround the selection.

   > *Note:*
   >
   > *You can also use the Edit>Transform submenu to apply specific transformations to a layer or selection.*

8. **Press Shift, click the top-right bounding box handle, and then drag down and left until the layer content is approximately two-thirds the original size.**

   The selection (in this case, the entire Rating layer) dynamically changes as you scale the layer. Pressing Shift while you drag a handle constrains the image proportions as you resize it. When you release the mouse button, the handles remain in place until you finalize ("commit") the transformation.

   The live cursor feedback shows the new dimensions of the transformed selection.

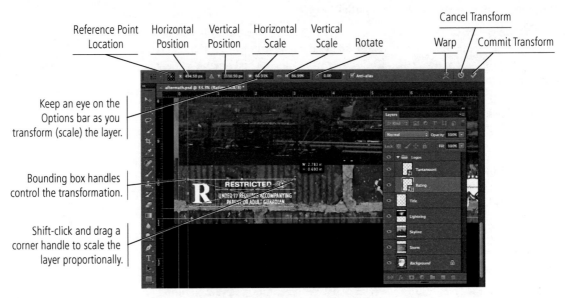

Reference Point Location · Horizontal Position · Vertical Position · Horizontal Scale · Vertical Scale · Rotate · Cancel Transform · Warp · Commit Transform

Keep an eye on the Options bar as you transform (scale) the layer.

Bounding box handles control the transformation.

Shift-click and drag a corner handle to scale the layer proportionally.

   While you're manually transforming a layer or selection, the Options bar shows the specifics. You can also type into these fields to apply specific numeric transformations.

9. **Press Return/Enter to finalize the transformation.**

   After finalizing the transformation, the bounding-box handles disappear.

10. **With the Rating layer still active, press Command/Control-T to enter Free Transform mode again and look at the Options bar.**

   Because the rating layer is a Smart Object layer, the W and H fields still show the scaling percentage based on the original.

The W and H fields still show the scaling you applied in Step 8.

11. **In the Options bar, choose the bottom-left reference point location.**

   The selected reference point defines the point around which transformations are made. By selecting the bottom-left point, for example, the bottom-left corner of the active selection will remain in place when you scale the selection in the next steps; the top-right corner will move based on the scaling you define.

12. **Click the Link icon between the W and H fields to constrain proportions during the transformation.**

13. Type 50 in the Options bar W field.

The bottom-left reference point is selected.

Click the Lock icon to constrain the height and width proportionally.

14. Click the Commit Transform button on the Options bar (or press Return/Enter) to finalize the transformation.

15. Collapse the layer group by clicking the arrow at the left of the group name.

Note:

If you press Return/Enter, you have to press it two times to finalize the transormation. The first time you press it, you apply the change to the active field; the second time, you finalize the transformation and exit Free Transform mode.

16. Save the file and continue to the next exercise.

TRANSFORM A REGULAR LAYER

Smart Object layers enable non-destructive transformations, which means those transformations can be changed or undone without affecting the quality of the layer content. Transforming a regular layer, on the other hand, is destructive and permanent.

1. With aftermath.psd open, hide all but the Storm layer. Click the Storm layer in the Layers panel to select it.

2. Choose Edit>Transform>Flip Horizontal.

The Transform submenu commands affect only the selected layer.

3. **Press Command/Control-T to enter Free Transform mode.**

   Some handles might not be visible within the boundaries of the document window. If necessary, zoom out so you can see all eight handles of the layer content.

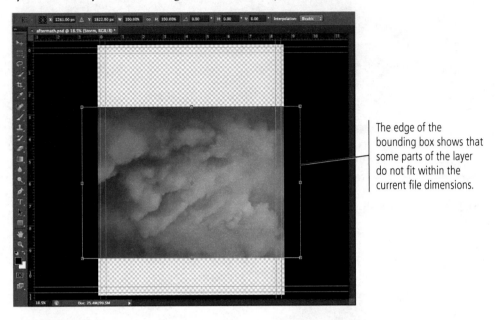

The edge of the bounding box shows that some parts of the layer do not fit within the current file dimensions.

4. **In the Options bar, choose the center reference point if it is not already selected.**

5. **Click the Link icon between the W and H fields to constrain the proportions.**

6. **Place the cursor over the W field label to access the scrubby slider for that field.**

The center reference point is selected.   Click the Link icon to constrain proportions.

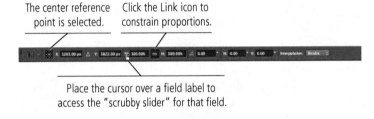

Place the cursor over a field label to access the "scrubby slider" for that field.

7. **Click and drag left until the W field shows 90%.**

8. **Press Return/Enter to finalize the transformation.**

9. **With the Storm layer still active, press Command/Control-T to re-enter Free Transform mode.**

   Once you commit the transformation on a regular layer, the transformation is final. Looking at the Options bar now, you can see that it shows the layer at 100% instead of the 90% from Step 7.

Re-entering Free Transform mode shows that the regular layer is again 100%, even after scaling.

10. **Press Esc to exit Free Transform mode without changing anything.**

11. **Save the file and continue to the next exercise.**

 ## TRANSFORM THE BACKGROUND LAYER

Your file currently has a number of layers, most of which were created by pasting or placing external files into the original file. Because every photograph and scan (and some images that you create from scratch in Photoshop) begins with a default locked Background layer, it is important to understand the special characteristics of that layer:

- You can't apply layer transformations, styles, or masks to the Background layer.

- You can't move the contents of the Background layer around in the document.

- If you delete pixels from the Background layer, the removed pixels will automatically be filled with the current background color.

- The Background layer cannot include transparent pixels, which are necessary for underlying layers to be visible.

- The Background layer is always the bottom layer in the stacking order; you can't add or move layers lower than the Background layer.

In the final composite file for this project, you need to flip the bricks image from top to bottom, remove the desert area from the hole in the bricks, and place the other photographs to appear through the hole in the wall. For any of these options to work properly, you need to convert the default Background layer to a regular layer.

Note:

If you transform a Smart Object layer, the scale percentage is maintained even after you finalize the change (unlike scaling a regular layer, where the layer re-calibrates so the new size is considered 100% once you finalize the scaling).

Note:

If you crop an image that includes a Background layer, the Background layer is automatically converted to a regular layer if the Delete Cropped Pixels option is not checked.

1. **With `aftermath.psd` open, hide the Storm layer and then show the Background layer.**

2. **Click the Background layer to select it and then choose Edit>Transform.**

   The Transform submenu commands are not available for the locked Background layer.

Note:

Although the Background layer exists by default in many files, it is not a required component.

Many commands are not available because the Background layer is locked.

3. **With the Background layer still selected, choose Image>Image Rotation> Flip Canvas Vertical.**

   To affect the locked background layer, you have to flip the actual canvas.

4. **Show the Logos layer group.**

   Because you flipped the canvas, the Tantamount and Ratings layers are also flipped upside-down. Rotating or flipping the entire canvas affects all layers in the file; this is obviously not what you want to do.

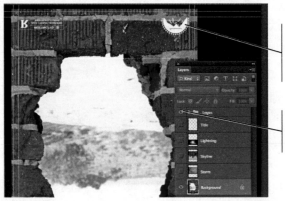

Because you flipped the canvas, the logos are now upside-down.

Showing the layer group shows all layers in that group.

5. **Choose Edit>Undo to restore the canvas to its original orientation.**

    The Undo command affects the last action you performed. Showing or hiding a layer is not considered an "action," so the Undo command simply un-flips the canvas. As you can see, though, the Logos group is again hidden, as it was when you flipped the canvas in Step 3.

6. **In the Layers panel, double-click the Background layer.**

7. **In the resulting New Layer dialog box, type `Bricks` in the Name field, then click OK.**

    Renaming the Background layer automatically unlocks and converts it to a regular layer.

Note:

The Undo menu command changes to reflect the action that will be affected. In this case, the actual command is Edit>Undo Flip Canvas Vertical.

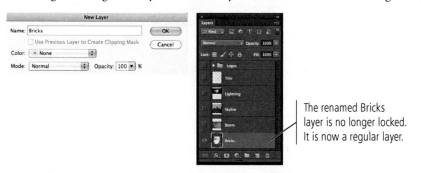

The renamed Bricks layer is no longer locked. It is now a regular layer.

8. **With the Bricks layer selected in the panel, choose Edit>Transform>Flip Vertical.**

    Because the layer is no longer locked, you can now access and apply the transform commands that affect only the selected layer.

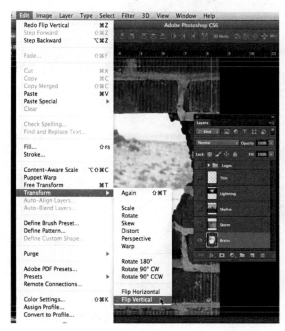
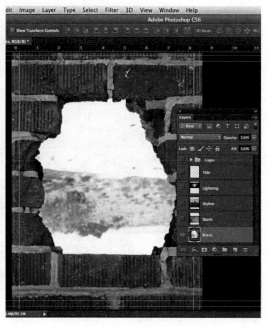

9. **Show all layers in the file.**

10. **Save the file and continue to the next stage of the project.**

Stage 3 Creating Complex Selections

At this stage of the project, you still have a few issues to resolve: some of the images are still randomly stacked on top of one another, and some images have areas that are hiding other images (the blue sky in the Skyline layer, for example). In this stage, you start fixing these problems.

Virtually any Photoshop project involves making some kind of selection. Making selections is so important, in fact, that there are no fewer than nine tools dedicated specifically to this goal, as well as a whole Select menu and a few other options for making and refining selections.

In an earlier lesson you learned how to use the Rectangular Marquee tool to draw simple selections. In the next series of exercises, you use several other selection methods to isolate pixels from their backgrounds (called **silhouetting**).

MAKE A FEATHERED SELECTION

1. **With aftermath.psd open, hide all but the Lightning layer. Click the Lightning layer to make it active.**

2. **Select the Lasso tool in the Tools panel.**

3. **Drag a rough shape around the lightning in the photo.**

   The lasso tools allow you to make irregular selections — in other words, selections that aren't just rectangular or elliptical. When you release the mouse button, the end point automatically connects to the beginning point of the selection.

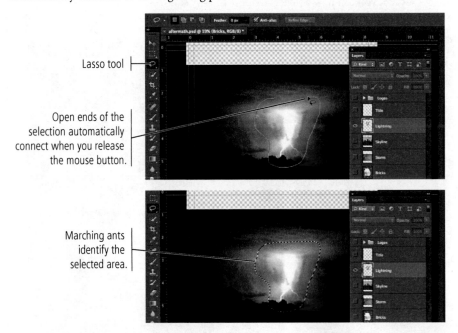

Lasso tool

Open ends of the selection automatically connect when you release the mouse button.

Marching ants identify the selected area.

4. **With the marching ants active, choose Select>Modify>Feather.**

   Feathering means to soften the edge of a selection so the image blends into the background instead of showing a sharp line around the edge. The Smooth, Expand, and Contract options in the Select>Modify submenu are self-explanatory; the Border option creates a specific number of pixels around the active selection (like the stroke/ border that surrounds a shape in an illustration program).

Note:

*You could also create a feathered selection by typing in the Feather field of the Options bar **before** drawing the selection marquee.*

5. **In the resulting dialog box, type 35 in the Feather Radius field. Click OK to return to the image window.**

   The Feather Radius defines the distance from solid to transparent. In the image window, there's no apparent difference in the selection because the marching ants can't show shades of a selection.

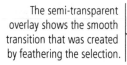

6. **Click the Quick Mask button at the bottom of the Tools panel to toggle into Quick Mask mode.**

   This mode creates a temporary red overlay (called an Alpha channel) that shows the graded selection. By default, the overlay is semi-transparent, which allows you to see the underlying image.

The semi-transparent overlay shows the smooth transition that was created by feathering the selection.

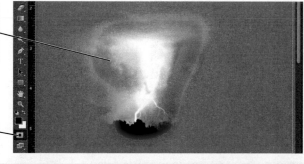

Quick Mask button

The Lasso Tools

PHOTOSHOP FOUNDATIONS

The basic **Lasso tool** works like a pencil, following the path where you drag the mouse.

The **Polygonal Lasso tool** creates selections with straight lines, anchoring a line each time you click the mouse. To close a selection area, you must click the first point in the selection.

The **Magnetic Lasso tool** snaps to edges of high contrast; you can use the Options bar to control the way Photoshop detects the edges of an image. **Width** is the distance away from the edge the cursor can be and still detect the edge; if you set this value higher, you can move the cursor farther from the edge. **Contrast** is how different the foreground can be from the background and still be detected; if there is a very sharp distinction between the foreground and background (as in the case of the white quill against the blue background in these sample images), you can set this value higher. **Frequency** is the number of points that will be created to make the selection; setting this number higher creates finer selections, while setting it lower creates smoother edges.

It isn't uncommon for a mouse to unexpectedly jump when you don't want it to — which can be particularly troublesome if you're drawing a selection with the Polygonal or Magnetic Lasso tools. If you aren't happy with your Polygonal or Magnetic Lasso selection, press Escape to clear the selection and then try again.

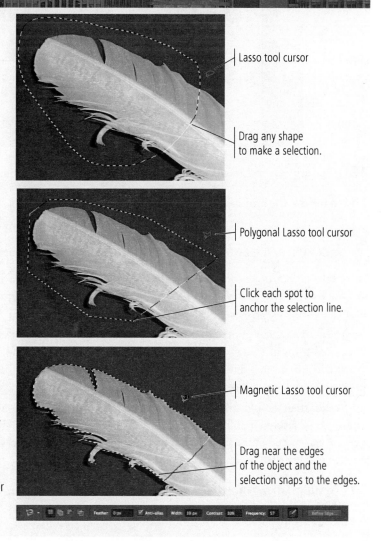

Lasso tool cursor

Drag any shape to make a selection.

Polygonal Lasso tool cursor

Click each spot to anchor the selection line.

Magnetic Lasso tool cursor

Drag near the edges of the object and the selection snaps to the edges.

7. **Click the Quick Mask button at the bottom of the Tools panel to toggle off the Quick Mask.**

8. **Choose Select>Inverse.**

   You want to remove the area around the lightning, so you have to select everything *other than* what you originally selected — in other words, the inverse of the previous selection.

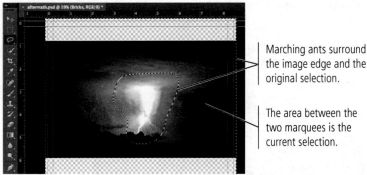

Marching ants surround the image edge and the original selection.

The area between the two marquees is the current selection.

Note:

Press Command/Control-Shift-I to invert the active selection.

9. **With the Lightning layer selected in the Layers panel, press Delete/Backspace.**

   Selection marquees are not particular to a specific layer. You have to make sure the correct layer is active before you use the selection to perform some action.

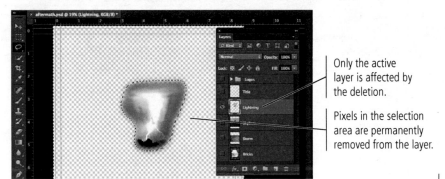

Only the active layer is affected by the deletion.

Pixels in the selection area are permanently removed from the layer.

10. **Choose Select>Deselect to turn off the active selection (marching ants).**

11. **Save the file and continue to the next exercise.**

Note:

Pressing Command/Control-D deselects the active selection.

SELECT A COLOR RANGE AND CREATE A LAYER MASK

As we said earlier, there are many selection options in Photoshop CS6, each with its own advantages and disadvantages. You have already used the marquee tools and lasso tools to select general areas of images.

Many images have both hard and soft edges, and/or very fine detail that needs to be isolated from its background (think of a model's blowing hair overlapping the title on the cover of a magazine). In this type of image, other tools can be used to create a very detailed selection based on the color in the image.

Rather than simply deleting pixels, as you did for the lightning image, another option for isolating object with a path is to create a **layer mask** that hides unwanted pixels. Areas outside the mask are hidden but not deleted, so you can later edit the mask to change the visible part of the image.

1. **With aftermath.psd open, hide all but the Skyline layer. Click the Skyline layer to make it active.**

2. **Choose the Magic Wand tool (under the Quick Selection tool). In the Options bar, make sure the New Selection button is active and set the Tolerance field to 32.**

The Magic Wand tool is an easy way to select large areas of solid color. The first four options in the Options bar are the same as those for the Marquee tools (New Selection, Add to Selection, Subtract from Selection, and Intersect with Selection).

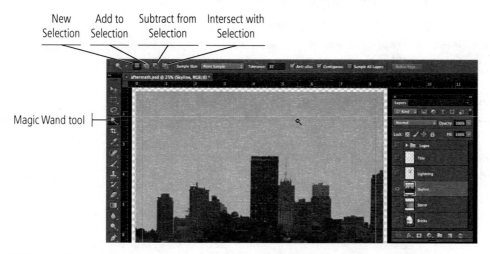

New Selection   Add to Selection   Subtract from Selection   Intersect with Selection

Magic Wand tool

Tolerance is the degree of variation between the color you click and the colors Photoshop will select; higher tolerance values select a larger range based on the color you click. If you're trying to select a very mottled background (for example), you should increase the tolerance; be careful, however, because increasing the tolerance might select too large a range of colors if parts of the foreground object fall within the tolerance range.

The **Anti-alias** check box, selected by default, allows edges to blend more smoothly into the background, preventing a jagged, stair-stepped appearance.

When **Contiguous** is selected, the Magic Wand tool only selects adjacent areas of the color; unchecking this option allows you to select all pixels within the color tolerance, even if some pixels are non-contiguous (for example, inside the shape of the letter Q).

By default, selections relate to the active layer only. You can check **Sample All Layers** to make a selection of all layers in the file.

The **Refine Edge** button opens a dialog box where you can use a number of tools to fine-tune the selection edge.

Note:

Anti-aliasing is the process of blending shades of pixels to create the illusion of sharp lines in a raster image.

3. **Click anywhere in the blue sky area of the image.**

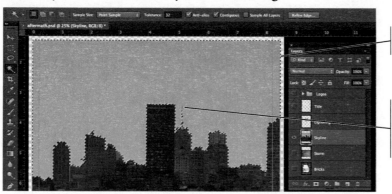

Marching ants indicate the selection area.

Fine areas of detail can't be distinguished by the marching ants, so you don't know if they're selected.

4. **Choose Select>Deselect to turn off the current selection.**

Although you could keep adding to the selection with the Magic Wand tool, the marching ants can't really show the fine detail.

5. **Choose Select>Color Range.**

6. **Make sure the Localized Color Clusters option is unchecked.**

7. **Choose White Matte in the Selection Preview menu (if it is not already).**

   By changing the Selection Preview, you can more easily determine exactly what is selected. You can preview color range selections in the image window as:

   - **None** shows the normal image in the document window.
   - **Grayscale** shows the entire image in shades of gray; selected areas are solid white and unselected areas are solid black.
   - **Black Matte** shows unselected areas in solid black; selected areas appear in color.
   - **White Matte** shows unselected areas in solid white; selected areas appear in color.
   - **Quick Mask** adds a partially transparent overlay to unselected areas.

Note:

Because the dialog box preview is so small, we prefer to rely on the preview in the document window, which is controlled in the Selection Preview menu at the bottom of the dialog box.

8. **Set the Fuzziness value to 25 and click anywhere in the blue sky (in the document window).**

   Fuzziness is similar to the Tolerance setting for the Magic Wand tool. Higher Fuzziness values allow you to select more variation from the color you click.

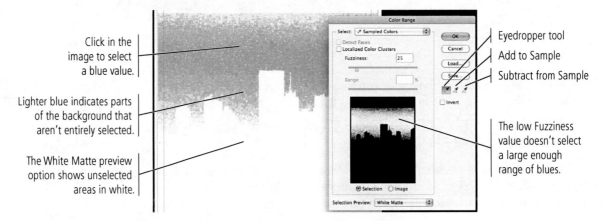

Click in the image to select a blue value.

Lighter blue indicates parts of the background that aren't entirely selected.

The White Matte preview option shows unselected areas in white.

Eyedropper tool

Add to Sample

Subtract from Sample

The low Fuzziness value doesn't select a large enough range of blues.

9. **Change the Fuzziness value to 80 and watch the effect on the dialog box preview.**

   Changing the Fuzziness value expands (higher numbers) or contracts (lower numbers) the selection. Be careful, though, since higher fuzziness values can eliminate fine lines and detail.

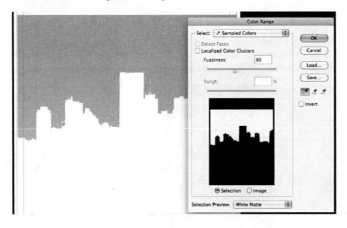

Note:

Depending on where you clicked, your selection might not exactly match what you see in our screen shot. For now, the important point is to know that the visible areas indicate the current selection.

PHOTOSHOP FOUNDATIONS

Selecting Localized Color Clusters

The **Localized Color Clusters** option in the Color Range dialog box can be used to select specific areas of a selected color. When this option is checked, the Range slider defines how far away (in physical distance) a color can be located from the point you click and still be included in the selection.

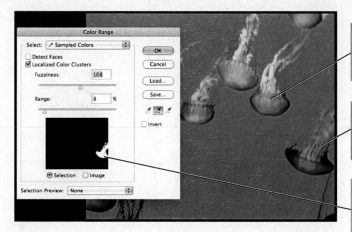

The same colors in other jellyfish are not selected because they are outside the reduced Range value.

We used a number of clicks with different Fuzziness values to sample the colors in this jellyfish.

Using Localized Color Clusters and a reduced Range value, we were able to isolate this jellyfish from its school.

Selection Presets

The Select menu at the top of the dialog box includes several presets for isolating specific ranges of primary colors (Reds, Yellows, Greens, Cyans, Blues, or Magentas), or specific ranges of color (highlights, midtones, or shadows).

If you select the **Skin Tones** preset, you can then activate the Detect Faces option at the top of the dialog box. By adjusting the Fuzziness slider, you can use this dialog box to make reasonably good selections of people's skin.

As you can see in this example, however, no automatic option is a perfect substitute when subjective decision-making is required. The tones in the rolling pin's reflection are very close to the color of skin, so they are included in the selection. This automatic selection method is still a good starting point, though, for making the complex selection of only a person's (or people's) skin.

Choose a preset from this menu.

When you choose the Skin Tones preset, you can also activate the Detect Faces option.

Some colors are close to skin tones, but are are not skin. You will have to manually edit the mask to correct these areas.

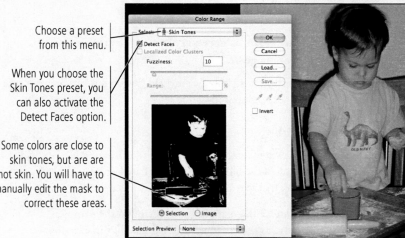

10. **In the Color Range dialog box, click the Add to Sample eyedropper. In the document window, click where parts of the blue sky are not shown in full strength.**

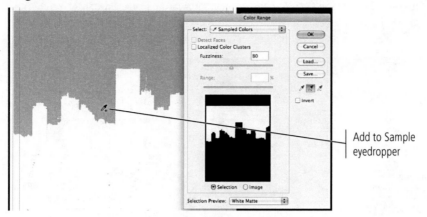

Add to Sample eyedropper

11. **Check the Invert box in the Color Range dialog box.**

Because your goal is to isolate the city and not the sky, it helps to look at what you want to keep instead of what you want to remove.

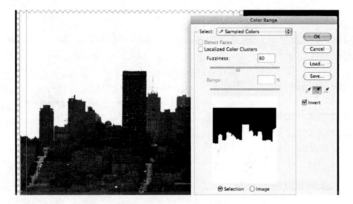

Note:

When the Color Range dialog box is open, you can press Command/Control to switch between the Selection and Image previews within the dialog box.

12. **Continue adding to (or subtracting from, if necessary) your selection until you are satisfied that all the blue sky is gone.**

You can also adjust the Fuzziness slider if necessary, but be sure you don't adjust it too far to include areas of the city.

13. **Click OK when you're satisfied with your selection.**

When you return to the image window, the marching ants indicate the current selection. In the Color Range dialog box, you selected the blue and inverted the selection — in other words, your selection is everything that isn't blue.

If you zoom out to see the entire file, you see the marching ants surround the canvas as well as the blue sky. Since the transparent area is not blue, it is included in the selection.

Marching ants surround the image edge.

14. Choose the Magic Wand tool in the Tools panel and choose the Subtract from Selection option on the Options bar.

15. Click anywhere in the transparent area (the gray-and-white checkerboard) to remove that area from the selection.

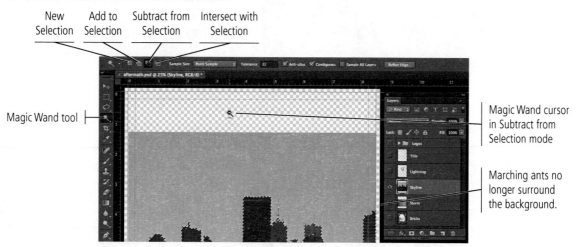

New Selection · Add to Selection · Subtract from Selection · Intersect with Selection

Magic Wand tool

Magic Wand cursor in Subtract from Selection mode

Marching ants no longer surround the background.

16. In the Layers panel, click the Add Layer Mask button.

A **layer mask** is a map of areas that will be visible in the selected layer. The mask you just created is a raster-based pixel mask, based on the active selection when you created the mask. This is a non-destructive way to hide certain elements of a layer without permanently deleting pixels; you can edit or disable the layer mask at any time.

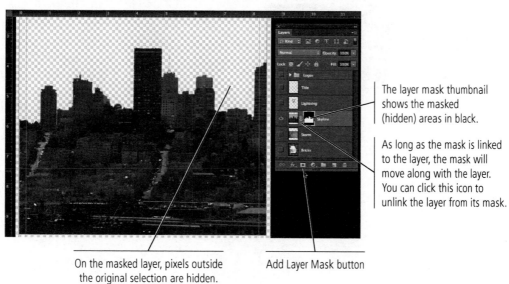

The layer mask thumbnail shows the masked (hidden) areas in black.

As long as the mask is linked to the layer, the mask will move along with the layer. You can click this icon to unlink the layer from its mask.

On the masked layer, pixels outside the original selection are hidden.

Add Layer Mask button

17. Control/right-click the mask thumbnail and choose Disable Layer Mask from the contextual menu.

You have to click the mask thumbnail to open the contextual menu for the mask.

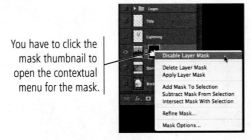

When you disable the mask, the background pixels are again visible. This is one of the advantages of using masks — the background pixels are not permanently removed, they are simply hidden.

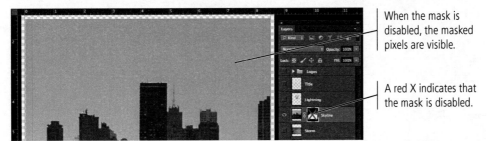

When the mask is disabled, the masked pixels are visible.

A red X indicates that the mask is disabled.

18. Control/right-click the mask thumbnail and choose Apply Layer Mask from the contextual menu.

This option applies the mask to the attached layer, permanently removing the masked pixels from the layer.

Note:

Creating selections, reversing them, and then deleting the pixels surrounding an object is a common method for creating silhouettes — but not necessarily the best method. Masks protect the original pixels while providing exactly the same result.

The masked pixels are permanently removed from the layer.

The mask is removed from the layer.

19. Choose Edit>Undo to restore the layer mask.

As you saw in the previous step, applying a mask permanently removes the masked pixels. This essentially defeats the purpose of a mask, so you are restoring it in this step.

20. Control/right-click the mask thumbnail and choose Enable Layer Mask from the contextual menu.

21. Save the file and continue to the next exercise.

MAKE AND REFINE A QUICK SELECTION

As you just saw, you can make selections based on the color in an image. This technique is useful when you want to select large areas of solid color, or in photos with significant contrast between the foreground and background. When the area you want to select has a complex edge, refining the selection edge can produce very detailed results.

1. **With aftermath.psd open, hide all but the Bricks layer. Click the Bricks layer to select it as the active layer.**

2. **Choose the Quick Selection tool (nested under the Magic Wand tool).**

3. **In the Options bar, make sure the Sample All Layers option is not checked.**

   You only want to select the area in the bricks layer (the hole in the wall), so you do not want to make a selection based on the content of other layers in the file.

4. **Click at the top area of the hole in the wall and drag down to the bottom edge of the hole.**

   The Quick Selection tool essentially allows you to "paint" a selection. As you drag, the selection expands and automatically finds the edges in the image.

Note:

If you stop dragging and then click in a nearby area, the selection grows to include the new area.

New Selection   Add to Selection   Subtract from Selection   Click to change the brush size and attributes.

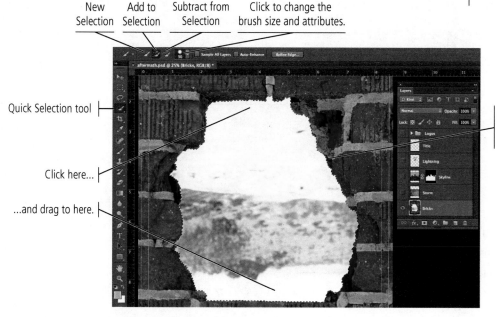

Quick Selection tool

Click here...

...and drag to here.

Marching ants surround the selected area.

5. **Click the Refine Edge button in the Options bar.**

6. **Click the View button. Choose the On White option from the menu if it is not already selected.**

   The preview options allow you to change the way your image appears in the document window while you refine the edges within the dialog box.

   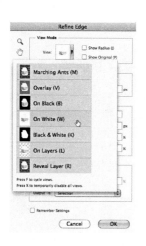

   - **Marching Ants** shows the basic standard selection.
   - **Overlay** shows the unselected areas with a Quick Mask overlay.
   - **On Black** shows the selection in color against a black background.
   - **On White** shows the selection in color against a white background.
   - **Black & White** shows the selected area in white and the unselected area in black.
   - **On Layers** shows only the selected area; unselected areas are hidden.
   - **Reveal Layer** shows the entire layer, with no visual indication of the selection.

7. **Experiment with the adjustments until you're satisfied with the selection edge.**

You want to include a small amount of darkness around the edge so that, when you invert the selection to remove the hole in the wall, there is no light halo effect left by the selection edge. We used the Shift Edge slider to slightly expand the selection edge.

- **Radius** is the number of pixels around the edge that are affected. Higher radius values (up to 250 pixels) improve the edge in areas of fine detail.

- **Smooth** reduces the number of points that make up your selection and, as the name suggests, makes a smoother edge. You can set smoothness from 0 (very detailed selection) to 100 (very smooth selection).

- **Feather** softens the selection edge, resulting in a transition that does not have a hard edge (in other words, blends into the background). You can feather the selection up to 250 pixels.

- **Contrast** is the degree of variation allowed in the selection edge. Higher Contrast values (up to 100%) mean sharper selection edges.

- **Shift Edge** shrinks or grows the selection edge by the defined percentage (from −100% to 100%).

- **Decontaminate Colors** can be checked to remove a certain percentage of color from the edge of a selection.

Note:

It might help to work with a closer view while you refine edges. You can use the Zoom and Hand tools in the Refine Edge dialog box to change the image view behind the open dialog box.

The On White preview shows the selected area on a white background.

The dark edge should be easily visible using the On White preview.

8. **At the bottom of the dialog box, choose the Layer Mask option in the Output To menu.**

This menu can be used to create a new layer or file (with or without a mask) from the selection. You want to mask the existing layer, so you are using the Layer Mask option.

9. **Click OK to accept your refined selection.**

The resulting layer mask hides areas that were not selected.

10. **Click the mask thumbnail in the Layers panel to select only the mask, and then open the Properties panel (Window>Properties).**

As you know, you want to remove the hole in the wall and not the wall. You selected the area in the hole to create the mask, but you now need to invert the mask.

Like the Options bar, the Properties panel is contextual. Different options are available in the panel depending on what is selected in the Layers panel.

When a layer mask is selected, you can manipulate a variety of properties related to the selected mask. (You will use different aspects of the Properties panel in later projects.)

11. **In the Properties panel, click the Invert button.**

This button reverses the mask, so now only the bricks are visible.

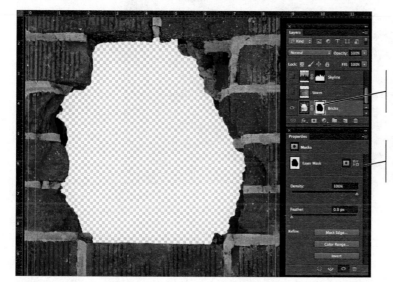

The layer mask must be selected in the Layers panel.

The Properties panel can be used to edit the selected mask.

12. **Save the file and continue to the next exercise.**

 ## ARRANGE LAYER POSITION AND STACKING ORDER

The ad is almost final, but a few pieces are still not quite in position. You already know you can use the Move tool to move the contents of a layer around on the canvas. You can move a layer to any position in the **stacking order** (the top-to-bottom position of a layer) by simply dragging it to a new position in the Layers panel.

1. **With aftermath.psd open, make all layers visible.**

2. **Click the Bricks layer in the Layers panel and drag up. When a heavy bar appears below the Title layer, release the mouse button.**

The heavy line indicates where the layer will be positioned when you release the mouse button.

Note:

Press Command/ Control-[(left bracket) to move a layer down in the stacking order.

Press Command/ Control-] (right bracket) to move a layer up in the stacking order.

Be careful: If the border appears around a layer group, releasing the mouse button would place the dragged layer inside of the group.

3. **With the Move tool active, check the Auto-Select option in the Options bar. Open the attached menu (to the right of the Auto-Select check box) and choose Layer.**

When Layer is selected in the Auto-Select menu, only the relevant layer will move even if it is part of a layer group. If you want all layers in a group containing the selected layer to move, you can choose Group in the menu.

4. **In the document window, click any pixel in the storm image, and drag until the image fills the top of the hole in the bricks.**

Make sure you click an area where no pixels from another layer are visible. (Because the layer mask on the Bricks layer hides the inner pixels, you can click within the mask shape to select the underlying layers.)

Check the Auto-Select option and choose Layer in the menu.

Click any pixel in the storm image and drag to move that layer's content.

Be careful to not click an area where a different layer is visible.

You don't have to first select a specific layer to move that layer's content.

5. **In the document window, click any pixel in the city image and drag until you are happy with the position of the layer content.**

6. **In the Layers panel, click the Lightning layer and drag it below the Skyline layer.**

7. **In the document window, click any pixel of the lightning image and drag to position the layer content so the lightning appears to strike one of the buildings.**

8. **In the document window, click any pixel in the title treatment and drag down so the title appears in the bottom half of the canvas.**

Your layers should appear in the same order as shown in the following image, with the Logos layer group at the top of the layer stack.

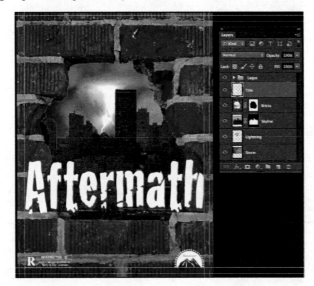

Note:

When the Move tool is active, you can move the selected object or layer 1 pixel by pressing the Arrow keys. Pressing Shift with any of the Arrow keys moves the selected object/layer by 10 pixels.

9. **Save the file and continue to the final stage of the project.**

Filtering Layers

When you work with complex files, you might find yourself with dozens — or even hundreds — of layers. Descriptive names can help you navigate through the layers, but you still have to scroll through the panel to find what you need.

Layer filtering, available at the top of the Layers panel, allows you to narrow down the panel to only layers that meet certain criteria — making it much easier to locate a specific layer.

When **Kind** is selected in the menu, you can use the associated buttons to show only certain types of layers (adjustment layers, smart objects, etc.).

Click this switch to turn filtering on and off.

Only layers that meet the defined filtering criteria appear in the panel.

When **Name** is selected, you can type in the attached field to find layers with names that include the text you enter in the field. The defined text string does not need to be at the beginning of the layer name; for example, typing "ti" would return both Rating and Title layers in the file for this project.

When **Effect** is selected, you can use the secondary menu to find only layers with a specified effect (applied using the Layer>Layer Style submenu).

Use this menu to filter layers by kind, name, effect, mode, attribute, or color.

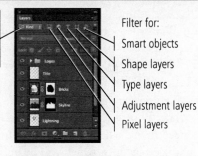

Filter for:

Smart objects

Shape layers

Type layers

Adjustment layers

Pixel layers

When **Attributes** is selected, you can choose from a number of layer attributes — visible, linked, clipped, etc.

When **Mode** is selected, you can use the secondary menu to find only layers to which a certain blending mode has been assigned.

When **Color** is selected, you can choose any of the built-in colors from the secondary menu. (These colors, which appear around the layer's visibility icon, can be assigned to individual layers in each layer's contextual menu.)

Stage 4 Saving Photoshop Files

At the beginning of the project, you saved this file in Photoshop's native format (PSD). However, many Photoshop projects require saving the completed file in at least one other format. Many artists prefer to leave all files in the PSD format since there is only one file to track. Others prefer to send only flattened TIFF files of their artwork because the individual elements can't be changed. Ultimately, the format (or formats, if the file is being used in multiple places) you use will depend on where and how the file is being placed.

Many Photoshop projects are pieces of a larger composition; the overall project defines the format you need to use when you save a complete project. The ad you just created, for example, will be placed in magazine layouts, which will be built in a page-layout application such as Adobe InDesign or QuarkXPress. Although the current versions of both industry-standard page-layout applications can support native layered PSD files, older versions can't import those native files. If a magazine is being designed in QuarkXPress 4, for example (and some still are), you can't place a layered PSD file into that layout. As the Photoshop artist, you have to save your work in a format that is compatible with the magazine layout.

As you know, the ad you created will be placed in multiple magazines, and different publishers have provided different file requirements. You need to save two different versions of the ad to meet those requirements.

 ## SAVE A LAYERED TIFF FILE

Some software that can't use native PSD files can use layered TIFF files, which allow you to maintain as much of the native information as possible in the resulting file.

1. **With aftermath.psd open, choose File>Save As.**

2. **If necessary, navigate to your WIP>Movie folder as the target location.**

    The Save As dialog box defaults to the last-used location. If you continued the entire way through this project without stopping, you won't have to navigate.

3. **In the Save As field, type _layered at the end of the current file name (before the .psd extension).**

Common File Formats

Photoshop, with the extension PSD, is the native format.

Photoshop EPS can maintain vector and raster information in the same file, and can maintain spot-color channels.

JPEG is a lossy compressed file format that does not support transparency.

Large Document Format, using the extension PSB, is used for images larger than 2 GB (the limit for PSD files); this format supports all Photoshop features including transparency and layers.

Photoshop PDF can contain all required font and image information in a single file, which can be compressed to reduce file size.

Photoshop 2.0 saves a flattened file that can be opened in Photoshop 2.0; all layer information is discarded.

Photoshop Raw supports CMYK, RGB, and grayscale images with alpha channels, and multichannel and LAB images without alpha channels; this format does not support layers.

PNG is a raster-based format that supports both continuous-tone color and transparency. It is sometimes used for print applications, but is more commonly used in digital publishing (specifically, Web design).

TIFF is a raster-based image format that supports layers, alpha channels, and file compression.

PHOTOSHOP FOUNDATIONS

4. **Click the Format menu and choose TIFF.**

5. **Make sure the Layers check box is selected in the lower half of the dialog box.**

   Because this file contains layers, this option is probably checked by default. If your file contained alpha channels, annotations, or spot colors, those check boxes would also be available. The As a Copy check box can be used if you want to save multiple versions of the same file with different options (which you will do in the next exercise).

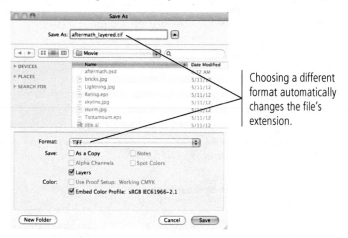

Choosing a different format automatically changes the file's extension.

6. **Leave the remaining options at their default values and click Save.**

7. **In the resulting TIFF Options dialog box, make sure the None image compression option is selected.**

   TIFF files can be compressed (made smaller) using one of three methods:

   - **None** (as the name implies) applies no compression to the file. This option is safe if file size is not an issue, but digital file transmission often requires files to be smaller than a full-page, multi-layered Photoshop file.

   - **LZW** (Lempel-Ziv-Welch) compression is **lossless**, which means all file data is maintained in the compressed file.

   - **ZIP** compression is also lossless, but is not supported by all desktop-publishing software (especially older versions).

   - **JPEG** is a **lossy** compression scheme, which means some data will be thrown away to reduce the file size. If you choose JPEG compression, the Quality options determine how much data can be discarded. Maximum quality means less data is thrown out and the file is larger. Minimum quality discards the most data and results in a smaller file size.

8. **Leave the Pixel Order radio button at the default value, and choose the Byte Order option for your operating system.**

    Pixel Order determines how channel data is encoded. The Interleaved (RGBRGB) option is the default; Per Channel (RRGGBB) is called "planar" order.

    Byte Order determines which platform can use the file, although this is somewhat deceptive. On older versions of most desktop-publishing software, Macintosh systems can read the PC byte order but Windows couldn't read the Macintosh byte order — which is why even the Macintosh system defaults to the IBM PC option. This option is becoming obsolete because most newer software can read either byte order. Nonetheless, some experts argue that choosing the order for your system can improve print quality, especially on desktop output devices.

    Save Image Pyramid creates a tiered file with multiple resolution versions; this isn't widely used or supported by other applications, so you can typically leave it unchecked.

    If your file contains transparency, the Save Transparency check box will be available. If you don't choose this option, transparent areas will be white in the saved file.

9. **In the Layer Compression area, make sure the RLE option is selected.**

    These three options explain — right in the dialog box — what they do.

10. **Click OK to save the file.**

    Photoshop warns you that including layers will increase the file size.

11. **Click OK to dismiss the warning and save the file.**

12. **Continue to the next exercise.**

Note:

If you don't see the warning, it's possible that someone checked the Don't Show Again check box. If you want to make sure that you see all warnings and messages, click Reset All Warning Dialogs in the General pane of the Preferences dialog box.

SAVE A FLATTENED TIFF FILE

Magazines using older page-layout applications need files that no longer maintain the layer information — called **flattened** files. You can flatten a file's layers manually using the Layers panel Options menu, or simply flatten the file during the Save As process.

1. **With aftermath_layered.tif open in Photoshop, choose File>Save As.**

    If you continued directly from the previous exercise, this is the version you just saved. If you quit before you began this exercise, make sure you open the TIFF version and not the PSD version from your WIP>Movie folder.

    Assuming that you started this exercise with the TIFF file from the previous exercise, the format and file name extension already reflect the TIFF options.

Note:

You can manually flatten a file by choosing Layer>Flatten Image.

2. **Uncheck the Layers check box.**

   The As a Copy box is now selected by default. A warning shows that the file must be saved as a copy when the Layers option is unchecked. This is basically a failsafe built into Photoshop that prevents you from overwriting your layered file with a flattened version.

Note:

Older desktop-publishing software doesn't always support compressed TIFF files. When saving for those workflows, you might have to save the file without compression, regardless of the resulting file size.

3. **In the Save As field, highlight the words "layered copy" and type flat.**

4. **Click Save. In the resulting TIFF Options dialog box, make sure the None compression option is selected and the Byte Order is set to IBM PC. At the bottom of the dialog box, make sure the Discard Layers and Save a Copy option is checked.**

5. **Click OK to save the second version of the file.**

6. **When the save is complete, choose File>Close. Click Don't Save when asked.**

Project Review

fill in the blank

1. _____ is likely to cause degradation of a raster image when it's reproduced on a printing press.

2. A _____ is a linked file that you placed into another Photoshop document.

3. The _____ is context sensitive, providing access to different functions depending on what tool is active.

4. The _____ is the final size of a printed page.

5. The _____ tool is used to draw irregular-shaped selection marquees.

6. The _____ tool is used to select areas of similar color by clicking and dragging in the image window.

7. The _____ tool can be used to drag layer contents to another position within the image, or into another open document.

8. When selecting color ranges, the _____ value determines how much of the current color range falls into the selection.

9. A _____ can be used to non-destructively hide certain areas of a layer.

10. _____ is a lossy compression method that is best used when large file size might be a problem.

short answer

1. Briefly describe the difference between raster images and vector graphics.

2. Briefly explain three separate methods for isolating an image from its background.

3. Briefly explain the concept of a layer mask.

Use what you learned in this project to complete the following freeform exercise.
Carefully read the art director and client comments, then create your design to meet the needs of the project.
Use the space below to sketch ideas; when finished, write a brief explanation of the reasoning behind your design.

art director comments

Tantamount Studios is pleased with your work on the *Aftermath* ad, and they would like to hire you again to create the ad concept and final files for another movie that they're releasing early next year.

To complete this project, you should:

❏ Download the **WC6_PB_Project1.zip** archive from the Student Files Web page to access the client-supplied title artwork and rating placeholder file.

❏ Find appropriate background and foreground images for the movie theme (see the client's comments at right).

❏ Incorporate the title artwork, logos, and rating placeholder that the client provided.

❏ Composite the different elements into a single completed file; save both a layered version and a flattened version.

client comments

The movie is titled *Above and Beyond*. Although the story is fictionalized, it will focus on the men who led the first U.S. Airborne unit (the 501st), which suffered more than 2000 casualties in the European theater of World War II.

We don't have any other images in mind, but the final ad should reflect the time period (the 1940s) of the movie. The 501st Airborne was trained to parachute into battle, so you should probably incorporate some kind of parachute image.

This movie is a joint venture between Sun and Tantamount, so both logos need to be included in the new ad. It isn't rated yet, so please use the "This Movie Is Not Yet Rated" artwork as a placeholder.

Create this ad big enough to fit on an 8.5 × 11″ page, but keep the live area an inch inside the trim so the ad can be used in different-sized magazines.

project justification

_____
_____
_____
_____
_____
_____
_____
_____
_____
_____
_____
_____
_____
_____
_____

Making selections is one of the most basic, and most important, skills that you will learn in Photoshop. Selections are so important that Photoshop dedicates an entire menu to the process.

As you created the movie ad in this project, you used a number of skills and techniques that you will apply in many (if not all) projects you build in Photoshop. You learned a number of ways to make both simple and complex selections — and you will learn additional methods in later projects. You also learned how to work with multiple layers, which will be an important part of virtually every Photoshop project you create, both in this book and throughout your career.

Composite images by dragging from one document to another

Transform a regular layer

Composite images by copying and pasting

Incorporate vector graphics into a raster image

Move layer content around on the canvas

Composite images by placing from Mini Bridge

Transform a Smart Object layer

Make a basic selection with a Marquee tool

Create a feathered selection to blend one layer into another

Create a silhouette using the Select Color Range utility

Create a silhouette using the Quick Selection tool

Refine a selection using the Refine Edges utility

Use a layer mask to hide pixels on a layer

Menu Image Correction

Your client is the owner of The Chateau, a five-star gourmet restaurant that has been operating in northern Los Angeles County for over five decades. The restaurant changes its menu frequently, so they currently use a chalkboard menu, presented on an easel at each table when guests are seated. The owner recently received a number of comments about the chalkboard menu being difficult to read, so he decided to create printed menus with the standard offerings and use the chalkboard to display the chef's daily specials.

This project incorporates the following skills:

❑ Repairing damaged images

❑ Understanding the relationship between tonal range and contrast

❑ Correcting image lighting and exposure problems

❑ Understanding how gray balance affects overall image color

❑ Correcting minor and severe image color problems

❑ Combining exposures into an HDR image

client comments

The Chateau is a unique destination restaurant that consistently wins awards from local and national food and wine reviewers. The restaurant was first opened in 1952 by Paul and Gina Roseman as a rest stop and diner for travelers along the Sierra Highway. While the restaurant remains in the family, it has evolved from home-style comfort food to more exotic fare such as wild game with a French twist.

The history of the restaurant is important to us. We have a Roseman family portrait — my great-grandparents — that we'd like to include on the back of the menu. The picture is a bit grainy and has some damage, though, and we'd like you to clean it up as much as possible. We also want to include a picture of the current executive chef, who is Paul and Gina's great-grandniece, in the same section. The only picture we have of her is very dark though, and we're hoping you can make it look better.

In addition, we've taken several pictures of different meals that Suzanne created. We want you to make sure they will look as good as possible when printed. You're the expert, so we trust that you know what needs to be done.

① Rosemans — touch up, fix damage

② Buffalo steak — fix brightness / contrast

③ Suzanne — lighten overall, add detail in shadows

④ Chicken — fix muddy / Exposure problem

⑤ Salmon — fix green cast throughout

⑥ Flan — fix red cast in plate

⑦ Pasta — bump contrast in midtones

⑧ Salad — correct color shift in reds/greens

⑨ Mill — exposures for better detail

art director comments

Digital images come from a wide variety of sources: scanned photographs and digital cameras are the two most common, as is the case for the client's images for this project. Some images can be used as is, or at least with only minor correction. Realistically, most professional photographers reshoot an image until they have one that doesn't need your help.

Unfortunately, however, not every project involves a professional photographer. Consumer-level cameras have come down in price and gone up in quality to the point where many non-professionals shoot their own photos without proper skill or knowledge. That means many of those images require a bit of help — and some require a lot.

Even when a professional photographer is involved, not every image comes from a perfectly lit studio. Location shots — where a subject is photographed in a "real-world" setting — can't always be captured perfectly. Those images usually need work as well. Fortunately, Photoshop provides a powerful toolset for solving most image problems, or at least improving the worst of them.

project objectives

To complete this project, you will:

❏ Remove grain with blur and sharpen techniques

❏ Heal severe scratches

❏ Clone out major damage

❏ Correct minor problems with the Brightness/Contrast adjustment

❏ Correct tonal range with the Levels adjustment

❏ Correct lighting problems with the Exposure adjustment

❏ Correct overall color problems with the Color Balance adjustment

❏ Correct precise color values with the Curves adjustment

❏ Combine multiple exposures with the Merge to HDR Pro utility

Stage 1 Retouching Damaged Images

Image repair is the process of fixing scratches, removing dust, making tears disappear, and generally putting broken or damaged pictures back together again. **Retouching**, on the other hand, is the technique of changing an image by adding something that wasn't there or removing something that was there. Damage can come from a wide range of sources: creases, scratches from any number of abrasive objects, water spots, and tape marks to name just a few. Other image problems such as photographic grain are a natural part of photographs (especially old ones), and dust is common (if not inevitable) whenever photographs are scanned.

There are many different ways to approach image repairs. As you complete the exercises in this stage of the project, you will use several tools — from basic to complex — to clean up damage in the client's family portrait from the early 1940s.

REMOVE GRAIN WITH BLUR AND SHARPEN TECHNIQUES

Photographic film is made up of microscopic grains of light-sensitive material. These grains capture the image information, which is eventually processed into a print or transparency. While not usually apparent in a standard photographic print, the grain in a photograph can become pronounced when scanned with a high-resolution scanner. Enlarging an image during scanning further enhances any grain that already exists.

When grain is evident in a digital image, the grain pattern can destroy fine detail and create a mottled appearance in areas of solid color or subtle tone variation. Slower-rated film typically has the smallest and least-evident grain, while faster film can produce significant graininess.

Sharpening and blurring techniques are the best methods for removing photographic grain. The techniques you use in this exercise work for any image with grain. Older images — such as the one your client wants to use — almost always have obvious grain problems that can be fixed to some degree; antique images can be fixed only just so much. The techniques you learn in this project produce very good results if you need to remove grain from modern scanned images.

1. **Download PS6_RF_Project3.zip from the Student Files Web page.**

2. **Expand the ZIP archive in your WIP folder (Macintosh) or copy the archive contents into your WIP folder (Windows).**

   This results in a folder named **Menu**, which contains the files you need for this project. You should also use this folder to save the files you create in this project.

3. **Open the file rosemans.jpg from your WIP>Menu folder.**

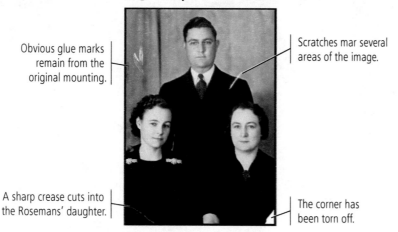

Obvious glue marks remain from the original mounting.

Scratches mar several areas of the image.

A sharp crease cuts into the Rosemans' daughter.

The corner has been torn off.

4. Choose View>Actual Pixels to view the image at 100%.

Grain is most obvious in large areas of solid (or nearly solid) color.

Grain in lighter areas can produce a sickly appearance in a person's face.

The Noise Filters

Noise is defined as random pixels that stand out from the surrounding pixels, either hurting the overall appearance of the image (as in the case of visible grains in an old photograph) or helping to prevent printing problems (as in the case of a gradient that extends across a large area). Photoshop includes several filters (Filters>Noise) that can add or remove noise.

The **Add Noise filter** applies random pixels to the image. Uniform distributes color values of noise between 0 and the defined amount. Gaussian distributes color values of noise along a bell-shaped curve. Monochromatic adds random pixels without affecting the colors in the image.

The **Despeckle** filter detects the edges in an image and blurs everything except those edges.

The **Dust & Scratches filter** reduces noise by comparing the contrast of pixels within the defined radius; pixels outside the defined threshold are adjusted.

The **Median filter** reduces noise by blending the brightness of pixels within a selection. The filter compares the brightness of pixels within the defined radius, and replaces pixels that differ too much from surrounding pixels with the median brightness value of the compared pixels.

The **Reduce Noise** filter provides far greater control over different aspects of noise correction. In Basic mode, you can remove luminance noise and color noise in the composite image.

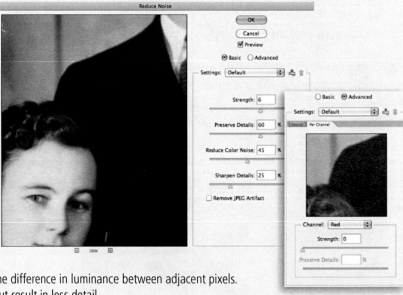

In Advanced mode, you can remove noise from individual color channels. (**Luminance noise**, also called grayscale noise, makes an image appear grainy; **color noise** usually appears as color artifacts in the image.)

- **Strength** controls the amount of luminance noise reduction.
- **Preserve Details** controls how carefully the filter compares the difference in luminance between adjacent pixels. Lower values remove more noise but result in less detail.
- **Reduce Color Noise** removes random color pixels from the image.
- **Sharpen Details** sharpens the image. Because the noise reduction process inherently blurs the image, this option applies the same kind of sharpening that is available in the Photoshop Sharpen filters.
- **Remove JPEG Artifacts** removes artifacts and halos caused by saving an image with a low JPEG quality setting (in other words, using a high lossy compression scheme).

5. **Choose Filter>Blur>Gaussian Blur.**

   All Photoshop blur filters work in essentially the same way: they average the brightness values of contiguous pixels to soften the image.

6. **Make sure Preview is checked and change the Radius field to 1.5 pixels.**

   The **Radius** field defines (in pixels) the amount of blurring that will be applied. Photoshop uses this value to average the brightness of a pixel with that of surrounding pixels. A radius value near 1 can soften an image and remove most photographic grain.

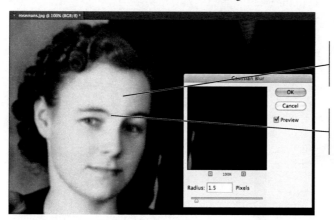

A small amount of Gaussian blur removes most of the photographic grain.

Areas of fine detail are also slightly blurred by the Gaussian Blur filter.

7. **Click OK to apply the Gaussian Blur to the image.**

   To remove the photographic grain, you had to blur the entire image; this means that areas of fine detail were also blurred. You can use a second technique — unsharp masking — to restore some of the lost edge detail.

The Blur Filters

The Filter>Blur menu includes a number of choices for applying corrective or artistic blurs to an image or selection.

Field Blur, **Iris Blur**, and **Tilt-Shift** open a special Blur Gallery interface.

Average finds the average color of an image or selection, and then fills the image or selection with that color to create a smooth appearance.

Blur and **Blur More** smooth transitions by averaging the pixels next to the hard edges of defined lines and shaded areas. When you apply these filters, you have no additional control: Blur is roughly equivalent to a 0.3-pixel radius blur, and Blur More uses approximately a 0.7-pixel radius.

Box Blur averages the color value of neighboring pixels. You can adjust the size of the area used to calculate the average value; a larger radius value results in more blurring.

Gaussian Blur blurs the selection by a specific amount.

Lens Blur adds blur to an image to create the effect of a narrower depth of field so some objects in the image remain in focus, while others areas are blurred.

Motion Blur includes an option for changing the blur angle, as well as a Distance value that defines the number of pixels to blur.

Radial Blur either spins the pixel around the center point of the image, or zooms the pixel around the center point based on the Amount setting. The farther a pixel is from the center point, the more the pixel is blurred. You can drag in the Blur Center window to move the center point of the blur.

Shape Blur uses a specific shape (**kernel**) to create the blur. Radius determines the size of the kernel; the larger the kernel, the greater the blur.

Smart Blur allows you to blur tones closely related in value without affecting edge quality. Threshold determines how closely pixels must be related in tone before being blurred. You can also specify a Quality level, and change the Mode setting. Using Edge Only mode, edges are outlined in white and the image is forced to black. Using Overlay Edges mode, the color image is blurred and edges are outlined in white.

Surface Blur blurs an image while trying to preserve edges. The Radius option specifies the size of the blur in whole numbers. The Threshold option controls how much the tonal values of neighboring pixels must differ before being blurred.

8. **Choose Filter>Sharpen>Unsharp Mask and make sure the Preview check box is active in the dialog box.**

Unsharp masking sharpens an image by increasing contrast along the edges in an image. **Amount** determines how much the contrast in edges will increase; typically, 150–200% creates good results in high-resolution images. **Radius** determines how many pixels will be included in the edge comparison; higher radius values result in more pronounced edge effects. **Threshold** defines the difference that is required for Photoshop to identify an edge. A threshold of 15 means that colors must be more than 15 levels different; using a higher Threshold protects the smooth tones in the faces, while still allowing detail in the faces (the eyes, for example) to be sharpened.

9. **Change the Amount to 150%, the Radius to 3.0 pixels, and the Threshold to 15 levels.**

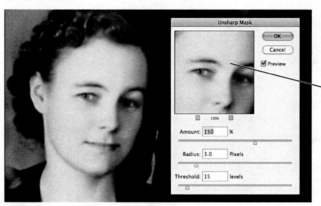

Drag here or click in the document window to change the visible area in the preview window.

10. **Click OK to apply the Unsharp Mask filter.**

11. **Choose File>Save As. Save the file as a native Photoshop file named `rosemans_working.psd` in your WIP>Menu folder. Continue to the next exercise.**

Remember, you have to choose File>Save As to save the file with a different name or format.

Note:

Using Gaussian Blur and Unsharp Masking in tandem is a common technique for cleaning up grainy images.

Note:

The degree of sharpening applied to an image is often a matter of personal choice; however, oversharpening an image produces a halo effect around the edges.

Note:

The Sharpen, Sharpen More, and Sharpen Edges filters apply sharpening with no user control.

The Smart Sharpen Filter

PHOTOSHOP FOUNDATIONS

The Smart Sharpen filter allows you to control the amount of sharpening that occurs in shadow and highlight areas.

Remove defines the algorithm used to sharpen the image. Gaussian Blur is the method used by the Unsharp Mask filter. Lens Blur detects edges and detail, and provides finer detail and fewer halos. Motion Blur tries to reduce the effects of blur due to movement at a defined angle.

The **More Accurate** check box processes the file more slowly for a more accurate blur removal.

In Advanced mode, you can use the Shadow and Highlight tabs to adjust sharpening of only those areas.

Fade Amount adjusts the amount of sharpening.

Tonal Width controls the range of tones that will be modified. Smaller values restrict the adjustments to only darker regions for shadows and only lighter regions for highlights.

Radius defines the size of the area around each pixel used to determine whether a pixel is in the shadows or highlights.

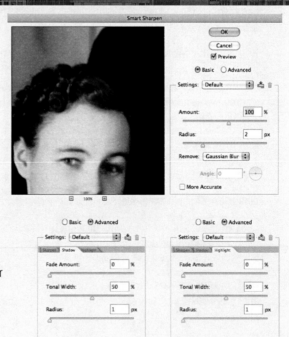

HEAL SEVERE SCRATCHES

The blur and sharpen routine from the previous exercise improved the client's image — the obvious grain is gone. Even though the edges are slightly less sharp than the original scan, they are sharp enough to produce good results when the image is printed. If you're working with images that aren't 70 years old, you will be able to produce far sharper edges using these same techniques.

There are still a number of problems in the image that require intervention. Photoshop includes several tools for changing the pixels in an image — from painting with a brush to nudging selections on a layer to using repair tools specifically designed for adjusting pixels based on other pixels in the image.

The **Spot Healing Brush tool** allows you to remove imperfections by blending the surrounding pixels. The **Healing Brush tool** has a similar function, except you can define the source pixels that will be used to heal a specific area. The **Patch tool** allows you to repair a selected area with pixels from another area of the image by dragging the selection area.

Note:

Throughout this project, you are going to clean up blemishes on images and make other adjustments that require looking at very small areas. It can be very helpful to clean your monitor so you don't mistake on-screen dust and smudges with flaws in the images you are adjusting.

1. With **rosemans_working.psd** open, view the image at 100%. Set up the document window so you can see the lower half of the image.

2. Select the Spot Healing Brush tool in the Tools panel.

3. In the Options bar, open the Brush Preset picker and choose a 20-pixel hard-edge brush. Choose the Proximity Match radio button.

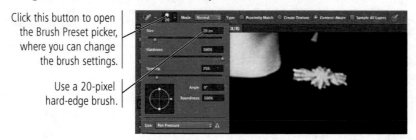

Click this button to open the Brush Preset picker, where you can change the brush settings.

Use a 20-pixel hard-edge brush.

The **Proximity Match** method uses the pixels around the edge of the selection to find an image area to use as a patch for the selected area. The **Create Texture** method uses all the pixels in the selection to create a texture for repairing the area. **Content Aware** mode attempts to match the detail in surrounding areas while healing pixels (this method does not work well for areas with hard edges or sharp contrast). If you select **Sample All Layers**, the tool pulls pixel data from all visible layers.

4. Place the cursor over the small white spot in the bottom-left corner of the image. Click immediately over the white spot to heal it.

The Spot Healing Brush tool shows the size of the selected brush.

5. Using the same technique, remove the remaining white spots from the dark areas of the Rosemans' clothing.

6. **Choose the Healing Brush tool (nested under the Spot Healing Brush tool).**

7. **In the Options bar, open the Brush Preset picker. Choose a small brush size that's slightly larger than the white spot on the girl's chin (we used 9 pixels).**

   When using the Healing Brush tool, the Mode menu determines the blending mode used to heal an area. The default option (Normal) samples the source color and transparency to blend the new pixels smoothly into the area being healed. The Replace mode preserves texture in the healed area when you use a soft-edge brush.

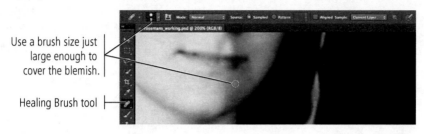

Use a brush size just large enough to cover the blemish.

Healing Brush tool

Note:

Multiple, Screen, Darken, Lighten, Color, and Luminosity modes have the same function as the blending modes for specific layers and brushes.

8. **Place the cursor directly below the spot you want to heal. Press Option/Alt and click to define the healing source.**

   Pressing Option/Alt with the Healing Brush tool changes the cursor icon to a crosshair, which you can click to select the source of the brush (the pixels that will be used to heal the spot where you next click).

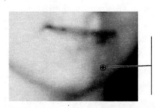

Pressing Option/Alt allows you to define the source pixels that will be used to heal the next spot you click.

Note:

You can use the bracket keys to enlarge (]) or reduce ([) the Healing Brush tool brush size.

Aligning the Healing Source

PHOTOSHOP FOUNDATIONS

When you work with the Healing Brush and Clone Stamp tools, you have the option to align the source to the cursor. If the Align option is turned off, the source starting point will be relative to the image. If the Align option is turned on, the source starting point will be relative to the cursor. The following images illustrate this idea.

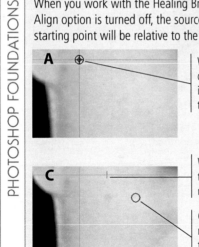

A We first Option/Alt-clicked at the guide intersection to define the healing source.

B The crosshair shows the source of the healing.

This circle shows the cursor location where we clicked with the Healing Brush tool.

C When the Aligned option is turned **on**, the source moves relative to the tool cursor.

Clicking farther to the right moves the source the same distance from its defined origin.

D When the Aligned option is turned **off**, the source remains in the same position even when the Healing Brush tool is clicked farther to the right.

9. **Place the cursor over the blemish on the girl's chin and click.**

Unlike the Spot Healing Brush tool, the Healing Brush tool allows you to define the source of the healing. By choosing nearby pixels as the healing source, the blemish on the girl's chin disappears, and that spot blends nicely into the surrounding pixels.

The Healing Brush tool blends colors from the source pixels (which you defined in Step 8) with colors in the area where you click. You can also change the source from Sampled (the pixels you defined by Option/Alt-clicking) to Pattern, which uses pixels from a defined pattern to heal the area. The Pattern option is a good choice for creating artistic effects, rather than healing blemishes in an existing photo.

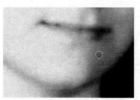

After clicking, the spot is healed using the source pixels.

10. **Save the file and continue to the next exercise.**

CLONE OUT MAJOR DAMAGE

The client's image has definitely been improved by removing the grain and healing the small blemishes, but four major areas of damage still need to be fixed. These larger areas require more control over the healing process, which the Clone Stamp tool provides.

The Clone Stamp tool paints one part of an image over another part, which is useful for duplicating objects or removing defects in an image. As with the Healing Brush tool, you can define the source that will be cloned when you click with the tool; the difference is that whole pixels are copied, not just their color values.

1. **With the file rosemans_working.psd open, zoom into the bottom-left corner (where the crease marks the image) and select the Clone Stamp tool.**

2. **In the Brush Preset picker (in the Options bar), choose a soft-edge brush large enough to cover the crease.**

When you are using the Clone Stamp tool, the Options bar combines brush options (brush size, blending mode, opacity, and flow) with healing options (alignment and sample source, which you used in the previous exercise).

Click to open the Brushes panel.   Click to open the Clone Source panel.   Click to ignore adjustment layers.

We are using an 80-pixel brush with 25% hardness.

Clone Stamp tool cursor

Clone Stamp tool

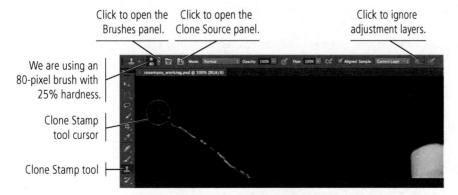

3. **In the Options bar, make sure the Aligned Sample option is turned on (checked).**

In this case, you want the cloning source to remain relative to the cursor, even if you stop and start several times. If you clone a large area relative to the same source origin (in other words, with the Align option turned off), you could end up with an unwanted pattern in the area you clone.

4. **Place the cursor directly above and to the right of the crease. Option/Alt-click to define the cloning source.**

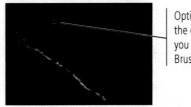

Option/Alt-click to define the cloning source, just as you did with the Healing Brush tool.

Note:

When using the Clone Stamp tool, hard-edge brushes can result in harsh lines where you clone pixels; soft-edge brushes can help prevent harsh lines from appearing.

5. **Click over an area of the crease and drag to clone out the crease.**

As you drag, notice that the source crosshairs move in relation to the Clone Stamp cursor. Because you turned on the Aligned Sample option in Step 3, you can stop and restart cloning, and the source will retain the same relative position to the tool cursor.

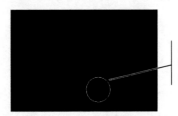

Drag with the Clone Stamp tool until the crease is no longer visible.

Note:

You can use the bracket keys to enlarge (]) or reduce ([) the Clone Stamp brush size.

6. **Use the same process to fill in the torn area in the bottom-right corner of the image.**

Note:

When you are cloning — especially large areas — it's usually a good idea to clone in small strokes or even single clicks. This method can help you avoid cloning in patterns or "railroad tracks" that do as much damage as good. When cloning large areas, it's also a good idea to frequently resample the clone source to avoid cloning the same pixels into a new noticeable pattern.

7. **Zoom into the scratch on the man's left shoulder.**

Cloning out damage in areas of solid color is fairly simple. This area presents a more difficult problem since the area you need to fix has an edge that must be maintained.

8. **In the Brush Preset picker, select a brush that just barely covers the edge of the man's jacket, and turn off the Aligned Sample option.**

To prevent cloning a hard edge, we used a 30-pixel brush with a 50% Hardness value.

9. **Place the cursor over the edge you want to reproduce and Option/Alt-click to define the source.**

Because the Aligned Sample option is turned off, each successive click uses the same source point.

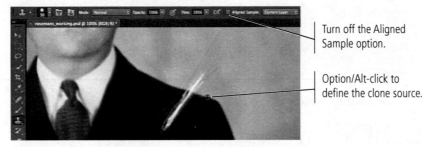

Turn off the Aligned Sample option.

Option/Alt-click to define the clone source.

10. **Place the cursor over the scratched pixels on the man's shoulder.**

As you move the Clone Stamp tool cursor, the source pixels move along with the tool cursor to give you a preview of what will happen when you click.

11. **Click without dragging when the cloned pixels appear to align properly with the area behind the scratch.**

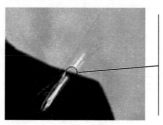

Clicking without dragging clones a 30-pixel area. Because the brush we chose has 50% hardness, the center (where the shoulder edge is) is clear, but the outside parts of the brush are feathered into the surrounding area.

Note:

If you're not happy with the result of a clone, simply undo the action (Command/Control-Z, or using the History panel) and try again. Cloning — especially edges — often takes more than one try to achieve the desired result.

12. **Move the cursor slightly to the left, again centering the cursor preview over the would-be edge, and click without dragging.**

With the Aligned Sample option turned off, you can click again to clone pixels from the same source.

13. **Repeat this process as necessary to clone out the remaining scratch along the man's shoulder.**

We clicked two more times to completely remove the scratch along the shoulder line.

14. **Choose the Lasso tool in the Tools panel. Draw a marquee around the scratches in the background, above the man's shoulder.**

Be careful to avoid the man's shoulder in the selection area.

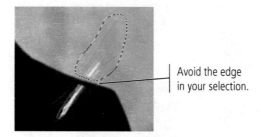

Avoid the edge in your selection.

15. **Choose Edit>Fill. Choose Content-Aware in the Use menu and click OK.**

Photoshop evaluates the image and determines what should be created inside the selection area. The fill might take a few seconds to process, so be patient.

16. **Choose Select>Deselect to turn off the selection marquee.**

    Content-Aware Fill works very well on areas of subtle shading, such as the backdrop in this image, or other areas where you do not need to maintain fine detail or edges in the selected area. If you try to use this option on a sharp edge, however, the Content-Aware Fill results are unpredictable. Other tools, such as the Clone Stamp tool, work better for retouching distinct edges.

Note:

Press Command/ Control-D to turn off a selection marquee.

17. **Use the same method as in Steps 14–15 to remove the scratches from the man's coat, and the scratches and glue residue on the left side of the photo.**

    At the ends of the image, it's okay to drag outside the edge of the canvas; Photoshop identifies the edge and snaps the selection edge to the canvas edge.

18. **Choose File>Save As and choose TIFF in the Format menu. Change the file name to `rosemans_fixed.tif` and save it with the default TIFF options in your WIP>Menu folder.**

19. **Close the file and continue to the next stage of the project.**

The Clone Source Panel in Depth

The Clone Source panel (Window>Clone Source) allows you to store up to five sources for the Clone Stamp or Healing Brush tool. These sources can be from any layer of any open image, which allows you to create unique blended effects by combining pixels from multiple layers or multiple files.

The Show Overlay options allow you to show (at the defined opacity) the source pixels on top of the area where you are cloning. For example, let's say you want to clone the gorilla into the giraffe photo. You would first define a clone source in the gorilla image, and then make the giraffe image active.

Store and access up to five sources from any layer of any open image.

Transform the offset, size, and angle of the clone source.

With the Show Overlay option checked, placing the Clone Stamp cursor over the giraffe image shows the gorilla on top of the giraffe. When you click in the giraffe image with the Clone Stamp tool, that area of the gorilla image will be cloned into the giraffe image; the overlay allows you to preview the areas of the source that will be cloned into the giraffe image.

If the Auto Hide option is checked, the overlay is only visible when the mouse button is not clicked. The Invert option reverses the overlay into a negative representation of the source image. You can also change the blending mode of the overlay from the default Normal to Darken, Lighten, or Difference.

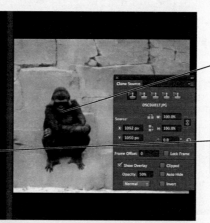

We defined a clone source here.

Using the overlay, you can see the Clone Stamp cursor in relation to the clone source. Clicking will clone this spot from the gorilla image into the giraffe image.

We defined a clone source here.

When the Clipped option is checked, the clone source appears only within the tool cursor area.

Stage 2 Correcting Lighting Problems

Before you start correcting problems with lighting and color, you should understand the different parts of an image, as well as the terms used to describe these areas.

- **Highlights** are defined as the lightest areas of the image that include detail. Direct sources of light such as a light bulb or reflected sunlight on water are called **specular highlights**; they should not be considered the highlights of an image.

- **Shadows** are the darkest areas of the image that still contain some detail; areas of solid black are not considered shadow tones.

- The shades between the highlights and shadows are the **midtones** (or **gamma**) of the image.

Contrast and saturation play an integral role in reproducing high-quality images. **Contrast** refers to the tonal variation within an image; an image primarily composed of highlights and shadows is a high-contrast image, while an image with more detail in the midtones is a low-contrast image.

Contrast is closely linked to **saturation**, which refers to the intensity of a color or its variation away from gray. The saturation of individual colors in an image, and the correct saturation of different colors in relation to one another, affects the overall contrast of the image. If an image is under- or oversaturated, the contrast suffers — detail is lost and colors appear either muted or too bright.

Note:

Image adjustments can be applied directly to the image pixels or as non-destructive adjustment layers using the Adjustments panel. In this project, you edit the actual image pixels; you use the adjustment layer method in Project 6: Advertising Samples.

CORRECT PROBLEMS WITH BRIGHTNESS/CONTRAST

Depending on the image, several tools are available for correcting problems related to images that are either too dark or too light. The most basic adjustment option — Brightness/Contrast — can fix images that need overall adjustment to brightness, contrast, or both. If an image requires more sophisticated adjustment, you should use one of the other adjustment options.

1. **Open the file buffalo.jpg from your WIP>Menu folder.**

   This image has an overall dark feel, probably caused by poor lighting or underexposure. The Brightness/Contrast adjustment can correct this problem.

2. **Choose Image>Adjustments>Brightness/Contrast and make sure the Preview option is checked.**

3. **Drag the Brightness slider to +35.**

   Increasing the overall brightness creates an immediate improvement in this image, although some areas of detail are still muddy.

4. **Drag the Contrast slider to +10.**

   Increasing the contrast brings out more detail in the food texture, which is the focal point of the image (pay particular attention to the meat).

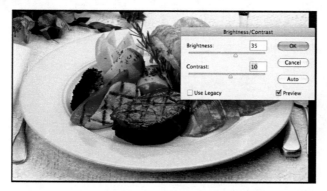

5. **Click OK to apply the change.**

6. **Save the file in your WIP>Menu folder as a TIFF file named `buffalo_fixed.tif` using the default TIFF options.**

7. **Close the file and continue to the next exercise.**

 ## CORRECT CONTRAST AND TONAL RANGE WITH LEVELS

The **tonal range** of an image is the amount of variation between the lightest highlight and the darkest shadow in a particular image. A grayscale image can contain 256 possible shades of gray. Each channel of a color image can also contain 256 possible shades of gray. To achieve the best contrast in an image, the tonal range of the image should include as many levels of gray as are available.

While the Brightness/Contrast option is a good choice for making basic adjustments, the Levels adjustment is the best approach for enhancing image detail throughout the entire tonal range. Using Levels, adjusting contrast is a three-step process:

- Determine the image's highlight areas (the lightest areas that contain detail).

- Determine the image's shadow areas (the darkest areas that contain detail).

- Adjust the gamma (the contrast in midtones of an image) to determine the proportion of darker tones to lighter tones.

1. **Open the file `chef.jpg` from the WIP>Menu folder.**

2. **Display the Histogram panel (Window>Histogram), and then choose Expanded View from the panel Options menu.**

   The Histogram panel can help you identify problems that need to be corrected. When you first display the panel, it probably appears in Compact view, which shows only the graphs for the individual color channels and the composite image.

   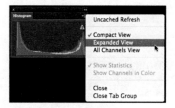

3. **In the Histogram panel, change the Channel menu to RGB.**

   The histogram — the chart that shows the distribution of tones — can display a single graph for the entire composite image (all channels combined) or for individual channels.

   In Expanded view, the panel shows the distribution of pixels from the darkest to the lightest portion of the image, for the entire image or for individual color channels.

   If you see a warning icon, click it to reset the cache.

   Choose from this menu to view and modify the histogram for individual channels.

   These shadow values are pushing out of the histogram "container," which shows that there is a problem in the shadow tones.

   The empty space at the left of the histogram indicates that some tones in the available range are not being used.

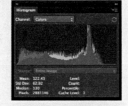

4. **If you see one, click the Warning icon in the upper-right corner of the Histogram panel to reset the cache.**

Every time you zoom in or out of an image, Photoshop stores the results of the display in a **cache** (a drive location that keeps track of what you're doing). The image you're looking at on the histogram often doesn't match the results on the drive. The Warning icon shows there's a problem; clicking the icon resets the image and rereads the cache.

Note:

If you see the Warning icon in the Histogram panel, click the icon to match the disk cache with what's happening in the live image.

5. **Choose Image>Adjustments>Levels and make sure Preview is checked.**

The Levels dialog box shows a histogram like the one shown in the Histogram panel.

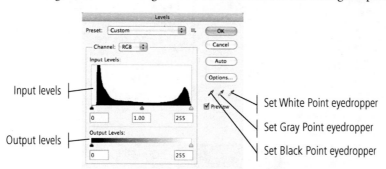

The Levels dialog box has two sets of sliders to control input levels and output levels. Each set has a black slider for adjusting the shadows in an image and a white slider to adjust highlights. The Input Levels slider also has a gray triangle in the center of the slider bar for adjusting gamma or midtones.

The Input sliders in the Levels dialog box correspond to the tonal range of the image. Any pixels that exist to the left of the Input Shadow slider are reproduced as solid black, and they have no detail; any pixels that exist to the right of the Input Highlight slider are reproduced as pure white.

Identifying Shadows and Highlights

PHOTOSHOP FOUNDATIONS

When you move the Shadow and Highlight sliders in the Levels dialog box, you change the **black point** and **white point** of the image — the points at which pixels become black or white. The goal is to find highlight and shadow points that maintain detail. Choosing a point that has no detail causes the area to turn totally white (highlight) or black (shadow) with no detail reproduced. In some images, it can be difficult to visually identify the black and white points in an image; in these cases you can use the Levels dialog box to help you find those areas.

If you press Option/Alt while dragging the Input Shadow or Input Highlight slider, the image turns entirely white or black (respectively). As you drag, the first pixels that become visible are the darkest shadow and the lightest highlight.

Once you identify the highlight and shadow points in the image, select the White Point eyedropper and click the highlight, and then select the Black Point eyedropper and click the shadow to define those two areas of the image.

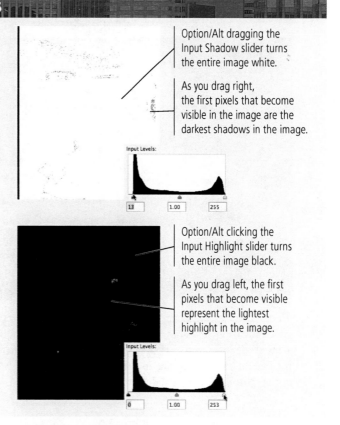

Option/Alt dragging the Input Shadow slider turns the entire image white.

As you drag right, the first pixels that become visible in the image are the darkest shadows in the image.

Option/Alt clicking the Input Highlight slider turns the entire image black.

As you drag left, the first pixels that become visible represent the lightest highlight in the image.

6. **Move the Input Shadow slider to the right until it touches the left edge of the curve.**

   This simple adjustment extends the colors in the image to take advantage of all 256 possible tones. This adjustment has a small effect on the shadow area of the image, but the majority of the colors in the image are still clustered near the shadow point (as you can see by the spike in the histogram).

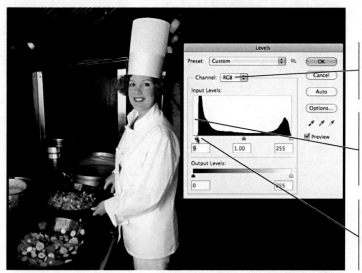

Choose from this menu to view and modify the histogram for an individual channel.

The white space at the left of the histogram indicates that some of the tones in the available range are not being used.

Dragging the Shadow Input slider to the left edge of the histogram extends the shadows into the full tonal range.

7. **Move the Input Gamma slider to the left until the middle box below the slider shows approximately 1.75.**

   The Input Gamma slider controls the proportion of darker tones to lighter tones in the midtones of an image. If you increase gamma, you increase the proportion of lighter grays in the image; this effectively increases contrast in lighter shades and lightens the entire image. If you decrease gamma, you extend the tonal range of darker shades; this allows those areas of the image to be reproduced with a larger range of shades, which increases the contrast in darker shades.

Note:

You can change input and output levels by moving the sliders, entering actual values in the boxes below the slider sets, or by using the eyedroppers to select the brightest and darkest points in the image.

Dragging the Gamma Input slider extends the range between the midtone and the highlights, creating greater contrast and showing more detail throughout the image.

   To decrease contrast in an image, you can adjust the Output sliders. This method effectively compresses the range of possible tones that can be reproduced, forcing all areas of the image into a smaller tonal range. Areas originally set to 0 are reproduced at the value of the Output Shadow slider; areas originally set to 255 are output at the value of the Output Highlight slider.

8. **Click OK to close the Levels dialog box.**

9. **Save the file in your WIP>Menu folder as a TIFF file named** `chef_fixed.tif`.

10. **Close the file and then continue to the next exercise.**

The Gradient Map Adjustment

The **Gradient Map adjustment** (Image>Adjustments>Gradient Map) enables you to create interesting artistic effects by mapping the tones of an image to the shades in a defined gradient.

In the Gradient Map dialog box, you can apply any defined gradient by clicking the arrow to the right of the gradient sample and choosing from the pop-up menu, or you can edit the selected gradient by clicking the sample gradient ramp. The **Dither** option adds random noise to the effect. If you check the **Reverse** option, image highlights map to the left end of the gradient, and image shadows map to the right end of the gradient, effectively reversing the gradient map.

The composite histogram of an RGB image starts at the darkest point and ends at the lightest point with 256 total possible tonal values. If you think of the gradient as having 256 steps from one end to the other, then you can see how the shades of the selected gradient map to the tones of the original image.

CORRECT LIGHTING PROBLEMS WITH THE EXPOSURE ADJUSTMENT

Many images are either over- or underexposed when photographed. If an image is under-exposed, it appears dark and lacks detail in the shadows. If an image is overexposed, it appears too light and lacks detail in the highlights. You can use the Exposure adjustment to correct exposure — and thus, the overall detail and contrast in the image.

Keep in mind, however, that Photoshop cannot create information that doesn't exist. If you have an underexposed image with no detail in the shadow areas, Photoshop cannot generate that detail for you. Some problems are simply beyond fixing.

The Exposure dialog box is designed to make tonal adjustments to 32- and 64-bit HDR (high dynamic range) images, but it also works with 8-bit and 16-bit images. The Exposure adjustment works by performing calculations in a linear color space (gamma 1.0) rather than the image's current color space.

Note:

HDR refers to high-density range (32- or 64-bit) images.

1. **Open chicken.jpg from your WIP>Menu folder.**

2. **Choose Image>Adjustments>Exposure and make sure Preview is checked.**

White Point eyedropper
Gray Point eyedropper
Black Point eyedropper

3. **Click the White Point eyedropper, and then click the white area on the top edge of the plate.**

The eyedroppers in the Exposure dialog box adjust the image's luminance (or the degree of lightness, from white to black). By adjusting the luminance only, you can change the lightness of the image without affecting the color.

- Clicking with the Black Point eyedropper shifts the point you click to black (0 luminance).
- Clicking with the White Point eyedropper shifts the point you click to white (100 luminance).
- Clicking with the Gray Point eyedropper shifts the point you click to gray (50 luminance).

Note:

The White Point and Gray Point eyedroppers affect the Exposure value. The Black Point eyedropper affects the Offset value.

Click here with the White Point eyedropper to define the white area of the image.

Clicking with the White Point eyedropper changes the Exposure setting.

4. **Drag the Gamma Correction slider left to extend the midtone range, which increases contrast and brings out detail in the image. (We used a setting of 1.25.)**

The Gamma slider adjusts the image midtones. Dragging the slider left lightens the image, improving contrast and detail in the midtones and highlights. Dragging the slider right darkens the image, extending the range and increasing detail in the shadows.

Extending the Gamma Correction value into the shadow range brings out more detail in the midtones.

5. **Click the Offset slider and drag very slightly left to add detail back into the midtones and shadows.**

The Offset slider lightens (dragged to the right) or darkens (dragged to the left) the shadows and midtones of the image. The white point (highlight) remains unaffected, but all other pixels are affected.

Decreasing the Offset value adds detail back into the shadows.

6. **Click OK to finalize the adjustment.**

7. **Save the file as a TIFF file named chicken_fixed.tif in your WIP>Menu folder.**

8. **Close the file and continue to the next stage of the project.**

Stage 3   Correcting Color Problems

You can't accurately reproduce color without a basic understanding of color theory, so we present a very basic introduction in this project. Be aware that there are entire, weighty books written about color science; we're providing the condensed version of what you absolutely must know to work effectively with files in any color mode.

Before starting to color-correct an image, you should understand how different colors interact with one another. There are two primary color models — RGB and CMYK — used to output digital images. (Other models such as LAB and HSB have their own purposes in color conversion and correction, but they are not typically output models.)

Additive vs. Subtractive Color

The most important thing to remember about color theory is that color is light, and light is color. You can easily prove this by walking through your house at midnight; you will notice that what little you can see appears as dark shadows. Without light, you can't see — and without light, there is no color.

The **additive color** model (RGB) is based on the idea that all colors can be reproduced by combining pure red, green, and blue light in varying intensities. These three colors are considered the **additive primaries**. Combining any two additive primaries at full strength produces one of the **additive secondaries** — red and blue light combine to produce magenta, red and green combine to produce yellow, and blue and green combine to produce cyan. Although usually considered a "color," black is the absence of light (and, therefore, of color). White is the sum of all colors, produced when all three additive primaries are combined at full strength.

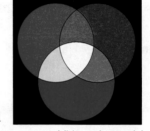 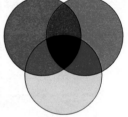

Additive color model   Subtractive color model

Reproducing color on paper requires **subtractive color theory**, which is essentially the inverse of additive color. Instead of adding red, green, and blue light to create the range of colors, subtractive color begins with a white surface that reflects red, green, and blue light at equal and full strength. To reflect (reproduce) a specific color, you add pigments that subtract or absorb only certain wavelengths from the white light. To reflect only red, for example, the surface must subtract (or absorb) the green and blue light.

Remember that the additive primary colors (red, green, and blue) combine to create the additive secondaries (cyan, magenta, and yellow). Those additive secondaries are also called the **subtractive primaries**, because each subtracts one-third of the light spectrum and reflects the other two-thirds:

- Cyan absorbs red light, reflecting only blue and green light.

- Magenta absorbs green light, reflecting only red and blue light.

- Yellow absorbs blue light, reflecting only red and green light.

A combination of two subtractive primaries, then, absorbs two-thirds of the light spectrum and reflects only one-third. As an example, a combination of yellow and magenta absorbs both blue and green light, reflecting only red.

Color printing is a practical application of subtractive color theory. The pigments in the cyan, magenta, yellow, and black (CMYK) inks are combined to absorb different wavelengths of light. By combining different amounts of the subtractive primaries, it's possible to produce a large range (or gamut) of colors.

Understanding Color Terms

PHOTOSHOP FOUNDATIONS

Many vague and technical-sounding terms are mentioned when discussing color. Is hue the same as color? The same as value? As tone? What's the difference between lightness and brightness? What is chroma? And where does saturation fit in?

This problem has resulted in several attempts to normalize color communication. A number of systems have been developed to define color according to specific criteria, including Hue, Saturation, and Brightness (HSB); Hue, Saturation, and Lightness (HSL); Hue, Saturation, and Value (HSV); and Lightness, Chroma, and Hue (LCH). Each of these models or systems plots color on a three-dimensional diagram, based on the elements of human color perception — hue, colorfulness, and brightness.

Hue is what most people think of as color — red, green, purple, and so on. Hue is defined according to a color's position on a color wheel, beginning from red (0°) and traveling counterclockwise around the wheel.

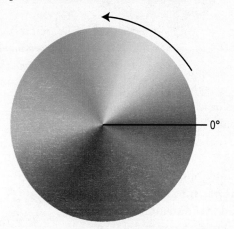

Saturation (also called "intensity") refers to the color's difference from neutral gray. Highly saturated colors are more vivid than those with low saturation. Saturation is plotted from the center of the color wheel. Color at the center is neutral gray and has a saturation value of 0; color at the edge of the wheel is the most intense value of the corresponding hue and has a saturation value of 100.

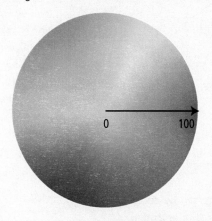

If you bisect the color wheel with a straight line, the line creates a saturation axis for two complementary colors. A color is dulled by the introduction of its complement. Red, for example, is neutralized by the addition of cyan (blue and green). Near the center of the axis, the result is neutral gray.

−100   0   +100

Chroma is similar to saturation, but chroma factors in a reference white. In any viewing situation, colors appear less vivid as the light source dims. The process of chromatic adaptation, however, allows the human visual system to adjust to changes in light and still differentiate colors according to the relative saturation.

Brightness is the amount of light reflected off an object. As an element of color reproduction, brightness is typically judged by comparing the color to the lightest nearby object (such as an unprinted area of white paper).

Lightness is the amount of white or black added to the pure color. Lightness (also called "luminance" or "value") is the relative brightness based purely on the black-white value of a color. A lightness value of 0 means there is no addition of white or black. Lightness of +100 is pure white; lightness of −100 is pure black.

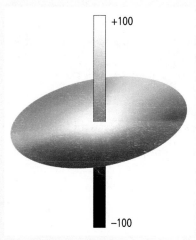

All hues are affected equally by changes in lightness.

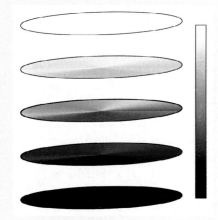

Although the RGB and CMYK models handle color in different ways, these two color models are definitely linked. RGB colors are directly inverse (opposite) to CMY colors, referring to the position of each color on a color wheel. The relationship between primary colors is the basis for all color correction.

Referencing a basic color wheel can help you understand how RGB colors relate to CMY colors. If you center an equilateral triangle over the color wheel, the points of the triangle touch either the RGB primaries or the CMY primaries. Adding together two points of the triangle results in the color between the two points. Red and blue combine to form magenta, yellow and cyan combine to form green, and so on.

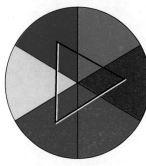

Opposite colors on the color wheel are called **color complements**. Using subtractive color theory, a color's complement absorbs or subtracts that color from visible white light. For example, cyan is opposite red on the color wheel; cyan absorbs red light and reflects green and blue. If you know green and blue light combine to create cyan, you can begin to understand how the two theories are related.

How does all this apply to color correction?

If you want to add a specific color to an image, you have three options: add the color, add equal parts of its constituent colors, or remove some of its complement color. For example, to add red to an image, you can add red, add yellow and magenta, or remove cyan. Conversely, this means that to remove a color from an image, you can remove the color itself, remove equal parts of its constituents, or add its complement. To remove cyan from an image, for example, you can remove cyan, remove blue and green, or add red.

Make sure you understand the relationships between complementary colors:

- To add red, add yellow and magenta or remove cyan.

- To add blue, add cyan and magenta or remove yellow.

- To add green, add cyan and yellow or remove magenta.

- To remove cyan, remove blue and green or add red.

- To remove yellow, remove green and red or add blue.

- To remove magenta, remove blue and red or add green.

Understanding Gray Balance

Understanding the concept of neutral gray is also fundamental to effective color correction. Once you correct the contrast (tonal range) of an image, many of the remaining problems can be at least partially (if not entirely) corrected by correcting the **gray balance**, or the component elements of neutral grays within an image.

In the RGB color model, equal parts of red, green, and blue light combine to create a shade of gray that is equal to the percentage of each component — R=0 G=0 B=0 creates pure black, while R=255 G=255 B=255 creates pure white. To correct an image in RGB mode, you should evaluate and correct the neutral grays so they contain equal percentages of the three primary colors.

Using the CMYK color model, equal percentages of cyan, magenta, and yellow theoretically combine to produce an equal shade of gray — C=0 M=0 Y=0 creates pure white, while C=100 M=100 Y=100 theoretically creates pure black. In practice,

Note:

Because white is a combination of all colors of light, white paper should theoretically reflect equal percentages of all light wavelengths. However, different papers absorb or reflect varying percentages of some wavelengths, thus defining the paper's apparent color. The paper's color affects the appearance of inks printed on that paper.

Note:

It might seem easiest to simply add or subtract the color in question, but a better result might be achieved by adding one color and subtracting another. For example, if an image needs less blue, simply removing cyan can cause reds to appear pink or cyan to appear green. Adding magenta and yellow to balance the existing cyan creates a better result than simply removing cyan.

Note:

An important point to remember is that any color correction requires compromise. If you add or remove a color to correct a certain area, you also affect other areas of the image.

however, the impurities of ink pigments — specifically cyan — do not live up to this theory. When you print an area of equal parts cyan, magenta, and yellow, the result is a muddy brown because the cyan pigments are impure. To compensate for the impurities of cyan, neutral grays must be adjusted to contain equal parts of magenta and yellow, and a slightly higher percentage of cyan.

 CORRECT COLOR CAST WITH THE COLOR BALANCE ADJUSTMENT

Color cast is the result of improper gray balance, when one channel is significantly stronger or weaker than the others. An image with improper gray balance has an overall predominance of one color, which is most visible in the highlight areas. The image that you will correct in this exercise has a strong green cast that needs to be removed.

1. **Open the file salmon.jpg from your WIP>Menu folder.**

2. **Display the Info panel (Window>Info).**

3. **If you don't see both RGB and CMYK color modes in the Info panel, choose Panel Options in the Info panel Options menu. Use the Info Panel Options dialog box to choose Actual Color for the First Color Readout and CMYK Color for the Second Color Readout, then click OK.**

Note:

This exercise relies purely on numbers to correct gray balance. To see an accurate preview of image color on screen, you should calibrate your monitor and create a monitor profile that you can load into Photoshop.

4. **Choose the Color Sampler tool (nested under the Eyedropper tool).**

5. **In the Options bar, choose 3 by 3 Average in the Sample Size menu.**

Instead of correcting based on individual pixel values, you can average a group of contiguous pixels as the sample value. Doing so prevents accidentally correcting an image based on a single anomalous pixel (a dust spot, for example).

Use this menu to define the sample size.

Color Sampler tool

Color Sampler tool cursor

The Info panel shows color values for the current cursor location, in both RGB and CMYK modes.

6. **Click the cursor on the lower-left plate lip to place a color sample.**

7. **Click to add a second sample point to the top-right plate lip.**

   The two samples show a strong predominance of green; the numbers in the Info panel reflect the visible color cast in the image.

Sample points are numbered in order of creation.

This is the color sample that we placed in Step 6.

The Info panel shows the values associated with each of the sample points you created.

Note:

The Color Sampler tool can place up to four sample points per image.

8. **Choose Image>Adjustments>Color Balance.**

   Color Balance is a basic correction tool that can effectively remove overall color cast. The Color Balance dialog box presents a separate slider for each pair of complementary colors. You can adjust the highlights, shadows, or midtones of an image by selecting the appropriate radio button; the Preserve Luminosity check box ensures that only the colors shift, leaving the tonal balance of the image unchanged.

Note:

To delete an existing sample point, make the Color Sampler tool active, press Option/Alt, and click a point when the cursor icon changes to a pair of scissors.

9. **Click the Highlights radio button in the Tone Balance section at the bottom of the Color Balance dialog box.**

   The focal point of this image is green spinach, which you don't want to affect. Instead, you need to remove the green cast from the highlight, where it is most obvious.

10. **Drag the Magenta/Green slider left until the middle field shows –10.**

    Remember, adding a color's complement is one method for neutralizing that color. Increasing magenta in the highlight areas neutralizes the green color cast.

The values after the "/" show the result of the changes; these will become the actual sample values if you click OK.

Changing the color balance brings the three values much closer to equal (called "in balance").

These fields correspond to the three color sliders. The middle field shows the Magenta/Green adjustment.

11. **Click OK to apply the adjustment.**

12. **Save the file in your WIP>Menu folder as a TIFF file named** `salmon_fixed.tif`**.**

13. **Close the file and continue to the next exercise.**

CORRECT GRAY BALANCE WITH CURVES

The Curves adjustment is the most powerful color-correction tool in Photoshop. If you understand the ideas behind curves, you can use this tool to remove color cast, enhance overall contrast, and even modify color values in individual channels.

The diagram in the Curves dialog box is the heart of the Curves adjustment. When you open the Curves dialog box, a straight diagonal line in the graph represents the existing color in the image.

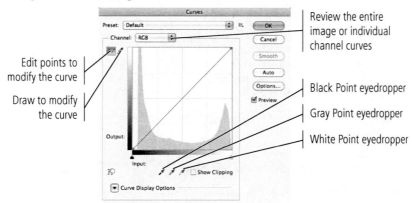

Edit points to modify the curve

Draw to modify the curve

Review the entire image or individual channel curves

Black Point eyedropper

Gray Point eyedropper

White Point eyedropper

The horizontal axis represents the input color value, and the vertical axis represents the output color value. The upper-right point is the maximum value for that color mode (255 for RGB images and 100 for CMYK images). The bottom-left corner of the curves grid is the zero point.

The color mode of the image determines the direction of the input and output scales. In both CMYK and RGB, 0 means "none of that color." However, remember the difference between the two different color modes:

- The additive RGB color model starts at black and adds values of each channel to produce different colors, so 0, 0, 0 in RGB equals black.

- The subtractive CMYK model starts with white (paper) and adds percentages of each ink (channel) to produce different colors, so 0, 0, 0, 0 in CMYK equals white.

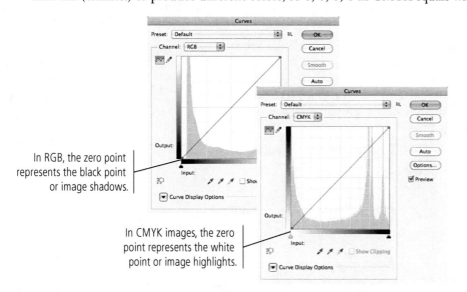

In RGB, the zero point represents the black point or image shadows.

In CMYK images, the zero point represents the white point or image highlights.

Note:

Remember, the additive colors (RGB) at full strength combine to create pure white, while the subtractive colors (CMYK) at full strength combine to create pure black.

Every curve is automatically anchored by a black point and a white point. (For RGB, the black point is at the bottom left and the white point is at the top right.) You can add points along the curve by simply clicking the curve. You can also move any point on the curve by clicking and dragging.

When you move points on the curve of an image (whether for the whole image or for an individual channel), you are telling Photoshop to, "Map every pixel that was [this] input value to [that] output value." In other words, using the following image as an example, a pixel that was 128 (the input value) will now be 114 (the output value). Because curves are just that — curves, and not individual points — adjusting one point on a curve changes the shape of the curve as necessary.

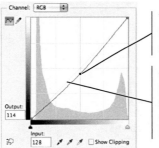

This point changes the input value of 128 to an output value of 114.

On either side of the adjusted point, the curve is adjusted to smoothly meet the other points on the curve (in this case, the black and white points).

1. **Open the file flan.jpg from the WIP>Menu folder.**

2. **Using the Color Sampler tool, place a sample point on the left plate lip.**

   This image has a strong red cast that needs to be neutralized. You can correct cast by removing the cast color or adding the other two primaries; the goal is equal (or nearly equal) parts of red, green, and blue in the neutral areas such as the plate lip.

   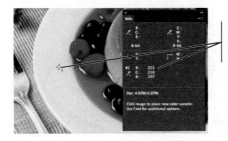

   The sample shows a strong red cast in what should be neutral areas.

   In the Info panel, the sample values show that the red channel has a value of 231, the green channel has a value of 210, and the blue channel has a value of 207. To fix the cast in this image, you will use the middle of these values (the green channel) as the target and adjust the other two curves.

3. **Choose Image>Adjustments>Curves and make sure the Preview option is checked in the Curves dialog box.**

4. **Choose Red in the Channel menu to display the curve for only the Red channel, and then click the line on the graph to place a point near the three-quarter grid intersection.**

   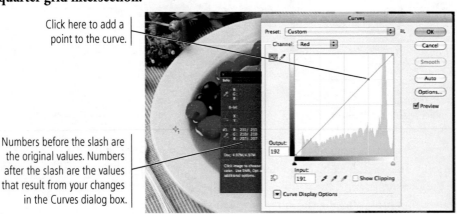

   Click here to add a point to the curve.

   Numbers before the slash are the original values. Numbers after the slash are the values that result from your changes in the Curves dialog box.

Note:

Easily recognizable "neutral" areas — such as the white plate in this image — are the best places to look for global color problems; fixing these will also fix many problem areas that you might not immediately recognize.

Note:

Your sample might be in a slightly different place, showing slightly different values. Use the values you see on your screen, rather than the numbers in our screen shots, to complete the following steps.

5. **With the new point selected on the curve, type the original Red value in the Input field (ours is 231).**

6. **Type the target value in the Output field (ours is the Green value of 210).**

The number after the slash shows that the Red value for this sample will be equal to the Green value when you click OK.

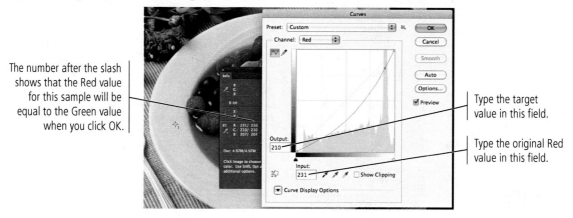

Type the target value in this field.

Type the original Red value in this field.

7. **In the Channel menu, choose the other channel that you need to adjust based on your sample values (ours is Blue). Add a point to the curve, and then adjust the input value to match your target output value (the original Green value, in our example). Using our sample point, we adjusted the 207 Input value to a 210 Output value.**

You can add the point anywhere along the curve; when you change the Input and Output values, the point automatically moves to that location along the curve.

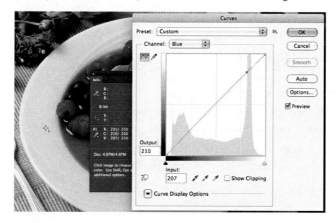

8. **Click OK to apply the changes and close the Curves dialog box.**

You can see how simply correcting gray balance has a significant impact on the image:

9. **Save the file in your WIP>Menu folder as a TIFF file named flan_fixed.tif.**

10. **Close the file and continue to the next exercise.**

PHOTOSHOP FOUNDATIONS

The On-Image Adjustment tool in the Curves dialog box allows you to make curve adjustments by interacting directly with the image (behind the dialog box).

When the On-Image Adjustment tool is active, clicking in the image places a point on the curve based on the pixel data where you clicked; you can then drag up or down within the image area to move that point of the curve (in other words, to change the output value of the selected input value).

You can add 14 points on a curve, and delete points by pressing Command/Control-delete.

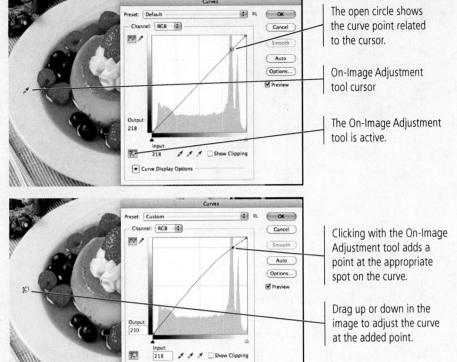

The open circle shows the curve point related to the cursor.

On-Image Adjustment tool cursor

The On-Image Adjustment tool is active.

Clicking with the On-Image Adjustment tool adds a point at the appropriate spot on the curve.

Drag up or down in the image to adjust the curve at the added point.

CORRECT CONTRAST WITH CURVES

Remember, contrast is essentially the difference between the values in an image. By adjusting the points on the curve, you increase the tonal range between those points — which means you also increase the contrast in that same range.

In the following image, Point A has an Input value of 167 and an Output value of 182. Point B has an Input value of 87 and an Output value of 62. Mathematically:

- Original tonal range (Input values): 167 to 87 = 80 available tones

- New tonal range (Output values): 182 to 62 = 120 available tones

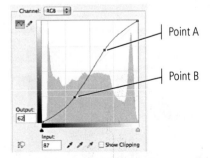

Point A

Point B

By making these two curve adjustments, we significantly increased the tonal range available for the image's midtones, which means we also significantly increased the contrast in the midtones. A steeper curve indicates increased tonal range and increased contrast. Notice, however, that the curves before Point B and after Point A are much shallower than the original curves, which means this change also significantly reduces the contrast in the shadow and highlight areas.

Points to Remember about Curves

Curves are very powerful tools, and they can be intimidating. To simplify the process and make it less daunting, keep these points in mind:

- Aim for neutral grays.
- You can adjust the curve for an entire image, or you can adjust the individual curves for each channel of the image.
- The horizontal tone scale shows the Input value, and the vertical tone scale shows the Output value.
- Changes made to one area of a curve affect all other areas of the image.
- The steeper the curve, the greater the contrast.
- Increasing contrast in one area inherently decreases contrast in other areas.

Curve Display Options

The Curve Display options allow you to control what is visible in the graph. (If you can't see the Curve Display options, click the button to the left of the heading.)

The Show Amount Of radio buttons reverse the input and output tone scales. Light is the default setting for RGB images; Pigment/Ink % is the default setting for CMYK images.

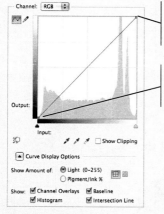

By default, the lightest point for an RGB image is in the top right.

The darkest point for an RGB image is in the bottom left.

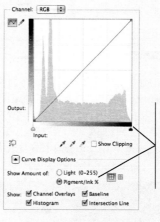

Choose Show Amount of Pigment/Ink % to reverse the tone scales. For an RGB image, the lightest point moves to the bottom left and the darkest point moves to the top right.

Other Curve Display Options determine what is visible in the actual graph:

When the Channel Overlays option is checked, each channel is represented on the graph by a separate line.

When the Baseline option is active, the original curve is represented by a gray line.

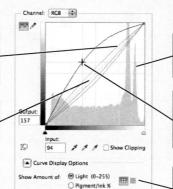

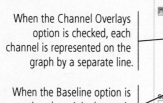

When the Histogram option is active, the image's tonal range is represented behind the graph.

When the Intersection Line option is active, crosshairs appear when you drag a point in the graph, which can help you more precisely adjust curve points.

Use these buttons to show a four-by-four grid or a ten-by-ten grid.

1. Open the file **pasta.jpg** from the WIP>Menu folder.

2. Choose Image>Adjustments>Curves and make sure Preview is checked.

3. Activate the Show Clipping option, click the black point on the bottom-left corner of the graph, and then drag until some pixels start to appear in the image (behind the dialog box).

We dragged the Input Black point just past the point where the histogram shows the darkest shadows in the image. (You performed this same action in the Levels dialog box when you adjusted the Input Shadow slider.) The Input and Output fields show that any pixels with an Input value of 13 will be output as 0; in other words, anything with an Input value lower than 13 will be clipped to solid black.

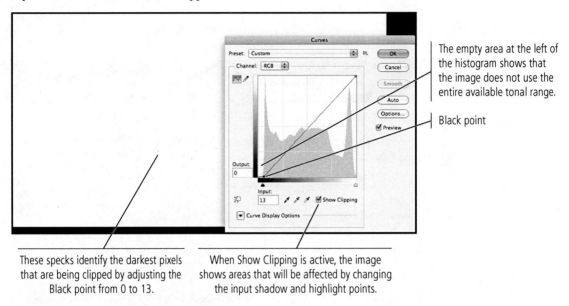

The empty area at the left of the histogram shows that the image does not use the entire available tonal range.

Black point

These specks identify the darkest pixels that are being clipped by adjusting the Black point from 0 to 13.

When Show Clipping is active, the image shows areas that will be affected by changing the input shadow and highlight points.

4. Repeat Step 3, dragging the White point left until the lightest areas of the image start to appear behind the dialog box.

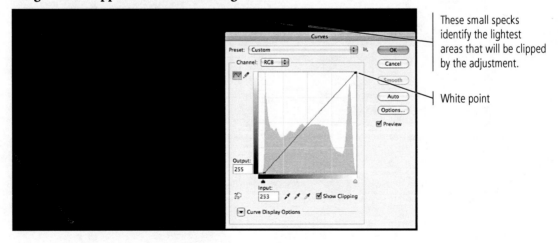

These small specks identify the lightest areas that will be clipped by the adjustment.

White point

5. **Turn off the Show Clipping option so you can see the actual image behind the dialog box.**

   Even this small change improved the image, but the midtones — especially in the pasta, which is the focal area of the image — need some additional contrast. To accomplish that change, you need to steepen the curve in the middle of the graph.

Note:

Contrast adjustments can have a major impact on color as well as on sharpness. Take particular note of the green basil leaves; no direct color adjustment was done to these two images, but the leaves are noticeably greener and brighter after you adjust the curves.

6. **Click the curve to create a point at the quartertone gridline and drag it slightly to the right.**

   We adjusted the curve point from an Input value of 81 to an Output value of 62.

Three-quartertone gridlines

Quartertone gridlines

7. **Click the curve at the three-quartertone gridline and drag the point to the left.**

   We adjusted the 175 Input value to a 190 Output value.

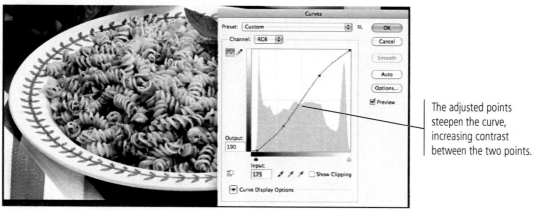

The adjusted points steepen the curve, increasing contrast between the two points.

8. **Click OK to apply the changes and close the dialog box.**

   Adjusting the contrast with curves improved the detail in the image and enhanced the overall image color.

9. **Save the file in your WIP>Menu folder as a TIFF file named pasta_fixed.tif.**

10. **Close the file and continue to the next stage of the project.**

Stage 4 Working with HDR Images

The human eye is extremely sensitive to subtle changes in light. In general, we can perceive detail in both light and dark areas — and areas in between — with a single glance. Camera sensors, on the other hand, are not so sensitive. If you look at most photographs, they typically have sharp detail in one of the ranges — highlights, midtones, or shadows, depending on the exposure and other settings used to capture the image. If a photograph favors highlights, details in shadow areas are lost (and vice versa).

To solve this problem, the concept of HDR (**high dynamic range**) images combines multiple photographs of different exposures into a single image to enhance the detail throughout the entire image — combining highlight, shadow, and midtone detail from various exposures to create an image more like what the human eye is capable of observing, rather than the more limited range that characterizes a digital camera's sensors.

The phrase "dynamic range" refers to the difference between the darkest shadow and the lightest highlight in an image.

- A regular 8-bit RGB photo has a dynamic range of 0–255 for each color channel (2^8 or 256 possible values). In other words, each pixel can have one of 256 possible values to describe the lightness of that color in that specific location.

- A 16-bit RGB photo allows 16 bits of information to describe the information in each pixel, allowing a dynamic range of 2^{16} or 65,536 possible values in each color channel.

- A 32-bit or HDR image allows 2^{32} possible values — more than 4 billion, which is signficantly larger than the visible spectrum of 16.7 million colors (thus, 32-bit dynamic range is sometimes referred to as "infinite").

USE MERGE TO HDR PRO

The last piece required to complete this project is an image of the antique waterwheel that is one of the hallmarks of the restaurant's exterior. Its location makes it very difficult to capture because the surrounding trees cast shadows even when the sun is at the best lighting angle. The photographer suggested using high dynamic range (HDR) photo techniques to capture the most possible detail in the scene, and has provided you with five photos taken at the same time, using different exposure settings.

1. **With no file open, choose File>Automate>Merge to HDR Pro.**

2. **In the resulting Merge to HDR Pro dialog box, click the Browse button.**

3. **Navigate to WIP>Menu>Mill Photos. Shift-click to select all five images in the folder and click Open.**

Note:

You can merge up to seven images with the Merge to HDR Pro utility.

4. **Make sure the Attempt to Automatically Align Source Images box at the bottom of the dialog box is checked, then click OK.**

   Because you are merging multiple images into a single one, there is a chance that one or more images might be slightly misaligned. (Even using a tripod, a stiff breeze can affect the camera just enough to make the different exposures slightly different.) When Attempt to Automatically Align Source Images is checked, Photoshop compares details in each image and adjusts them as necessary to create the resulting merged image.

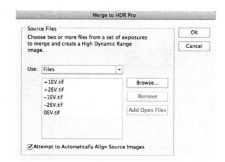

5. **Read the resulting message, then click OK.**

   HDR images are best created from Camera RAW files, which can maintain significantly more data than the TIFF or JPEG formats. In many cases, however, you will have to use non-RAW files because that is what your photographer or client will provide to you. The merge process still works very well with JPEG and TIFF files.

6. **If you don't see a histogram on the right side of the dialog box, open the Mode menu and choose 32 Bit.**

   The resulting dialog box shows each selected image as a thumbnail at the bottom. By default, all selected images are included in the merge. You can exclude specific exposures by unchecking the box for that image.

   If you work with HDR, you need to realize that most computer monitors are not capable of displaying 32-bit image depth. When you merge to a 32-bit image, you can use the White Point Preview slider to change the dynamic range that is visible on your screen, but this has no effect on the actual data in the file — it affects only the current display of the image data.

Note:

The merge process might take a minute or two to complete, so be patient.

7. **Check the Remove Ghosts option on the right side of the dialog box.**

When an HDR image contains movement, merging the individual exposures can blur the areas where that movement occurs — such as the water dripping off the wheel in this image. When you check Remove Ghosts, the software uses one of the exposures (highlighted in green) to define detail in the area of motion; you can change the key exposure by simply clicking a different image in the lower pane.

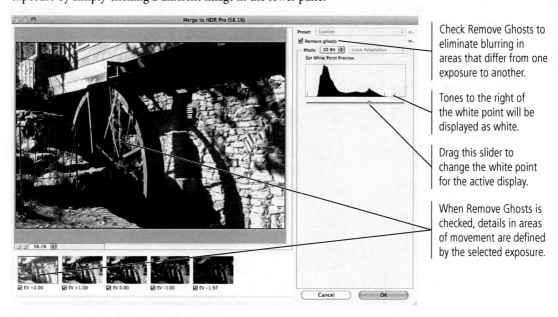

Check Remove Ghosts to eliminate blurring in areas that differ from one exposure to another.

Tones to the right of the white point will be displayed as white.

Drag this slider to change the white point for the active display.

When Remove Ghosts is checked, details in areas of movement are defined by the selected exposure.

8. **Open the Mode menu and choose 8 Bit.**

32-bit images can store a tremendous amount of information, which creates images with far more detail than you see in a conventional 8-bit photograph. However, one significant disadvantage of such images is that they cannot be separated for commercial printing. If you're going to use an HDR image in a print application — such as the cover of this menu — you need to apply the process of **tone mapping** to define how the high dynamic range will be compressed into the lower dynamic range that is required by the output process.

9. **Leave the secondary menu set to Local Adaptation.**

You can use the other options to apply less specific tone mapping to the image. Equalize Histogram and Highlight Compression have no further options. The Exposure and Gamma option allows you to define specific values for only those two settings.

When the Local Adaptation method is selected, you can change the values for a number of specific options to map the tones in the HDR image to a lower dynamic range.

10. **Open the Preset menu and choose Photorealistic.**

The application includes a number of standard settings, including several variations of monochromatic, photorealistic, and surrealistic. Each preset changes the values of the Local Adaptation sliders to create the desired effect.

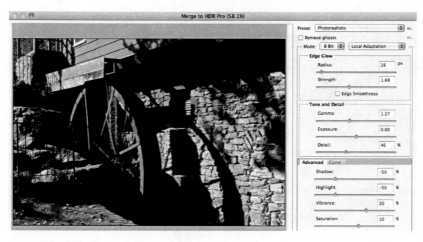

11. **Experiment with the different sliders until you are satisfied with the result.**

Tone mapping is a largely subjective process, and different end uses can influence the settings that you apply to a specific image. You should understand the following information as you experiment with the various settings:

- **Radius** defines the size of the glowing effect in areas of localized brightness.

- **Strength** determines the required tolerance between tonal values before pixels are no longer considered part of the same brightness region.

- **Gamma** values lower than 1.0 increase details in the midtones, while higher values emphasize details in the highlights and shadows.

- **Exposure** affects the overall lightness or darkness of the image.

- **Detail** increases or decreases the overall sharpness of the image.

- **Shadow** and **Highlight** affect the amount of detail in those areas of the image. Higher values increase detail and lower values reduce detail.

- **Vibrance** affects the intensity of subtle colors, while minimizing clipping of highly saturated colors.

- **Saturation** affects the intensity of all colors from –100 (monochrome) to +100 (double saturation).

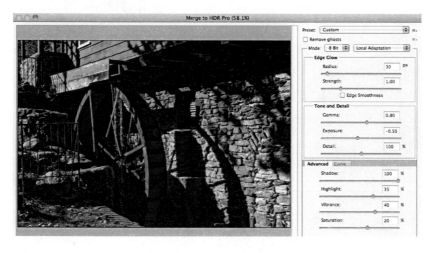

Note:

You can create your own presets by clicking the button to the right of the Preset menu and choosing Save Preset in the resulting menu.

12. **Click OK to finalize the process.**

Because you chose 8 Bit in the Mode menu of the Merge to HDR Pro dialog box, the resulting image is an 8-bit RGB image (as you can see in the document tab).

13. **Save the file in your WIP>Menu>Mill Images folder as a native Photoshop file named mill_merged.psd, then close it.**

fill in the blank

1. The _____ filter locates pixels that differ in value from surrounding pixels by the threshold you specify; it sharpens an image by increasing contrast along the edges in an image.

2. _____ is defined as random pixels that stand out from the surrounding pixels.

3. The _____ blends colors from user-defined source pixels with colors in the area where you click.

4. The _____ paints one part of an image over another part, which is useful for duplicating specific objects or removing defects in an image.

5. _____ are direct sources of light such as a light bulb or reflected sunlight on water; they should not be considered the highlights of an image.

6. _____ refers to the tonal variation within an image.

7. A _____ is a visual depiction of the distribution of colors in an image.

8. _____ is defined according to a color's position on a color wheel, beginning from red (0°) and traveling counterclockwise around the wheel.

9. _____ (also called "intensity") refers to the color's difference from neutral gray.

10. _____ (also called "luminance" or "value") is the amount of white or black added to the pure color.

short answer

1. Explain the concept of neutral gray.

2. List three important points to remember when working with curves.

3. Briefly explain the concepts of minimum printable dot and maximum ink coverage.

Use what you learned in this project to complete the following freeform exercise.
Carefully read the art director and client comments, then create your design to meet the needs of the project.
Use the space below to sketch ideas; when finished, write a brief explanation of the reasoning behind your design.

art director comments

The tourism board director dined at The Chateau recently. In a conversation with the restaurant owner, he mentioned a new project about local architecture. Mr. Roseman, pleased with your work on the menu images, recommended you for the job.

To complete this project, you should:

❏ Find at least 10 photos of different architectural styles throughout the Los Angeles metropolitan area.

❏ Use photo retouching techniques to clean up any graffiti and trash that is visible in the images.

❏ Use correction techniques to adjust the tonal range and gray balance of the images.

client comments

Over the next year, we're planning on publishing a series of promotional booklets to show tourists that L.A. is more than just Hollywood.

Each booklet in the series will focus on an 'interest area' such as fine art or — for the first one — architecture. The city has a diverse architectural mix, from eighteenth-century Spanish missions to 1920s bungalows to the Walt Disney Concert Hall designed by Frank Gehry in the 1990s.

We'd like at least ten pictures of different landmarks or architectural styles, corrected and optimized for printing on a sheetfed press. If possible, we'd also like some historical images to include in a 'building a metropolis' section on the first couple of pages.

Of course, Los Angeles is a large city, and cities have their problems — not the least of which are graffiti and garbage. We are trying to attract tourists, not turn them away. Make sure none of the images show any graffiti or blatant litter; if these problems are visible in the images you select, give them a good digital cleaning.

project justification

_____
_____
_____
_____
_____
_____
_____
_____
_____
_____
_____
_____
_____
_____

As with many other skills, it takes time and practice to master image correction techniques. Understanding the relationship between brightness and contrast, and how these two values affect the quality of reproduction in digital images, is the first and possibly most critical factor in creating a high-quality image. An image that has too much contrast (a "sharp" image) or not enough contrast (a "flat" image) translates to an unsatisfactory print.

A basic understanding of color theory (specifically complementary color) is the foundation of accurate color correction. Effective color correction relies on the numbers, rather than what you think you see on your monitor. As you gain experience in correcting images, you will be better able to predict the corrections required to achieve the best possible output.

Remove photographic grain with blur and sharpen techniques

Use the Healing Brush and Spot Healing Brush tools to correct scratches

Use the Clone Stamp tool to remove major damage

Correct contrast and tonal range using the Levels adjustment

Correct minor color problems using the Brightness/Contrast adjustment

Correct gray balance using the Curves adjustment

Correct lighting problems with the Exposure adjustment

Correct overall color cast using the Color Balance adjustment

Correct contrast with the Curves adjustment

Use Merge to HDR Pro to find detail in multiple exposures

Adobe Flash is the industry-standard application for building animations and other interactive content. Mastering the tools and techniques of the application can significantly improve your potential career options.

Typical Flash work ranges from simply moving things around within a space to building fully interactive games and Web sites, complete with sound and video files. Flash is somewhat unique in the communications industry because these different types of work often require different sets of skills — specifically, a combination of both visual creativity and logical programming. Depending on the type of application you're building, you should have a basic understanding of both graphic design and ActionScript code.

Our goal in this book is to teach you how to use the available tools to create various types of work that you might encounter in your professional career. As you complete the projects, you explore the basic drawing techniques, and then move on to more advanced techniques such as adding animation and interactivity — two core functions that make multimedia one of the most popular elements of modern electronic communication.

The simple exercises in this introduction are designed to let you explore the Flash user interface. Whether you are new to the application or upgrading from a previous version, we highly recommend that you follow these steps to click around and become familiar with the basic workspace.

 EXPLORE THE FLASH INTERFACE

Much of the Flash interface functions in the same way as the Photoshop user interface. Panels can be opened, moved, and grouped in the same manner, and you can save custom workspaces to call specific sets of panels. The first time you launch the application, you'll see the default workspace settings defined by Adobe. When you relaunch after you or another user has quit, the workspace defaults to the last-used settings — including specific open panels and the position of those panels on your screen. Because Flash has a different basic purpose than Photoshop, there are some inherent differences that you should recognize.

1. **Download the WC6_RF_InterfaceFL.zip archive from the Student Files Web page.**

2. **Expand the ZIP archive in your WIP folder (Macintosh) or copy the archive contents into your WIP folder (Windows).**

   This results in a folder named **Interface_FL**, which contains all of the files you need for this project.

3. **In Flash, open the Window menu and choose Workspace>Essentials.**

   Remember: Saved workspaces, accessed in the Window>Workspace menu or in the Workspace switcher on the Application bar, provide one-click access to a defined group of tools.

4. Choose Window>Workspace>Reset 'Essentials'.

As in Photoshop, saved workspaces in Flash remember the last-used state; to restore the saved state of the workspace, you have to use the Reset option.

The Welcome Screen appears by default when no file is open, unless you (or someone else) checked the Don't Show Again option. The Welcome Screen provides quick access to recently opened files, and links for creating a variety of new documents. If you don't see the Welcome Screen when no files are open, you can turn this feature back on by choosing Welcome Screen in the On Launch menu of the General pane of the Preferences dialog box. After you quit and relaunch the application, the Welcome Screen reappears.

Macintosh users: You cannot turn off the Application frame in Flash.

Note:

When no file is open in Flash, only a few menus are available in the Menu bar. Others become available only when a file is open.

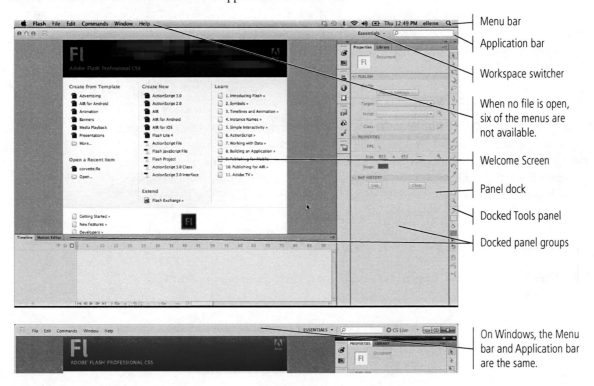

Menu bar

Application bar

Workspace switcher

When no file is open, six of the menus are not available.

Welcome Screen

Panel dock

Docked Tools panel

Docked panel groups

On Windows, the Menu bar and Application bar are the same.

5. On the right side of the workspace, click the Tools panel title bar and drag away from the dock into the middle of the workspace.

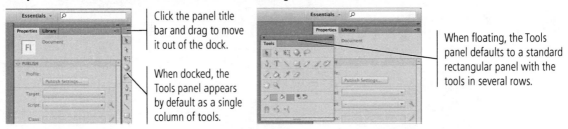

Click the panel title bar and drag to move it out of the dock.

When docked, the Tools panel appears by default as a single column of tools.

When floating, the Tools panel defaults to a standard rectangular panel with the tools in several rows.

6. Click the Tools panel title bar and drag left until a blue line appears on the left edge of the workspace.

This step docks the Tools panel on the left edge of the workspace.

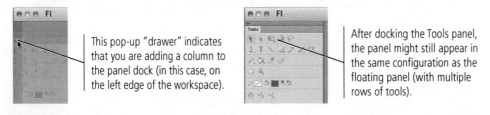

This pop-up "drawer" indicates that you are adding a column to the panel dock (in this case, on the left edge of the workspace).

After docking the Tools panel, the panel might still appear in the same configuration as the floating panel (with multiple rows of tools).

FLASH FOUNDATIONS

In addition to a wide variety of panels, Flash CS6 includes 30 tools — a large number that indicates the power of the application. You can change the docked Tools panel to more than one column by dragging the right edge of the panel. When the Tools panel is floating, it defaults to show the various tools in rows.

You learn how to use these tools as you complete the projects in this book. For now, you should simply take the opportunity to identify the tools and their location on the Tools panel. The image to the right shows the icon, tool name, and keyboard shortcut (if any) that accesses each tool. Nested tools are shown indented and the names appear in italics.

Keyboard Shortcuts & Nested Tools

When you hover your mouse over a tool, the pop-up tooltip shows the name of the tool and a letter in parentheses. Pressing that letter activates the associated tool (unless you're working with type, in which case pressing a key adds that letter to your text). If you don't see tooltips, check the General pane of the Preferences dialog box; the Show Tooltips check box should be active. (Note: You must have a file open to see the tooltips and access the nested tools.)

When you hover the mouse cursor over the tool, a tooltip shows the name of the tool.

Any tool with an arrow in the bottom-right corner includes related tools nested below it. When you click a tool and hold down the mouse button, the nested tools appear in a pop-up menu. If you choose one of the nested tools, that variation becomes the default choice in the Tools panel.

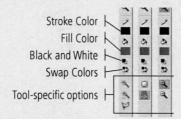

This arrow means the tool has other nested tools.

Click and hold down the mouse button to show the nested tools.

Tool Options

In addition to the basic tool set, the bottom of the Tools panel includes options that control the fill and stroke colors, as well as options that change depending on the selected tool.

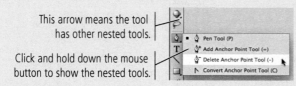

Stroke Color
Fill Color
Black and White
Swap Colors
Tool-specific options

Customizing the Tools Panel

Flash offers a unique feature that makes it easy to customize the Tools panel (Flash>Customize Tools Panel on Macintosh or Edit>Customize Tools Panel on Windows).

If you click a tool icon in the left side of the dialog box, all tools nested in that space display in the Current Selection list. If you add a tool from the Available Tools list, it becomes nested under the selected tool. To remove a tool from the default Tools panel, select the tool name in the Current Selection list and click Remove.

Selection tool (V)
Subselection tool (A)
Free Transform tool (Q)
Gradient Transform tool (F)
3D Rotation tool (W)
3D Translation tool (G)
Lasso tool (L)
Pen tool (P)
Add Anchor Point tool (=)
Delete Anchor Point tool (-)
Convert Anchor Point tool (C)
Text tool (T)
Line tool (\)
Rectangle tool (R)
Oval tool (O)
Rectangle Primitive tool (R)
Oval Primitive tool (O)
PolyStar tool
Pencil tool (Y)
Brush tool (B)
Spray Brush tool
Deco tool (U)
Bone tool (M)
Bind tool
Paint Bucket tool (K)
Ink Bottle tool (S)
Eyedropper tool (I)
Eraser tool (E)
Hand tool (H)
Zoom tool (Z)

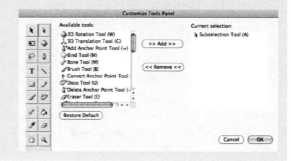

7. **If your Tools panel shows multiple tools in the same row, click the right edge of the Tools panel and drag left until all the tools appear in a single column.**

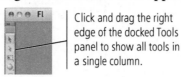

Click and drag the right edge of the docked Tools panel to show all tools in a single column.

8. **Continue to the next exercise.**

 EXPLORE THE FLASH DOCUMENT WINDOW

There is far more to using Flash than arranging panels around the workspace. What you do with those panels — and even which panels you need — depends on the type of work you are doing in a particular file. In this exercise, you open a Flash file and explore the interface elements that you will use to create digital animations.

1. **In Flash, choose File>Open.**

2. **Navigate to your WIP>InterfaceFL folder and select `capcarl.fla` in the list of available files.**

   The Open dialog box is a system-standard navigation dialog. Press Shift to select and open multiple contiguous (consecutive) files in the list. Press Command/Control to select and open multiple non-contiguous files.

3. **Click Open.**

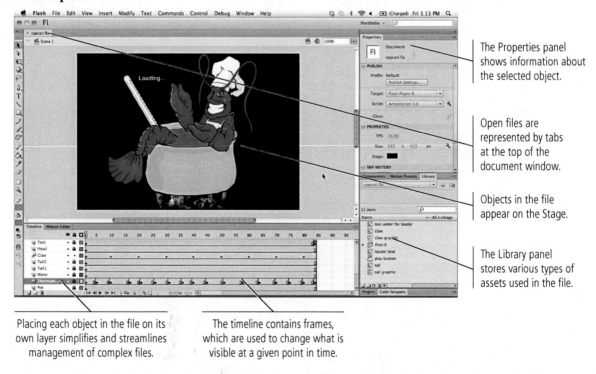

The Properties panel shows information about the selected object.

Open files are represented by tabs at the top of the document window.

Objects in the file appear on the Stage.

The Library panel stores various types of assets used in the file.

Placing each object in the file on its own layer simplifies and streamlines management of complex files.

The timeline contains frames, which are used to change what is visible at a given point in time.

4. **Above the top-right corner of the Stage, open the View Percentage menu and choose Fit in Window.**

5. **Click the bar that separates the Stage area from the Timeline panel. Drag up to enlarge the panel and show all the layers in the file.**

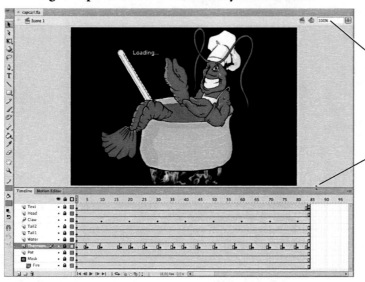

The Fit in Window command enlarges or reduces the view percentage to fill the available space in the document window.

Click here and drag up to show all the layers in the file.

Customizing Flash Behavior

Keyboard Shortcuts and Menus

Different people use Flash for various reasons, sometimes using a specific, limited set of tools to complete only one type of project. In addition to customizing the workspace and the Tools panel, you can also customize the various keyboard shortcuts used to access different commands (Flash>Keyboard Shortcuts on Macintosh or Edit>Keyboard Shortcuts on Windows). Once you have defined custom menus or shortcuts, you can save your choices as a set so you can access the same custom choices again without having to redo the work.

Delete Set

Export Set as HTML

Rename Set

Duplicate Set

Use this menu to access saved sets.

Use this menu to view different groups of commands.

Application Preferences

You can also customize the way many of the program's tools and options function. The left side of the Preferences dialog box (Flash>Preferences on Macintosh or Edit>Preferences on Windows) allows you to display the various sets of preferences available in Flash. As you work your way through the projects in this book, you will learn not only what you can do with these collections of Preferences, but also why and when you might want to use them.

6. Review the Timeline panel.

The Timeline panel is perhaps the most important panel in Flash. It represents the passage of time within your animation, and it enables you to control what happens to objects in your file, as well as when and where changes occur.

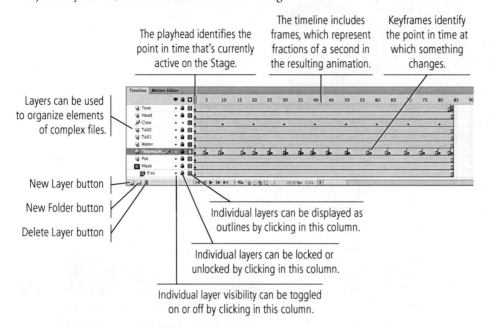

The playhead identifies the point in time that's currently active on the Stage.

The timeline includes frames, which represent fractions of a second in the resulting animation.

Keyframes identify the point in time at which something changes.

Layers can be used to organize elements of complex files.

New Layer button

New Folder button

Delete Layer button

Individual layers can be displayed as outlines by clicking in this column.

Individual layers can be locked or unlocked by clicking in this column.

Individual layer visibility can be toggled on or off by clicking in this column.

7. Choose the Selection tool from the Tools panel and click the lobster's right claw on the Stage.

Although we will not discuss all 20+ Flash panels here, the Properties panel deserves mention. This important panel is **context sensitive**, which means it provides various options depending on what is selected on the Stage.

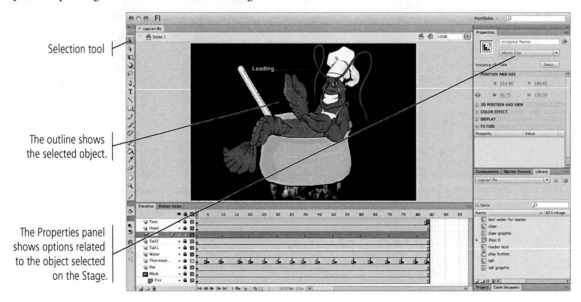

Selection tool

The outline shows the selected object.

The Properties panel shows options related to the object selected on the Stage.

8. Click the playhead above the timeline frames and drag right.

This technique of dragging the playhead above the timeline is called **scrubbing**.

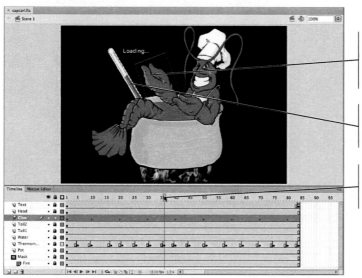

As you drag right, the claw moves back and forth in a waving motion (based on objects on the Claw layer).

The mercury in the thermometer rises (based on objects on the Thermometer layer).

Drag the playhead to preview animation in the document window.

9. Click the gray area outside of the Stage to deselect everything, then press Return/Enter.

One final reminder: throughout this book, we list differing commands in the Macintosh/Windows format. On Macintosh, you need to press the Return key; on Windows, press the Enter key. (We will not repeat this explanation every time different commands are required for the different operating systems.)

This keyboard shortcut plays the movie on the Stage from the current location of the playhead. If the playhead is already at the end of the frames, it moves back to Frame 1 and plays the entire movie.

10. Press Command-Return/Control-Enter.

Instead of simply playing the movie on the Stage, you can preview the file to see what it will look like when exported. This keyboard shortcut, which is the same as choosing Test Movie in the Control menu, exports a SWF file from the existing FLA file so you can see what the final file will look like.

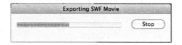

In the Flash Player window, you see some animated elements that did not appear when you played the movie on the Stage. This is a perfect example of why you should test actual animation files rather than relying only on what you see on the Stage. (This is especially true if you did not create the file, as in this case.)

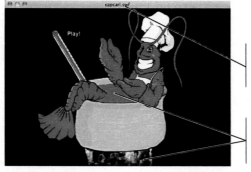

The exported SWF file appears in a Flash Player window and begins playing.

Some animation does not play on the Stage, but does play in the Player window.

Note:

When a movie is playing on the Stage, press the Escape key to stop the playback.

Note:

The Controller panel (Window>Toolbars> Controller) enables you to control movie playback on the Flash Stage, using buttons similar to those on DVD players.

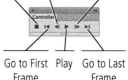

Step Back One Frame   Step Forward One Frame

Stop

Go to First Frame   Play   Go to Last Frame

The Controller panel only affects the Flash Stage. It does not affect files open in the Flash Player window.

11. **Close the Player window and return to Flash.**

12. **Click the Close button on the capcarl document tab. If asked, click Don't Save/No to close the file without saving.**

Click here to close the file.

Note:

Press Command/ Control-W to close the active file.

Clicking the Close button on the Application frame closes all open files and quits the application.

Application frame
Close button (Macintosh)

Application frame
Close button (Windows)

Understanding Auto-Recovery

FLASH FOUNDATIONS

In the General pane of the Preferences dialog box, the Auto-Recovery option is turned on by default. Auto-recovery files are saved every 10 minutes by default; you can use the field to change this interval.

When auto-recovery is turned on, a copy of the active file is saved with the word "RECOVER_" appended to the beginning of the defined file name. (If you haven't saved a file yet, the auto-recovery file is saved in the application's Temp folder.)

If the application or system crashes before you intentionally save and close the file, you will be asked if you want to restore the auto-recovery file when you relaunch Flash. When you intentionally close the active file, the recovery files are deleted.

If auto-recovery is not enabled for a particular file, you will see a warning after the defined interval, asking if you want to enable auto-recovery for that file.

(Remember: Preferences are accessed in the Flash menu on Macintosh and in the Edit menu on Windows.)

Most Flash projects require some amount of zooming in and out, as well as navigating around the document within its window. As we show you how to complete different stages of the workflow, we usually won't tell you when to change your view percentage because that's largely a matter of personal preference. You should understand the different options for navigating around a Flash file, however, so you can easily and efficiently get to what you want, when you want to get there.

Zoom Tool

You can click with the Zoom tool to increase the view percentage in specific, predefined intervals (the same intervals you see in the View Percentage menu in the top-right corner of the document window). Pressing Option/Alt with the Zoom tool allows you to zoom out in the same predefined percentages. If you drag a marquee with the Zoom tool, you can zoom into a specific location; the area surrounded by the marquee fills the available space in the document window.

Click with the Zoom tool to zoom in.

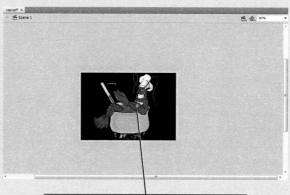

Option/Alt-click with the Zoom tool to zoom out.

Draw a marquee with the Zoom tool…

…to fill the document window with the selected area.

View Menu

The View>Magnification menu also provides options for changing the view percentage, including their associated keyboard shortcuts. (The Zoom In and Zoom Out options step through the same predefined view percentages you see by clicking with the Zoom tool.)

Zoom In	Command/Control-equals (=)
Zoom Out	Command/Control-minus (–)
100%	Command/Control-1
Show Frame	Command/Control-2
Show All	Command/Control-3
400%	Command/Control-4
800%	Command/Control-8

View Percentage Field

In addition to the predefined view percentages in the menu, you can also type a specific percentage in the View Percentage field in the top-right corner of the document window.

Hand Tool

If scroll bars appear in the document window, you can use the Hand tool to drag the file around within the document window. The Hand tool changes the visible area in the document window; it has no effect on the actual content of the image.

When using a different tool other than the Text tool, you can press the Spacebar to temporarily access the Hand tool.

Double-clicking the Hand tool in the Tools panel fits the Stage to the document window.

Talking Kiosk Interface

You were hired to create an animated introduction for a shopping mall information kiosk. The Flash-based animation must feature a character who offers shoppers assistance in finding various facilities. Each button should also offer audio instructions that explain the link's purpose. As part of the Flash development team, your job is to prepare the interface artwork that will be handed off to the programmer, who will script the interactivity.

This project incorporates the following skills:

❏ Importing and managing artwork from Adobe Illustrator

❏ Using the Library panel to manage a complex file

❏ Building a frame-by-frame animation

❏ Editing various button states

❏ Importing sound files into Flash

❏ Adding event and stream sounds to the Flash timeline

❏ Controlling volume and duration of sound

❏ Applying built-in sound effects

❏ Synchronizing sound to animation

❏ Defining sound compression settings

client comments

Throughout the facility grounds, we are replacing all of the static "You Are Here" maps with interactive kiosks that will help users more quickly find the shops they are looking for.

I'd like the interface to be personal — a person actually talking to the user. We thought about the video route, but I'm convinced an animated character would be better (plus we won't have to pay an actor to use her image).

The interface should provide a link to four different categories of shops: Shoes & Apparel, Home Furnishings, Music & Electronics, and Casual & Fine Dining. We might break it down into more specific categories later, but the important point for now is to get the first version of this thing into use quickly.

art director comments

I already had all of the kiosk components created. I need you to assemble everything in Flash and prepare the various elements for the programmer, who will create all of the necessary code and links.

The artwork was created in Adobe Illustrator. Our illustrator is fairly knowledgeable about Flash requirements, so you should be able to import the artwork without too many problems. He even created the basic appearance of the navigation buttons, so you'll just need to modify those rather than create them from scratch.

When I reviewed the sound files, it seemed like the background music was very loud compared to the spoken intro. You should fix the music so the talking is audible above the background.

The lip-syncing part of the interface requires some careful attention to detail, but overall, it isn't a difficult job. Just take your time and try to make the mouths follow the words.

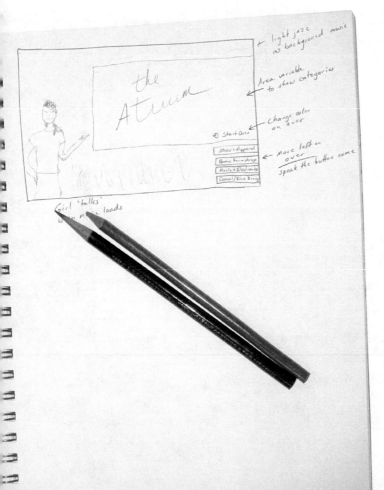

project objectives

To complete this project, you will:

❏ Create symbols from imported Illustrator files

❏ Place and manage instances of symbols on the Stage

❏ Control timing using keyframes

❏ Add visual interactivity to button symbols

❏ Import sound files into Flash

❏ Add event and stream sounds to a movie

❏ Use the start and stop sync methods for button sounds

❏ Edit a sound envelope to control volume and duration

❏ Swap graphics at precise moments in time

❏ Define sound compression settings

Stage 1 Working with Symbols

Although Flash can be used to create extraordinary interactive content, the program can also create extremely large files that take a very long time to download. (The size of a file is often referred to as a file's **weight**.) Users will not wait for more than a few seconds to download a file, so you should always try to keep file weight to a minimum — and that's where symbols come into play.

Symbols are objects that can be used repeatedly without increasing file size. The original symbol resides in the Library panel; **symbol instances** are copies of the symbol that you place onto the Stage. Although a regular graphic object adds to the overall file weight every time you use it on the Stage, a symbol counts only once no matter how many times you use it — which can mean dramatically smaller file sizes.

As another benefit, changes made to the content of an original symbol reflect in every placed instance of that symbol. For example, if you have placed 40 instances of a bird symbol, you can simultaneously change all 40 birds from blue jays to cardinals by changing the primary symbol in the Library panel.

A third benefit of symbols is that you can name placed instances, which means those instances can be targeted and affected by programming — one of the keys to animation and interactive development.

Note:

There are three primary types of symbols — graphic, movie clip, and button — and a number of other types of assets, such as audio and video files. In Flash, all of these assets are automatically stored in the Library panel.

FLASH FOUNDATIONS

The Library Panel in Depth

Assets in Flash are stored in the Library panel. Additional information about each asset is listed on the right side of the panel, including the name by which an asset can be called using ActionScript (AS Linkage), the number of instances in the current file (Use Count), the date the asset was last modified (Date Modified), and the type of asset (Type). To show the additional information, you can either make the panel wider or use the scroll bar at the bottom of the panel. In addition to storing and organizing assets, the Library panel has a number of other uses:

- Each type of asset is identified by a unique icon. Double-clicking a symbol icon enters into Symbol-Editing mode, where you can modify the symbol on its own Stage. Double-clicking a non-symbol icon (sounds, bitmaps, etc.) opens the Properties dialog box for that file.

- You can use the Library menu to switch between the libraries of currently open files.

- The Preview pane shows the selected asset. If the asset includes animation, video, or sound, you can use the Play and Stop buttons to preview the file in the panel. (The Stage background color appears in the Preview pane; if you can't see the Play button, move your mouse over the area of the button to reveal it.)

- If a file has a large number of assets (which is common), you can use the Search field to find assets by name.

- Clicking the Pin button to the right of the Library menu attaches the current library to the open Flash file.

- Clicking the New Library Panel button opens a new version of the Library panel, which allows you to view multiple libraries at one time.

- Clicking the New Symbol button opens the Create New Symbol dialog box, where you can define the name and type of the new symbol you want to create.

- Clicking the New Folder button adds a new folder in the current file's library.

- Clicking the Properties button opens a dialog box that shows information about the selected library asset.

- Clicking Delete removes an asset from the library. Placed instances of that symbol are deleted from the file.

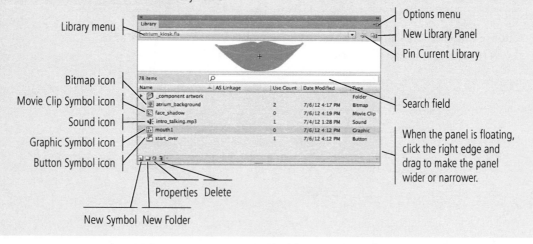

Library menu — Library / atrium_kiosk.fla

Options menu
New Library Panel
Pin Current Library

Bitmap icon
Movie Clip Symbol icon
Sound icon
Graphic Symbol icon
Button Symbol icon

78 items
Name / AS Linkage / Use Count / Date Modified / Type
_component artwork — Folder
atrium_background — 2 — 7/6/12 4:17 PM — Bitmap
face_shadow — 0 — 7/6/12 4:19 PM — Movie Clip
intro_talking.mp3 — 1 — 7/4/12 1:28 PM — Sound
mouth1 — 0 — 7/6/12 4:12 PM — Graphic
start_over — 1 — 7/6/12 4:12 PM — Button

Search field

When the panel is floating, click the right edge and drag to make the panel wider or narrower.

Properties Delete

New Symbol New Folder

IMPORT ADOBE ILLUSTRATOR ARTWORK

You can use the built-in Flash tools to draw complex custom artwork. In many cases, however, your work in Flash will incorporate files that were created in other applications. For example, illustrations and other vector graphics for animation are typically created in Adobe Illustrator. This project incorporates a number of external files, which you need to import into your Flash file.

1. **Download WC6_RF_Project3.zip from the Student Files Web page.**

2. **Expand the ZIP archive in your WIP folder (Macintosh) or copy the archive contents into your WIP folder (Windows).**

   This results in a folder named **Atrium**, which contains the files you need for this project. You should also use this folder to save the files you create in this project.

3. **In Flash, create a new Flash document for ActionScript 3.0 using the default settings in the New Document dialog box.**

   You can choose File>New, or use the Create New ActionScript 3.0 option in the Welcome Screen.

4. **Choose File>Save. Save the file in your WIP>Atrium folder as a Flash document named atrium_kiosk.fla.**

   In this project, you will use the Tools, Properties, Library, Align, and Timeline panels. You should arrange your workspace to best suit your personal preferences.

5. **Review the Properties and Library panels.**

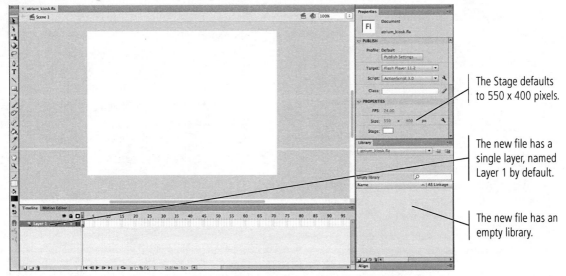

The Stage defaults to 550 x 400 pixels.

The new file has a single layer, named Layer 1 by default.

The new file has an empty library.

6. **Choose File>Import>Import to Stage. Navigate to the file interface.ai in the WIP>Atrium folder and click Open.**

7. **In the top-left section of the resulting dialog box, review the contents of the file that you are importing.**

The list of imported elements will make more sense if you're familiar with Adobe Illustrator. If you're not, the best choice is usually to import everything and review it carefully once it is in the Flash file.

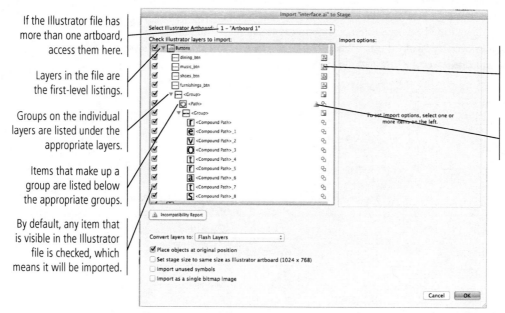

If the Illustrator file has more than one artboard, access them here.

Layers in the file are the first-level listings.

Groups on the individual layers are listed under the appropriate layers.

Items that make up a group are listed below the appropriate groups.

By default, any item that is visible in the Illustrator file is checked, which means it will be imported.

This icon identifies a graphic symbol, which can be created in Adobe Illustrator.

Some Illustrator objects can't be reproduced by the Flash drawing model.

8. **Click the path with the warning icon in the list, and review the information on the right side of the dialog box.**

Many objects created in Illustrator are fully compatible with Flash drawing capabilities, so they are imported as regular drawing objects. Any objects that don't fit into the Flash drawing model — primarily, ones with some type of applied transparency — are imported in a way that allows Flash to maintain the integrity of the overall artwork. Effects that cannot be reproduced by Flash display a warning icon in the list of elements.

Note:

Learn more about Adobe Illustrator in the companion book of this series, **Adobe Illustrator CS6: The Professional Portfolio***.*

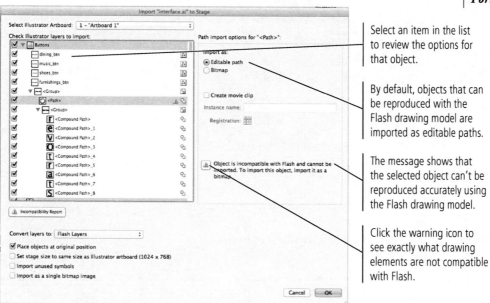

Select an item in the list to review the options for that object.

By default, objects that can be reproduced with the Flash drawing model are imported as editable paths.

The message shows that the selected object can't be reproduced accurately using the Flash drawing model.

Click the warning icon to see exactly what drawing elements are not compatible with Flash.

9. **With the incompatible path selected, choose the Bitmap radio button in the Import As area.**

Importing the object as a bitmap preserves its appearance, but you won't be able to edit the vector paths that make up the shape.

Bitmaps are typically larger files than vector graphics, which means that bitmaps require more time to download. Be careful when you use bitmaps in a Flash movie, especially one that will be downloaded over the Internet; very large bitmap files in the library can still affect the file's overall download time. (Because this project will be placed on a kiosk rather than downloaded over the Internet, file size is not a significant issue.)

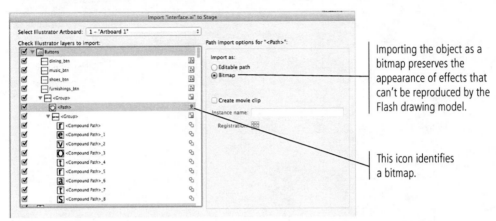

Importing the object as a bitmap preserves the appearance of effects that can't be reproduced by the Flash drawing model.

This icon identifies a bitmap.

10. **Click the arrow to the left of the Buttons layer name to collapse that layer. Review the rest of the items in the list.**

We prepared this Adobe Illustrator file very carefully to meet the requirements of this Flash project, including assigning descriptive names to all layers and groups. Many illustrators will not provide this level of detail in their files.

Illustrator objects that do not directly correlate to Flash drawing objects, such as shapes with applied transparency settings, are automatically converted to movie clip symbols when imported to Flash.

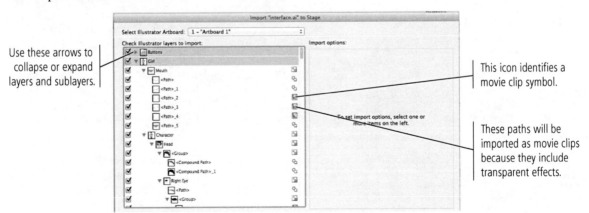

Use these arrows to collapse or expand layers and sublayers.

This icon identifies a movie clip symbol.

These paths will be imported as movie clips because they include transparent effects.

11. **At the bottom of the dialog box, choose Flash Layers in the Convert Layers To menu.**

This option maintains the existing layers from the original artwork; each Illustrator layer becomes a layer in the Flash file. This is useful if you aren't sure about what you're importing; you can always change or delete imported layers if you don't need them.

You can also choose Single Flash Layer, which flattens all objects onto a single layer (named according to the imported file name), or choose Keyframes to add each layer as a keyframe on the default Layer 1.

Note:

You will learn about keyframes in Stage 2 of this project.

12. **Check the Place Objects at Original Position option.**

Using this option places the imported artwork at the same relative position where it appeared on the Illustrator artboard (the "page" or drawing space). For example, if a square is placed 1 inch from the top and left edges of the artboard, it will be placed 1 inch from the top and left edges of the Stage. When this option is not checked, the imported artwork is centered in the document window, regardless of the position of the Flash Stage.

> Convert layers to: Flash Layers
> ☑ Place objects at original position
> ☑ Set stage size to same size as Illustrator artboard (1024 x 768)
> ☐ Import unused symbols
> ☐ Import as a single bitmap image

It is important to note that the relative position of imported artwork is maintained, regardless of your selection here. In other words, all imported objects appear in the same place (relative to each other) as in the Illustrator file. The import process treats all objects in the import as a single group for the purposes of the import only; this option simply controls the imported artwork's position relative to the Stage.

Note:

The options at the bottom of the dialog box remember the last-used settings. Some of the choices we define in Steps 11–15 might already be set on your computer.

13. **Check the Set Stage to Same Size as Illustrator Artboard option.**

The Illustrator artboard is the area that defines the physical dimensions of the file, just as the Stage defines the physical size of a Flash file. This option shows the dimensions of the imported file's artboard; if you know the Illustrator file was created to the correct dimensions — as it was in this case — you can use this option to automatically change the Stage size to match the imported artwork.

14. **Uncheck the Import Unused Symbols option.**

Illustrator can be used to create graphic and movie clip symbols (but not buttons), which are stored in a file's Symbols panel. This can include symbols that are not placed in the file, but which might be necessary for the overall project. If you don't know what a file contains, you can check this option to be sure all of the necessary bits are imported; you can always delete unwanted symbols once they have been imported. For this project, we are telling you that all required symbols in the imported artwork are placed on the artboard.

15. **Uncheck the Import as a Single Bitmap Image option.**

If this option is checked, the entire file is flattened and converted to a bitmap image; you would not be able to access any of the components of the imported artwork.

16. **Click OK to import the Illustrator artwork.**

17. **Fit the Stage in the document window, then click away from all objects on the Stage to deselect them.**

All objects are automatically selected after being imported to the Stage. Deselecting them allows you to review the Flash file's properties.

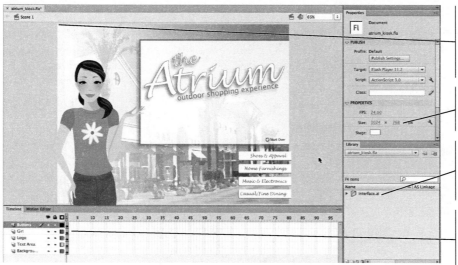

The imported artwork is aligned to the top-left corner of the Stage, matching its relative position on the original Illustrator artboard.

With nothing selected, the Properties panel shows the adjusted Stage size.

A folder (named the same as the imported file) is added to the library, containing all the pieces necessary for the imported artwork.

Five layers are added to the Timeline panel, named the same as the layers in the original Illustrator file.

18. **In the Library panel, click the arrow to the left of the interface.ai folder to expand it, and then click the arrows to expand all but the Girl folder.**

Imported assets are sorted by layer; folder names match the imported layer names to help you understand where different pieces are required. A separate folder for Illustrator Symbols is included.

Note:

The Girl folder includes a long list of paths and groups that were imported as movie clips to preserve transparency effects that were applied in the Illustrator file. We did not include that folder in this instruction simply because the list is so long.

Click the arrows to expand or collapse folders.

Bitmap icon

Graphic symbol icon

Movie clip symbol icon

This bitmap image was placed on the Background layer in Illustrator.

This bitmap image was created by the Import process to solve incompatibility problems.

These graphic symbols were created in the Illustrator file.

These movie clips were created by the Import process to maintain the appearance of transparent effects.

19. **In the Library panel, collapse the subfolders in the interface.ai folder.**

20. **Save the file and continue to the next exercise.**

Illustrator File Import Preferences

FLASH FOUNDATIONS

You can define the default options for importing native Illustrator files in the AI File Importer pane of the Preferences dialog box. (Remember, preferences are accessed in the Flash menu on Macintosh and in the Edit menu on Windows.) Most of these options will become clearer as you work through this project and learn more about the different types of symbols. In some cases, the options refer to specific features in the native application.

- **Show Import Dialog Box** is checked by default. If you uncheck this option, Illustrator files will import using the default options defined here (without showing the Import dialog box).

- If **Exclude Objects Outside Artboard** is checked, objects outside the artboard (Illustrator's "page") are unchecked by default in the Import dialog box.

- If **Import Hidden Layers** is checked, all layers in the file (including ones that are not visible) are listed in the Import dialog box.

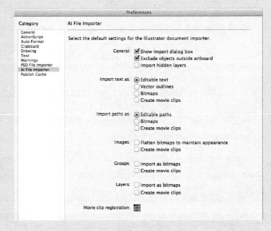

- The **Import Text As** options define how text objects in the Illustrator file import into the Flash file. Editable Text, selected by default, imports text objects that you can edit using the Flash Text tool. If you choose Vector Outlines, text objects import as a group of vector shapes; you cannot edit the text in these objects (other than manipulating the vector paths). If you choose Bitmaps, text objects import as raster objects that cannot be edited with either the Text tool or the Subselection tool.

- The **Import Paths As** options determine the default behavior for how vector paths in the Illustrator file are added to the Flash file. Editable Paths means you can use the Flash Subselection tool to manipulate the anchor points and handles on the imported paths; if you select the Bitmaps option, you will not be able to edit the vector paths within Flash.

- **Images** placed in an Illustrator file are maintained when the file imports into Flash; if you select an image in the Import dialog box, you can choose to flatten the bitmap file or automatically create a movie clip. You can use the Images preference options to automatically check the related boxes in the Import dialog box.

- **Groups** and **Layers** from the Illustrator file are listed separately in the Import dialog box. You can use the Groups and Layers preference options to automatically check the Import as Bitmap and Create Movie Clip options in the Import dialog box.

- **Movie Clip Registration** defines the default registration option for objects you import as movie clip symbols.

In addition to importing files to the Flash Stage, you can also import external files directly into the Flash file's Library panel. This option is particularly useful when certain objects aren't going to be placed on the main Stage, or if you don't yet know how you will use a particular object.

1. **With atrium_kiosk.fla open, choose File>Import>Import to Library. Navigate to the file mouths.ai in the WIP>Atrium folder and click Open.**

   When you import an Illustrator file directly to the Library panel, most of the options are the same as for importing to the Stage. The Place Objects at Original Position and Set Stage Size to Same Size as Illustrator Artboard options are not available because they do not apply to files that only exist (for now) in the file's library.

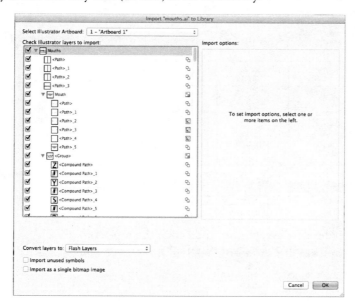

2. **Click OK to import the artwork to the library.**

   The Library panel shows that the resulting object was imported as a graphic symbol. Nothing is added to the Stage or the timeline.

3. **In the Library panel, click the mouths.ai item to select it.**

   The top portion of the panel shows a preview of the selected item.

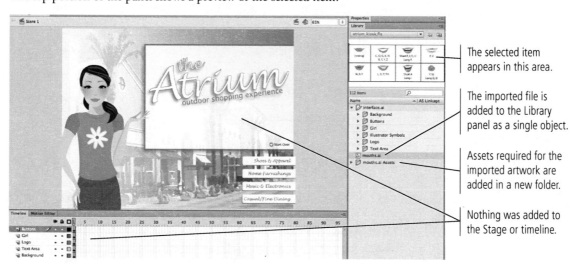

The selected item appears in this area.

The imported file is added to the Library panel as a single object.

Assets required for the imported artwork are added in a new folder.

Nothing was added to the Stage or timeline.

4. **Save the file and continue to the next exercise.**

CONVERT OBJECTS TO SYMBOLS

You now have a number of assets in your file's Library panel. The mouths.ai graphic contains eight groups of graphics — the different mouth shapes that you will use later in this project to synchronize the character to a sound file. For the process to work, you need to separate each mouth shape into a distinct symbol so the correct artwork can be placed at the appropriate point in the file.

1. **With atrium_kiosk.fla open, choose the Selection tool. Double-click the mouths.ai symbol icon to enter into the symbol.**

   Every symbol technically has its own Stage, which is theoretically infinite and separate from the main Stage of the base file. When you double-click the symbol icon in the Library panel, you enter **Symbol-Editing mode** for that symbol; other elements of the base file are not visible on the Stage.

The Edit bar shows that you are now working on the mouths.ai Stage (called **Symbol-Editing mode**).

When you first enter into the symbol, all artwork in the symbol is selected.

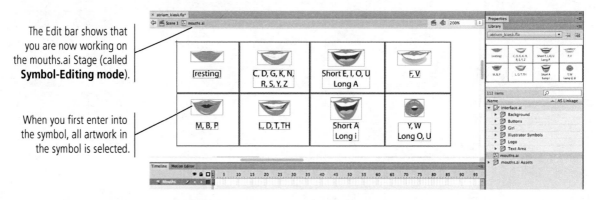

2. **Click away from the artwork to deselect everything, then click the top-left mouth shape to select that group (but not the word "resting").**

   Grouping in the original artwork is maintained in the imported artwork.

3. **Control/right-click the selected artwork and choose Convert to Symbol from the contextual menu.**

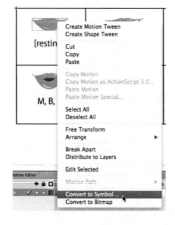

Note:

You can also drag an object onto the Library panel to open the Convert to Symbol dialog box for that object.

4. **In the resulting dialog box, type mouth1 in the Name field and choose Graphic in the Type menu.**

   A graphic symbol is the most basic type of symbol. It is typically used for objects that will simply be placed on the Stage. (A graphic symbol can include animation; you will explore these options in Project 5: Ocean Animation.) The type of animation you create in the third stage of this project — simply swapping one symbol with another at various points in time — is ideally suited to graphic symbols.

5. **Select the center point in the registration proxy icon.**

The registration grid affects the placement of the symbol's registration point, which is the 0,0 point for the symbol. (This will make more sense shortly when you begin editing symbols on their own Stages.)

6. **Click OK to create the new symbol.**

The Properties panel now shows that the selected object is an instance of the mouth1 symbol, which has been added to the Library panel.

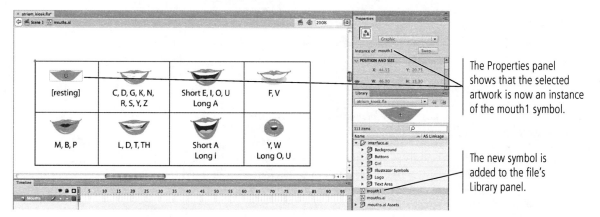

The Properties panel shows that the selected artwork is now an instance of the mouth1 symbol.

The new symbol is added to the file's Library panel.

7. **Click the second mouth shape (to the right) to select it. Control/right-click the group and choose Convert to Symbol.**

The Convert to Symbol dialog box remembers the last-used settings. The Type menu is already set to Graphic, and the center registration point is already selected.

8. **Type mouth2 in the Name field and click OK.**

9. **Repeat Steps 7–8 to convert the rest of the mouth shapes into symbols, working from left to right across the top row and then left to right across the bottom row.**

10. **Click Scene 1 in the Edit bar to return to the main Stage.**

11. **Using the Selection tool, click the mouth shape on the Stage to select it.**

The selected object is a group. It is not an instance of any symbol.

12. **In the Timeline panel, add a new layer immediately above the Girl layer. Name the new layer Mouths.**

    When you selected the mouth shape in Step 11, the layer containing the object (Girl) automatically became the active layer. When you click the New Layer button in this step, the new layer is automatically added above the previously selected layer. The new layer is also automatically selected as the active layer.

13. **Click mouth1 in the Library panel and drag an instance onto the Stage.**

14. **Use the Selection tool to drag the placed instance to the same position as the mouth group on the underlying Girl layer.**

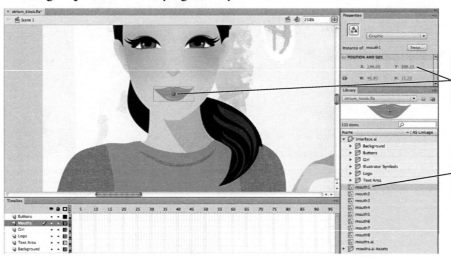

The X and Y fields show the position of the instance's registration point.

Drag the symbol from the Library panel to the Stage to place an instance on the active layer.

15. **Hide the Mouths layer, select the mouth group on the Girl layer and delete it, and then show the Mouths layer again.**

16. **Save the file and continue to the next exercise.**

Note:

Don't confuse the symbol registration point (the crosshairs) with the transformation point (the hollow circle).

CREATE A BUTTON SYMBOL

Buttons, one of the three main symbol types in Flash, are interactive assets that change when a user interacts with them. A button symbol has four "states":

- A button's **Up state** (also referred to as the idle or default state) is the basic appearance of a button when a user first loads a file.

- The **Over state** occurs when a mouse pointer rolls over a button. (When a user places a mouse cursor over a rollover area, the cursor often turns into a pointing finger or some other custom shape.)

- The **Down state** occurs when a user clicks a button.

- The **Hit state** defines the size of a rollover area (**hot spot**) of a button.

Note:

Buttons can be both animated and idle at the same time; idle simply means that no one has passed over or clicked the button with the mouse pointer.

This file includes five buttons. Four were created as symbols in the Illustrator artwork, and one was imported onto the Stage as a group.

1. **With atrium_kiosk.fla open, use the Selection tool to select the group containing the words "Start Over".**

2. **Control/right-click the selected group and choose Convert to Symbol in the contextual menu.**

3. **In the resulting dialog box, type start_over in the name field. Choose Button in the Type menu and choose the center registration point (if it is not already selected).**

4. **Click OK to create the new symbol.**

   Because you created the symbol from objects on the Stage, the Properties panel shows that the selection is automatically an instance of the new symbol.

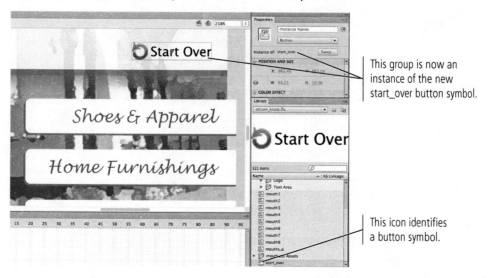

This group is now an instance of the new start_over button symbol.

This icon identifies a button symbol.

5. **Double-click the Start Over button on the Stage to enter into the symbol.**

   This method of editing a symbol is called **editing in place**. Other objects on the Stage are still visible, but they are screened back and cannot be accessed.

   As we explained earlier, a button is a special type of symbol with four distinct states. Each possible state is represented as a frame in the special Button symbol timeline.

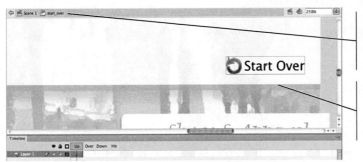

The Edit bar shows that you are editing on the start_over button symbol Stage.

Editing a symbol in place means you can see — but not access — the other objects on the Stage.

6. **In the Timeline panel, Control/right-click the Over frame of Layer 1 and choose Insert Keyframe from the contextual menu.**

   A **keyframe** defines a point where something changes. If you want to make something appear different from one frame to the next — whether inside a symbol or on the main Stage — you need to place a keyframe at the point where the change should occur.

Control/right-click the Over frame for Layer 1.

Note:

You can also insert a keyframe by choosing Insert>Timeline> Keyframe, or pressing F6.

7. **Make sure the Over frame is selected in the Timeline panel, then double-click the words "Start Over" in the graphic to enter into that group.**

   The contents of the Over frame will appear when the user's mouse moves over the button area. You are going to change the color of the letters in this button.

8. **Double-click any letter in the group to access the individual letters that make up the group.**

   Remember, Flash remembers the groupings from the original Illustrator file. Depending on how a file was created, you might have to enter into a number of nested groups before you get to the level you need.

9. **With the individual letter shapes selected, use the Fill Color swatch in the Tools or Properties panel to change the fill color to a medium blue.**

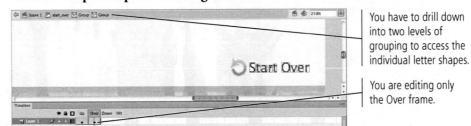

You have to drill down into two levels of grouping to access the individual letter shapes.

You are editing only the Over frame.

10. **Click Scene 1 in the Edit bar to return to the main Stage.**

    Even if you have drilled into multiple levels of Symbol-Editing mode, you can return to the main Stage with a single click on the Edit bar. You can also return to any particular nesting level by clicking a specific item (called "breadcrumbs") in the Edit bar.

Note:

You will test the button's functionality in the next exercise.

11. **Save the file and continue to the next exercise.**

DEFINE A HIT FRAME

In the previous exercise, you changed the color of button text in the Over frame. However, there is still a problem — the button currently works only if the mouse pointer touches the icon or one of the letter shapes. If the pointer lies between two letters, for example, the button fails to activate.

All spaces within the button should be active. Moving the pointer close to or on top of the button should trigger the desired action. To resolve the problem, you need to define the Hit frame, which determines where a user can click to activate the button.

1. **With atrium_kiosk.fla open, choose Control>Enable Simple Buttons to toggle that option on.**

   This command allows you to test button states directly on the Flash Stage.

2. **Check the current condition of the Start Over button by positioning the pointer between the two words in the button.**

   There are "dead" areas within the button that don't cause the color change to occur. (You might need to zoom in to verify this problem.)

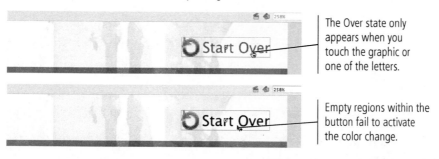

The Over state only appears when you touch the graphic or one of the letters.

Empty regions within the button fail to activate the color change.

3. **Choose Control>Enable Simple Buttons to toggle that option off.**

   When this option is active, you can't select a button instance on the Stage — which means you can't double-click the button to edit the symbol in place.

4. **Double-click the Start Over button on the Stage to edit the symbol in place.**

5. **Control/right-click the Hit frame and choose Insert Keyframe from the contextual menu.**

   The **Hit frame** defines the live area of the button, or the area where a user can click to activate the button. Objects on this state do not appear in the movie; you only need to define the general shapes.

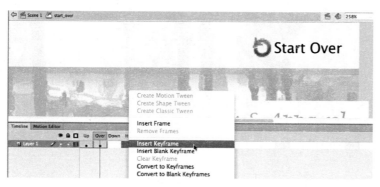

Note:

Using a button symbol mimics a four-frame Flash animation; it is the basic concept behind all Flash buttons. You add keyframes, you modify the content of each frame, and then Flash displays the appropriate frame when the user hovers over the object, clicks the object, or — in the case of the Hit frame — approaches the object.

6. **Choose the Rectangle tool from the Tools panel.**

7. **Change the fill color to some contrasting color, then turn off the Object Drawing option.**

   Because merge-drawing shapes drop to the back of the stacking order, this method allows you to still see the button artwork in front of the "hit" shape.

8. **Draw a rectangle that covers the entire contents of the button.**

   We used a red color that contrasted with the blue text, but any color will work because the Hit frame content doesn't appear on the Stage when you play the movie.

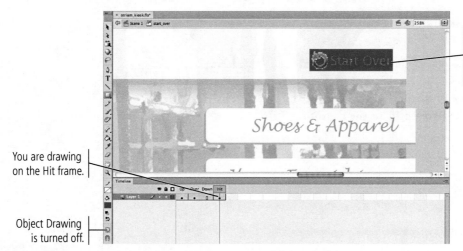

The merge-drawing shape is created behind other objects on the layer.

You are drawing on the Hit frame.

Object Drawing is turned off.

9. **Click Scene 1 in the Edit bar to return to the main Stage.**

10. **Choose Control>Enable Simple Buttons to toggle the option back on, then place the mouse cursor between the words in the button.**

    Now the button works even if you hover over the white areas or between the letters. The Hit frame rectangle determines the live (hit) area of the button.

Now the button works even if you hover between the words.

11. **Save the file and continue to the next exercise.**

Using Different Symbol-Editing Modes

You can edit symbols in three different ways: in Symbol-Editing mode, in place on the Stage, or in a separate window.

You're already familiar with Symbol-Editing mode, the discrete Stage that appears when you double-click a symbol in the Library panel; the name of the symbol appears to the right of the Scene name in the Edit bar, indicating that you're working on the symbol instead of the main scene. You can also access this option by Control/right-clicking a placed instance on the Stage and choosing Edit.

In basic Symbol-Editing mode, the name of the symbol appears above the Stage in the Edit bar.

When editing a symbol on its own Stage, other placed objects are not visible.

Shoes & Apparel

The second option, editing in place, means you can edit a symbol while still seeing other objects on the Stage. If you double-click a symbol on the Stage, you can edit the symbol in the context of the larger movie (as shown by the symbol name in the Edit bar). You can also access this option by Control/right-clicking a placed symbol instance and choosing Edit in Place.

Editing in place is a variant of Symbol-Editing mode, so the name of the symbol appears above the Stage.

When editing a symbol in place, other placed objects remain visible but screened back.

Start Over

Shoes & Apparel

Home Furnishings

When editing a symbol in place, it is easy to forget that you are actually editing the symbol — including all placed instances of that symbol. Any changes you make will also affect other placed instances, even though those instances are not directly accessible in the document window.

The third option, editing in a separate window, opens the symbol in its own document window. Only the symbol name appears above the Stage; there is no preceding scene. You can access this option by Control/right-clicking an instance on the Stage and choosing Edit in New Window in the contextual menu.

When editing the symbol in a new window, there is no associated scene; only the symbol name appears above the Stage.

The document tabs show that you are editing in a second instance of the file containing the symbol.

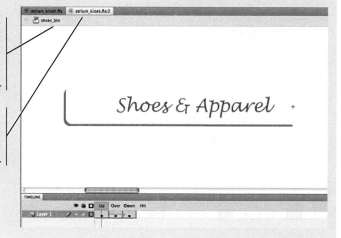

Shoes & Apparel

EDIT SYMBOL PROPERTIES

The control buttons, which you imported as graphic symbols from the external file library, are the final pieces of artwork for your Flash movie. Illustrator, however, does not create button symbols; you now need to convert the imported graphic symbols into the necessary button symbols.

1. **With atrium_kiosk.fla open, choose Control>Enable Simple Buttons. Make sure that option is toggled off.**

   Remember, you can't select a button on the Stage if this control is toggled on.

2. **In the Library panel, expand the Illustrator Symbols folder (inside the interface.ai folder) if necessary. Control/right-click the shoes_btn symbol icon in the Library panel and choose Properties from the contextual menu.**

3. **In the Symbol Properties dialog box, choose Button in the Type menu, and then click OK.**

Note:

The Symbol Properties dialog box is nearly the same as the Create New Symbol dialog box; it does not have registration options, because that has already been defined for the symbol. To move the symbol artwork relative to the registration point, you can edit the symbol on its Stage.

4. **Using the Selection tool, click the Shoes & Apparel button on the Stage to select it.**

5. **In the Properties panel, open the top menu and choose Button.**

   Unlike changing the content of a symbol, changes to the symbol type do not reflect in placed instances. When you change the type of a symbol that has already been placed on the Stage, you also have to change the instance type in the Properties panel.

Choose Button in this menu to change the behavior of the placed instance.

The symbol now shows the button icon instead of the original graphic icon.

6. **Repeat Steps 2–5 to convert the remaining three graphic symbols to buttons.**

7. **Save the file and continue to the next exercise.**

EXPLORE THE SYMBOL REGISTRATION POINT

Now that the buttons are symbols rather than graphics, you can define the various states of the buttons. You are going to edit the artwork so the buttons seem to move when the mouse cursor rolls over the hit area.

1. **With `atrium_kiosk.fla` open, double-click the Shoes & Apparel button instance to edit the symbol in place.**

   The crosshairs in the middle of the symbol artwork identify the **symbol registration point**; all measurements for placed instances begin at this location.

Symbol registration point

When editing the symbol, the X and Y fields show the position of the top-left corner relative to the symbol's registration point.

2. **In the Align panel, make sure the Align To Stage option is active and then click the Align Right Edge button.**

   The right edge of the symbol artwork is now aligned to the symbol registration point. Because you are editing the symbol in place, you can see the effect of the new alignment relative to the overall file artwork. This illustrates that the registration point is fixed, and the artwork is the thing that moves — not the other way around.

Note:

Use the Align panel with the Align To Stage option active to align the placed object to the symbol's registration point.

3. **Click Scene 1 in the Edit bar to return to the main Stage.**

4. **With the Shoes & Apparel button selected, click the current X value in the Properties panel to access the field.**

5. **Type 1034 in the highlighted X field and press Return/Enter to apply the change.**

   As we explained earlier, the symbol registration point is the origin of measurements for placed instances. When you change the X position, you are defining the horizontal location of the symbol registration point for the selected instance.

   The Stage for this file is 1024 pixels wide (as defined by the imported Illustrator artboard); you are placing the right edge of the button 10 pixels past the Stage edge.

On the main Stage, the X and Y fields define the position of the registration point for the instance.

In the next few steps, you will use this position as the basis for changing the object's position when a user moves the cursor over the button (i.e., triggers the Over frame).

6. **Double-click the Shoes & Apparel button again to enter back into the symbol Stage.**

7. **Insert a new keyframe on the button's Over frame. With the Over keyframe selected, click the button artwork to select it.**

   The object must be selected to change its properties. Selecting the frame in the timeline also selects the object on that frame.

8. **In the Properties panel, click the current X value in the Properties panel to access the field.**

Click the field to access the current value.

You should be working on the Over keyframe.

9. **Place the insertion point after the existing value and type –10 after the existing value. Press Enter to move the selected object.**

   Using mathematical operators makes it easy to move an object a specific distance without manually calculating the change:

   - Subtract from the X position to move an object left.
   - Add to the X position to move an object right.
   - Subtract from the Y position to move an object up.
   - Add to the Y position to move an object down.

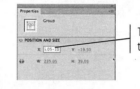

Type –10 after the current value.

The new X value moves the artwork 10 pixels to the left.

10. **Click Scene 1 in the Edit bar to return to the main Stage.**

11. **Repeat Steps 1–10 for the three remaining buttons.**

12. **Choose Control>Enable Simple Buttons to toggle the option back on. Move your mouse cursor over the buttons to test the Over state functionality.**

13. **Save the file and continue to the next exercise.**

Note:

Because this button artwork includes a solid-filled white rectangle, you don't need to define a separate hit frame. The artwork itself is sufficient to trigger the button.

ORGANIZE YOUR LIBRARY WITH FOLDERS

Library folders work the same as layer folders; they help you organize and structure complex files. Movies often contain dozens or even hundreds of assets — and the more complex a movie becomes, the more useful it is to clearly organize those assets. Although this step isn't strictly necessary, it is always a good idea to organize your work so you can more easily organize your thoughts and processes going forward.

1. **With atrium_kiosk.fla open, expand the interface.ai folder in the Library panel.**

2. **Click the Illustrator Symbols folder (inside the interface.ai folder) and drag down to the empty area at the bottom of the panel.**

   This moves the Illustrator Symbols folder to the first level of the library. The symbols, which are placed on the Stage, are not affected by the move.

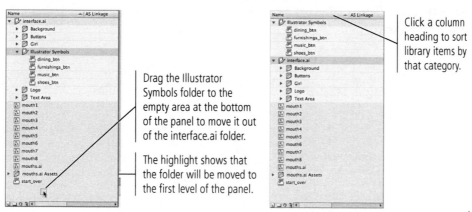

Drag the Illustrator Symbols folder to the empty area at the bottom of the panel to move it out of the interface.ai folder.

The highlight shows that the folder will be moved to the first level of the panel.

Click a column heading to sort library items by that category.

3. **Double-click the Illustrator Symbols folder name to highlight the name. Type buttons to change the folder name.**

4. **Click the start_over button symbol icon and drag it into the Buttons folder.**

5. **Double-click the interface.ai folder name to highlight the name. Type component artwork to change the folder name.**

Note:

If your Library panel is too short to show an empty area below the current assets, Control/ right-click any of the existing first-level assets and choose Paste. The pasted symbols are pasted at the same level as the asset where you Control/ right-click.

6. **Click the mouths.ai Assets folder and drag it into the Component Artwork folder.**

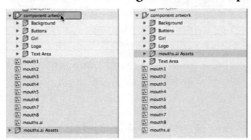

7. **Click the empty area at the bottom of the panel to deselect all assets and folders.**

8. **Click the New Folder button at the bottom of the Library panel. Type mouth graphics as the new folder name.**

   The new folder is added at the main level of the library, alphabetized with other items at the same level. If you didn't deselect in Step 7, the new folder would have been created at the same nesting level as the selected item.

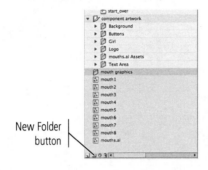

New Folder button

9. **Click the mouth1 symbol to select it, then Shift-click the mouth8 symbol to select it and all files in between.**

   Press Shift to select multiple contiguous items in the panel, or press Command/Control to select multiple, non-contiguous items.

10. **Click the icon of any selected file and drag into the mouth graphics folder.**

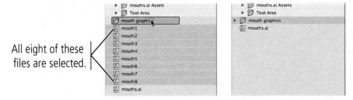

All eight of these files are selected.

11. **Click the mouths.ai graphic symbol and click the panel's Delete button.**

    Although you used this artwork to create the individual mouth symbols, this symbol is not used in the file, so it can be safely deleted from the library. If you delete a symbol that is used in the file, the placed instances will also be deleted from the file.

Delete button

12. **Collapse all library folders, then save the file and continue to the next stage of the project.**

Stage 2 Working with Sound

Sound files can be categorized into three basic types: uncompressed, compressed (lossless), and compressed (lossy). **Uncompressed sound files** encode all sounds with the same number of bits per unit of time. In an uncompressed format, two sound files of the same duration — whether a symphony or a simple beep — have the same size (which is typically very large). Such files are commonly used for archiving or other situations where file size is not an issue.

Note:

Compression is the process of removing data to reduce file size.

Lossless compression sound files lose no data during compression; these files are smaller than uncompressed files, but not as small as lossy compression file formats. **Lossy compression sound files** lose some data but retain good sound quality; a large number of these files can be stored in relatively small amounts of space.

Flash handles most major audio formats, including the ones most commonly used today:

- The **MP3** format is the most commonly used audio format. This format compresses a music file in the most efficient manner, so file size is reduced without compromising quality. MP3 playback does require more processing power than other formats because the data has to be decoded every time the file plays.

- The **WAV** format is an uncompressed format with very high quality. This file type can be used in Flash animations for desktop applications, but should be avoided for Web-based movies because the files are huge and take a long time to download.

- The **AIFF** format (Audio Interchange File Format) is common on Macintosh computers. This format is generally uncompressed, so file sizes are large compared to the MP3 format. AIFF files are suitable for applications specifically targeted for Macintosh computers.

- The **Audio** (AU) file format, developed by Sun Microsystems, transmits sound files over the Internet and can be played in Java programs. These files are smaller than AIFF and WAV formats, but the quality of sound is not as good as regular WAV files.

- The **QuickTime** (MOV) format is technically a video format, but it can also include audio.

IMPORT SOUND FILES

In general, there are three methods for incorporating sound into a Flash movie. Sounds in a file's library can be placed directly on the timeline, or you can use code to call a library sound based on a particular event. You can also use code to load and play external sound files (those that don't exist in the Flash library).

In this project, you will use the timeline method to add the various sounds that are needed for the kiosk to function properly. The first step is to import the necessary sound files into the Flash library.

1. **With atrium_kiosk.fla open, choose File>Import>Import to Stage. In the resulting dialog box, select all files in the WIP>Atrium>Audio folder, then click Open.**

2. Open the Library panel and review the contents.

Sound files do not exist on the Stage. Even though you chose Import to Stage, the sound files are automatically imported into the file's Library panel.

3. Click the New Folder button at the bottom of the Library panel. Rename the new folder audio.

4. Command/Control-click all six imported audio files and drag them into the audio folder.

5. Expand the audio folder so you can see the available files.

6. Save the file and continue to the next exercise.

Note:

It's always a good idea to keep your library well organized while developing a file with numerous assets.

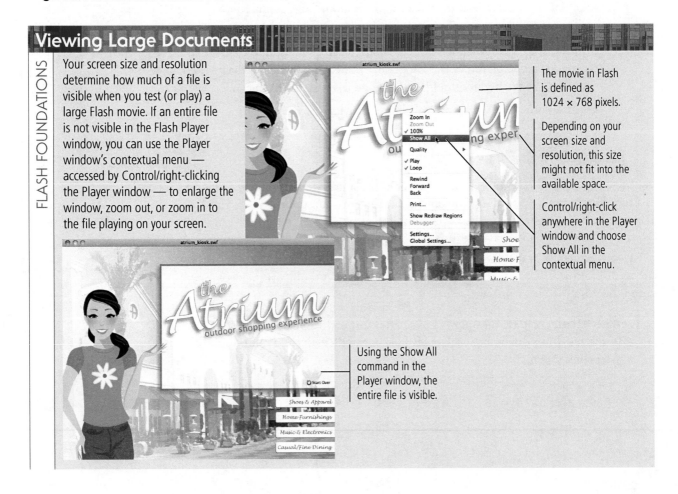

Viewing Large Documents

FLASH FOUNDATIONS

Your screen size and resolution determine how much of a file is visible when you test (or play) a large Flash movie. If an entire file is not visible in the Flash Player window, you can use the Player window's contextual menu — accessed by Control/right-clicking the Player window — to enlarge the window, zoom out, or zoom in to the file playing on your screen.

The movie in Flash is defined as 1024 × 768 pixels.

Depending on your screen size and resolution, this size might not fit into the available space.

Control/right-click anywhere in the Player window and choose Show All in the contextual menu.

Using the Show All command in the Player window, the entire file is visible.

Event sounds are "timeline independent" — they play independently of the movie timeline. They are downloaded completely and stored in the user computer's memory; this means they can be played repeatedly (including continuously looping) without having to redownload the file.

Note:

Because event sounds must be downloaded completely before they can play, they can cause buffering delays in playback.

1. **With the file atrium_kiosk.fla open, click to select the atrium_jazz.mp3 file in the Library panel.**

   This file will be the background music for the entire file. It will play in an infinite loop as long as the kiosk file is open.

2. **Click the Play button in the top-right corner of the Preview area.**

   You can use the Library panel to hear imported sounds before they are used on the Stage.

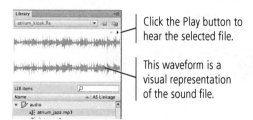

Click the Play button to hear the selected file.

This waveform is a visual representation of the sound file.

3. **Select the Frame 1 keyframe on the Background layer.**

4. **In the Sound section of the Properties panel, choose atrium_jazz.mp3 in the Name menu.**

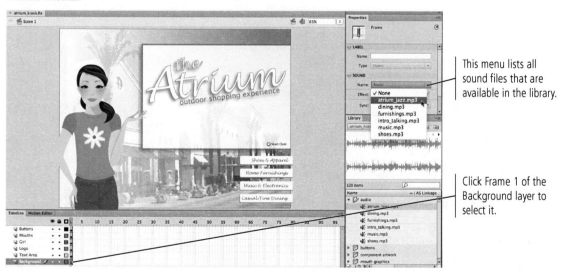

This menu lists all sound files that are available in the library.

Click Frame 1 of the Background layer to select it.

5. **In the Sync menu, choose Event.**

   Event sounds default to the Repeat 1 method, which means the sound plays one time. You can change the number in the Repeat field to play the sound a specific number of times.

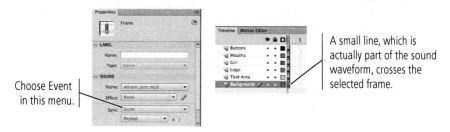

Choose Event in this menu.

A small line, which is actually part of the sound waveform, crosses the selected frame.

6. Choose Control>Test Movie>In Flash Professional.

This command opens the file in a separate Flash Player window. (You will use this command frequently as you develop this and most Flash projects.) Although the sound waveform only appears on Frame 1 of the Background layer, the entire sound plays from start to finish when you test the movie file.

Note:

Press Command-Return/ Control-Enter to test the movie in a Flash Player window.

The Test Movie command opens the file in a Flash Player window, showing what the exported movie would look — and sound — like.

7. Close the Player window and return to Flash.

8. With Frame 1 of the Background layer selected, choose Loop in the menu under the Sync menu (in the Sound area of the Properties panel).

Using the Loop method, the event sound plays continuously as long as the movie remains open.

9. Press Command-Return/Control-Enter to test the movie again.

The background sound now plays from start to finish, and then repeats to create a continuous background sound track.

10. Close the Player window and return to Flash.

11. Save the file and continue to the next exercise.

EDIT A SOUND ENVELOPE TO CONTROL VOLUME

Although Flash is not intended to be a sound-editing application, you can apply a limited number of effects to control the volume and length of sounds on the Flash timeline. These options are available in the Effect menu of the Properties panel when a sound is attached to a keyframe.

1. **With atrium_kiosk.fla open, click Frame 1 of the Background layer to select the frame where you attached the sound in the previous exercise.**

2. **In the Properties panel, open the Effect menu and choose Custom to open the Edit Envelope dialog box.**

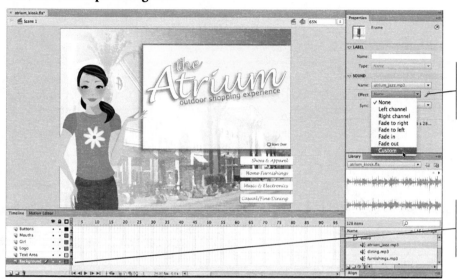

Clicking the Edit Sound Envelope button has the same result as choosing Custom in the Effect menu.

Frame 1 of the Background layer must be selected to access the sound settings.

The Edit Envelope dialog box shows the waveforms for each channel in a sound file. (In many cases, both channels have the same waveform.) You can view the sound waves by seconds or frames, and you can zoom in or out to show various portions of the sound.

The left and right channels refer to sound output systems that have more than one speaker — one on the left and one on the right. You can apply different settings to individual channels to create an effect of aural depth. For example, fading a car sound out for the left channel and in for the right channel helps to reinforce a visual that moves the car from left to right across the Stage.

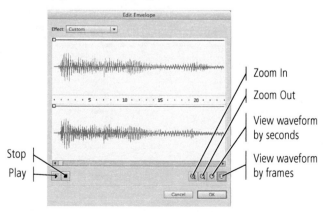

Zoom In

Zoom Out

View waveform by seconds

View waveform by frames

Stop

Play

3. **Click the Frames button to show the sound based on frames (if this isn't already active).**

4. **In the left channel area (the top waveform), click the handle on the left end of the waveform, and drag down to below the existing waveform.**

Note:

Click the envelope line to add a new handle to the envelope. Click an existing handle and drag it away from the window to remove a point from the envelope.

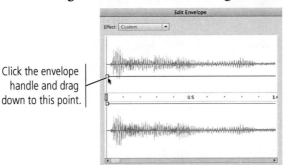

Click the envelope handle and drag down to this point.

Editing Sound Files

FLASH FOUNDATIONS

Applying Built-in Sound Effects

The Effect menu in the Properties panel lists a number of common sound envelope effects built into Flash. These sound effects do not alter the sound in the files; they simply control how the sound data plays.

- **Left Channel** plays only the left channel of the sound.
- **Right Channel** plays only the right channel of the sound.
- **Fade to Right** gradually lowers the sound level of the left channel, and then gradually raises the sound level of the right channel.
- **Fade to Left** gradually lowers the sound level of the right channel, and then gradually raises the sound level of the left channel.

- **Fade In** gradually raises the sound level at the beginning of the sound file.
- **Fade Out** gradually lowers the sound level at the end of the sound file.
- **Custom** opens the Edit Envelope dialog box, where you can define your own sound effects.

Editing Sound Duration

Although it is usually a better idea to edit sound files in a true sound-editing application, you can also use the Edit Envelope dialog box to shorten the duration of a sound file.

When you first open the Edit Envelope dialog box, the Time In Control bar appears at the left side of the waveform. If you use the scroll bar below the waveforms to find the end of the waveform, you will see the Time Out Control bar, which marks the end of the sound. You can drag these control bars to change the starting and ending point of the selected sound.

Warning: Be very careful editing the duration of sound files in Flash. There are known problems with sounds playing from the original starting point and cutting off in the middle, rather than honoring the defined Time In and Time Out points. In many cases, the edited sounds play normally when tested on the Stage in Flash, but the problem is evident when you test your movie in the Flash Player window.

Time In Control bar

Use the scroll bar to find the Time Out Control bar at the end of the waveform.

Parts of the waveform to the left of the Time In Control bar or right of the Time Out Control bar will not be included in the movie.

5. **Repeat Step 4 for the right channel (the bottom waveform).**

By lowering the envelope handles, you reduced the volume of the sound file.

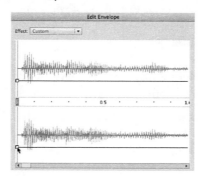

6. **Click OK to close the Edit Envelope dialog box and apply the change.**

7. **Save the file and continue to the next exercise.**

USE THE START AND STOP SYNC METHODS FOR BUTTONS

The four category buttons will link to different screens in the kiosk. Each button needs to trigger a sound that plays when the user's mouse rolls over the button. To achieve this result, you can attach the relevant sound to each button using the same technique you applied in the previous exercise. Because of the four-frame nature of button symbols, however, a few extra steps are required to make the sounds play only when you want them to play.

1. **With `atrium_kiosk.fla` open, choose Control>Enable Simple Buttons to make sure that option is toggled on.**

2. **In the Library panel, double-click the shoes_btn symbol icon to enter Symbol-Editing mode for that symbol.**

   Remember, you can edit a symbol by double-clicking the symbol icon. This is especially useful when the Enable Simple Buttons feature is toggled on, because you can't select buttons on the Stage in that mode.

3. **Select the Over frame of Layer 1. In the Properties panel, choose shoes.mp3 in the Sound menu and set the Sync menu to Event.**

You are attaching the sound to the button's Over frame.

4. **Click Scene 1 in the Edit bar to return to the main Stage.**

5. **Move your mouse cursor over the Shoes & Apparel button to hear the attached sound.**

Moving the mouse over the button triggers the Over state, including the attached sound file.

6. **Move your mouse cursor away, and then move back over the Shoes & Apparel button to trigger the sound again.**

   When the mouse re-enters the button area — triggering the Over frame — the message plays again. (Because the sound is very short, this might not be apparent unless you move the mouse back into the button area very quickly.)

7. **Double-click the shoes_btn symbol icon to enter back into the button Stage. Select the Over frame, then change the Sound Sync menu to Start.**

   The Start sync option is similar to the Event method. The difference is that the Start method allows only one instance of the same sound to play at a time; this prevents the overlap problem caused by the Event method.

   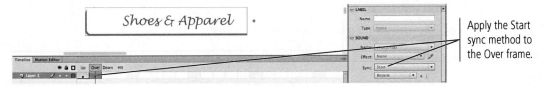

   Apply the Start sync method to the Over frame.

8. **Control/right-click the Down frame and choose Insert Keyframe from the contextual menu.**

9. **In the Properties panel, choose shoes.mp3 in the Sound menu and choose Stop in the Sync menu.**

   The Stop option stops all instances of the selected sound from playing. When a user clicks the Shoes & Apparel button, the sound triggered on the Over frame will stop playing.

   Apply the Stop sync method to a keyframe on the Down frame.

10. **Click Scene 1 to return to the main Stage.**

11. **Repeat the same basic process to add the appropriate event sounds to the other three navigation buttons:**
    - Double-click the button symbol icon to enter the symbol's Stage.
    - Select the Over frame and attach the appropriate sound file using the Start sync option.
      - For the Home Furnishings button, use the furnishings.mp3 sound file.
      - For the Music & Electronics button, use the music.mp3 sound file.
      - For the Casual/Fine Dining button, use the dining.mp3 sound file.
    - Add a keyframe to the Down frame.
    - Attach the same sound you used for the Over frame, and apply the Stop sync option.

12. **If you haven't done so already, click Scene 1 in the Edit bar to return to the main Stage.**

13. **Roll your mouse cursor over the four buttons to test all four sounds. Click each to make sure the sounds stop when they're supposed to.**

14. **Save the file and continue to the next stage of the project.**

Stage 3 Creating Frame Animations

The basic underlying premise of animation is that objects change over time — from complex transitions in color, shape, and opacity to moving a character to a new position. The most basic type of animation is to simply replace one object with another at specific points in time; you will create this type of animation in this stage of the kiosk project to make it seem like the girl is talking.

Repositioning or replacing objects on successive frames results in the appearance of movement when you watch an animation; in reality, your brain is being fooled — you're simply seeing a series of images flash before your eyes (hence the application's name). Your brain thinks it's seeing movement, when in fact it's simply processing a series of still images displayed in rapid succession.

To make an animation appear to run continuously, you can **loop** it so it starts over at Frame 1 after reaching the last frame. (In fact, as you will see, looping is the default state of an animation; you have to use code to prevent the timeline from automatically looping in the exported file.)

To create animation, you need to understand several terms and concepts:

- The Flash Timeline panel shows a visual depiction of the passage of time. Each fraction of a second is represented by a frame (the rectangles to the right of the layer names). The **playhead** indicates the current point in time, or the frame that is visible on the Stage.

- The number of frames in one second (called **frames per second**, **FPS**, or **frame rate**) determines the length and quality of the overall animation. New Flash files default to 24 fps, which is the standard frame rate of most film movies in the United States (although HD formats range as high as 120 fps). Animations only for the Web are commonly developed at 15 fps.

- A **keyframe** indicates the point in time at which something changes. If you want to change something, you need to insert a keyframe at the appropriate moment on the timeline.

- Regular frames between keyframes have the same content as the preceding keyframe.

Note:

The term **playhead** is a throwback to the days when animation and video were shown on physical tape-reading machines. The playhead is the component under which the tape moves, and the tape is read by the player. By sliding the tape back and forth underneath the playhead, an animator could make a movie run forward and backward.

ADD STREAMING SOUND

Unlike the event sounds that you used in the previous exercises, **stream sounds** play as soon as enough data is downloaded (called **progressive downloading**) to the user's computer. Stream sounds cannot be saved on a user's computer; the sound file must be redownloaded every time it is played. Stream sounds are linked to the timeline, which means they stop playing if the timeline stops (i.e., they are "timeline dependent").

1. **With atrium_kiosk.fla open, add a new layer named Talking immediately above the Mouths layer.**

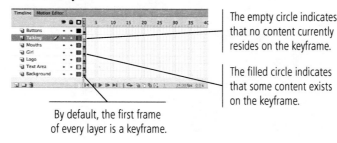

The empty circle indicates that no content currently resides on the keyframe.

The filled circle indicates that some content exists on the keyframe.

By default, the first frame of every layer is a keyframe.

Note:

Because stream sounds are typically larger files (longer sounds equal more data and larger file size), the quality of these sounds might be poor for users who have slow Internet connections.

2. **Select the Frame 1 keyframe of the Talking layer.**

3. **In the Properties panel, choose intro_talking.mp3 from the Sound menu and choose Stream in the Sync menu.**

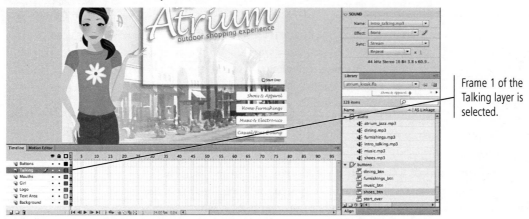

Frame 1 of the Talking layer is selected.

4. **Press Command-Return/Control-Enter to test the movie.**

The background sound plays as expected, but the intro_talking sound does not. Remember, stream sounds are related to the position of the playhead on the timeline (they are timeline dependent). Because this file currently has only one frame, the playhead has nowhere to move, so the sound file does not play in the Player window.

5. **Close the Player window and return to Flash.**

6. **In the timeline, Control/right-click Frame 95 of the Talking layer and choose Insert Frame from the contextual menu.**

Frame numbers appear in the frame ruler at the top of the timeline.

Control/right-click Frame 95 of the Talking layer to open the contextual menu.

When you add a new frame, you extend the layer's timeline to the point where you place the new frame. The red playhead above the timeline shows the currently active frame.

You can now see the entire waveform of the sound that is attached to Frame 1 of the Talking layer. As you can see, however, none of the graphics are visible on the Stage, because you have not added frames to the other layers. In other words, objects on those layers don't yet exist at Frame 95.

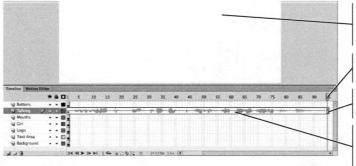

Other layers are not yet extended to Frame 95, so the graphics on those layers are not visible.

The playhead shows the currently active frame.

Adding a frame extends the layer's timeline.

The waveform on the Talking layer, which extends to Frame 91, is now entirely visible.

7. Click Frame 95 of the Buttons layer to select it, then press F5.

This keyboard shortcut inserts a new frame at the selected location on the timeline; it is the same as choosing Insert Frame from the contextual menu.

After adding the new frame to the Buttons layer, objects on that layer are now visible at Frame 95. The other graphics are still not visible because those layers do not yet have frames at Frame 95.

Note:

If you are using a laptop that has system-specific functions assigned to the Function keys, you can either press FN plus the required function key, or use the menu commands (in the Insert>Timeline submenu) to insert frames and keyframes.

You can also insert a frame, keyframe, or blank keyframe by Control/right-clicking a specific frame in the Timeline panel and choosing from the contextual menu.

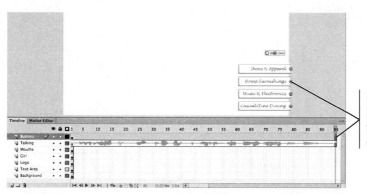

Objects on the Buttons layer are visible once that layer has been extended to Frame 95.

8. Click Frame 95 of the Mouths layer, then Shift-click Frame 95 of the Background layer.

9. Press F5 to add new frames to all five selected layers.

Because all of the layers now "exist" on Frame 95, all of the kiosk graphics are now visible on the Stage.

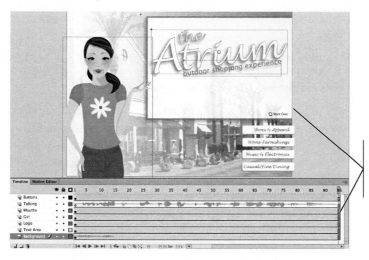

Because all layers now extend to Frame 95, all graphics in the interface are visible on the Stage.

10. Click Frame 1 of any layer to move the playhead to the beginning of the timeline.

The playhead identifies the current point in time on the Flash timeline. If you don't move the playhead back to Frame 1, the background sound will not play.

11. Press Return/Enter to test the movie on the Flash Stage.

You should now hear two sounds: the character talking and the background music. The background music is an event sound (not related to the playhead), so it loops continuously.

Pressing Return/Enter causes the playhead to move, playing the movie directly on the Stage.

When a movie is playing on the Stage, pressing Return/Enter stops the playback but does not stop sounds that are playing.

12. **Press the Escape key (ESC) to stop the background music.**

13. **Press Command-Return/Control-Enter to test the movie in a Player window.**

    The movie plays entirely through, and then starts over again (**loops**) — this is what would happen in the actual exported file.

    To make the timeline play only once, you have to use code to intentionally stop the playhead from looping. This code will be implemented by your developer partner after you are finished creating the lip-syncing animation.

14. **Close the Flash Player window and return to Flash.**

15. **Save the file and continue to the next exercise.**

Note:

You can choose Control>Loop Playback to allow the playhead to loop on the Flash Stage.

PREPARE FOR LIP SYNCING

If you have ever watched cartoons, you have probably seen the results of the time-consuming and painstaking work involved in synchronizing a character's movements to sounds. Realistic lip syncing is an extremely complex art that requires precise attention to detail, as well as in-depth study of behavioral movement. Other projects, such as this one, do not call for the precision and detail required for lifelike animation; rather, they use representative movements to create the effect of a character talking.

1. **Sit or stand in front of a mirror.**

2. **Say the following sentence slowly, paying careful attention to the shape of your mouth for each syllable:**

    Need help? Use the buttons to find exactly what you're looking for.

Note:

To better understand how to sync lip movements to sounds, you should study the different facial movements that are involved in spoken sound (called phonology).

3. **With atrium_kiosk.fla open in Flash, expand the mouth graphics folder in the Library panel.**

    The illustrator for this project created eight different mouth shapes to represent the various "talking" sounds.

4. **Click each mouth symbol in the Library panel and review the shapes.**

    Note that each symbol was created with the registration point at the center.

Symbol	Use for:	Symbol	Use for:
mouth1	Silent, M, B, P	mouth5	M, B, P
mouth2	C, D, G, J, K, N, R, S, Y, Z	mouth6	L, D, T, Th
mouth3	Short E, I, O, U Long A	mouth7	Short A, E Long I
mouth4	F, V	mouth8	Ch, Sh, Qu, W Long O, U

5. **In the timeline layers area, double-click the icon to the left of the Talking layer name to open the Layer Properties dialog box.**

6. **Choose 300% in the Layer Height menu and click OK.**

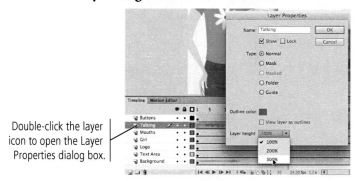

Double-click the layer icon to open the Layer Properties dialog box.

It's easier to sync movement to sound when you can see the variations in the sound file. By enlarging the layer height, you can see the peaks and valleys of the waveform directly on the timeline.

7. **Continue to the next exercise.**

CREATE LIP SYNC ANIMATION

While lip syncing might seem complicated, it's actually quite simple — you show the graphic that supports the sound heard at a particular frame on the timeline. Because the different mouth shapes for this project have already been created, the most difficult part of the process is determining which shape to place at which point on the timeline.

1. **Click Frame 1 above the timeline to reset the playhead to the beginning of the movie.**

2. **Click the playhead and drag quickly to the right.**

   Dragging the playhead, a technique called **scrubbing the timeline**, allows you to manually preview portions of an animation. Because the sound on the Talking layer is a stream sound, you hear the sound as you drag the playhead. The background music — an event sound — is not related to the playhead, so scrubbing the playhead does not play the background music.

   As you drag the playhead from Frame 1, you hear the first sound in the spoken message beginning at Frame 4 (also indicated by the rise in the waveform).

Click the playhead and drag right to find the first spoken sound.

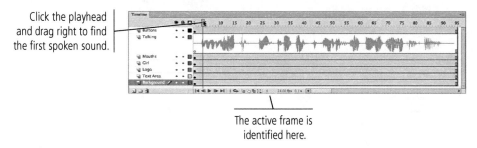

The active frame is identified here.

3. **Control/right-click Frame 3 of the Mouths layer and choose Insert Keyframe from the contextual menu.**

Note:

You can also press the F6 key to add a new keyframe to the selected frame.

Remember, a keyframe is the point at which something changes. In this case, you are going to change the mouth shape, so you need to add a keyframe at the appropriate point in time (when the mouth begins to move to make the spoken sound).

Content on the preceding frame is automatically duplicated on the new keyframe.

Note:

You can use the Insert Blank Keyframe command to add a blank keyframe to the timeline that (as the name suggests) has no content.

Although the sound begins at Frame 4, people's mouths usually start moving before actual words are spoken. You are adding a keyframe one frame earlier than the sound to accommodate for this behavior.

4. **Click the mouth symbol on the Stage to show its properties in the Properties panel.**

The object on the selected keyframe is selected on the Stage.

The Properties panel shows the name of the symbol being used.

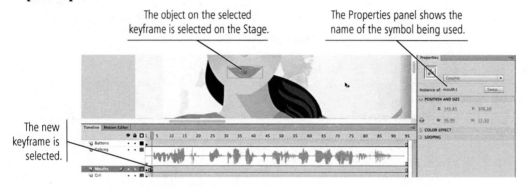

The new keyframe is selected.

5. **With the mouth shape on the Frame 3 keyframe selected, click the Swap button in the Properties panel.**

Lip syncing requires one primary task: swapping symbols to show the graphics that correlate to the sound at that particular moment.

6. **In the Swap Symbol dialog box, choose the mouth2 graphic symbol.**

This is the mouth that correlates to the "N" sound at the beginning of the word "Need".

7. **Click OK to close the Swap Symbol dialog box.**

    The new mouth now appears on Frame 3. The mouth symbol (mouth1) on the previous keyframe will remain visible until the playhead reaches Frame 3.

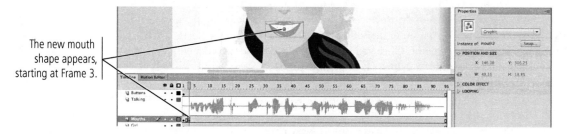

The new mouth shape appears, starting at Frame 3.

8. **Drag the playhead right to find the next significant change in sound.**

    The brief pause between the words "need" and "help" suggests a change in the speaker's mouth position at Frame 8.

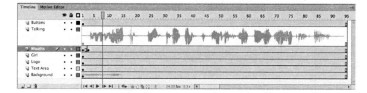

9. **Insert a new keyframe at Frame 8 of the Mouths layer.**

10. **With the mouth on the Frame 8 keyframe selected, click the Swap button in the Properties panel. In the Swap Symbol dialog box, choose the mouth5 symbol and click OK.**

    This mouth shape is nearly closed, so it works well for the brief pause between words. It correlates to the short "I" sound, but it also works well as a good transition shape between a wide-open mouth and a closed mouth.

11. **Insert a new keyframe at Frame 10 of the Mouths layer. Open the Swap Symbol dialog box, and replace the mouth shape with the mouth3 symbol.**

    This shape correlates to the "short e" sound in "help". (The "h" sound typically blends into the vowel sound.)

12. **Return the playhead to Frame 1 and press Return/Enter to play the movie on the Stage.**

So far you have only three changes in the character's mouth, but you should begin to see how the different symbols appear at the appropriate points in the playback. In general, lip syncing in Flash is a relatively simple process. The hardest parts are determining when to change the graphics in relation to the sound, and deciding which shape best suits the animation at any given point. Once you have determined these two elements, the actual syncing process is simply a matter of swapping symbols.

13. **Press the Escape key to stop the background music playback.**

14. **Applying the same process you used to create the first three mouth changes, continue scrubbing the playhead to identify points of change. Insert keyframes and swap symbols on the Mouths layer at the appropriate locations. In our example, we used the following locations and symbols:**

Frame	Symbol	Frame	Symbol	Frame	Symbol
15	mouth1	43	mouth4	64	mouth3
23	mouth8	46	mouth3	66	mouth2
27	mouth2	48	mouth2	68	mouth8
30	mouth6	50	mouth3	70	mouth2
31	mouth1	52	mouth2	72	mouth6
33	mouth3	55	mouth7	74	mouth2
36	mouth6	57	mouth2	79	mouth4
39	mouth2	60	mouth6	82	mouth8
41	mouth8	62	mouth2	84	mouth2

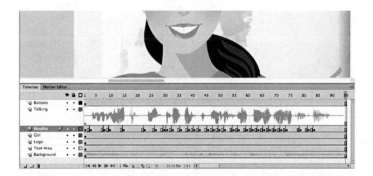

15. **Return the playhead to Frame 1, then press Return/Enter test the animation.**

By swapping the mouth symbol at various points on the timeline in relation to the sounds on the Talking layer, you now have a character who appears to be talking.

16. **Save the file and continue to the next exercise.**

DEFINE SOUND COMPRESSION SETTINGS

Before you export the final movie file, you should optimize the sounds to produce the smallest possible files while still maintaining the best possible quality. You can define default export settings for all stream sounds and all event sounds, but you can also experiment with different compression settings for individual sound files in the library.

1. **With atrium_kiosk.fla open, Control/right-click the atrium_jazz.mp3 file in the Audio folder of the Library panel. Choose Properties from the contextual menu.**

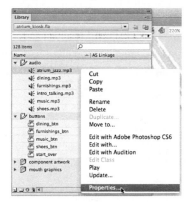

2. **In the resulting Sound Properties dialog box, make sure the Options tab is active at the top of the dialog box.**

3. **Choose MP3 in the Compression menu. If available, uncheck the Use Imported MP3 Quality option.**

   Flash supports five sound compression options:

   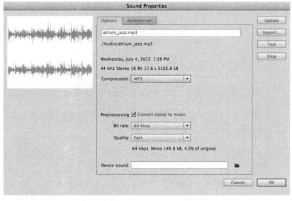

   - **Default.** This option uses the global compression settings (mp3, 16kbps, mono) defined in the Publish Settings dialog box when you export your SWF file. If you select Default, no additional export settings are available.

   - **MP3.** Over the past few years, this format has become a *de facto* standard for audio on the Web. MP3 compression produces small files with very good quality, but it can cause problems for older computers with limited processing power.

   - **ADPCM.** This option converts sounds into binary data. ADPCM encoding is not as efficient as MP3 compression, but it is useful if you need to export a file to be compatible with older versions of Flash (version 3 or lower).

   - **Raw.** This option does not compress the audio data, which results in very large file sizes. This option should only be used for files that will be delivered on the desktop instead of over the Internet.

     ADPCM and Raw use less processing power on each playback than MP3. They are recommended for very short (small) sounds that are played back rapidly. A shooting game in which guns fire many times a second, for example, might benefit from encoding the gun sound in ADPCM or Raw; the cost in file size would probably be less than 1k, and processor performance would be significantly enhanced.

   - **Speech.** This option uses a compression algorithm designed specifically for compressing spoken sounds. Sounds compressed with this option are converted to mono sounds (instead of stereo). Speech-compressed sounds require Flash Player 6 or higher.

Note:

The Preprocessing check box, enabled by default, converts stereo sounds to mono sounds.

4. **Choose 48 kbps in the Bit Rate menu.**

   Depending on the selected compression option, you can also change the bit rate or the sample rate to affect the quality of the exported sound.

   - The **Sample Rate** menu is available for ADPCM, Raw, and Speech compression; lower sample rates decrease file size, but can also decrease sound quality. The 22 kHz setting is recommended for reasonably good quality of most sounds.

   - The **Bit Rate** menu is available for MP3 compression. This option determines the bits per second in the exported sound. Higher bit rates result in better sound quality. Most experts recommend at least 20 kbps for speech, and 48 kbps for reasonably good quality of complex sounds such as music.

Note:

Flash cannot increase the sample rate or bit rate of an imported sound above its original settings.

5. **Choose Best in the Quality menu.**

   Three quality options — in order of file size (from small to large) and quality (from low to high) — are available for MP3 sounds: Fast, Medium, and Best.

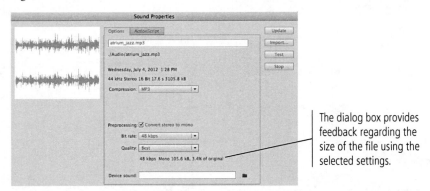

   The dialog box provides feedback regarding the size of the file using the selected settings.

6. **Click OK to change the export settings for the selected sound file.**

7. **Open the Sound Properties dialog box for the intro_talking sound file.**

8. **Choose Speech in the Compression menu.**

9. **Choose 11 kHz in the Sample Rate menu, and then click the Test button.**

   When the sound plays, you might notice some popping or hissing noises behind the spoken message.

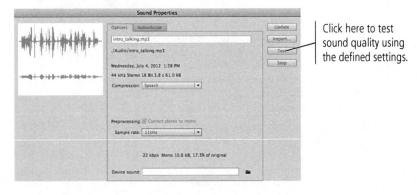

   Click here to test sound quality using the defined settings.

Note:

You can change the default sound export settings in the Publish Settings dialog box.

10. **Choose 44 kHz in the Sample Rate menu, and then click the Test button.**

    This sample rate results in much better quality. Because this kiosk will not be downloaded over the Internet, the larger file size is not a problem.

11. **Click OK to apply the new compression settings for this sound file.**

12. **Save the Flash file and close it.**

Project Review

fill in the blank

1. In a Button symbol, the _____ defines the area where a user can click to trigger the button.

2. _____ to edit a symbol in place on the Stage.

3. The _____ marks the location of the defined X and Y values of a placed instance.

4. A(n) _____ defines the point in time when a change occurs.

5. _____ is the number of animation frames that occur in a second.

6. _____ sounds are timeline independent; they must download completely before they play.

7. _____ sounds are timeline dependent; they play as soon as enough of the data has downloaded to the user's computer.

8. The _____ sync method prevents more than one instance of the same sound from playing at the same time.

9. You can use the _____ dialog box to change the length of a specific sound file.

10. Use the _____ option to replace one symbol with another at a specific frame.

short answer

1. Briefly describe at least three uses of the Library panel.

2. Briefly explain the difference between event sounds and stream sounds.

3. Briefly explain the concept of lip syncing, as it relates to symbols and the Flash timeline.

Use what you learned in this project to complete the following freeform exercise.
Carefully read the art director and client comments, then create your own design to meet the needs of the project.
Use the space below to sketch ideas; when finished, write a brief explanation of your reasoning behind your final design.

art director comments

Your client is a company that provides technical support for children's online video games. The owner wants an introduction page for that site similar to the kiosk interface, with a talking character that identifies the options.

To complete this project, you should:

❑ Download the client's supplied files in the **WC6_PB_Project3.zip** archive on the Student Files Web page.

❑ Review the client-supplied sound and artwork files.

❑ Develop a site intro page with a talking robot and two different buttons.

❑ If you use the client's artwork, import the file into Flash and create movie clips as necessary from the different elements.

❑ If you don't use the supplied file, create or find artwork as appropriate.

client comments

We want to build a new introduction page to our video game site. We're using a robot avatar throughout the video game site, and want that character to be featured on the intro page — I even recorded the intro message with a "mechanical" sounding voice. (Feel free to re-record the audio if you want to, as long as the message stays the same.)

I found a robot illustration that I like, but I'm not an artist; I'd be happy to review other artwork if you have a better idea. I also want you to develop some kind of background artwork that makes the piece look like a cohesive user interface.

You need to include two buttons: one that links to online technical support and one that links to a telephone support page.

In the final file, I want the robot to look like it's talking, but I also want the robot to point to the related buttons when the appropriate part of the intro sound plays.

project justification

_____
_____
_____
_____
_____
_____
_____
_____
_____
_____
_____
_____
_____
_____

Project Summary

This project introduced many of the basic concepts and techniques of animating objects in Flash. You learned about frames and keyframes, as well as two different types of symbols that will be used in many Flash projects, both throughout this book and in your professional career. You also learned how to import artwork that was created in Adobe Illustrator — a very common workflow in the graphic design/animation market.

You should understand how frames on the Flash timeline relate to the passage of actual time, and how keyframes are used to make changes at specific points in an animation. You should also understand the basic concept of symbols and instances, including the different ways to edit the conent of a specific symbol. You will build on these skills as you complete the rest of the projects in this book.

This project also showed you how to add audio content to a movie — placing a looped sound in the background of a file, triggering specific sounds with a button's Over state, and even synchronizing graphics to a spoken message.

Import artwork from Adobe Illustrator files

Add an event sound that loops continuously in the background

Edit a sound envelope to control the sound volume

Add a streaming sound as the interface introduction

Create symbols from imported artwork

Synchronize graphics to sound to create a "talking" effect

Attach and control button sounds

Edit button symbols to change different button states

Animated Internet Ads

Your client wants to create a series of ads to place on Web sites that are used by existing and potential customers. They have asked you to create a short animation rather than just a static image, in hopes of attracting more attention when the ad appears in a browser with other content.

This project incorporates the following skills:

❑ Creating shape tweens to animate changes in shape and color

❑ Creating classic tweens to animate changes in position and opacity

❑ Adding text to a Flash movie

❑ Adapting file content to match different file dimensions

❑ Using a Flash project to manage assets for multiple files

❑ Publishing a file to SWF for distribution

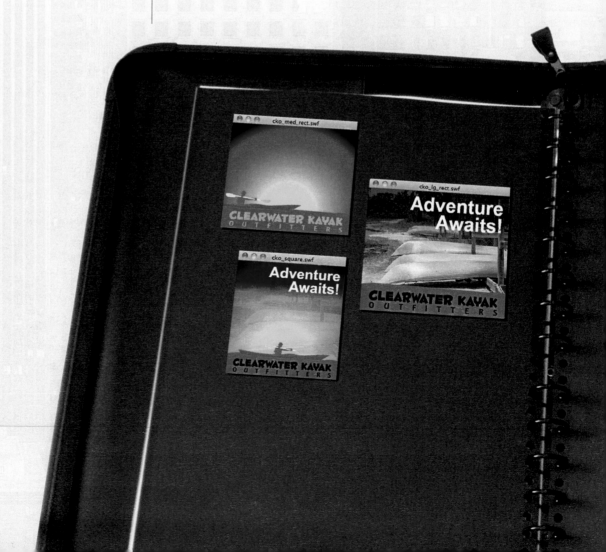

client comments

We've provided you with our logo and an image that we want to use in the ads. Since these are going to be placed into a variety of Web sites, we want some kind of animation that might help catch a user's eye.

Most of the sites where we're planning on advertising use standard ad sizes. I'm not sure exactly which sizes we're going to purchase, but we do like the rectangle and square shapes better than the narrow banners.

We might decide on some of the other options later, but we'd like to get started with three common sizes:

- 300 × 250 pixels
- 336 × 280 pixels
- 250 × 250 pixels

art director comments

Flash includes predefined templates for most of the common ad sizes, so that's the easiest way to start the first file.

I want you to animate different aspects of the client's logo over the course of the animation. The kayaker is ideally suited to move across the stage. He should paddle across the stage while the sun rises. Halfway through, he should pause and wait until the tagline appears, then move the rest of the way across while the image gradually appears in place of the sunrise.

After you create the initial ad, you can use several built-in techniques to repurpose the content for other sizes. You should also take advantage of the Project panel to manage assets that will be used in more than one file, so it will be easier to make universal changes in any of the shared assets.

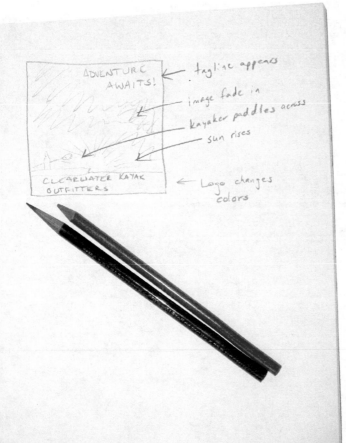

project objectives

To complete this project, you will:

❏ Create a file based on a template

❏ Create a shape tween

❏ Tween an object's color

❏ Create a classic tween

❏ Tween an object's opacity

❏ Stop the animation timeline

❏ Create and control a text object

❏ Define font embedding

❏ Control object stacking order

❏ Create a Flash project

❏ Scale content to document properties

❏ Edit a shared symbol

❏ Publish files to SWF

Stage 1 Animating Symbols

Animation — the true heart of Flash — can be created in a number of different ways. To create the animated ads for this project, you will use **shape tweening** and **classic tweening**.

If you completed Project 3: Talking Kiosk Interface, you already learned a bit about symbols in general, specifically button and graphic symbols. In this project, you work with movie clip symbols. Both graphic symbols and movie clip symbols can include animation, but movie clips offer a number of advantages over graphic symbols.

Movie clips are **timeline independent**; the animation contained in a movie clip requires only a single frame on the timeline where it is placed (called the **parent timeline**). A movie clip timeline might include 500 frames, but the entire animation will play on a single frame of the parent timeline.

An animated graphic symbol, on the other hand, is **timeline dependent**; it requires the same number of frames on the parent timeline that are present inside the symbol's timeline. In other words, a 500-frame animation inside the graphic symbol requires 500 corresponding frames on the timeline where the symbol is placed.

Because movie clip timelines function independently of the parent timeline, you can more easily incorporate animations of different duration onto the same parent timeline.

Planning a movie

When you start any new project, you should begin by analyzing what you need to accomplish. A bit of advance planning can help you avoid unnecessary rework and frustration — in the project planning phase, you can determine, for example, that an independent movie clip is a better option than animating an object directly on the main timeline.

The ad that you are going to create in this project has the following plan or **storyboard**:

- The entire animation should last four seconds.

- The logotype will change from white to dark blue throughout the entire four-second animation.

- The kayaker will move across the Stage throughout the entire four-second duration, pausing halfway until the client's tagline appears.

- The sun is going to rise while the kayaker moves across the Stage. The sunrise animation should be finished when the kayaker gets halfway across the Stage.

- An image will gradually appear to replace the sunrise.

This information tells you a number of things about what you need to do:

- The finished ad requires four separate animations — the logo changing colors, the moving kayaker, the sunrise, and the image fading in.

- Each animation requires different timing. The sunrise and the image fade-in each occupy only half the time of the moving kayaker.

- The animations also require different starting points. The sunrise and the moving kayaker need to start as soon as the file opens. The image fade-in doesn't start until the sunrise animation is complete.

As you complete this project, you are going to use movie clip symbols and timeline frames to achieve the stated goals.

CREATE AN AD FILE

The final goal of this project is three separate ads that can be placed on Web sites where your client has decided to advertise. Because Internet ads typically use standard sizes, Flash includes those sizes as templates in the New Document dialog box.

In the first stage of this project, you are going to create the initial ad using one of the defined templates. Later you will use Flash's built-in tools to repurpose the existing content into the other required ad sizes.

1. **Download WC6_RF_Project4.zip from the Student Files Web page.**

2. **Expand the ZIP archive in your WIP folder (Macintosh) or copy the archive contents into your WIP folder (Windows).**

   This results in a folder named **Kayaks**, which contains the files you need for this project. You should also use this folder to save the files you create in this project.

3. **Choose File>New. In the New Document dialog box, click the Templates tab to display those options.**

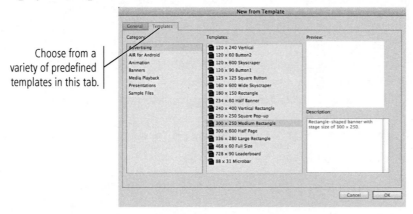

Choose from a variety of predefined templates in this tab.

4. **Select Advertising in the left pane, then select the 300 × 250 Medium Rectangle option in the right pane.**

   Flash includes templates for a number of standard file sizes, including the most common ads that are placed on the Internet.

5. **Click OK to create the new file.**

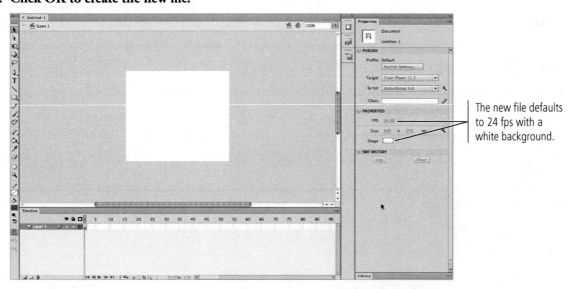

The new file defaults to 24 fps with a white background.

6. **Choose File>Import>Import to Stage. Select `cko_logo.ai` (in the WIP>Kayaks folder) and click Open.**

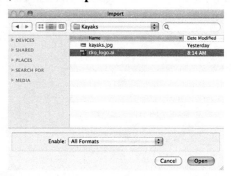

7. **Review the options in the Import to Stage dialog box.**

This Illustrator file was created with four layers, each containing a different element of the logo. As you complete this project, you will use several techniques to animate different parts of the logo artwork.

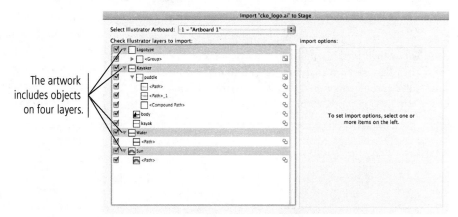

The artwork includes objects on four layers.

8. **At the bottom of the dialog box, choose the following options:**

- **Convert Layers To**   **Flash Layers**
- **Place Objects at Original Position**   **Checked**

  Although you will move the various logo components as you complete this project, you are importing them at their original positions so you can see the logo as it was designed before you make changes.

- **Set Stage Size...**   **Unchecked**

  You created this Flash file at a specific file size to meet specific needs, so you are not converting the Stage to match the imported artwork.

- **Import Unused Symbols**   **Unchecked**

  The Illustrator file does not include any unused symbols. (In a professional environment, it is a good idea to open the Illustrator file and review its contents, if possible, before importing into Flash.)

- **Import as a Single Bitmap Image**   **Unchecked**

  Beginning in the next exercise, you are going to change several of the paths that make up the logo. If you converted the artwork to a single bitmap, you would not be able to access the individual paths that you need to change.

9. **Click OK to import the artwork to the Stage.**

The Flash file now includes four layers, matching the layers in the original Illustrator file. All the imported artwork is automatically selected.

The imported artwork is centered in the document window.

Each separate object has its own bounding box.

Four layers were added to the file.

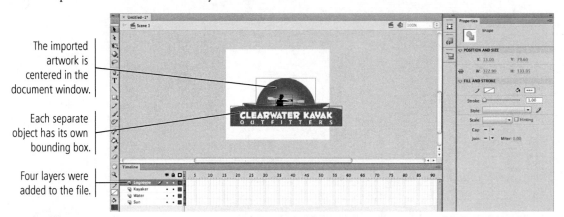

10. **Using the Selection tool, drag the selected artwork until the bottom edge snaps to the bottom edge of the Stage, and the artwork appears to be centered horizontally.**

Each logo component, identified by the various bounding boxes, is an individual object (or group). If you tried to use the Align panel to align the artwork to the bottom and center of the Stage, each individual component would be aligned to the bottom of the Stage; the objects' positions relative to one another would not be maintained.

Note:

Because these objects all reside on different layers, you can't use the Group command to treat them as a single object for positioning purposes.

Use the Selection tool to move all selected objects at one time without changing their positions relative to one another.

11. **Click away from everything on the Stage to deselect everything.**

12. **In the Properties panel, click the Stage swatch and choose Black from the pop-up color panel.**

13. **Click the FPS hot text to access the field, and change the FPS to 15.**

The ads you are creating are only going to be distributed over the Internet; 15 fps is high enough for good-quality display. (Higher frame rate would result in larger file sizes that are unnecessary for this type of file, and could be problematic for users with slower download speeds.)

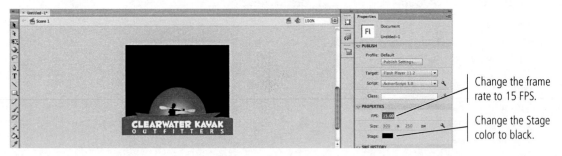

Change the frame rate to 15 FPS.

Change the Stage color to black.

14. **Save the file as cko_med_rect.fla in your WIP>Kayaks folder, then continue to the next exercise.**

CREATE A SHAPE TWEEN

A **shape tween** allows you to convert one shape into another over time. You define the starting and ending shape, then Flash creates the in-between frames (hence the name "tween") that create the appearance of continuous movement when the finished animation plays.

You will use this type of tween to create the sunrise animation, as well as change the colors of the logotype.

1. **With `cko_med_rect.fla` open, use the Selection tool to select the sun object on the Stage.**

2. **Open the Color panel.**

   This object was created with a gradient fill. You are going to edit the gradient so the edge of the shape blends smoothly into the Stage background color.

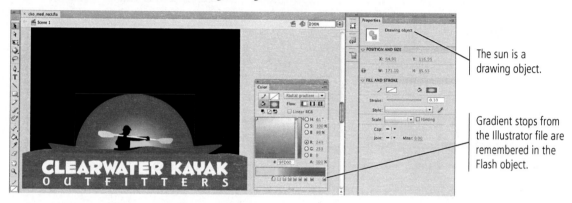

The sun is a drawing object.

Gradient stops from the Illustrator file are remembered in the Flash object.

3. **Click the right gradient stop to select it, then change the Alpha value of the selected stop to 0.**

   Alpha refers to transparency; a value of 0 means something is entirely transparent.

   This step makes the last gradient stop entirely transparent. Colors between the next-to-last and last stop will now transition from entirely opaque (100% Alpha) to entirely transparent (0% Alpha), which allows the object to blend into the background without a harsh edge.

Change the Alpha value of the last stop on the gradient.

4. **Control/right-click the selected object and choose Convert to Symbol.**

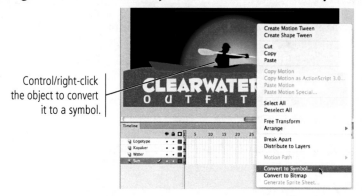

Control/right-click
the object to convert
it to a symbol.

5. **In the resulting dialog box, type sun_mc in the Name field, choose Movie Clip in the Type menu, and choose the bottom-center registration point.**

You are using the bottom-center registration point because you want the sun object to grow out from that point.

6. **Click OK to create the new symbol.**

When you create a symbol from existing artwork, the original object is automatically converted to an instance of that symbol.

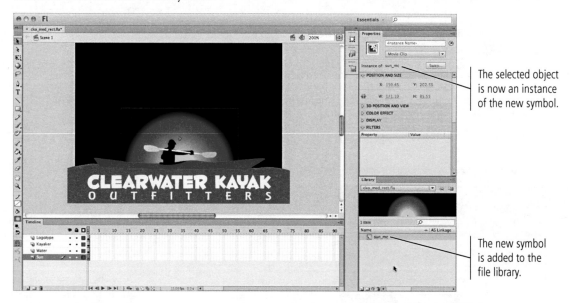

The selected object
is now an instance
of the new symbol.

The new symbol
is added to the
file library.

7. **Double-click the instance on the Stage to enter into Symbol-Editing mode.**

You are editing this symbol in place because you need to be able to see the shape's size relative to the Stage on which it is placed.

8. **Select Frame 30 in the timeline, then press F6 to add a new keyframe.**

The completed ad needs to last four seconds. At 15 fps, the entire ad will require 60 frames; the sunrise should take half that time to complete, so this movie clip needs 30 frames.

When you add a keyframe to a layer, the contents of the previous keyframe are automatically copied to the new keyframe. You can edit the contents on each keyframe independently, without affecting the same contents on other keyframes.

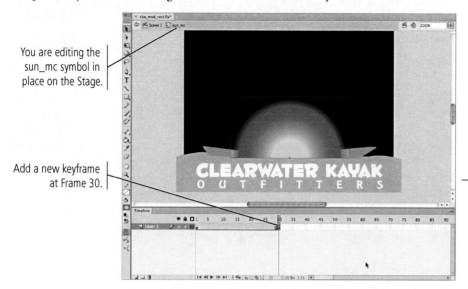

You are editing the sun_mc symbol in place on the Stage.

Add a new keyframe at Frame 30.

Note:

If you can't use, or don't have, Function keys, you can use the Insert> Timeline submenu, or the frame's contextual menu, to insert a frame, keyframe, or blank keyframe.

Note:

Remember, keyframes are required when an object needs to change in some way at a given point in time.

9. **Choose the Free Transform tool.**

10. **With Frame 30 selected in the timeline and the sun object selected on the Stage, move the transformation point to the object's bottom-center bounding-box handle.**

When you create the animation, you want the sun to appear as if it is growing out from the horizon. To accomplish this, you are going to make the sun shape larger, using the bottom-center point as the anchor.

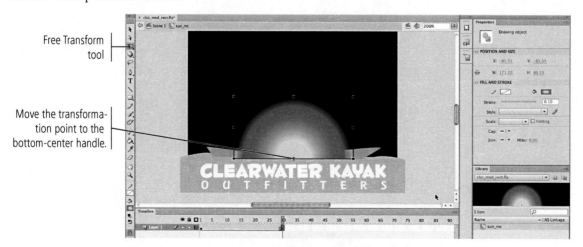

Free Transform tool

Move the transformation point to the bottom-center handle.

11. **Zoom out so you can see the area around the Stage on all four sides.**

Feel free to zoom in and out as necessary while you complete the projects in this book.

12. Open the Transform panel. At the top of the panel, make sure the Constrain icon is active.

When the Constrain icon appears as two connected chain links, the object's width and height are linked to maintain object's original aspect ratio. If this icon is a broken chain, you can change one value without affecting the other.

Note:

The Transform panel can be used to make precise numerical changes, or simply to monitor the changes you make with the Free Transform tool.

13. Place the cursor over the existing Width value. When you see the scrubby-slider cursor, click and drag right to enlarge the object until none of the black background color is visible.

Although you can use the Properties panel to change an object's height and/or width, those changes apply from the top-left corner of the selection instead of the defined transformation point that you set in Step 10. Changes made through the Transform panel respect the defined transformation point, so this is a better option for making this type of change.

Note:

This technique of dragging to change a property value is called **scrubbing**.

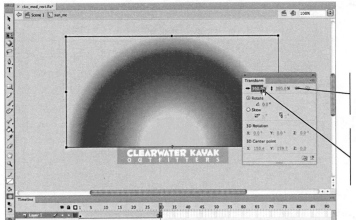

Make sure the Constrain icon appears as a linked chain.

Scrub the Width value until the object obscures the entire black background.

14. Control/right-click any frame between Frame 1 and Frame 30, and choose Create Shape Tween from the contextual menu.

In the timeline, Flash identifies the shape tween with green frames and an arrow between keyframes.

Note:

You can't create a shape tween for a group.

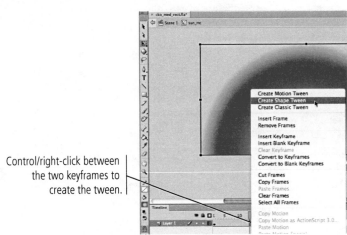

Control/right-click between the two keyframes to create the tween.

15. Click Frame 1 in the timeline to move the playhead back to the beginning of the animation.

16. **Press Return/Enter to play the animation on the Stage.**

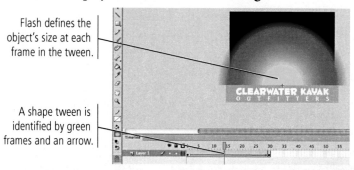

Flash defines the object's size at each frame in the tween.

A shape tween is identified by green frames and an arrow.

Understanding Transformation Options

The Transform Panel

At times, you might need to apply very specific numeric transformations, such as scaling an object by a specific percentage. Rather than manually calculating new dimensions and defining the new dimensions in the Properties panel, you can use the Transform panel to make this type of change.

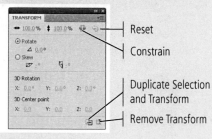

Reset

Constrain

Duplicate Selection and Transform

Remove Transform

When you change a value in the Transform panel, press Return/Enter to apply the change, or click the Duplicate Selection and Transform button to make a copy of the object and apply the change to the copy.

Keep in mind that all transformations made in the Transform panel apply around the defined transformation point.

The Modify>Transform Submenu

The Modify>Transform submenu has a number of valuable options for transforming objects.

Free Transform displays a set of eight bounding box handles, which you can drag horizontally or vertically to scale, stretch, skew, and rotate an object. During a free transform, an object's overall shape is maintained (an oval remains an oval, a square remains a square, and so on).

Distort displays a set of eight bounding box handles. If you drag one of the corner handles, you can "stretch" the object out of its original shape. For example, you can drag one corner of a rectangle to create a polygon with odd angles.

Scale and Rotate opens a dialog box where you can define specific scale percentages or rotation angles. You can also use the **Rotate 90°** (Clockwise and Counterclockwise) options for a selected object.

Envelope adds control handles to the object's anchor points, which you can use to warp the shape. You can drag the handles to reshape the connecting curves, and/or drag the anchor points to new positions to create an entirely different shape than the original.

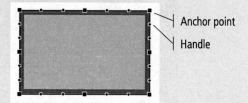

Anchor point

Handle

Scale is a subset of Free Transform. You can see the eight bounding box handles, but you can only scale or stretch the object; you can't rotate or skew it.

Rotate and Skew are also subsets of Free Transform. You can see the eight bounding box handles, but you can only skew or rotate the object; you can't scale or stretch it.

Flip Horizontal or **Flip Vertical** options allow you to flip objects on either axis.

Even though you can transform objects, Flash remembers the object's original size and shape. You can remove any transformation — except envelope distortion — from drawing objects and symbol instances using the **Remove Transform** option. (You can't remove a transformation from a merge-drawing object after you have deselected the object.)

To remove an envelope distortion, you have to choose Modify>Combine Objects>Delete Envelope.

17. Click Scene 1 in the Edit bar to return to the main Stage.

Remember, pressing Return/Enter plays the *current* timeline on the Stage. Because the main timeline has only one frame, this command would have no effect. Testing a movie on the Stage does not initiate the timeline of movie clips that are placed on the Stage.

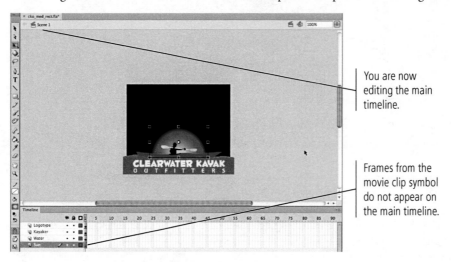

You are now editing the main timeline.

Frames from the movie clip symbol do not appear on the main timeline.

18. Save the file and continue to the next exercise.

TWEEN AN OBJECT'S COLOR

Changing an object from one color to another is a common animation task. This is simply accomplished using a shape tween, using the same method you used to change the size of the sun symbol.

1. With `cko_med_rect.fla` open, use the Selection tool to select the logotype on the Stage.

2. Control/right-click the selected group and choose Convert to Symbol.

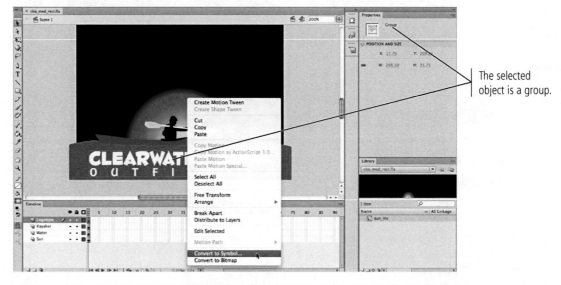

The selected object is a group.

3. Type `logo_mc` in the Name field and choose Movie Clip in the Type menu.

4. Click OK to create the new symbol.

In this animation, you are simply going to change the color of the text. Because nothing is moving, the symbol registration point does not matter; you can leave it at the default location.

5. Double-click the symbol instance on the Stage to enter into it.

6. With the logotype selected on the Stage, choose Modify>Ungroup.

You can't create a shape tween with a group, so you first have to ungroup the letters. After ungrouping, you can see that each letter is a separate drawing object.

Note:

You chould also choose Modify>Break Apart (or press Command/Control-B) to accomplish the same general effect.

You are editing the logo_mc symbol in place on the Stage.

7. Click Frame 60 in the timeline to select it, then press F6 to add a new keyframe.

When you add or select a frame on the timeline, the frame becomes the active selection.

This is deceptive because the objects' bounding boxes are still visible, suggesting that they are selected — even though they are not.

Note:

If you aren't sure what is actually selected, look at the top of the Properties panel.

8. Click the filled area of any of the drawing objects on the Stage to make them the active selection.

To edit an object's properties, you first have to remember to intentionally reselect the object(s) on the Stage.

After adding the keyframe, the Properties panel shows that the frame is selected.

The bounding boxes of objects on the selected frame are visible.

Click any filled area inside any bounding box to make the drawing objects the active selection.

In addition to changing object properties in a shape tween, you can also create a **shape tween** to change one shape into another over time (as the name suggests). A shape tween requires two existing keyframes — one with the starting shape and one with the ending shape.

If you Control/right-click between two keyframes, choosing Create Shape Tween generates the shape tween; the tween frames automatically change the shape of the object as necessary to convert Shape A into Shape B. The following illustrations show a simple shape tween that changes a blue square into a green circle.

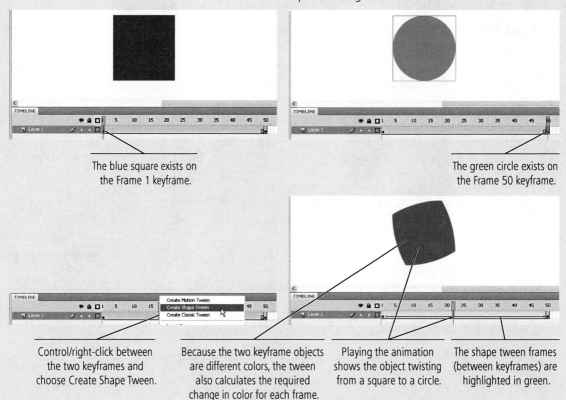

The blue square exists on the Frame 1 keyframe.

The green circle exists on the Frame 50 keyframe.

Control/right-click between the two keyframes and choose Create Shape Tween.

Because the two keyframe objects are different colors, the tween also calculates the required change in color for each frame.

Playing the animation shows the object twisting from a square to a circle.

The shape tween frames (between keyframes) are highlighted in green.

In many cases, shape tweens don't work exactly as expected. In the previous examples, the shape tween animation twists the square shape over time into the circle

shape. If you want the square corners to simply move without twisting (for example), you can use **shape hinting** to control the change that occurs in a shape tween.

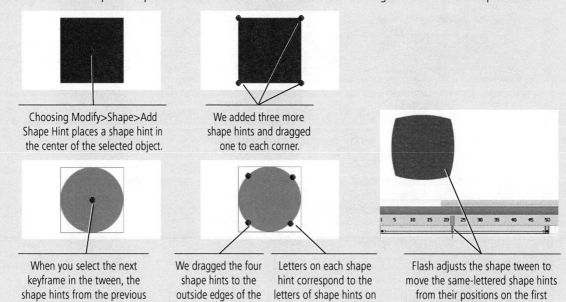

Choosing Modify>Shape>Add Shape Hint places a shape hint in the center of the selected object.

We added three more shape hints and dragged one to each corner.

When you select the next keyframe in the tween, the shape hints from the previous keyframe are already in place in the middle of the object.

We dragged the four shape hints to the outside edges of the circle on Frame 50.

Letters on each shape hint correspond to the letters of shape hints on the first keyframe object.

Flash adjusts the shape tween to move the same-lettered shape hints from their positions on the first keyframe object to their positions on the second keyframe object.

9. **Using the Color panel, change the objects' fill color to #000033.**

After ungrouping, click any of the active objects to select them.

Use the Color panel to change the fill color to #000033 with 100% Alpha.

10. **Control/right-click any frame between Frame 1 and Frame 60, and choose Create Shape Tween from the contextual menu.**

Although you did not change the objects' shapes, a shape tween is still an appropriate method for changing an object's color over time.

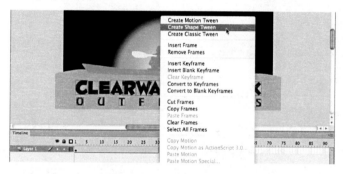

11. **Move the playhead to Frame 1, then press Return/Enter to test the animation on the Stage.**

12. **Click Scene 1 in the Edit bar to return to the main Stage.**

Again, there is only one frame on the main timeline, so there is nothing to play. Remember, a movie clip symbol operates independently of the main timeline; you can't view the movie clip's animation directly on the Flash stage.

13. **Save the file and continue to the next exercise.**

CREATE A CLASSIC TWEEN

As you can probably guess, there is much more to animation than changing an object's shape or color. In this exercise, you will create very simple classic tweens that move the kayaker across the Stage, and use keyframes to control the movement's timing.

1. **With `cko_med_rect.fla` open, click the Kayaker layer in the timeline to select all objects on the layer.**

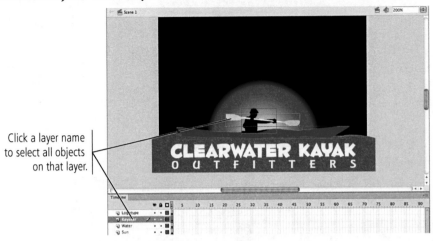

Click a layer name to select all objects on that layer.

2. **Control/right-click the selected objects and choose Convert to Symbol.**

3. **In the resulting dialog box, type `kayaker_mc` in the Name field. Choose Movie Clip in the Type menu and choose the right-center registration point. Click OK to create the new symbol.**

Extending the Length of the Timeline

FLASH FOUNDATIONS

If you create animations with very long timelines, you might need to extend the timeline beyond what is available by default. To accomplish this, scroll the timeline all the way to the right, and then add a regular frame to the layer near the end of the visible timeline.

When you add a frame after the last visible frame, the timeline scroll bar moves to the middle of the panel, indicating that more frames are now available in the timeline. You can then scroll again to the new end of the timeline and add another frame, which again extends the length of the available timeline. Continue this process until you have the number of frames you need.

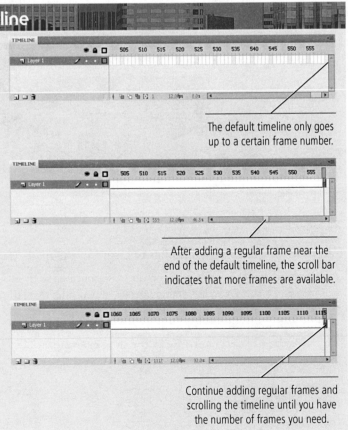

The default timeline only goes up to a certain frame number.

After adding a regular frame near the end of the default timeline, the scroll bar indicates that more frames are available.

Continue adding regular frames and scrolling the timeline until you have the number of frames you need.

4. **With the new symbol instance selected on the Stage, change the X value in the Properties panel to 0.**

   Remember, the X and Y properties define the position of a symbol's registration point. Because you chose the right-center registration point, changing the X value to 0 moves the kayaker entirely off the Stage.

You are editing the symbol
instance on the main timeline.

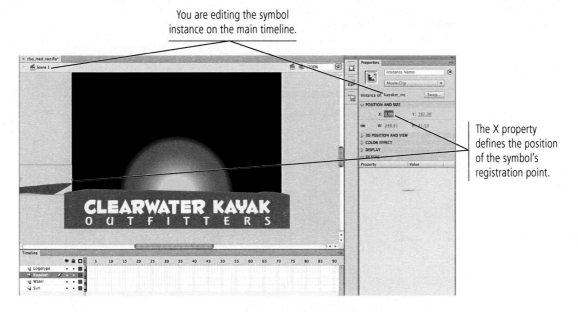

The X property
defines the position
of the symbol's
registration point.

5. **Click Frame 30 of the Kayaker layer and press F6 to add a new keyframe.**

6. **Click the kayaker symbol instance to select it, then scrub the X property in the Property panel until the instance is approximately centered on the Stage (as shown here).**

Other objects are not
visible because those
layers don't yet exist
on Frame 30.

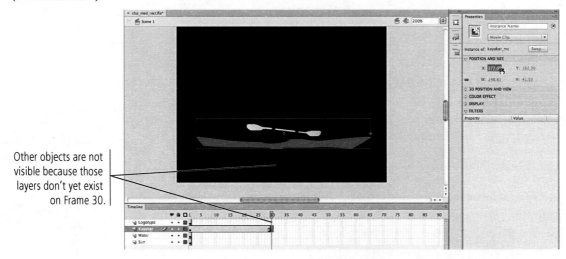

7. **Control/right-click any frame between Frame 1 and 30 of the Kayaker layer and choose Create Classic Tween from the contextual menu.**

A classic tween is one method for creating motion in a Flash animation. Like the shape tweens you created already, you have to define the starting and ending keyframes, then create the tween; Flash automatically determines the instance's position on the in-between frames.

In Project 5: Ocean Animation, you will learn about Motion Tweens, which provide far more control over numerous aspects of a tween. You should understand what a classic tween is, though, so you can recognize one if you find one in a file — especially files created in older (pre-CS4) versions of the software.

Note:

This is called a "classic" tween because this technique was available in previous versions of the application that did not include the Flash Motion Editor.

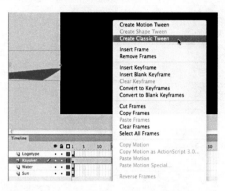

In the timeline, Flash identifies the classic tween with blue frames and an arrow between keyframes.

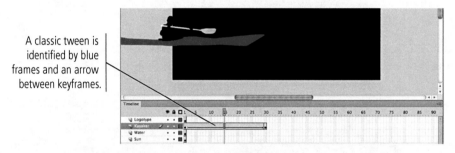

A classic tween is identified by blue frames and an arrow between keyframes.

8. **Select Frame 38 on the Kayaker layer, then press F6 to add another keyframe.**

Remember: when you add a new keyframe, Flash duplicates the content on the previous keyframe. By adding this keyframe at Frame 38, you are holding the symbol instance in place for approximately half a second.

9. **Select Frame 60 of the Kayaker layer and add a new keyframe.**

10. **Select the symbol instance on the Stage, then change the X property in the Properties panel until the instance is entirely past the right edge of the Stage.**

Note:

We say "approximately half a second" because the frame rate in this file is 15 fps, which is not equally divisible by 2. Because you can't have half a frame, you are using slightly more than half a second for the pause in animation.

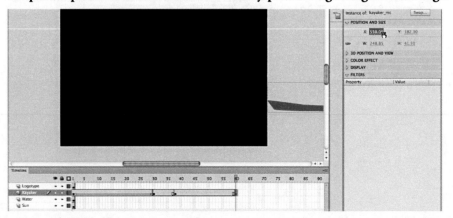

11. Control/right-click any frame between Frame 38 and 60 of the Kayaker layer and choose Create Classic Tween from the contextual menu.

The new tween occupies the entire range of frames between the keyframes that you defined on Frames 38 and 60.

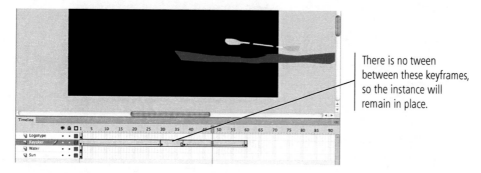

There is no tween between these keyframes, so the instance will remain in place.

12. Select Frame 60 of the Logotype layer. Press Command/Control, then click Frame 60 of the Water and Sun layers to add them to the active selection.

You can press Shift to select contiguous frames, or press Command/Control to select non-contiguous layers.

Although two of these layers contain animated movie clips, those movie clips' timelines do not transfer to the main movie timeline. They will not exist in the main movie beyond Frame 1 unless you extend those layers' timelines on the main Stage.

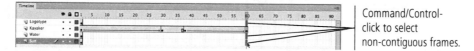

Command/Control-click to select non-contiguous frames.

13. Press F5 to add regular frames to the three selected layers.

This extends all three layers to Frame 60, so their content will be visible throughout the entire animation.

14. Click Frame 1 to select it, then press Return/Enter to test the animation on the timeline.

Remember, you can't see the sunrise and logotype animations because those are created inside the individual symbols. To see all three animations together, you have to test the movie in the Flash Player window. (You will do this after you create the final required animation in the next exercise.)

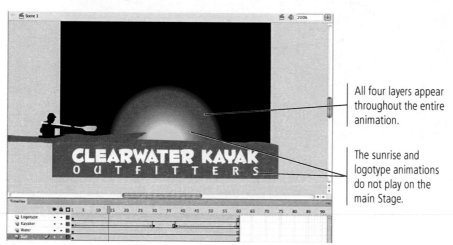

All four layers appear throughout the entire animation.

The sunrise and logotype animations do not play on the main Stage.

15. Save the file and continue to the next exercise.

TWEEN AN OBJECT'S OPACITY

The last required animation for this movie is an image that fades in after the sun finishes rising. In this exercise you will create a new layer on the timeline and use a blank keyframe to prevent the image from appearing too early.

1. **With cko_med_rect.fla open, create a new layer named Photo directly above the Sun layer.**

2. **Control/right-click Frame 30 on the new layer and choose Insert Blank Keyframe.**

   You are inserting a blank keyframe before placing the image onto the Stage at Frame 30, so the preceding frames (1–29) will remain blank — preventing the image from appearing until halfway through the movie.

3. **With the blank keyframe on Frame 30 selected, choose File>Import>Import to Stage.**

4. **Choose the file kayaks.jpg in your WIP>Kayaks folder, then click Open.**

5. **Align the image to the top of the Stage, centered horizontally.**

   Unlike the imported Illustrator artwork, you can use the Align panel to move the image into the correct position.

6. **Choose the Free Transform tool, then move the image's transformation point to the top-center bounding-box handle.**

   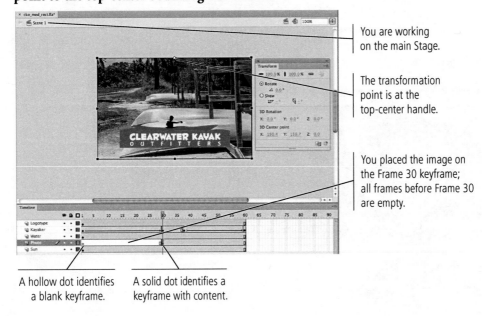

   You are working on the main Stage.

   The transformation point is at the top-center handle.

   You placed the image on the Frame 30 keyframe; all frames before Frame 30 are empty.

   A hollow dot identifies a blank keyframe.

   A solid dot identifies a keyframe with content.

7. **Using the Transform panel, reduce the image scale (proportionally) until the bottom edge is just hidden by the blue shape that makes up the water.**

You can't animate a bitmap object; to cause this image to appear gradually over time, you first need to convert it to a symbol.

Because you moved the transformation point, the top-center point of the image remains in place when you scale it.

8. **Control/right-click the image and choose Convert to Symbol. In the resulting dialog box, type `photo_mc` in the Name field, and choose Movie Clip in the type menu. Click OK to create the new symbol.**

You are not animating the instance's position, so the registration point doesn't matter.

Symbols have a number of properties that are not available for bitmap or drawing objects. In this case you are going to edit and animate the Color Effect property to change the alpha (transparency) value of the symbol over time.

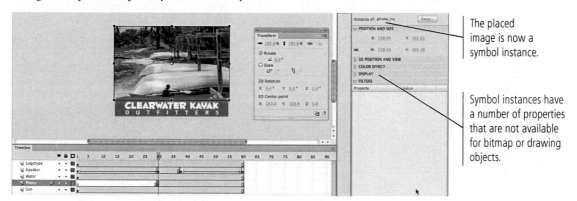

The placed image is now a symbol instance.

Symbol instances have a number of properties that are not available for bitmap or drawing objects.

9. **In the Properties panel, expand the Color Effect options, then choose Alpha in the Style menu. In the secondary Alpha field that appears, change the Alpha value to 0.**

Remember, the Alpha value controls an object's opacity; a value of 0 means the object is not visible.

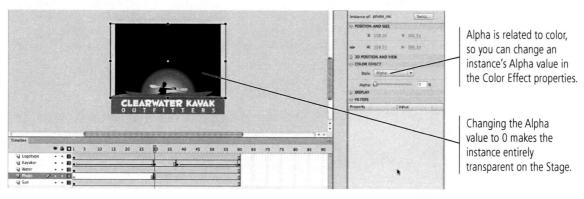

Alpha is related to color, so you can change an instance's Alpha value in the Color Effect properties.

Changing the Alpha value to 0 makes the instance entirely transparent on the Stage.

10. **Add a new keyframe to Frame 60 of the Photo layer.**

FLASH FOUNDATIONS

With one or more frames selected in the timeline, you can use the Properties panel to control a number of options.

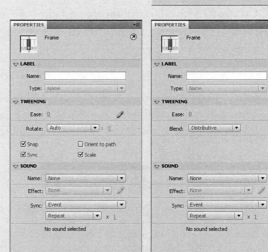

- **Name field.** Frames are sequentially numbered by default; you can also assign text-based labels to specific frames so you can more easily remember where in the timeline a specific action occurs. For example, "Arc_Tween" is more descriptive than "Frame 54."

- **Type menu.** If you assign a frame label, you can use this menu to treat the label as a regular name, as an anchor that can be targeted in a hyperlink, or as a comment.

- **Sound options.** The Properties panel includes several options for controlling sound files. You used these options in Project 3: Talking Kiosk Interface.

Classic and Shape Tween Properties

When a classic or shape tween is applied to selected frames, you can use the Properties panel to control a number of options related to the tween itself.

- **Ease.** This option is used to change the speed of movement as an object moves through a tween. You can set negative or positive values to increase or decrease speed at a consistent rate, or you can click the Edit button to define custom Ease values with different speeds at different points in the tween.

- **Rotate menu.** By default, an object simply moves from one place to another through the tween frames. You can choose Auto in the Rotate menu to rotate the object one time over the length of the tween; the object will turn in the direction that requires the least change. You can also exert greater control by choosing CW (clockwise) or CCW (counterclockwise), and then defining a specific number of times the object should rotate throughout the tween.

- **Snap option.** When this option is checked, the registration point of the tweened object attaches to the motion path.

- **Sync option.** This option synchronizes the number of frames in a tween within a graphic symbol to match the number of frames on the timeline where the graphic symbol is placed. With this option checked, replacing the animated symbol in the first frame of the tween replaces the symbol in all tweened frames.

- **Orient to Path.** If you are using a motion path, you can check this option to orient the baseline (bottom edge) of an object to the motion path.

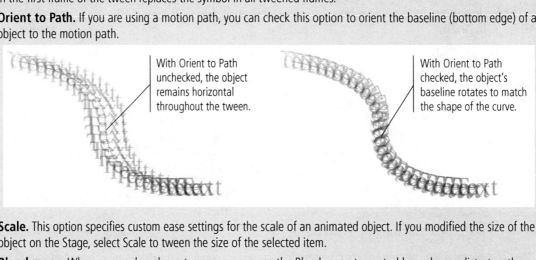

With Orient to Path unchecked, the object remains horizontal throughout the tween.

With Orient to Path checked, the object's baseline rotates to match the shape of the curve.

- **Scale.** This option specifies custom ease settings for the scale of an animated object. If you modified the size of the object on the Stage, select Scale to tween the size of the selected item.

- **Blend menu.** When you apply a shape tween, you can use the Blend menu to control how shapes distort as they change from one shape to another. Distributive, the default option, creates smoother shapes throughout the transition. The Angular option can produce better results if the starting and ending shapes have sharp corners that you want to preserve throughout the transition.

11. **Click the symbol instance's transformation point to select the instance on the Stage.**

The symbol instance is not visible because its Alpha value is currently 0; you can still use the transformation point to select it.

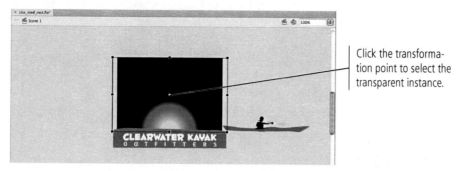

Click the transformation point to select the transparent instance.

12. **In the Properties panel, change the Alpha value to 100%.**

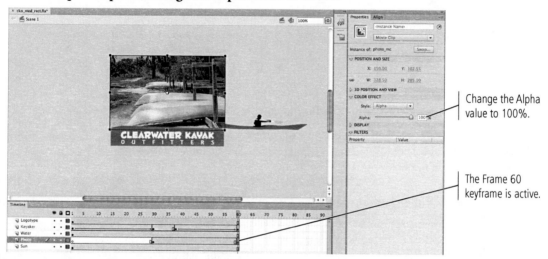

Change the Alpha value to 100%.

The Frame 60 keyframe is active.

13. **Control/right-click anywhere between Frames 30 and 60 in the Photo layer and choose Create Classic Tween.**

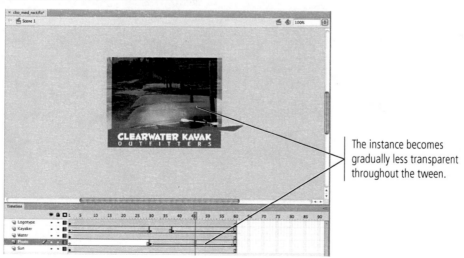

The instance becomes gradually less transparent throughout the tween.

14. **Save the file and continue to the next exercise.**

STOP THE ANIMATION TIMELINE

Remember, movie clips each have their own timelines, which are independent of other movie clips and of the main movie timeline. As soon as the playhead reaches the end of the timeline in each symbol, it automatically returns to the beginning and plays again (called **looping**). To prevent this, you have to add the Stop command to the timeline.

1. **With `cko_med_rect.fla` open, press Command-Return/Control-Enter to test the movie in the Flash Player window.**

   As you can see, the four animations in your movie play repeatedly. You should also notice that the sun rises twice in the time it takes the logotype to change colors and the kayaker to move out of the movie area.

All four animations in the movie loop repeatedly.

2. **Close the Flash Player window and return to Flash.**

3. **In the timeline, select Frame 60 of the Kayaker layer.**

   It really doesn't matter what layer you selected because the Stop command applies to the entire timeline. Any animation on this timeline — the main movie timeline — will be stopped when the playhead reaches Frame 60.

4. **Open the Code Snippets panel and expand the Timeline Navigation folder.**

   The Code Snippets panel is intended to make it easier for non-programmers to add a certain level of interactivity to a Flash movie. Different types of common commands are available, grouped into logical sets or folders. Each item includes a plain-English name.

Expand the various folders to find the available commands.

Click these icons to find more information about the selected snippet.

You can find more information about a snippet by clicking the icons to the right of the selected item in the panel.

Clicking the ⓘ icon shows a description of the selected snippet.

Clicking the ⟨⟩ icon shows the code that will be added by the selected snippet.

5. **Double-click Stop at this Frame in the Code Snippets panel.**

The Actions panel opens and shows the code that is required to stop the timeline from playing more than once.

A new Actions layer is added at the top of the layer stack on the main timeline. A small "a" in the selected keyframe (Frame 60) indicates that code exists on that frame.

Note:

Although we are not going to go into any depth about code until Project 5: Ocean Animation, this is a fundamental requirement for many Flash animations. The Code Snippets panel makes it easy to add the necessary code without any programming knowledge.

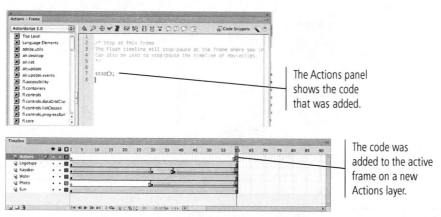

The Actions panel shows the code that was added.

The code was added to the active frame on a new Actions layer.

6. **Press Command-Return/Control-Enter to test the animation in the Flash Player window.**

The kayaker and photo animations play once and stop; however, the two movie clip animations continue to loop. It is important to note that the stop command does not stop movie clip animations that are placed on the current timeline.

Remember, movie clip timelines are independent of other movie clips and of the main timeline; you have to add the stop command to each symbol timeline to prevent them from looping.

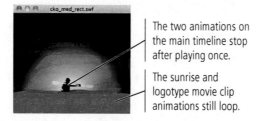

The two animations on the main timeline stop after playing once.

The sunrise and logotype movie clip animations still loop.

7. **Close the Flash Player window and return to Flash.**

8. **In the Library panel, double-click the sun_mc icon to enter into the symbol.**

9. **Select Frame 30 in the timeline, then double-click Stop at this Frame in the Code Snippets panel.**

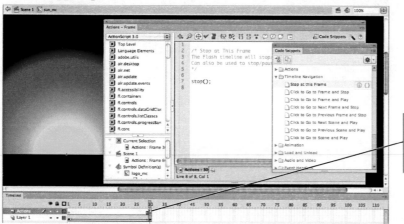

You are adding the Stop command to Frame 30 of the sun_mc symbol.

10. **In the Library panel, double-click the logo_mc symbol icon to enter into that symbol.**

When you use the Library panel to enter into a symbol, you don't need to return to the main movie Stage before entering into a different symbol. You can simply double-click the symbol icons to navigate from one symbol to another.

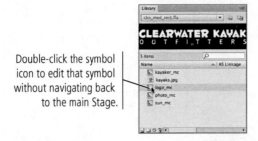

Double-click the symbol icon to edit that symbol without navigating back to the main Stage.

11. **Select Frame 60 in the timeline, then double-click Stop at this Frame in the Code Snippets panel.**

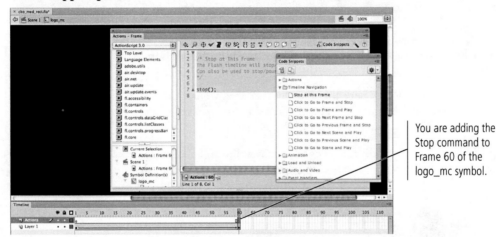

You are adding the Stop command to Frame 60 of the logo_mc symbol.

12. **Click Scene 1 in the Edit bar to return to the main Stage.**

13. **Press Command-Return/Control-Enter to test the movie in Flash Player.**

All four animations now play once and stop.

14. **Close the Flash Player window and return to Flash.**

15. **Save the file and continue to the next stage of the project.**

Stage 2 Working with Text

One of the more frustrating aspects of Web design is working with text elements; this is because the appearance of type is sometimes dependent on the available fonts on a user's computer. Flash movies are not subject to this limitation because used fonts can be embedded in the exported SWF file; you can use any font in a Flash file, and it will appear exactly as expected in the movie as long as it is embedded.

To do this, you can use the Properties panel Text Engine menu to create a Classic Text object. In this case, you create one of three specific types of text object:

- **Static text** is placed, kerned, aligned, and manually edited with the Text tool. This type of text does not change.

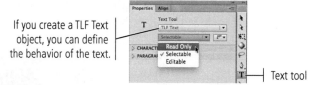

If you create a Classic Text object, you can also define the type of text.

Text tool

- **Dynamic text** is basically an area into which information can be read; this type of text object can be named and addressed by code, which means the content can be changed as the result of a certain action.

- **Input text** is a field in which users can type to submit information (as in an online form).

Flash CS6 also supports Text Layout Framework (TLF) text, which makes it very easy to add text to a movie by clicking and dragging with the Text tool. You have a wide range of formatting options that define the behavior of the frame, as well as the appearance of text within the frame. Using TLF text, you don't need to specify whether the object is static or dynamic. Rather, you can determine whether text in the area is Read-Only, Selectable, or Editable.

If you create a TLF Text object, you can define the behavior of the text.

Text tool

CREATE A NEW TEXT OBJECT

Your client wants a very simple text message added to the top of the ad. The message shouldn't appear until halfway through the animation, so you will again use blank keyframes to prevent the message from appearing until it should.

1. **With `cko_med_rect.fla` open in Flash, choose View>Magnification>Fit in Window.**

2. **Add a new layer named `Text` above the Logotype layer. Select the Text layer as the active layer.**

3. **Control/right-click Frame 37 on the Text layer and choose Insert Blank Keyframe in the contextual menu.**

    You are going to add the text object to this new blank keyframe. On Frames 1–36, the layer remains empty.

4. **Choose the Text tool in the Tools panel.**

5. **At the top of the Properties panel, choose TLF Text in the Text Engine menu and choose Read Only in the Text Type menu.**

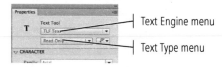

Text Engine menu

Text Type menu

6. **In the Character section of the Properties panel:**

   - **Change the Family menu to a sans-serif font such as Arial or Helvetica.**

   - **Choose a Bold, Black, or Heavy variation of the selected font in the Style menu.**

   - **Click the current Size link to access the field. Type 24 in the field and press Return/Enter.**

   - **Make sure the Leading menu is set to % and change the associated value to 90.**

   - **Click the Color swatch to open the Swatches panel. Choose white (#FFFFFF) as the text color, and make sure the Alpha value is 100%.**

   - **Choose Readability in the Anti-Alias menu.**

7. **In the Paragraph section of the Properties panel, click the Align to End option.**

   Any formatting you define before clicking with the Text tool will be applied in the new text area.

8. **Click near the top-left corner of the Stage and drag to create a rectangular text area in the top half of the Stage.**

   To include text in a movie, you first have to create an area to hold the text characters. As you drag, notice that dragging affects only the width of the rectangle. The area's minimum height is determined by the currently defined text formatting options.

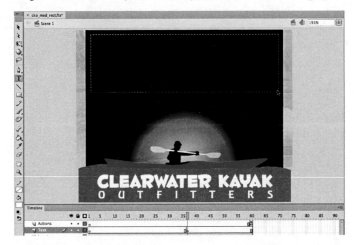

   When you release the mouse button, the text area appears as a white box. When the insertion point is flashing, you can type in the box to add text.

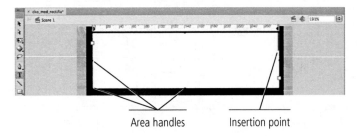

   Area handles   Insertion point

9. **Type** Adventure Awaits!.

The text appears in the text area you just created, using the character and paragraph formatting options that you already defined. (Because you chose white as the text color, the text appears gray in the area so you can see it as you type.)

10. **Choose the Selection tool, and then expand the Position and Size options in the Properties panel. Make sure the Constrain icon to the left of the W and H fields is broken, then change the properties of the selected text area to:**

X: 10	**Y: 10**
W: 280	**H: 50**

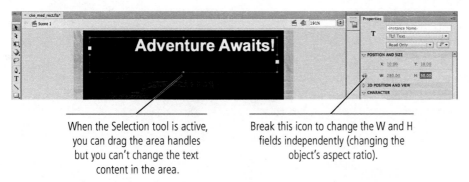

When the Selection tool is active, you can drag the area handles but you can't change the text content in the area.

Break this icon to change the W and H fields independently (changing the object's aspect ratio).

Using the Position and Size properties, you can define specific numeric parameters for the area. You can also reposition a text area by clicking inside the area with the Selection tool and dragging to a new location, or resize the area by dragging any of the handles that appear on the outside edges of the object.

11. **In the Character section of the Properties panel, change the Size value to 40.**

When a text area is selected, changes to character and paragraph formatting apply to all text inside the area. You can change the formatting of only certain characters by highlighting the target characters with the Text tool before making changes in the Properties panel.

Overset text icon

The red plus sign icon (called the **overset text icon**) on the bottom-right corner of the area indicates that more text exists than will fit into the defined space. You can either change the size of the area to accommodate all of the text, or click the overset text icon to "load" the cursor with the rest of the text; once loaded with the overset text, clicking again on the Stage creates a second linked text area to contain the overset text.

12. **Click the bottom-center handle of the text area and drag down until all of the text is visible.**

    When you drag a text area handle with the Selection tool, text formatting is not affected.

Click the handle and drag down
to change the area height.

13. **Click away from the text area to deselect it.**

14. **Save the file and continue to the next exercise.**

Controlling Text Properties

FLASH FOUNDATIONS

A number of text formatting options are available in the Properties panel when the Text tool is active and TLF text is selected in the Text Engine menu. (If you create a Classic Text object, many of these options are not available.)

Character Options

- **Family and Style menus.** As with any computer application, the font defines the appearance of the text. The entire list of fonts installed on your machine appears in the Family menu. The Style menu lists available variants of the selected font (Bold, Italic, etc.).

- **Embed button.** This button allows you to embed selected fonts or specific characters to ensure that text will appear on users' computers in the font you define.

- **Size.** The size of the text (in points) can be changed in the Font Size field or selected from the menu.

- **Leading.** This defines the distance between the bottom of one line of text and the bottom of the next line of text. You can define leading based on a percentage of the applied type size, or using a specific value.

- **Color.** This swatch changes the fill color of selected characters.

- **Letter Spacing (Tracking) field.** This option is used to increase or decrease the spacing between a selected range of characters.

- **Highlight.** This swatch defines the color immediately behind the selected text.

- **Auto Kern check box.** You can uncheck this option to prevent Flash from applying a font's default kerning values in static text.

- **Anti-aliasing menu.** This menu determines the level of anti-aliasing applied (if any).

- **Rotation menu.** This option changes the orientation of text within the area.

- **Type Style buttons.** These buttons change the style of text to (from left) underlined, ~~strikethrough~~, superscript (such as the TH in 4th), and subscript (the 2 in H_2O).

Paragraph Options

- **Paragraph Alignment buttons.** Text can be aligned to the start (left), center, or end (right) of its containing area, or it can be justified so all lines fill the available horizontal space. If you use the Justify options on the right, you can also determine how the last line in the paragraph is formatted (start, centered, end, or forced to fill the horizontal space).

- **Margins.** These options define how far text is placed from the left and right edges of the containing area.

- **Indent.** This option defines how far the first line of the paragraph is indented from the left edge of the remaining text in the same paragraph.

- **Spacing.** These options define how much space is added above or below each paragraph.

- **Text Justify.** When using justified paragraph alignment, this menu determines how extra space is distributed: between individual letters or only between words.

FLASH FOUNDATIONS

When an existing text area is selected, other options become available for controlling the selected text.

Advanced Character Options

- **Link.** If you want selected text to act as a hyperlink, you can type the destination URL in this field.

- **Target.** This menu defines where the hyperlink target will open: in the same browser window (_self), in a new blank browser window (_blank), in the parent container of the SWF file (_parent), or in the main browser window that contains the frame with the link (_top).

- **Case.** This menu can be used to change text to all UPPER CASE, all lower case, or SMALL CAPS.

- **Digit Case.** This option can be used to apply Lining or Old Style character glyphs in place of regular numbers (if those options exist in the applied font).

- **Digit Width.** This option controls the horizontal spacing of number characters. Tabular forces all digits to occupy the same amount of space. Proportional allows each number to occupy only the space that is required for the digit shape.

- **Ligatures.** This option can be used to control the replacement of select character pairs (for example, fl or ff) with a single-character representation of those letters.

- **Break.** This menu can be used to force each selected character onto a new line (All), allow text to break naturally where necessary (Any), or prevent selected text from breaking across multiple lines (No Break).

- **Baseline Shift.** This option raises selected characters away from the invisible line on which the bottoms of characters rest.

- **Locale.** This menu defines the language that is used for selected text.

Container and Flow Options

- **Behavior.** This menu can force text to only a Single Line of text, in which all text appears on one line regardless of return characters; display Multiline wrapped text in which text will reflow in the container if you change its width; or Multiline No Wrap text, in which new lines require pressing Return/Enter as you type.

- **Max Chars.** If you define the text type as Editable, you can use this value to limit how much text can be typed in an area.

- **Columns.** You can use this option to create multiple columns in a single text area. If you use multiple columns, you can also define the gutter width, or the space between columns.

- **Padding.** These fields define how far text is placed from the edge of the containing area (sometimes called text inset, especially in applications such as Adobe InDesign).

- **Border Color** and **Background Color.** These swatches can be used to apply different colors to the text area.

- **1st Line Offset.** This menu can be used to adjust the position of the first line of text in the area, either by a specific distance or based on attributes of the applied font and formatting (Ascent and Line Height).

🖐 DEFINE FONT EMBEDDING

When you use text in a movie, the fonts you use must be available to other users who open your file. If not, the users' systems will substitute some font that is available — which can significantly change the appearance of your movie. To solve this potential problem, you can embed fonts into your movies so the required fonts are always available.

1. With `cko_med_rect.fla` open, select the Text tool.

2. Click inside the heading text area to place the insertion point and reveal the formatting for that area.

3. **In the Character section of the Properties panel, click the Embed button.**

This button opens the Font Embedding dialog box. The currently applied font is automatically selected in the Family and Style menus.

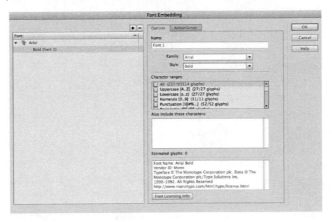

Note:

Keep in mind that embedding fonts adds to the resulting file size and increases the download time of Flash movies. The font outline (embedded character) is stored as part of the SWF file, so repeatedly using the same character of the same font in the movie does not increase the file size (the same theory as using instances of symbols). Keeping the number of fonts in a movie to a minimum ensures a faster-loading movie.

4. **Change the Name field to** `Heading Font`.

5. **In the Character Ranges list, check the Uppercase, Lowercase, and Punctuation options.**

Remember, embedding characters from fonts increases the resulting file size. You know only letters and punctuation were used in this document, so you can limit the embedded characters to only these ranges rather than embedding every possible character of the font.

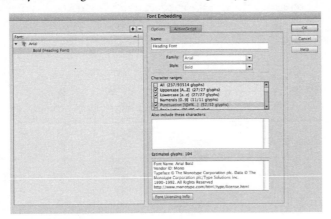

Note:

The item on the left side of the dialog box won't reflect the new name until you click away from the Name field.

6. **Click OK to close the dialog box.**

7. **Review the Library panel.**

When you embed a font into the file, it is added to the file's library.

The embedded font is added to the file's library.

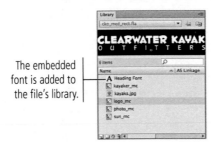

8. **Press Command-Return/Control-Enter to test the file in the Flash Player.**

9. **Read the resulting warning, then click OK.**

When you use TLF text in a file, it requires an external file called a Runtime Shared Library (RSL). Flash warns you about the issue when you test a file containing TLF text.

An RSL stores assets that are common to multiple files. Other SWF files can all refer to the external RSL file, so the common assets don't need to be separately embedded in each SWF file. The RSL is downloaded once, and multiple SWFs can then refer to those shared assets without the need to constantly re-download the same assets. This allows SWF files to be smaller and more efficient.

When the SWF file runs, it first looks for the RSL on the local machine, then on the Adobe.com Web site, then in its own directory on the host server. In many cases, the download process for RSLs is virtually transparent. However, on devices that don't already have the RSL available (cached), users might be prompted to allow the SWF file Internet access to download the file from Adobe's site.

You can avoid this issue by embedding the RSL directly into your SWF file, which means it will automatically be available as soon as the SWF file is run. This does increase the file size, though, so you should carefully weigh your options and requirements before embedding the RSL into each SWF file.

10. **Click OK to dismiss the warning message.**

When the movie ends, you might notice a problem — the white text is difficult to read when the image is entirely opaque. You will solve this problem in the next exercise.

11. **Close the Flash Player window and return to Flash.**

12. **Save the file and continue to the next exercise.**

CONTROL OBJECT STACKING ORDER

It is not uncommon for designers to use individual layers for every single object in the file — which makes things much easier to find as long as you use descriptive layer names.

You should also understand, however, that stacking order applies to multiple objects that are created on the same layer. Drawing objects and symbols exist from bottom to top in the order they were created *on a single layer*. It is easy to create something in the wrong order, but fortunately, Flash makes it relatively easy to rearrange the stack.

Note:

Merge-drawing shapes are always created at the back of the stacking order, behind any other objects on the layer (symbol instances, object-drawing shapes, type areas, etc.).

1. **With cko_med_rect.fla open, select Frame 37 of the Text layer.**

2. **Choose the Rectangle tool, and make sure Object-Drawing mode is active.**

3. **In the Color panel, change the Stroke color to None. Open the Fill color palette and choose the white-to-black linear gradient swatch.**

4. **Click the left gradient stop to select it, then change the Alpha value to 0%.**

5. **Click the right gradient stop to select it, and drag it to the 50% point along the gradient. Change the stop color to #000033, and change the Alpha value to 50%.**

The Rectangle tool is active.

Object-drawing mode is toggled on.

Frame 37 of the Text layer is active.

Set the left gradient stop to 0% Alpha.

Move the right gradient stop to the middle of the gradient. Set it to #000033, 50% Alpha.

6. **With Frame 37 of the Text layer selected, click and drag to create an object that fills the top half of the Stage.**

The gradient defaults to fill the object from left to right.

The gradient goes from entirely transparent to 50% transparent (the Alpha value of each stop on the gradient).

7. **Choose the Gradient Transform tool in the Tools panel, then click the gradient-filled rectangle to reveal the gradient-editing handles.**

Gradient Transform tool

Rotation handle

Width handle

8. **Rotate the gradient 90° counterclockwise, then use the gradient width handle to make the gradient the same size as the object's height.**

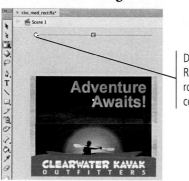

Drag the Gradient Rotate handle to rotate the gradient 90° counterclockwise...

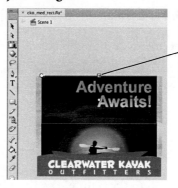

... then drag the Gradient Width handle down until the gradient width is the same as the shape height.

9. **Using the Selection tool, select the gradient-filled rectangle.**

As you can see, the gradient-filled shape is currently on top of the text object. You want the text to appear on top of the gradient, so you need to rearrange the object stacking order.

10. **Choose Modify>Arrange>Send to Back.**

Options in the Modify>Arrange submenu control the stacking order of objects on the active layer. These options have no effect on the relative stacking of objects on different layers.

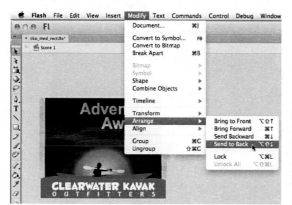

By placing the gradient-filled rectangle behind the text object but in front of the underlying layers, the white text will be more easily visible when the background photo is entirely visible at the end of the animation.

11. **Save the file and continue to the next stage of the project.**

Stage 3 **Working with a Flash Project**

The first ad required for this project is now complete. However, the entire job calls for three versions of the same ad, using different standard ad sizes but the same content in each ad. Rather than simply creating a new file and then copying the existing content into it, you can use the Project panel to define a new project, which will allow you to share assets across multiple files.

 CREATE A FLASH PROJECT

The Flash Project panel provides an easy interface through which you can share assets across multiple Flash files. This is useful whenever you need to make multiple versions of the same movie, whether it is a series of ads that will be placed on the Internet, or an application interface that you need to optimize for multiple different devices.

1. With **cko_med_rect.fla** open, open the Project panel (Window>Project).

2. Open the Projects menu and choose New Project.

3. In the resulting dialog box, type **Kayak Ads** in the Project Name field.

4. Click the Folder icon to the right of the Root Folder field to open a navigation dialog box.

    You can't drag this navigation box away from the panel; if necessary enlarge the Project panel until you can see the dialog box.

    The root folder is the folder on your computer that contains (or will contain) the files that are part of the project.

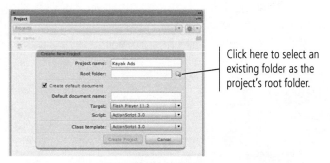

Click here to select an existing folder as the project's root folder.

5. **Macintosh: In the Choose a Folder dialog box, navigate to your WIP>Kayaks folder and click Choose.**

    Windows: In the Browse for Folder dialog box, navigate to your WIP>Kayaks folder and click OK.

Macintosh

Windows

6. **In the Create New Project dialog box, uncheck the Create Default Document option.**

When Create Default Document is checked, Flash automatically generates a new file that will be placed in the defined root folder. In this case, you already have a file that you want to include in the project, and you will create other files based on the existing ad; you don't need to check this option.

Uncheck this option.

7. **Click Create Project.**

When the process is complete, all Flash files in the WIP>Kayaks folder appear in the Projects panel. The tab for the open document now shows that the open file is part of the Kayak Ads project file. The AuthortimeSharedAssets.fla file stores assets that you want to share across multiple files.

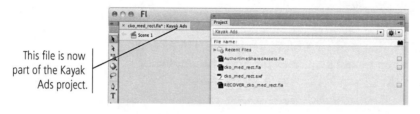

This file is now part of the Kayak Ads project.

Note:

The SWF file is the result of testing the file in the Flash Player window. You will overwrite it later when you publish your files.

8. **Open the Library panel for the active file.**

When a file is part of a Flash Project, the Library panel includes an option to share specific symbols.

9. **Check the Link option for all four symbols in the file.**

After you check an item, you might notice a brief "Saving" message. When you opt to share a symbol, that symbol is copied into the AuthortimeSharedAssets.fla file; any changes you make to the symbol are actually made inside that authortime file, and then propagated out to placed instances in all files within the project.

You do not need to share all symbols in every project file. In this case, however, you do want all pieces of the ad to be the same in all versions, so you are sharing all four symbols.

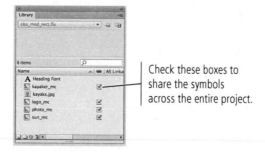

Check these boxes to share the symbols across the entire project.

10. **Save the file, then continue to the next exercise.**

SCALE CONTENT TO DOCUMENT PROPERTIES

To complete the entire assignment, you need two more versions of the ad: one is a slightly larger rectangle size (336 × 280 px), and one is a 250 × 250-pixel square.

You could use the New Document dialog box to create the file using the built-in templates, then copy and paste all of the necessary content from one file to another. However, that process is time-consuming and introduces the potential for error since you need to copy the entire timeline as well as the objects on the Stage.

In this exercise, you will use the existing file as the basis for the other two files.

1. **With `cko_med_rect.fla` open, make sure nothing is selected on the Stage and the Selection tool is active.**

2. **In the Properties panel, click the Edit Document Properties button.**

With nothing selected on the Stage, click here to open the Document Settings dialog box.

3. **In the resulting dialog box, change the Width dimension to 336 px and change the Height dimension to 280 px. Check the Scale Content with Stage option, then click OK.**

Make sure this option is checked.

Because the new file dimensions have the same width-to-height aspect ratio (6:5), the objects in the new file are easily scaled up, and require no further manipulation to function properly. By using the existing file as the basis of the new one, the Scale Content with Stage option made the entire process possible in only a few clicks.

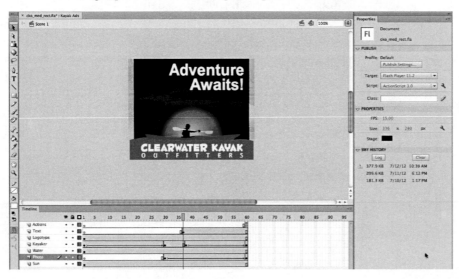

4. **Save the file as `cko_lg_rect.fla` in your WIP>Kayaks folder.**

   Because you saved the file in the defined root folder of the Kayak Ads project, the new file should now appear in the Project panel as part of the project file.

5. **If you don't see the new file in the Project panel, open the panel Options menu and choose Refresh.**

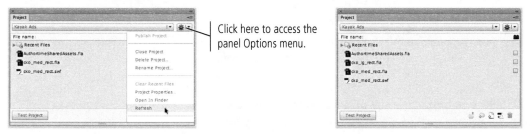

Click here to access the panel Options menu.

6. **Save and close the Flash file, then continue to the next exercise.**

MANUALLY ADJUST CONTENT TO DOCUMENT PROPERTIES

In the last exercise, you created a new file by adjusting the document properties of an existing file, allowing Flash to scale objects as necessary to meet the new document size. Because the new file size had the same aspect ratio, you did not need to make any further changes other than saving the file with a new name.

In many cases, the new file size will not have the same aspect ratio as the original. In this situation, you will have to make some manual adjustments to keep the content in the same general position as in the original.

1. **In the Project panel, double-click `cko_med_rect.fla` to open that file.**

   You can use the Project panel to open any file in the active project.

2. **With `cko_med_rect.fla` open, deselect everything on the Stage and then click the Edit Document Properties button in the Properties panel.**

3. **In the resulting dialog box, change the Width and Height dimensions to 250 px. Check the Scale Content with Stage option, then click OK.**

   In this case, the new file does not use the same aspect ratio as the original. As you can see, Flash is not able to interpret the necessary positions of all elements in the file. Although this is a good start, you still need to make some adjustments manually.

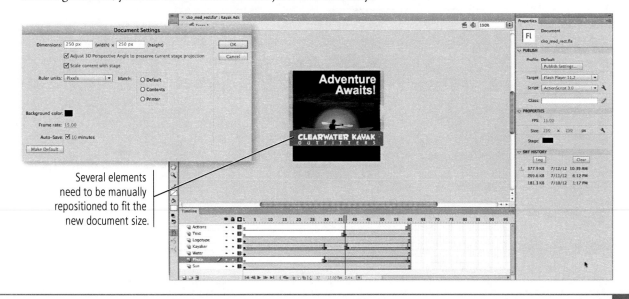

Several elements need to be manually repositioned to fit the new document size.

4. **Save the file as `cko_square.fla` in your WIP>Kayaks folder.**

   By immediately saving the new file with a different name, you avoid accidentally changing something in the wrong file.

5. **Click Frame 1 in the timeline to move the playhead to the beginning of the movie.**

6. **In the Timeline panel, Command/Control-click to select the Logotype, Kayaker, Water, and Sun layers.**

   You need to move the content on all four of these layers down to the bottom of the adjusted Stage. You don't want to move the Photo layer content because you want it to remain attached to the top of the Stage.

7. **Using the Selection tool, click any of the selected objects on the Stage, press Shift, and drag down until the water aligns with the bottom of the Stage.**

   By moving the content on all four layers at once, you maintain the same relative positions between the selected objects.

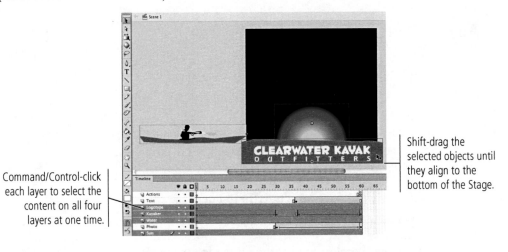

Command/Control-click each layer to select the content on all four layers at one time.

Shift-drag the selected objects until they align to the bottom of the Stage.

8. **Press Return/Enter to play the movie on the Stage.**

   You should notice the kayaker symbol instance moves up and away from the water as the playhead progresses. If you review the timeline, remember that this layer has four separate keyframes, each of which define a specific position in a classic tween. To keep the kayaker paddling straight across the Stage, you have to change the instance's position on each keyframe in the layer.

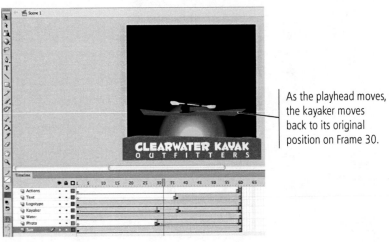

As the playhead moves, the kayaker moves back to its original position on Frame 30.

9. **Return the playhead to Frame 1 on the timeline, then click the kayaker symbol instance to select it.**

10. In the Properties panel, note the instance's Y position.

In our example, the Y position is 193.90. If yours is different, you should use the exact value from your file in the following steps. The point is to make the instance's Y (vertical) position consistent in all keyframes.

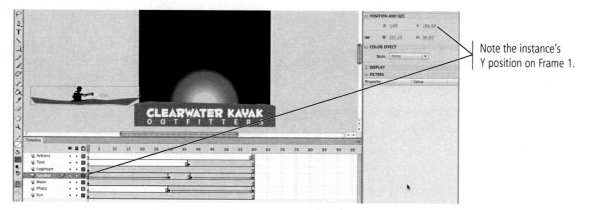

Note the instance's Y position on Frame 1.

11. Click Frame 30 of the Kayaker layer, then click the symbol instance on the Stage to select it.

12. In the Properties panel, change the Y position to the same value you noted in Step 10.

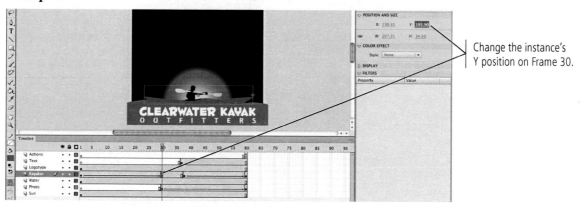

Change the instance's Y position on Frame 30.

13. Repeat Steps 11–12 for the two remaining keyframes on the Kayaker layer.

When you get to Frame 60, you should notice another problem — the photo no longer fills the background area. (This was harder to see when the image was entirely or semitransparent). You now need to adjust the photo to fill the space.

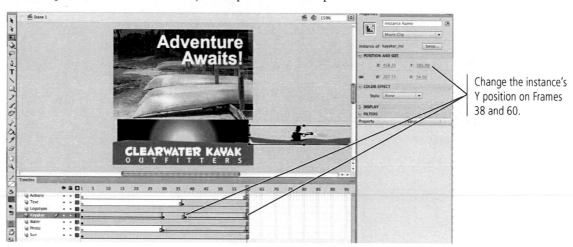

Change the instance's Y position on Frames 38 and 60.

14. **Select Frame 30 on the Photo layer, then select the symbol instance on the Stage.**

    The first keyframe (Frame 1) on the Photo layer is blank; the image doesn't exist on that frame, so you don't need to edit that keyframe.

    Remember, this image is actually an instance of a symbol, which you created from the original bitmap image.

15. **Choose the Free Transform tool, then move the transformation point of the instance to the top center handle.**

16. **Using the Transform panel, scale the instance proportionally until the bottom edge is just hidden by the top edge of the water shape.**

    Be careful when you scale bitmap images, especially making them larger. Bitmap images have a fixed resolution, which means enlarging them can significantly reduce the quality.

    If you remember the first part of this project, you actually reduced the image before creating the symbol instance. Enlarging this particular instance above 100% still keeps the image smaller than the original bitmap's physical dimensions, so you should not see any significant lack of quality in this case.

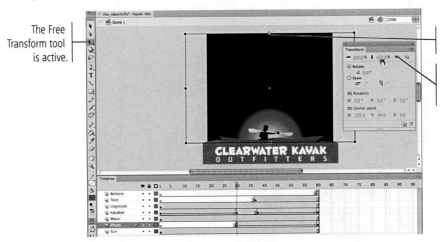

The Free Transform tool is active.

Move the transformation point to this handle.

Make sure this chain is linked to scale the instance proportionally.

17. **Repeat Steps 14–16 for the instance on the Frame 60 keyframe.**

    You should apply the exact same transformation on Frame 60 as you did on Frame 30. Rather than scrubbing the values in the Transform panel, you can click one of the existing values to enter the field, constrain the two dimensions, and then type the exact same value that you applied in Step 16.

18. **Save the file and continue to the next exercise.**

EDIT A SHARED SYMBOL

As we explained earlier, changes in shared symbols propagate to all instances in the project's files — one of the benefits to using the Project panel. In this exercise, you will edit a shared symbol in the project file so the change is applied to every instance in any file in the project.

1. **With cko_square.fla open, double-click the kayaker_mc symbol icon in the Library panel to edit that symbol.**

   The symbol Stage reflects the defined background color of the open file; as you can see, it is difficult to see the black shape of the kayaker's body against the black background. You are going to change the shape's color to be more easily visible against the background.

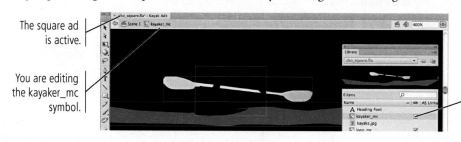

The square ad is active.

You are editing the kayaker_mc symbol.

The Link option is active for all four symbols in the file.

2. **Using the Selection tool, click away from all objects on the Stage to deselect them, then click the shape of the kayaker's body to select it.**

3. **Using the Properties or Color panel, change the Fill and Stroke colors of the selected drawing object to #666666.**

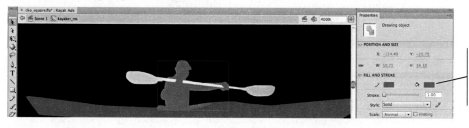

Change the Fill and Stroke colors of the selected drawing object.

4. **Click Scene 1 in the Edit bar to return to the main Stage.**

5. **Save the file and close it.**

6. **In the Project panel, double-click the cko_med_rect.fla file to open it.**

   Remember, earlier you checked the Link option for the kayaker_mc symbol, which means it is a shared asset in the entire project. The kayaker_mc symbol instance in the medium rectangle ad now shows the same change that you made when the square ad file was open.

The symbol instance is changed in the medium rectangle ad as well.

7. **Save the active file, than continue to the next exercise.**

   You do not have to open each project file for the changes to apply. When you publish the files in the next exercise, you will see the same change in the large rectangle ad.

PUBLISH THE AD FILES

Exporting a document refers to publishing it in a form that can be viewed in another application. The File>Export menu has three options: Export Image, Export Selection, and Export Movie.

- If you choose **Export Image**, you can save your file as a static graphic (with no animation) in formats such as GIF or JPEG.

- **Export Selection** saves the active selection as a Flash XML Graphics (FXG) file, which is an XML-based graphics file format for vector graphics.

- **Export Movie** allows you to create a file (or sequence of files) that includes animation, which can be placed into an HTML document created in another application. A number of formats are available in the Format/ Save As Type menu. Each format has distinct uses, advantages, and disadvantages.

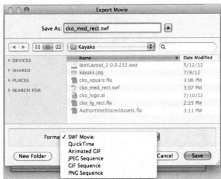

  - **SWF Movie.** A Flash movie file can be placed into an HTML file, or it can be used in another Flash application.

  - **QuickTime.** Selecting this option opens the Export QuickTime MOV dialog box, where you can set options such as dimensions, Stage color, last frame reached, time elapsed, and others.

  - **Animated GIF.** Files exported in this format preserve all the animations in a single file. You can specify various options, such as dots per inch (dpi), image area, colors, and animation for the resulting GIF file. Setting the dpi is the same as setting the dimensions of the image; the number of times the animation needs to repeat can also be defined (0 creates an endless loop).

  - **JPEG Sequence.** Selecting this option allows the file to be exported in the JPEG format. The Match Movie option matches the size of the exported file with that of the original document. When you use any of the sequence options, each frame of the movie is exported as a separate image.

  - **GIF Sequence.** This format exports the files in GIF format, except the files are generated in a sequence for each frame animation. The animated GIF format exports a single file that contains all of the animations; this option generates a sequence of files.

  - **PNG Sequence.** This option saves the files in the Portable Network Graphics (PNG) format, which supports transparency for objects that might need to be placed on various backgrounds. You can specify options such as dimension, resolution, colors, and filters.

  - **Windows AVI (Windows only).** This option exports the movie in the Windows format and results in huge file sizes. Choosing this option opens the Export Windows AVI dialog box, where you can set options such as dimensions and quality of the movie.

  - **WAV Audio (Windows only).** This option exports only the sound file from the current document. You can specify the sound frequency and format of the sound file (stereo, mono, etc.), as well as ignore event sounds if you don't want them in the exported file.

You can also use the Publish option (File>Publish) to generate a Flash SWF file, as well as a number of other formats. When you publish a file, the resulting output is based on the active options in the Publish Settings dialog box.

1. **With `cko_med_rect.fla` open, choose File>Publish Settings.**

   Rather than simply choose File>Publish, you are using this dialog box to first review the settings that will apply when you publish the files.

2. **In the Publish options on the left side of the Publish Settings dialog box, make sure the Flash (.swf) option is selected.**

3. **Uncheck all other options in the left side of the dialog box.**

   If the HTML Wrapper option is checked, the publish process also generates an HTML file that includes the necessary code for opening the SWF file in a browser window. Because these ads will be distributed for insertion into other sites, the HTML option is not necessary.

Note:

The Win Projector and Mac Projector options generate platform-specific executable applications, which can function without the Flash Player.

ActionScript Settings button

4. **At the top of the dialog box, click the ActionScript Settings button.**

5. **In the resulting Advanced ActionScript 3.0 Settings dialog box, make the Library Path options visible in the lower half of the dialog box.**

6. **Choose Merged into Code in the Default Linkage menu.**

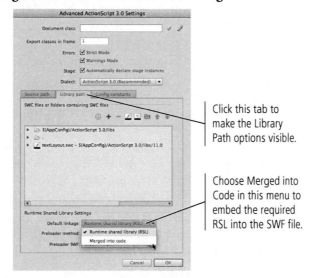

Click this tab to make the Library Path options visible.

Choose Merged into Code in this menu to embed the required RSL into the SWF file.

As we explained earlier, TLF text objects require an RSL file to function properly. To avoid problems with the file not being available, you are merging the RSL code directly into the published SWF file.

Keep in mind that this will significantly increase the size of each resulting SWF file; we are simply showing you how to embed the code for illustration purposes.

Understanding SWF Publish Settings

The Publish Settings dialog box (File>Publish Settings) contains all the necessary settings for publishing files from Flash.

- The **Profile** menu lists all available saved profiles, which save defined publish settings for easier access. You can use the attached Profile Options button to create, import, export, and manage saved profiles.

- The **Player** menu allows you to export the Flash movie to be compatible with an earlier version of the Flash Player, Adobe AIR 1.1, or various versions of Flash Lite.

- **Script** specifies which version of ActionScript (1, 2, or 3) is or will be used in the file. Clicking the ActionScript Settings button opens a dialog box where you can specify the path of an external ActionScript file.

The **Publish** list on the left side of the dialog box lists the available formats that can be exported; the Flash (.swf) and the HTML Wrapper formats are selected by default. When you click a specific format in the Publish list, options related to that format appear on the right side of the dialog box.

When **Flash (.swf)** is selected in the Publish list, options on the right side of the dialog box determine how the animation is exported.

- The **Output File** field shows the default file name, based on the FLA file name, that will be used for the exported file. By default, exported files are created in the same location as the FLA file you are exporting; you can click the folder icon next to a file name to specify a different publishing location. (This is available for all publishing formats.)

- **JPEG Quality** specifies the quality of exported JPEG images. Lower values result in smaller file sizes, but also lower image quality; as the quality increases, so does the size of the file. The **Enable JPEG Deblocking** option helps smooth the appearance of JPEG files with very high levels of compression.

- The **Audio Stream** and **Audio Event** options show the current sound export settings for stream and event sounds (respectively). Clicking either link opens the Sound Settings dialog box, where you can change the compression format, quality, and bit rate options for each type of sound.

(A streaming sound plays as soon as enough data is downloaded; the sound stops playing as soon as the movie stops. An event sound does not play until it downloads completely, and it continues to play until explicitly stopped.)

- If **Override Sound Settings** is checked, the default options in the Audio Stream and Audio Event settings override any settings that are defined for individual sound files in the file's library.

- **Export Device Sounds** allows you to export sounds for mobile devices, encoded in the device's native format rather than a standard format.

- **Compress Movie** reduces the size of the exported file, which also reduces download time. Compressed files can only be played in Flash Player 6 or later.

- **Include Hidden Layers** allows you to export hidden layer information in the exported file.

- **Include XMP Metadata** exports any metadata that is entered in the File Info dialog box (File>File Info).

- **Generate Size Report** creates a text file with information about the amount of data in the final Flash content.

- **Omit Trace Statements** allows Flash to ignore trace options, which are ActionScript functions that display the results of certain code in the Output panel.

- **Permit Debugging** allows you to debug your SWF file and allows other users to debug your SWF file remotely. You can also define a password, which other users will have to enter in order to debug the file.

- **Protect from Import** prevents others from importing your SWF file. This option also allows you to protect your SWF file with a password.

- **Password** is activated if you select the Protect from Import or the Permit Debugging option. You can specify a password that other users must enter in order to import the file or debug the movie.

- **Local Playback Security** options provide security for your application. If you select Access Local Files Only, your SWF file can interact only on the local machine. If you choose Access Network Only, your SWF file can communicate with resources only on the network and not on the local machine.

- **Hardware Acceleration** options can be used to speed up the graphics performance of the exported movie.

FLASH FOUNDATIONS

HTML Wrapper options relate to publishing a Flash document on the Web. In this case, you might need an HTML file that will embed your SWF file.

- The **Templates** menu contains various Flash templates in which an HTML file can be published. Selecting a template and then clicking the Info button shows a dialog box with information about the selected template.

- If you select **Detect Flash Version**, you can use the Version fields to define which is required. Detection code is embedded in the resulting file to determine if a user has the required version. If not, a link is provided to download the latest version of the Flash player. (Some templates do not support the Flash detection code.)

- The **Size** options define the dimensions of the resulting HTML file. You can choose Match Movie to use the size of the Flash Stage, or define specific width and height (in pixels or percent).

- The **Paused at Start** option keeps the SWF file from being played unless the user clicks to initiate the movie.

- The **Loop** option causes the Flash content to repeat after it reaches the final frame, so the movie plays in a continuous loop.

- The **Display Menu** option enables a shortcut when the user Control/right-clicks the SWF file in the browser. Deselecting this option shows only About Flash in the shortcut menu.

- Selecting the **Device Font** option displays users' system fonts instead of the fonts used in the SWF file, if those fonts are unavailable in the user's system.

- **Quality** specifies the quality of the SWF content embedded in the HTML file. Auto Low gives preference to document loading rather than quality, but also tries to improve the quality of the SWF file. Auto High treats loading and quality equally; when the loading speed is reduced, quality is compromised. The remaining three options are self-explanatory; lower quality settings mean higher compression, smaller file sizes, and faster download times.

- **Window Mode** sets the value of the wmode attribute in the object and embed HTML tags. Window does not embed window-related attributes in the HTML tags; the background of the Flash content is opaque. Opaque Windowless sets the background of the Flash content to opaque, which allows HTML content to appear on top of Flash content. Transparent Windowless sets the background of the Flash content to transparent.

- The **Show Warning Messages** option displays all warning and error messages whenever a setting for publishing the content is incorrect.

- **Scale** controls the display of Flash content when you change the dimension of the Flash content in the HTML file. Default (Show All) displays the entire document in the specified area. No Border fits the document in the specified area and maintains the quality of the SWF file by avoiding distortion. Exact Fit fits the entire SWF file in the specified area, but compromises the quality of the SWF file. No Scale prevents the Flash content from being scaled in the HTML file.

- **HTML Alignment** aligns the Flash content in the browser window. The Default option displays the SWF file in the center of the browser; you can also choose Left, Right, Top, or Bottom.

- **Flash Vertical and Horizontal Alignment** set the alignment of Flash content within the HTML file.

7. **Click OK to close the Advanced ActionScript 3.0 Settings dialog box, then click OK again to close the Publish Settings dialog box.**

8. **Save the open file (cko_med_rect.fla) and close it.**

9. **Repeat Steps 1–8 for the other two ad files in the project.**

   Publish settings are file-specific, so you have to define these options for each file that will be published.

10. **If you don't see all three ad files in the Project panel, choose Refresh in the panel Options menu.**

11. **In the Project panel, check the Publish Items boxes for the three ad files.**

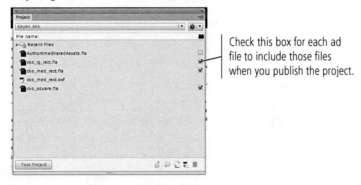

Check this box for each ad file to include those files when you publish the project.

12. **Open the panel Options menu and choose Publish Project.**

When the process is complete, all three SWF files now appear in the panel — one for each ad file you created.

13. **Close the Project panel.**

fill in the blank

1. A(n) _____ timeline functions independently of other symbols in the same file.

2. _____ are required when an object needs to change in some way at a given point in time.

3. The _____ can be used to scale an object proportionally with respect to the object's defined transformation point.

4. A(n) _____ can be used if you need to change an object's color over time.

5. A(n) _____ is identified by blue frames and an arrow in the timeline.

6. _____ is simple text that does not change.

7. _____ is essentially a text area that can be populated with the contents of an external file.

8. _____ solves the potential problem of used fonts not being available on a user's computer.

9. The _____ option allows you to change objects' size based on the edited document settings.

10. _____ is the default extension for exported file movies.

short answer

1. Briefly explain how a movie clip symbol relates to the primary timeline of a file.

2. Briefly explain one method for creating multiple versions of the same file, with different file sizes.

3. Briefly explain the purpose of the AuthortimeSharedAssets.fla file in a Flash project.

Use what you learned in this project to complete the following freeform exercise.
Carefully read the art director and client comments, then create your own design to meet the needs of the project.
Use the space below to sketch ideas; when finished, write a brief explanation of your reasoning behind your final design.

art director comments

Our agency has been hired to create a series of animated videos explaining scientific principles for children.

To complete this project, you should:

❑ Research the topics you are going to model and determine what (if any) data will be required to create a scientifically accurate illustration.

❑ Create or locate images or graphics that will result in a "kid-friendly" learning experience.

❑ Develop the animations so they can be placed into an existing Web site, using a 600 × 800 file size.

client comments

We would like you to create a series of videos over the next year (as the grant funds become available). The first one we want is an illustration of gravity. We're not entirely sure how it should look or function. We kind of like the legend of Isaac Newton sitting under an apple tree, when an apple fell on his head. If you could figure out how to make that work, great. If not, we're happy to consider other solutions.

As more funds become available, we're also going to want movies to illustrate other scientific principles. Our current list includes tectonic plate movement, tidal patterns, volcanic eruptions, and friction.

It will be easier to secure the secondary grants for later projects if we can include a specific plan for the different programs. Once you finish the gravity illustration (which we already have the money for), can you sketch out plans for at least two others?

project justification

_____
_____
_____
_____
_____
_____
_____
_____
_____
_____
_____
_____
_____
_____

The ability to control object shape and movement is one of the most important functions in designing animations. In this project, you used a number of basic techniques for animating object properties, including size, color, and position. As you complete the next projects in this book, you will expand on the knowledge from this chapter, learning new ways to animate multiple properties at once. The skills and knowledge from this project, however, apply to any animation — understanding frame rate, keyframes, and timeline independence are essential to being a successful animator.

This project also introduced the concept of adding text to a movie. Many Flash projects will involve some text, even if that text is eventually converted into drawing objects; you now know how to create and format text to communicate a client's message directly within a Flash file.

Finally, you learned techniques for creating multiple variations of the same file, using built-in tools to automate as much of the work as possible. These techniques and skills can be helpful whenever you need multiple versions of a single file — whether you need to create multiple different-sized ads or different versions for various mobile device sizes.

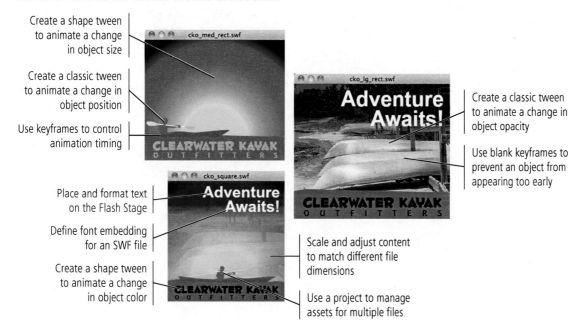

Create a shape tween to animate a change in object size

Create a classic tween to animate a change in object position

Use keyframes to control animation timing

Create a classic tween to animate a change in object opacity

Use blank keyframes to prevent an object from appearing too early

Place and format text on the Flash Stage

Define font embedding for an SWF file

Create a shape tween to animate a change in object color

Scale and adjust content to match different file dimensions

Use a project to manage assets for multiple files

Ocean Animation

Your client, Bay Ocean Preserve, wants to add an interactive animation to the kids' side of its Web site. As part of the Flash development team, your job is to build the required animations, and then add the necessary controls to make the buttons function as expected.

This project incorporates the following skills:

- ❏ Importing and managing artwork from Adobe Photoshop
- ❏ Importing symbols from external Flash file libraries
- ❏ Understanding the different types of Flash symbols
- ❏ Building frame-by-frame animations
- ❏ Creating motion tweens to animate various object properties
- ❏ Creating an animated armature
- ❏ Animating in three dimensions
- ❏ Preparing symbol instances for scripting
- ❏ Adding basic button controls to instances on the Stage

Our organization focuses on natural resource conservation and habitat preservation on the central California coast. This area is home to a number of endangered species, and we work to educate people about observing those creatures without interacting and interfering with them.

We've been told that some kind of interactivity will be an important part of capturing a younger audience. Although we think cartoon fish dancing across the screen would minimize the seriousness of our message, we understand that we have to do something to make the site more interesting for children.

We were thinking about an "aquarium" screen saver we used to have, and we thought that kind of thing would be a good balance between user interactivity and pointless arcade games.

Since the client clearly wants to avoid a cartoon look, I had the staff artist create some fish and other illustrations that are fairly realistic. I also found a good photo of a turtle that will work well with the other elements.

One of the animations — the swaying kelp forest — should play constantly, and will not be controlled by buttons.

Three animations will be controlled by the buttons. First, a fish hiding in a cave will blow bubbles. Second, a turtle will swim across the scene and get bigger, to create the effect of swimming closer. Finally, a school of different fish will swim in the other direction, in a "train" across the scene.

One other animation — the organization's logo — will play as soon as the file opens, and then not again until the entire file is reset.

The programming for this isn't very complicated, so you should be able to create it with Flash's built-in Code Snippets.

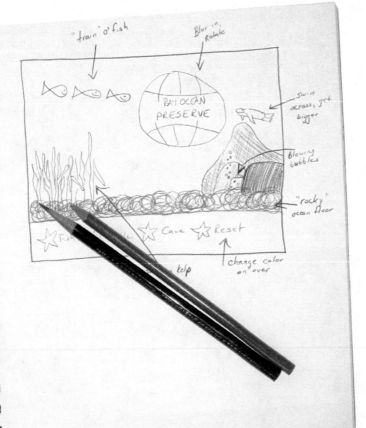

To complete this project, you will:

❏ Create symbols from imported Photoshop artwork

❏ Import symbols from other Flash files

❏ Place and manage instances of symbols on the Stage, and control the visual properties of those symbols

❏ Control timing using keyframes

❏ Create animated movie clip symbols

❏ Generate motion tweens to animate changes in object properties

❏ Use the Motion Editor to numerically control properties at specific points in time

❏ Animate a bone armature

❏ Animate an object in three-dimensional space

❏ Add interactivity to button symbols

Stage 1 **Importing Bitmaps and Symbols**

In this project, much of the artwork was created in Adobe Photoshop — a common workflow. It's important to understand that artwork from a Photoshop file is imported into Flash as bitmap objects, which are raster images that can result in large file sizes. Fortunately, the Flash symbol infrastructure means that objects in a file's library are downloaded only once; you can use multiple instances of a symbol without increasing overall file size.

You should also keep in mind that the quality of a bitmap object is defined by its resolution. Bitmap objects can typically be reduced in size, but enlarging them much beyond 100% could significantly reduce the image quality.

Finally, it's important to realize that Flash is designed to create files that will be viewed on a digital screen. Flash recognizes the actual number of pixels in a bitmap image rather than the defined pixels per inch (ppi). If you import a 3″ × 3″ bitmap image that is saved at 300 ppi (typical of print-quality images), that image is 900 pixels × 900 pixels high. In Flash, the image is still 900 pixels × 900 pixels, but those same pixels occupy 12.5″ at a typical screen resolution of 72 ppi.

IMPORT ADOBE PHOTOSHOP ARTWORK

Importing a Photoshop file to the Flash Stage is very similar to importing an Illustrator file. Because of the different nature of the two applications, however, you have fewer options when you work with Photoshop files.

1. **Download FL6_RF_Project4.zip from the Student Files Web page.**

2. **Expand the ZIP archive in your WIP folder (Macintosh) or copy the archive contents into your WIP folder (Windows).**

   This results in a folder named **Aquarium**, which contains the files you need for this project. You should also use this folder to save the files you create in this project.

3. **In Flash, create a new Flash document for ActionScript 3.0.**

4. **Choose File>Save. Save the file in your WIP>Aquarium folder as a Flash file named ocean.fla.**

5. **Open the Flash Preferences dialog box and click PSD File Importer in the list of categories.**

6. **Choose Lossless in the Compression menu at the bottom of the dialog box, and click OK.**

   When you import a Photoshop file, you can define the compression settings for each resulting bitmap object. By default, Flash applies lossy compression, which can create smaller file sizes but can also degrade the quality of resulting images. By changing the setting in the Preferences dialog box, you are changing the default setting that will be applied to all bitmap objects that are created when you import a Photoshop file to the Flash Stage. This means you won't have to change the option for individual objects.

> *Note:*
>
> *Learn more about Adobe Photoshop in the companion book of this series, **Adobe Photoshop CS6: The Professional Portfolio**.*

> *Note:*
>
> *Preferences are accessed in the Flash menu on Macintosh or the Edit menu on Windows.*

Choose Lossless in this menu.

7. **Choose File>Import>Import to Stage. Navigate to the file `ocean.psd` in your WIP>Aquarium folder and click Open/Import.**

8. **In the resulting dialog box, click the first item in the list of Photoshop layers, and then review the options on the right.**

   Flash recognizes individual layers in the native Photoshop file; objects on each individual layer will be imported as separate bitmap objects. For each layer/bitmap object, you can choose to automatically create a movie clip instance from the imported artwork.

Each layer in the Photoshop file will be imported as a separate bitmap object.

Layer groups are recognized, and can be maintained in the imported artwork.

If you select multiple layers in the list, you can merge those layers into a single bitmap object.

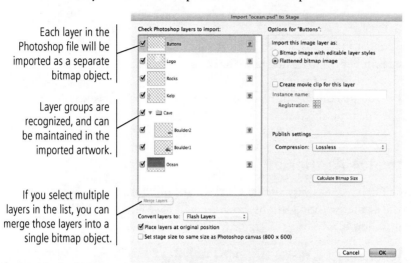

Note:

When artwork is created in Photoshop, each object that needs to be managed separately in Flash should be created on a separate Photoshop layer.

Photoshop File Import Preferences

You can define the default options for importing native Photoshop files in the PSD File Importer pane of the Preferences dialog box. (Remember, preferences are accessed in the Flash menu on Macintosh and in the Edit menu on Windows.) Most of these options will become clearer as you work through this project and learn more about the different types of symbols. In some cases, the options refer to specific features in the native application.

- The **Import Image Layers As** options determine whether applied layer styles are editable (if possible) in the Flash file. Photoshop layer styles include blending modes, drop shadows, beveling, and others.

- The **Import Text Layers As** options determine how Photoshop text layers are managed. These options are the same as the Import Text As options for importing Illustrator files. The default here, however, is to import Photoshop text layers as flattened bitmap images, which means you can't edit the text or the vector letter shapes.

- The **Import Shape Layers As** options determine how vector-based shape layers in the Photoshop file import into Flash. If you choose Editable Paths and Layer Styles, vector shapes in the Photoshop file are imported as vector paths; styles applied to the shape layer in Photoshop are imported as styles in the Flash file (if those styles are supported by Flash). If you choose Flattened Bitmap Images, Photoshop shape layers are flattened in Flash, which means you cannot access or edit the vector information within the Flash file.

- **Layer Groups** and **Merged Bitmaps** in the native Photoshop file can be automatically converted to a single movie clip if these options are checked.

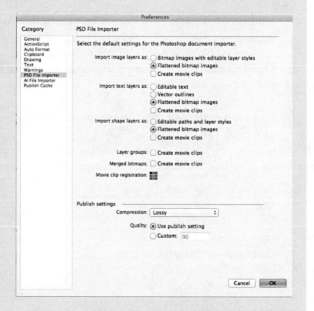

- **Movie Clip Registration** defines the default registration options for any objects you import as movie clip symbols.

- **Publish Settings** defines the type of compression applied and the quality of the resulting files.

FLASH FOUNDATIONS

9. **Click the Cave item in the list of layers and review the options.**

   If a Photoshop file includes a layer group, the group is recognized in the Import dialog box. You can choose to create a single movie clip from the entire layer group, and name the instance that is placed on the stage.

10. **Check the Create Movie Clip for this Layer option. In the Instance Name field, type cave_mc, and choose the bottom-right registration option.**

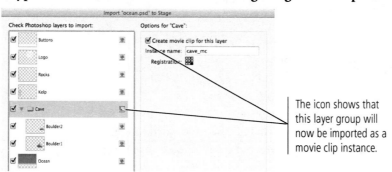

The icon shows that this layer group will now be imported as a movie clip instance.

Note:

If you don't choose the Create Movie Clip option, the layer group is maintained in the imported artwork as a layer group in the Flash timeline.

11. **Make sure Flash Layers is selected in the Convert Layers To menu. Check the options to place layers at their original position, and to set the stage size to match the Photoshop canvas.**

    These options have the same general purpose as the similar options when you import a native Illustrator file. (The Photoshop document area is called the canvas; the Illustrator document area is an artboard.)

12. **Click OK to complete the import process, and review the results.**

    If you had not chosen to make a movie clip instance from the layer group, those layers would have been imported as a layer group in the Flash timeline. The default Layer 1 from the original file is maintained at the bottom of the layer stack.

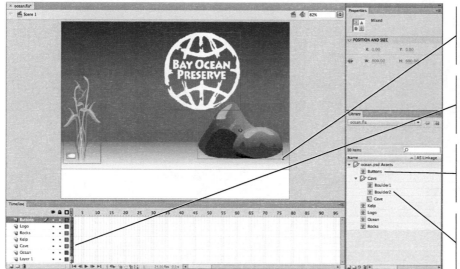

The symbol registration point indicates that this object is an instance of a movie clip symbol.

Because you created a movie clip instance from the layer group, only one layer is created to contain the instance.

Each resulting bitmap exists inside a folder that is named based on the imported Photoshop file.

Objects from the Cave layer group are nested in a folder that is named based on the layer group name.

13. **Select Layer 1 and click the Delete button at the bottom of the Timeline panel.**

14. **Save the file and continue to the next exercise.**

COPY ASSETS FROM EXTERNAL LIBRARIES

When objects already exist in a Flash file, it is a fairly simple process to copy them from one file to another. If both files are open, you can simply copy a symbol instance from the Stage of one file and paste it into the Stage of the other file; the necessary assets are automatically pasted into the library of the second file. You can also simply open the Library panel of an external file, which enables you to access the assets in that library without opening the second file's Stage.

1. **With `ocean.fla` open, choose File>Open. Navigate to `creatures.fla` (in the WIP>Aquarium folder) and click Open.**

   When more than one file is open, each file is represented by a tab at the top of the document window. You can click any document tab to make that file active.

2. **In the Library panel, Shift-click to select the Fish1, Fish2, and Turtle items in the library. Control/right-click one of the selected items and choose Copy from the contextual menu.**

Note:

Press Shift to select multiple consecutive items in a dialog box or panel. Press Command/Control to select multiple non-contiguous items.

The document tabs show that there are two open files.

The Library panel shows the library for the currently active file.

3. **Click the Library menu at the top of the Library panel and choose ocean.fla to display that file's library.**

Use this menu to switch between the libraries of all open files.

4. **Control/right-click the empty area at the bottom of the Library panel (below the existing assets) and choose Paste from the contextual menu.**

   The Air bitmap item is also pasted because it is used in the Fish2 movie clip.

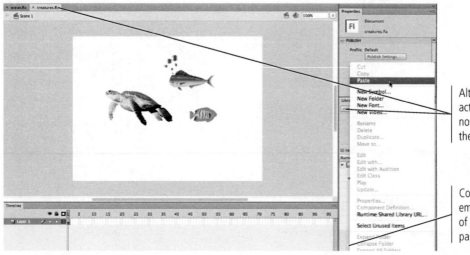

Although creatures.fla is active, the Library panel now shows the library of the ocean.fla file.

Control/right-click the empty area at the bottom of the Library panel to paste the copied items.

5. **Click the Close button on the creatures.fla document tab to close that file.**

   None of the pasted symbols is added to the Stage; they are only placed in the ocean.fla file's library.

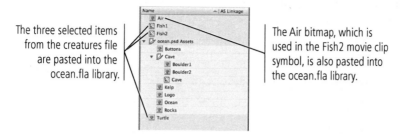

The three selected items from the creatures file are pasted into the ocean.fla library.

The Air bitmap, which is used in the Fish2 movie clip symbol, is also pasted into the ocean.fla library.

6. **With ocean.fla still open, choose File>Import>Open External Library.**

7. **Select buttons.fla (in the WIP>Aquarium folder) and click Open.**

   You can use this option to open the library of another file without opening the external FLA file. The external library opens as a separate panel; the file name is included in the panel tab.

Note:

The keyboard command for opening an external library is Command/Control-Shift-O.

8. **Shift-click the Reset, Showcave, Showfish, and Showturtle button symbols.**

9. **Click any of the selected items and drag to the ocean.fla Library panel.**

   The files don't disappear from the external library; they're simply duplicated in the ocean.fla Library panel. The Starfish bitmap object is also copied because it is used in the four button symbols.

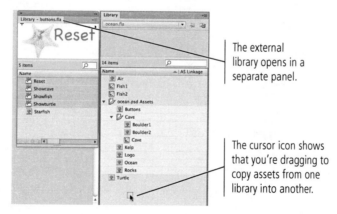

The external library opens in a separate panel.

The cursor icon shows that you're dragging to copy assets from one library into another.

10. **Click the Close button of the buttons.fla Library panel to close the external file's library.**

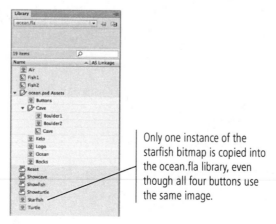

Only one instance of the starfish bitmap is copied into the ocean.fla library, even though all four buttons use the same image.

11. **Save the ocean.fla file and continue to the next exercise.**

The four buttons for this project need to be placed across the bottom of the Stage, aligned to appear equally distributed across the Stage area. The Align panel makes it very easy to position multiple selected objects relative to one another.

1. **With ocean.fla open, select the Buttons layer to make it active.**

2. **Drag instances of the four button symbols to the middle of the Stage, arranged so they do not overlap.**

3. **Select the placed Showfish button instance. Using the Properties panel, position the instance at X: 20, Y: 510.**

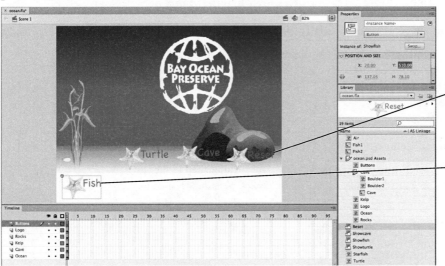

Place the symbols (from left to right) Showfish, Showturtle, Showcave, and Reset across the Stage.

Use the Properties panel to position the Showfish button instance.

4. **Using the Selection tool, Shift-click to select all four button instances on the Stage.**

5. **In the Align panel, turn off the Align To Stage option and then click the Align Bottom Edge button.**

The Align options position objects based on the selected edge. Because you used the Align Bottom Edge button, the selected objects are all moved to the bottom edge of the bottommost object in the selection.

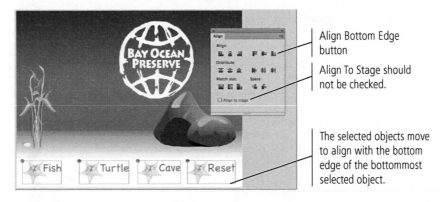

Align Bottom Edge button

Align To Stage should not be checked.

The selected objects move to align with the bottom edge of the bottommost selected object.

Note:

Many of the steps required in the first stage of this project reinforce the techniques you already learned if you completed the first three projects in this book. Creating symbols and positioning objects on the Stage are fundamental skills that will be important in virtually any Flash project.

6. **Select only the Reset button and set the X position to 605.**

7. **Select the four placed button instances.**

8. **In the Align panel, click the Space Evenly Horizontally button.**

This option calculates the overall space across the selection, then shifts the objects so the same amount of space appears between each object in the selection. Because the buttons are different widths, this option creates a better result than the distribution options.

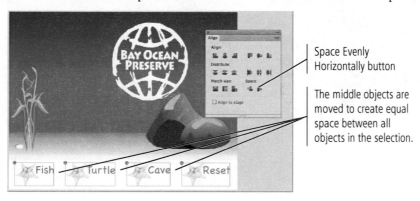

Space Evenly Horizontally button

The middle objects are moved to create equal space between all objects in the selection.

9. **Save the file and continue to the next exercise.**

 ## TRANSFORM SYMBOLS AND INSTANCES

Placed instances of a symbol are unique objects, which means they can be manipulated separately without affecting other instances of the symbol. Each instance remains linked to the primary symbol, however, so transforming the actual symbol affects all placed instances of that symbol.

1. **With ocean.fla open, Control/right-click the Kelp object on the Stage and choose Convert to Symbol from the contextual menu.**

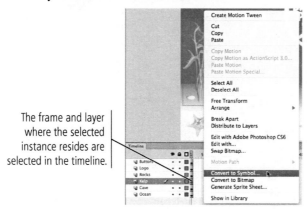

The frame and layer where the selected instance resides are selected in the timeline.

2. **In the resulting dialog box, type Seaweed in the Name field and choose Movie Clip in the Type menu. Choose the bottom-center registration point and click OK.**

Remember, the name of the actual symbol is only used internally while you develop the file. The specific names of instances on the Stage are more important, as you will see later when you add ActionScript to control the various pieces of this movie.

The Properties panel now shows that the selected object is an instance of the Seaweed symbol, which has been added to the Library panel.

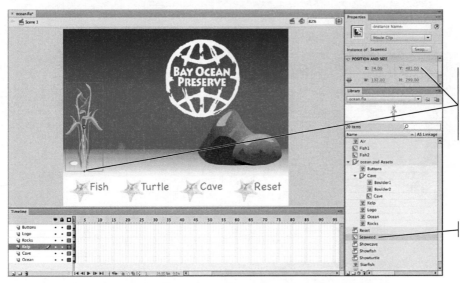

You defined bottom-center registration for this symbol, so measurements are based on the bottom-center point of the instance.

There's the new symbol.

3. **Using the Selection tool, Option/Alt-click the existing instance and drag right to clone a second instance of the Seaweed symbol.**

4. **Repeat Step 3 to clone one more instance.**

5. **Deselect everything on the Stage. Choose the Free Transform tool in the Tools panel and click the middle Seaweed instance to select it.**

   The Free Transform tool is used to change the size or shape of an object. Remember, all transformations are applied around the transformation point.

Note:

If the Free Transform tool is active when you click and drag to move an object, make sure you don't click the object's transformation point before you drag the object.

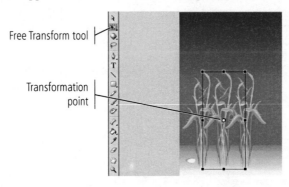

Free Transform tool

Transformation point

6. **Drag the transformation point until it snaps to the bottom-center bounding box handle.**

7. **Click the top-center bounding box handle and drag down to make the selected instance shorter.**

   Transformations applied to individual instances have no effect on the original symbol or on other placed instances.

Note:

You can also press Option/Alt and drag a center handle to transform the object around the opposite bounding-box handle, without moving the transformation point.

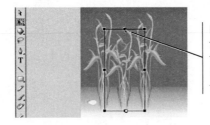

Because the bottom-center is the transformation point, dragging the top-center handle makes the instance shorter without moving the bottom of the instance.

8. **In the Library panel, double-click the Seaweed symbol icon to enter into the symbol.**

The crosshairs in the bottom center identify the **symbol registration point**, or the location of X:0, Y:0 for placed instances; all measurements for placed instances begin at this location.

Even though you changed the transformation point of one placed instance on the main Stage, the transformation point remains in the center of the object on the symbol Stage. The transformation point is specific to each placed object or instance.

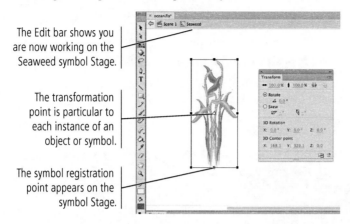

The Edit bar shows you are now working on the Seaweed symbol Stage.

The transformation point is particular to each instance of an object or symbol.

The symbol registration point appears on the symbol Stage.

9. **With the Free Transform tool still selected, drag the transformation point until it snaps to the bottom-center bounding box handle of the object on the symbol's Stage.**

10. **Show the Transform panel (Window>Transform).**

11. **In the Transform panel, make sure the Link icon is not active and then change the Scale Height value to 80%.**

If the Link icon shows two solid chain links, changing the height of the object would proportionally affect the width of the object (and vice versa). Because you only want to change the height, you need to break the Link icon.

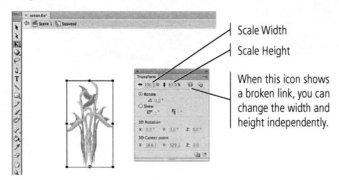

Scale Width

Scale Height

When this icon shows a broken link, you can change the width and height independently.

12. **In the Edit bar, click Scene 1 to return to the main Stage.**

When you modify the original symbol, the changes ripple through all placed instances.

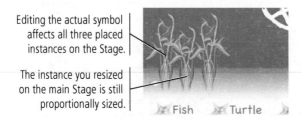

Editing the actual symbol affects all three placed instances on the Stage.

The instance you resized on the main Stage is still proportionally sized.

13. **Save the file and continue to the next exercise.**

When you imported the project artwork, the two pieces of the cave were created on separate layers — in a layer group — because you need to place a fish inside the cave, stacked between the two boulders. If the two boulders had existed on a single layer, the result would have been a single bitmap object, which could not be broken apart in Flash to accomplish the desired effect.

1. **With ocean.fla open, use the Selection tool to click the Cave movie clip instance on the Stage.**

2. **In the Properties panel, change the X position of the instance to 850.**

   If the cave objects had been placed in the correct position in the Photoshop file, the imported bitmap objects would have been clipped at the Stage edge. If you create artwork in Photoshop, make sure pieces are entirely inside the Canvas edge if you don't want them clipped when they are imported into Flash.

Note:

Remember, the symbol registration point marks the location of the defined X and Y values on the main Stage.

Because you defined the bottom-right corner as the symbol's registration point, that point is positioned at X: 850.

3. **Double-click the Cave movie clip instance on the Stage to edit the symbol in place on the Stage.**

   Because this movie clip (and instance) was created based on a layer group in the imported artwork, the layers that made up the group are maintained in the symbol timeline.

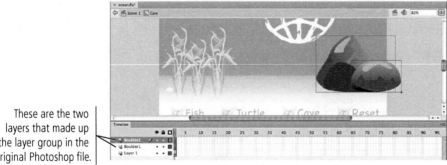

These are the two layers that made up the layer group in the original Photoshop file.

4. **Change the name of Layer 1 to Fish.**

5. **Drag an instance of the Fish2 movie clip symbol onto the Stage, near the existing cave pieces.**

   Because the Fish layer is below the two Boulder layers, the Fish2 instance should be at least partially hidden by the two pieces of the cave.

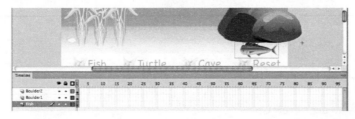

6. **In the Timeline panel, drag the Fish layer above the Boulder 1 layer.**

The Fish2 instance is now between the two pieces of the cave.

7. **Drag the Fish2 instance so only the head appears to the left of the front rock.**

In the second stage of this project, you will learn a number of techniques for creating animations — including making this fish blow bubbles that rise up and off the Stage.

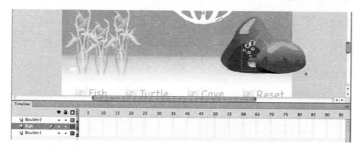

8. **Click Scene 1 in the Edit bar to return to the main Stage.**

9. **Save the file and continue to the next exercise.**

Use the Spray Brush

Although you could simply place multiple instances of the Rock bitmap without converting it to a formal symbol, you can use the Spray Brush tool to quickly and easily add numerous instances of the object.

1. **With ocean.fla open, Control/right-click the Rock bitmap on the Stage. Choose Convert to Symbol in the contextual menu.**

2. **In the resulting dialog box, type Gravel in the Name field. Choose Graphic in the Type menu, select the center registration point, and click OK.**

You are going to create many instances of this symbol as decoration on the Stage. Because you don't need to address the instances with script, you don't need to name the instances. You also don't need to animate anything inside the Gravel symbol, so the Graphic type is appropriate.

3. **Choose the Spray Brush tool (nested under the Brush tool) in the Tools panel.**

Use the Properties panel to define what will be sprayed and how it will spray.

Spray Brush tool

Spray Brush tool cursor

4. **In the Properties panel, click the Edit button in the Symbol area. Choose Gravel in the resulting dialog box, and then click OK.**

5. **Check the Random Scaling, Rotate Symbol, and Random Rotation options. Change the Brush Width and Height values to 75 pixels.**

6. **In the timeline, make sure the Rocks layer is active. Zoom out so you can see the entire Stage, and some of the surrounding area on the left and right.**

7. **Click the left edge of the Stage over the brown area of the gradient. Hold down the mouse button and drag slowly to the right across the entire Stage.**

    The dozens (or even hundreds, depending on how you dragged) of instances do not significantly increase the file size because the symbol needs to download only once.

Using the Random Scaling, Rotate Symbol, and Random Rotation options, you used a single symbol to create a field of ocean rocks.

Because the Buttons layer is higher than the Rocks layer, the bottom edges of the sprayed instances are hidden.

Each time you click and drag with the Spray Brush tool, the resulting instances are grouped. If you click again to add more rocks, you will have more than one group of rock instances.

8. **Save the file and continue to the next exercise.**

Note:

You have to enter into the group (double-click) to access the individual instances.

ORGANIZE YOUR LIBRARY WITH FOLDERS

Folders make it easy to organize the assets that make up a movie, and easy to find the assets you need.

1. **With ocean.fla open, click the Library panel to activate it.**

2. **In the Library panel, change the name of the ocean.psd Assets folder to Bitmaps.**

   Changing a library folder name has no effect on placed instances of the symbols inside that folder.

3. **Select the two bitmap objects in the nested Cave folder and move them into the first-level Bitmaps folder.**

   Moving symbols to a new location in the Library panel has no effect on placed instances of the moved symbols.

4. **Select the three bitmap objects in the first level of the library and drag them into the Bitmaps folder.**

5. **Drag the nested Cave folder from the Bitmaps folder to the main level of the Library panel.**

6. **Change the Cave folder name to Movie Clips, then drag the three movie clip symbols from the main level of the Library into the Movie Clips folder.**

Drag the nested folder to the empty area at the bottom of the panel to move it to the first level of the library.

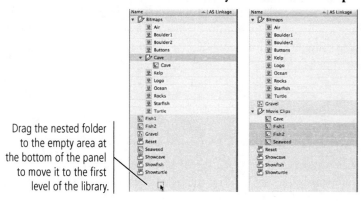

7. **Create a new folder named Buttons at the first level of the library. Drag the four button symbols into the new folder.**

   New folders are created at the same nesting level as the current selection. To create a new folder at the first level of the library, click the empty area at the bottom of the panel to deselect any files before clicking the New Folder button.

8. **Create another new folder named Graphics at the main level of the Library folder. Drag the one remaining graphic symbol into the folder.**

Note:

In this case, we're using simple names for the symbol folders. The names you assign to symbol (or layer) folders aren't functional; they just need to make sense to you (or other people working with your files).

9. **Save the file and continue to the next stage of the project.**

Stage 2 Animating Symbols

In Project 3: Talking Kiosk Interface, you created simple animation by swapping symbols at specific points in time; although nothing technically changed position, replacing one object with another is still considered "animation." In Project 4: Animated Internet Ads, you used classic tweening to move objects across the Stage; this technique creates smooth motion by defining the start point keyframe, end point keyframe, and path shape. In this project, you learn several different techniques for creating various types of animation, including animating specific properties of an object.

CREATE A BASIC FRAME ANIMATION IN A MOVIE CLIP SYMBOL

Movie clips are animated symbols that reside on a single frame of the timeline. In its simplest form, a movie clip can include a solitary fish swimming across the ocean; at its most complex, a movie clip can include fully interactive elements in a video game. In this exercise, you create the most basic type of animation — a frame animation.

1. **With ocean.fla open, choose the Selection tool and make sure nothing is selected on the Stage.**

2. **In the Properties panel, change the FPS hot text to 15 frames per second.**

   Using 15 fps for a movie — especially one that's going to run on the Web — provides decent quality. The default 24 fps is not necessary for standard computer viewing, and could create files that require too much processing power for some users.

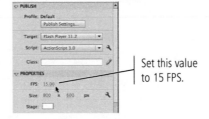

Set this value to 15 FPS.

3. **On the Stage, double-click the Cave symbol instance to enter into the symbol Stage (edit in place).**

4. **Double-click the placed Fish2 instance to enter into the nested symbol. Click away from the selected objects, and then select only the air bubbles.**

   All of the bubbles together are a single bitmap object; you don't need to select each individual bubble shape.

   When you first enter into a symbol, all objects in the symbol are automatically selected. You are going to move only the bubbles, which are an instance of the Air bitmap object that is placed inside the Fish2 symbol. You are editing in place on the main Stage so you can see when the bubbles are entirely outside the Stage area.

   Note:

   You can also Control/ right-click a frame in the timeline and choose Insert Keyframe from the contextual menu, or choose Insert>Timeline> Keyframe.

5. **In the timeline, click Frame 7 to select it, then press F6 to insert a new keyframe.**

   As you already know, **keyframes** are special frames where something happens to an object: it appears or disappears, changes size, moves to another position, changes color, and so on. When you add a new keyframe, regular frames are automatically added immediately before the previous keyframe; objects on the preceding keyframe will remain in place until the playhead reaches the new keyframe.

You are working on the Fish2 symbol, which is nested inside the Cave symbol.

When you add a keyframe, regular frames are automatically added directly before it.

6. **With Frame 7 selected in the timeline, deselect the fish graphic, and then reposition the air bubbles graphic directly above the original position.**

   When you select a keyframe, all objects on that keyframe are automatically selected (just as when you first enter into the symbol). You can Shift-click the fish instance to deselect that object, leaving only the air bubbles object selected.

With the Frame 7 keyframe active, move the bubbles up from their previous position.

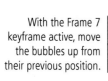

7. **Repeat Steps 5–6 six more times, adding a new keyframe every seven frames and moving the air bubbles up until they are outside the top edge of the Stage.**

Because you're editing the symbol in place, you can see how far you need to move the bubbles until they are outside the Stage area. If you edited this symbol on its own Stage, you would have to guess about positioning, return to the main Stage to test your guess, return to the symbol to add more frames, return to the main Stage to test again, and so on.

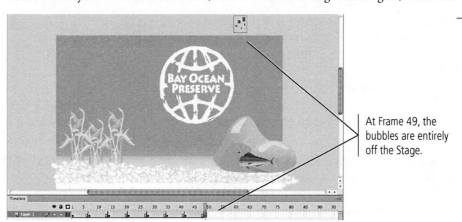

At Frame 49, the bubbles are entirely off the Stage.

Note:

If you change an object on a regular frame in the middle of a movie, all frames between the two surrounding keyframes (or the nearest preceding keyframe and the final frame) reflect that change.

8. **Select Frame 56 on the timeline and press F5 to add a regular frame.**

This regular frame at Frame 56 extends the timeline by half a second, which prevents the bubbles from reappearing in the fish's mouth (Frame 1) immediately after they move past the top of the Stage (Frame 49).

9. **Click the playhead above the timeline and drag left and right.**

Scrubbing the playhead allows you to look at specific sections of a movie over time so you can see if they work the way you expect.

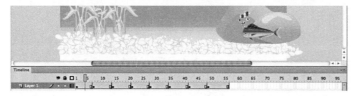

10. **Click Scene 1 in the Edit bar to return to the main Stage.**

11. **Press Command-Return/Control-Enter to test the movie.**

You can see the air bubbles moving up in a continuous loop. Even though the primary Stage has only one frame, the movie clip's timeline continues to play as long as the movie remains open.

The animation plays in the Flash Player window.

Note:

Remember from Project 3: Animated Internet Ads, you can't preview the animation inside a movie clip on the main Stage. You have to test the file in the Flash Player window to see the animation.

12. **Close the Flash Player window and return to Flash.**

13. **Save the file and continue to the next exercise.**

CREATE A MOTION TWEEN

Creating the appearance of continuous, fluid movement requires a slightly different position or shape (depending on what you are animating) on every frame in an animation. Rather than defining each individual frame manually — which could take days, depending on the length of your animation — you can let Flash define the frames that are in between two keyframes (the tween frames).

Flash incorporates technology that makes it very easy to define smooth animations by simply moving a symbol object around on the Stage.

1. With **ocean.fla** open, create a new layer named Turtle immediately above the Logo layer. Select the Turtle layer as the active layer.

2. Drag an instance of the turtle bitmap image from the Library panel onto the Stage. Use the Transform panel to scale the instance uniformly to 50%, and then position it beyond the right edge of the Stage, higher than the Cave instance.

3. Control/right-click the turtle instance and choose Convert to Symbol from the contextual menu.

4. In the resulting dialog box, type Swimmer in the Name field, choose Movie Clip in the Type menu, and choose the center registration point.

5. Click the Folder link. Select the Existing Folder radio button and choose Movie Clips in the list. Click Select to return to the Convert to Symbol dialog box, and then click OK to create the new symbol.

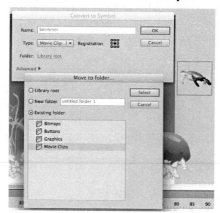

6. Click Frame 90 on the Turtle layer and press F5 to add a new regular frame.

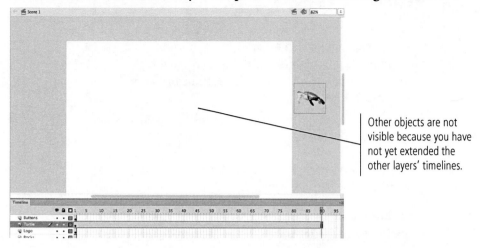

Other objects are not visible because you have not yet extended the other layers' timelines.

7. Control/right-click any frame on the Turtle layer and choose Create Motion Tween.

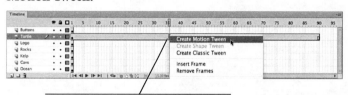

Control/right-click anywhere on the timeline between keyframes to add a motion tween between keyframes (or between a keyframe and the final frame on that layer).

Note:

We enlarged our workspace by collapsing docked panels to icons so we could see the entire Stage and all 90 frames in the timeline.

8. Click Frame 90 to select that frame.

Flash creates a motion tween in the frames between keyframes. Because Frame 1 is the only keyframe on this layer, the motion tween is created between Frame 1 and the last frame on the layer.

9. Select the Turtle image located at the right of the Stage, and drag it off the left edge of the Stage.

A new keyframe is automatically added on Frame 90 to mark the new position of the Swimmer symbol. A line — the motion path — shows the path of movement from the symbol's position on Frame 1 to its position on Frame 90. The small dots along the motion path correspond to the frames within the tween.

When you edit symbols on a tween layer, the position of the playhead is crucial. When you change any property of an object on a tween layer, a property keyframe is automatically inserted at the current frame. Flash generates the tween frames based on the change in the property value between the active keyframe and the previous one.

Note:

The motion path line corresponds to the color of the layer containing the path.

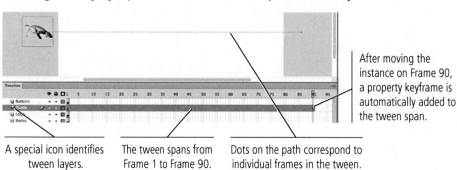

After moving the instance on Frame 90, a property keyframe is automatically added to the tween span.

A special icon identifies tween layers.

The tween spans from Frame 1 to Frame 90.

Dots on the path correspond to individual frames in the tween.

10. Click Frame 1 to move the playhead back to the beginning of the timeline, and then press Return/Enter to play the timeline on the Stage.

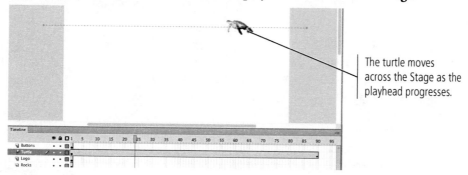

The turtle moves across the Stage as the playhead progresses.

11. Move the playhead to Frame 90, then click the turtle instance to select it. Scale the selected instance to 200% of its current size. If necessary, use the Selection tool to reposition the resized turtle so it is entirely outside the edge of the Stage.

The term "motion path" is deceptive because you can animate much more than just motion when you apply a motion tween. By scaling the object on Frame 90, you told Flash to change both the symbol size and position as the timeline progresses.

Note:

Because you scaled the object to 50% before you created the Swimmer symbol, resizing this instance to 200% restores the bitmap to its original size.

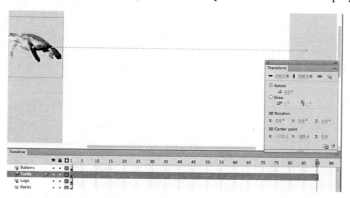

12. Return the playhead to Frame 1, and then press Return/Enter to play the timeline on the Stage.

Now the turtle gets larger as it moves across the stage, creating the effect of the turtle swimming closer. Flash automatically calculates the appropriate position and size of the symbol for all frames between the Frame 1 and Frame 90 keyframes.

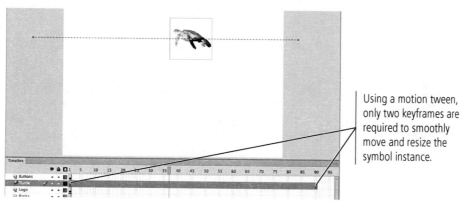

Using a motion tween, only two keyframes are required to smoothly move and resize the symbol instance.

13. Save the file and continue to the next exercise.

Onion skinning, accessed through a set of buttons at the bottom of the timeline, is a technique that allows you to view more than one frame of an animation at a time.

- Clicking the **Onion Skin** button toggles the feature on or off.
- Clicking the **Onion Skin Outlines** button turns all visible skins to outlines (or wire frames). Combining outlines and onion skins allows you to clearly see the components of your animations without fills or (true-weight) strokes.
- Clicking the **Edit Multiple Frames** button allows you to edit multiple frames at the same time: moving an entire animation, for example, or simply changing single frames within a tween. Without this feature, you would have to move objects one frame at a time. With the feature, you can see previous or subsequent frames, which often helps when you're fine-tuning an animation and you need to move an object in one frame relative to its position in other frames.
- Clicking the **Modify Markers** button allows you to select from a range of predefined skins, or turn onion skinning off. You can choose to have onion skins span two frames, five frames, or all frames. You can also manually adjust the onion skin markers and bypass these presets.

The following illustrations show a simple motion tween that moves the oval symbol across the Stage, from left to right.

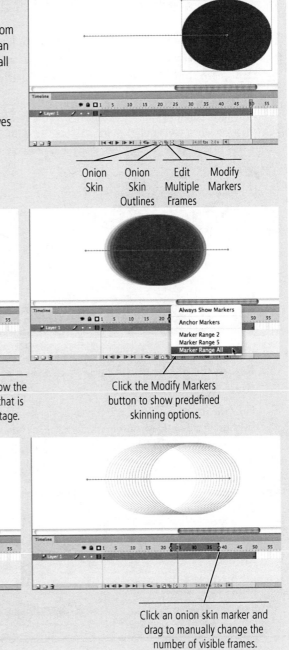

Onion Skin | Onion Skin Outlines | Edit Multiple Frames | Modify Markers

When the Onion Skin feature is active, you can see multiple frames at once (around the playhead).

These markers show the range of frames that is visible on the Stage.

Click the Modify Markers button to show predefined skinning options.

When Onion Skin Outlines is active, frames within the visible onion skin display as wireframes.

Click an onion skin marker and drag to manually change the number of visible frames.

FLASH FOUNDATIONS

EDIT THE SHAPE OF THE MOTION PATH

As you learned in the previous exercise, moving an object and changing its size (or other properties) can be as simple as creating a motion tween and adjusting the symbol at specific frames on the timeline. You don't need to manually create keyframes because Flash adds them for you whenever you change the symbol at a particular point in the timeline. In this exercise, you work with the motion path line, which can be edited like any other line in Flash — giving you precise control over the course of a tween.

1. **With ocean.fla open, click the Swimmer symbol on the Stage to select it and reveal the related motion path.**

2. **Move the Selection tool cursor near the center of the motion path until you see a curved line in the cursor icon. Click near the path and drag up to bend the motion path.**

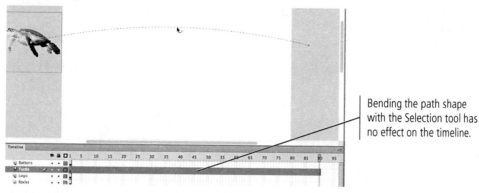

Bending the path shape with the Selection tool has no effect on the timeline.

3. **Return the playhead to Frame 1 on the timeline, and then press Return/Enter to play the timeline.**

   The turtle now follows the new shape of the motion path.

4. **Click Frame 45 of the Turtle layer to select that frame. Using the Selection tool, click the Swimmer symbol instance and drag down.**

   Flash automatically adds another keyframe to the motion tween to mark the instance's position at that point; the motion path bends again to reflect the defined position for the turtle at the selected frame. Flash adds an anchor point to the path at the new keyframe.

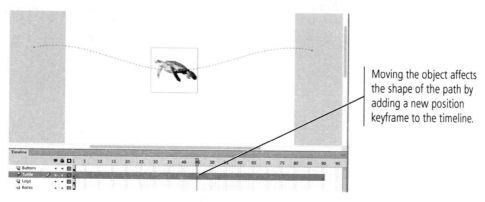

Moving the object affects the shape of the path by adding a new position keyframe to the timeline.

5. **Choose the Subselection tool in the Tools panel, and then click the new anchor point in the middle of the path.**

   The Selection tool selects entire paths. The Subselection tool selects the anchor points and handles that make up a shape.

Controlling Animation Speed with Easing

Physical objects are subject to physical laws; in the real world, friction, momentum, and mass (among other things) affect how an object moves. A bouncing ball is a good example of these laws. If you throw a ball at the ground, how hard you throw the ball determines its beginning speed. When the ball hits the ground, it transfers energy to the ground and then rebounds, causing the ball to move away from the ground (its first bounce), at which point it is moving slightly faster than when you threw it. As the ball arcs through the bounce it slows down, then starts to drop and hits the ground again, repeating the process in ever-decreasing arcs until it finally gives up its energy and then stops. The speed of the ball changes when the energy behind the ball changes.

In animation terms, these changes in speed are called **easing**. In Flash, you can control easing in the Properties panel when a tween is selected in the timeline.

- Positive Ease values decrease the distance of movement on subsequent frames, causing the object to slow down as it moves through the tween.

- Negative Ease values increase the distance of movement on subsequent frames, causing a moving object to speed up through the tween.

- Ease values closer to 100 or −100 result in greater apparent changes in speed.

The accompanying illustrations show a simple 50-frame motion tween that moves a circle symbol across the Stage.

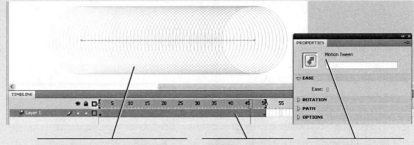

We turned on onion skins for all frames to show the position of the symbol at each frame in the tween.

We clicked inside the tween span to select the motion tween.

The Properties panel shows options related to the selected tween.

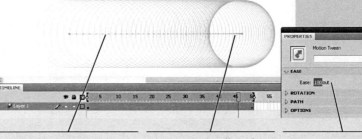

By increasing the Ease value, the object moves farther on earlier frames than on later frames.

This creates the effect of the object slowing down over the course of the animation.

The Properties panel shows the positive Ease value as "out" — it slows down.

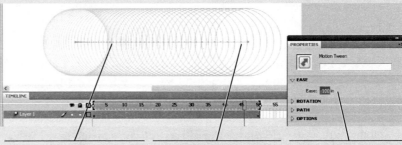

By decreasing the Ease value, the object moves farther on later frames than on earlier frames.

This creates the effect of the object speeding up over the course of the animation.

The Properties panel shows the negative Ease value as "in" — it speeds up.

6. Click the selected anchor point and drag left.

Moving the anchor point changes the shape of the motion path, just as it does when you edit a regular Bézier curve. You can also adjust the handles of the point to change the shape of the motion path between the two connecting anchor points (the selected point and the point at the left end of the path).

When you change the position of the anchor point, notice that the number of dots (representing frames in the tween) on either side of the point remains unchanged. Because you effectively shortened the left half of the path, the same number of frames display over a shorter distance than the same number of frames to the right of the selected point. In effect, you made the turtle swim faster in the first half of the animation (moving a longer distance) and slower in the second half (moving a shorter distance).

Note:

You can use the Convert Anchor Point tool to convert a smooth anchor point on a motion path to a corner anchor point, allowing you to change directions in the tween.

Note:

By default, motion paths are created with a non-roving keyframe property, which means the anchor points along the path are attached to specific keyframes in the timeline.

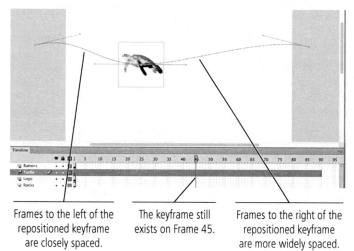

Frames to the left of the repositioned keyframe are closely spaced.

The keyframe still exists on Frame 45.

Frames to the right of the repositioned keyframe are more widely spaced.

7. Control/right-click anywhere within the motion tween (in the timeline), and choose Motion Path>Switch Keyframes to Roving in the contextual menu.

When you choose this option, the dots along the path redistribute to equal spacing across the entire length of the tween, and the keyframe from Frame 45 is removed from the layer timeline. The shape of the path is not affected.

A roving-property keyframe is not attached to any particular frame in the tween. This type of keyframe allows you to create a custom-shaped motion path with consistent speed throughout the tween.

Note:

If you convert keyframes to roving, frames are redistributed along the entire span of the tween. If you then convert the frames back to non-roving, the location of keyframes added to the tween is determined by the location of anchor points on the path.

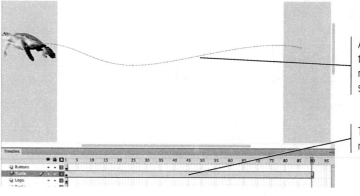

After choosing the Roving option, the frames along the path are redistributed to be equally spaced across the entire path.

The property keyframe is removed from the timeline.

8. Save the file and continue to the next exercise.

In Flash CS6, the motion tween includes all information for the animation, including the length of the animation and specific object properties at various points along the path. A motion path is actually a specific type of object rather than simply a guide; the Properties panel shows a number of options that relate to the selected motion tween.

Because a motion tween is an actual object, you can attach any symbol to the path by simply dragging a new symbol onto the Stage when the motion tween layer is selected.

Use this field to define a name for the motion path instance.

Use Ease values to speed up or slow down an animation over time.

Use this option to rotate a symbol X number of times as it moves along the motion path.

Check this option to rotate the object so its bottom edge follows the contour of the path.

Use these options to change the position and size of the overall path.

Check this option to synchronize the number of frames in a tween within a graphic symbol to match the number of frames on the timeline where the graphic symbol is placed.

We dragged the Fish 3 symbol onto the Stage while the motion path layer was active.

A warning asks if you want to replace the current symbol on the selected motion path.

After clicking OK in the warning, the Fish 3 symbol follows the same motion path.

A special icon identifies a motion path layer.

Flash includes a number of predefined motion presets (Window>Motion Presets), which you can use to add common animations to your files. You can also save your own motion presets by Control/right-clicking an existing motion path and choosing Save as Motion Preset from the contextual menu. (User-defined presets are stored and accessed in a Custom folder in the Motion Presets panel. Custom presets do not include previews.)

COPY AND PASTE FRAMES

Your turtle currently swims from right to left across the Stage. When the animation loops, however, it would seem to miraculously jump back to the right and swim across again. For a more realistic effect, you are going to make a copy of the motion path animation and reverse it so the turtle swims back across the Stage before the animation loops.

1. **With ocean.fla open, Control/right-click anywhere in the Turtle layer motion tween and choose Copy Frames from the contextual menu.**

   You could also use the options in the Edit>Timeline submenu, but the standard Edit menu commands (and the related keyboard shortcuts) do not work when you want to copy or paste frames in the timeline.

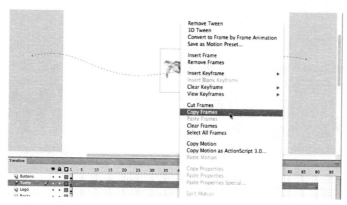

2. **Control/right-click Frame 95 of the Turtle layer and choose Paste Frames.**

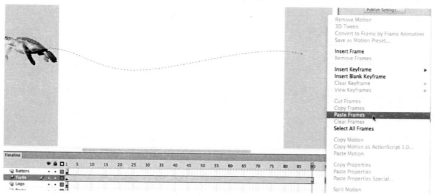

Note:

You are allowing five extra frames between the time the turtle leaves and then re-enters the Stage area (ostensibly enough time for it to turn around before it swims back).

   You pasted an exact copy of the selected frames (the motion tween) — including the position of the symbol at various keyframes. In other words, the turtle is on the right at Frame 95 and on the left at Frame 184 (the end of the pasted animation).

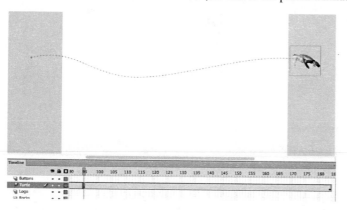

3. **Control/right-click anywhere between Frame 95 and Frame 184 and choose Reverse Keyframes.**

   Reversing the keyframes moves the turtle to the left at Frame 95 and the right at Frame 184.

4. **Select the Frame 95 keyframe in the timeline. Click the turtle instance with the Selection tool, then choose Modify>Transform>Flip Horizontal.**

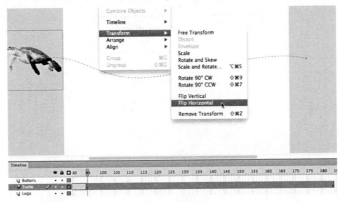

   For the turtle to realistically swim back across the Stage, you have to flip the symbol instance to face in the correct direction.

5. **Click Frame 184 to make that the active frame. With the turtle on the Frame 184 keyframe selected, choose Modify>Transform>Flip Horizontal again.**

   The turtle now faces to the right throughout the entire second half of the animation.

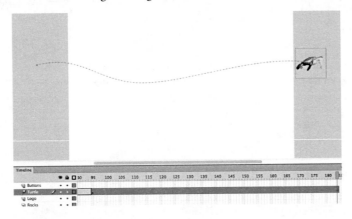

6. **Add new regular frames to Frame 184 of the remaining layers on the timeline.**

   Remember, you have to manually extend each layer so they will all exist throughout the length of the entire animation.

7. Click Frame 1 to reposition the playhead, then press Return/Enter to play the movie on the Stage.

The air bubbles in the Cave movie clip instance do not move because that animation exists only inside the movie clip timeline.

8. Save the file and continue to the next exercise.

USE THE MOTION EDITOR

In addition to making changes on the Stage, you can also use the Motion Editor panel to define specific changes to specific properties at specific points in time. In this exercise, you use the Motion Editor to animate the seaweed with a tween that creates the effect of a smooth, swaying motion.

1. With **ocean.fla** open, double-click the Seaweed symbol icon in the Library panel to enter into the symbol Stage.

2. In the timeline, select Frame 40 and press F5 to insert a new regular frame.

You can also Control/right-click the frame and choose Insert Frame from the contextual menu.

3. Control/right-click anywhere between Frame 1 and Frame 40 and choose Create Motion Tween.

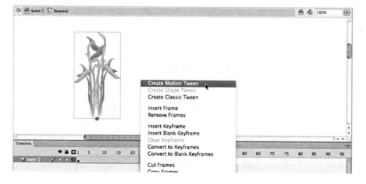

4. Read the resulting message.

Motion tweens only work with symbol instances. As you see in the warning dialog box, Flash can automatically convert the placed bitmap instance to a movie clip symbol.

5. **Click OK in the message to create a symbol from the selected object.**

   You are not creating this tween on the main Stage because you want the animation to loop continuously regardless of the position of the playhead on the main timeline. Even though you are already inside of a symbol, you need to create a nested symbol structure for the motion tween to work properly.

6. **In the Library panel, change the name of Symbol 1 to Seaweed Sway, and then move the symbol into the Movie Clips folder.**

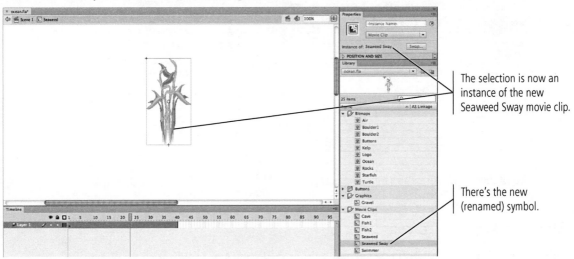

The selection is now an instance of the new Seaweed Sway movie clip.

There's the new (renamed) symbol.

7. **Choose the Free Transform tool in the Tools panel. Select the object on the Stage, and drag the transformation point to the bottom-center handle.**

8. **Open the Motion Editor panel (Window>Motion Editor). If it is grouped with the Timeline panel, click the Motion Editor tab and drag it away from the group so you can see both panels at once.**

9. **Move the playhead to Frame 10. In the Motion Editor panel, scroll until you find the Skew X option. Click the hot text for that option and change the value to 5°.**

   The concept here is the same as in the previous exercise: select the frame, and then change the object properties to what you want at that particular point in time. The difference is that you're using the Motion Editor panel to easily define numeric values for specific properties at specific points in time.

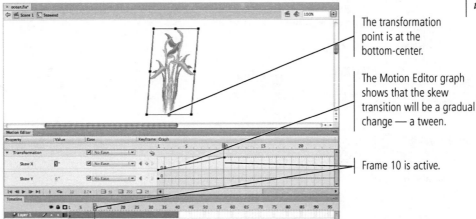

The transformation point is at the bottom-center.

The Motion Editor graph shows that the skew transition will be a gradual change — a tween.

Frame 10 is active.

The Motion Editor Panel in Depth

The Motion Editor panel can control any property that can be animated in a motion tween. All available properties are listed in the left side of the panel. The right side shows a graph with the number of frames defined in the bottom-left corner; the active frame, and the value of each property at that frame, appears at the left edge of the graph. (You can change the number of viewable frames in the bottom-left corner of the dialog box to see an overview of the entire path animation.)

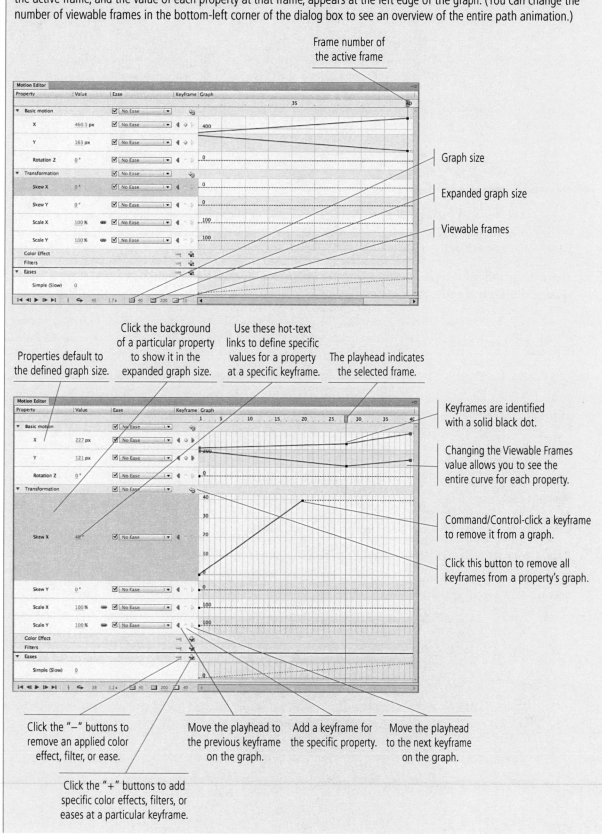

Frame number of the active frame

Graph size

Expanded graph size

Viewable frames

Properties default to the defined graph size.

Click the background of a particular property to show it in the expanded graph size.

Use these hot-text links to define specific values for a property at a specific keyframe.

The playhead indicates the selected frame.

Keyframes are identified with a solid black dot.

Changing the Viewable Frames value allows you to see the entire curve for each property.

Command/Control-click a keyframe to remove it from a graph.

Click this button to remove all keyframes from a property's graph.

Click the "–" buttons to remove an applied color effect, filter, or ease.

Move the playhead to the previous keyframe on the graph.

Add a keyframe for the specific property.

Move the playhead to the next keyframe on the graph.

Click the "+" buttons to add specific color effects, filters, or eases at a particular keyframe.

10. Move the playhead to Frame 30 in the timeline. In the Motion Editor panel, change the Skew X value to –5°.

You don't need to manually move the skew back to 0°; the tween frames do that for you.

Note:

Selecting a different frame in either panel changes the selected frame in the other panel.

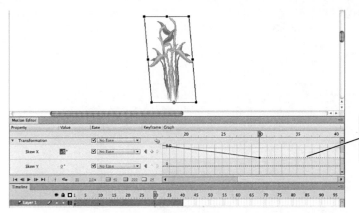

The dotted lines show the projected value of the property at specific frames.

As you can see by the dotted line after the Frame 30 keyframe, the Skew X transition would stay at –5° until the animation looped, when it would jump back to 0°. To avoid this jump, you need to manually set the skew back to 0° at the last keyframe.

11. Move the playhead to Frame 40 in the timeline. In the Motion Editor panel, change the Skew X value to 0°.

Note:

The object must be selected to change its properties. Selecting the frame in the timeline also selects the object on that frame.

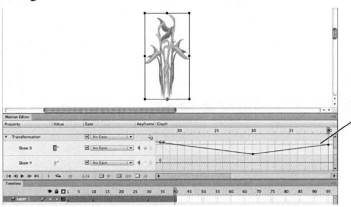

The animation will now flow smoothly from –5° to 0° before it loops back to Frame 1.

12. Click Scene 1 in the Edit bar to return to the main Stage.

13. Press Command-Return/Control-Enter to test the movie in a Player window.

Because you created the animation inside of the Seaweed movie clip symbol, all three instances of the symbol sway continuously as long as the animation is open.

14. Close the Player window and return to Flash. Save the file and continue to the next exercise.

Both graphics and movie clips can include animation. However, there are two fundamental differences in the capabilities of the two symbol types.

First, movie clip symbol instances can be named, which means they can be addressed by code. You can write scripts to control the timeline within a movie clip symbol independently of other objects in the file. Graphic symbol instances can't be named, which means you can't affect them with code.

Second, if you create animation inside of a graphic symbol, the timeline where you place the instance determines how much of the graphic symbol's animation plays. In other words, frames in the graphic symbol must correspond to frames on the parent timeline (they are "timeline dependent").

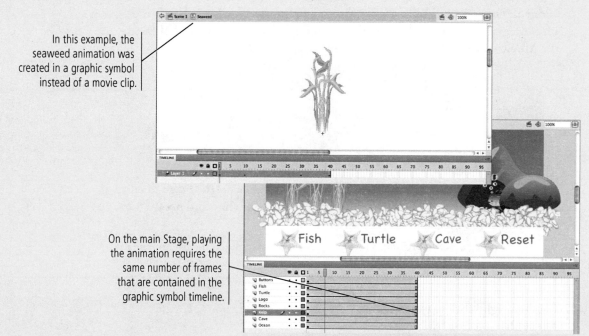

In this example, the seaweed animation was created in a graphic symbol instead of a movie clip.

On the main Stage, playing the animation requires the same number of frames that are contained in the graphic symbol timeline.

In the example here, the 40-frame seaweed animation was created in a graphic symbol (as you can see in the Edit bar above the symbol Stage). For the instances on the main Stage to play properly, you need to extend all of the layers to 40 frames (above right).

If the parent timeline includes more frames than the graphic symbol (as in the example on the right, where the main timeline has 94 frames) the graphic symbol's timeline will play slightly less than 2.5 times before looping back to the beginning — causing a visible jump in the animation.

If you have a number of animations of different length, you should use movie clip symbols, which function independently of the timeline where they are placed and can loop continuously regardless of the length of other animations on the same parent timeline.

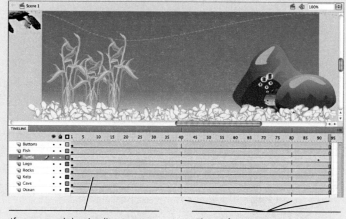

If you extend the timeline to create other animations, the graphic symbol animation repeats as long as the timeline allows.

The 40-frame seaweed animation would play 2 full times plus 14 frames before the main timeline looped back to Frame 1.

ANIMATE EFFECTS AND FILTERS

In addition to changing the common symbol properties — position, size, etc. — a motion tween can be used to animate a number of other options. Effects and filters, which can add visual interest to most objects on the Stage, can also be animated to change over time. In this exercise, you are going to cause the client's logo to fade into view over time, changing from blurry to clear and fully visible.

1. **With `ocean.fla` open, choose the Selection tool. Control/right-click the logo instance on the Stage and choose Convert to Symbol.**

2. **Name the new symbol BOP, choose Movie Clip as the type, and choose the center registration point. Use the Folder link to place the new symbol inside the Movie Clips folder. Click OK to create the symbol.**

3. **Using the Selection tool, double-click the Logo instance on the Stage to edit the symbol in place. Select Frame 60 on the Layer 1 timeline and press F5 to add a new regular frame.**

    Because movie clips are self-contained animations, every movie clip in the file can last a different amount of time. You also need to be able to control this animation separately from other animations, which is why you are creating the tween inside of the symbol.

4. **Control/right-click between Frame 1 and Frame 60 and choose Create Motion Tween from the contextual menu.**

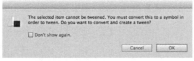

5. **Click OK in the resulting warning. Rename the new Symbol 1 as BOP Animated, and then move the symbol into the Movie Clips folder.**

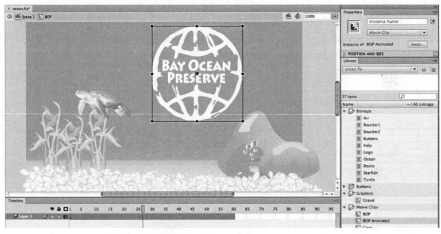

6. **Move the playhead to Frame 1 in the timeline, and then click the symbol instance on the Stage to select it.**

7. **In the Properties panel, open the Style menu in the Color Effect section and choose Alpha. Drag the resulting slider all the way to the left to change the Alpha value to 0.**

   If you don't see the Style menu, click the arrow to the left of the Color Effect heading.

   The Alpha value controls an object's opacity; a value of 0 means the object is not visible.

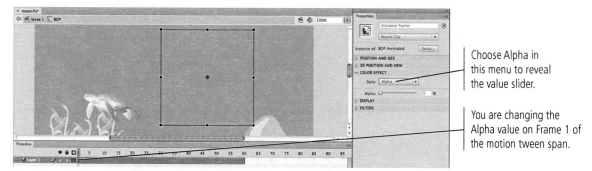

Choose Alpha in this menu to reveal the value slider.

You are changing the Alpha value on Frame 1 of the motion tween span.

8. **Move the playhead to Frame 30 on the Layer 1 timeline, and then click the symbol registration point on the Stage to select the symbol instance.**

   Because the current Alpha value is 0, you can't see the actual object to select it; you have to rely on the registration point to select the instance on the Stage.

9. **In the Properties panel, change the Alpha value back to 100.**

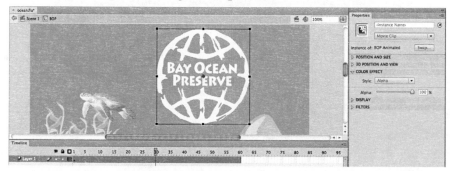

10. **With the instance selected on the Stage, open the Motion Editor panel (if necessary) and move the playhead to Frame 1.**

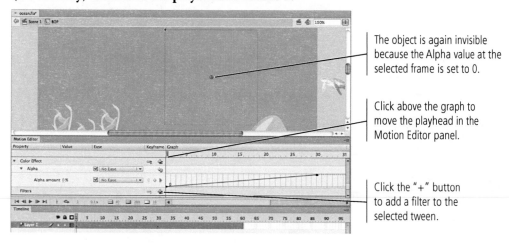

The object is again invisible because the Alpha value at the selected frame is set to 0.

Click above the graph to move the playhead in the Motion Editor panel.

Click the "+" button to add a filter to the selected tween.

11. Scroll through the Motion Editor properties until you find the Filters option. Click the "+" button for Filters and choose Blur from the resulting menu.

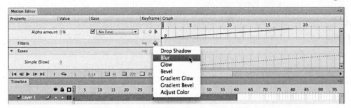

12. Make sure the Blur X and Blur Y values are linked, and then change the Blur X value to 30 px.

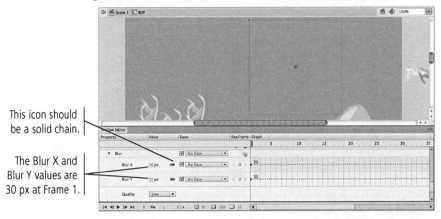

This icon should be a solid chain.

The Blur X and Blur Y values are 30 px at Frame 1.

13. Move the playhead to Frame 30 in the timeline. In the Motion Editor panel, click the Add Keyframe button for the Blur X property, and then change the Blur X value to 0 px.

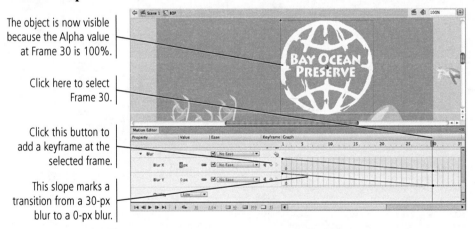

The object is now visible because the Alpha value at Frame 30 is 100%.

Click here to select Frame 30.

Click this button to add a keyframe at the selected frame.

This slope marks a transition from a 30-px blur to a 0-px blur.

14. Return the playhead to Frame 1, and then press Return/Enter to preview the animation.

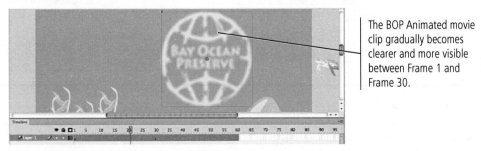

The BOP Animated movie clip gradually becomes clearer and more visible between Frame 1 and Frame 30.

15. Save the file and continue to the next exercise.

ANIMATE IN 3D

As you know, you can change the X (left/right) and Y (up/down) properties to move an object around the Stage. Flash CS6 adds the third dimension — the Z dimension (near/far or front/back) — so you can animate movie clips in three dimensions.

1. **With ocean.fla open, make sure you are editing the BOP movie clip in the Edit in Place mode.**

2. **Move the playhead to Frame 45 in the timeline, and then choose the 3D Rotation tool in the Tools panel.**

   When a movie clip is selected with the 3D Rotation tool, a visual indicator overlays the selected instance. Each axis (X, Y, or Z) is controlled by a different aspect of the overlay.

3D Rotation tool

3D Rotation Overlay

   If you look carefully, you can see the related axis in the cursor icon when you move over a specific element in the overlay graphic.

The green line represents the Y axis.

The red line represents the X axis.

The blue circle represents the Z axis.

3. **Click the Y Axis overlay and drag right to rotate the movie clip around the Y axis.**

The shaded area of the overlay shows how far you have rotated the object.

4. **In the Motion Editor panel, make sure the graph view shows at least 60 frames.**

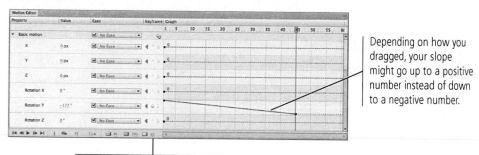

Depending on how you dragged, your slope might go up to a positive number instead of down to a negative number.

Change this Viewable Frames option to 60 to show the entire graph.

5. Review your Rotation X, Rotation Y, and Rotation Z properties.

Simply dragging the overlay allows you to rotate the object, but it is not guaranteed to produce the results you want. Before you finalize the animation, you should use the Motion Editor graph to verify that what you get is what you want (a single, full revolution).

6. In the Motion Editor panel, make sure the Rotation Y property is –180 (one half of an entire revolution), and the other two rotation properties are 0.

The negative value causes the rotation to occur from left to right. Positive values cause the rotation to occur from right to left.

Note:

If you use a mouse with a scroll wheel, be very careful scrolling through the Motion Editor panel. The menus and hot-text values in the panel are also scrollable. If your cursor moves over one of these values or menus as you try to scroll, you will inadvertently change the values or menu where you scroll.

7. Move the playhead to Frame 60 in the timeline. In the Motion Editor panel, click the Add Keyframe button for the Rotation Y property and change the value for that keyframe to –360.

Using the negative number, you are causing the object to make one full revolution; the constant downslope in the Motion Editor panel confirms this. If you had simply used 0, the object would revolve halfway, then go back in the opposite direction for the second half of the revolution. Because the slope is steeper from Frames 45–60, the second half of the rotation will occur more rapidly than the first half of the rotation.

8. **Select Frame 30 in the Motion Editor, and then click the Rotation Y Add Keyframe button. Change the value of the new keyframe to 0.**

The two halves of the revolution will now occur at the same speed; none of the revolution will take place until the logo is entirely visible and unblurred.

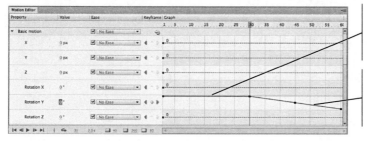

The flat line shows that the Rotation Y value will not change until the playhead reaches Frame 30.

The constant downslope shows that the object will make one complete revolution in the same direction.

9. **Click Scene 1 in the Edit bar to return to the main Stage.**

10. **Press Command-Return/Control-Enter to test the animation.**

Because the Rotation Y value is a continuous slope, the logo completes one entire revolution in the same direction between Frame 30 and Frame 60.

11. **Save the file and continue to the next exercise.**

WORK WITH THE BONE TOOL

The Bone tool can be used to link symbols to one another in a "chain" effect, or to define complex motion for simple objects. As the name implies, you use the Bone tool to create "bones" and "joints" where the bones connect. In this exercise, you use the Bone tool to create a school of fish that swims in a line across the Stage.

1. **With ocean.fla open, create a new layer named Fish above the Turtle layer in the main timeline.**

2. **Choose Insert>New Symbol. Name the new symbol School and choose Movie Clip as the symbol type. Use the Folder link to place the new symbol inside the Movie Clips folder. Click OK to create the new symbol.**

When you use the New Symbol dialog box to create a new symbol from scratch, there is no registration point option because there is no existing art that must be placed in reference to the symbol registration point. When you add objects to the symbol, you can position them relative to the symbol registration point on the Stage.

3. **Using the Selection tool, drag a copy of the Fish1 movie clip onto the symbol Stage. Align the top-right corner of the instance to the symbol registration point.**

When you use the Insert>New Symbol command, the Stage automatically switches to a new blank symbol Stage.

4. **Press Option/Alt, click the Fish1 instance, and then drag left to clone a second instance of the first Fish1. Repeat this process to add two more Fish1 instances.**

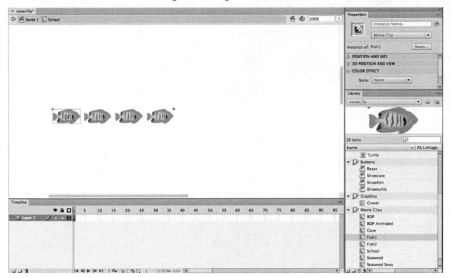

5. **Click Scene 1 in the Edit bar to return to the main Stage.**

6. **With Frame 1 of the Fish layer selected, drag an instance of the School movie clip symbol onto the Stage. Position the School instance in the top half of the Stage, but entirely outside the left edge of the Stage.**

7. **Double-click the placed School instance to edit the symbol in place on the Stage.**

   You're going to make this school of fish swim across the top of the movie. Editing the symbol in place allows you to see how far you need to move the fish to ensure they go all the way across the ocean.

8. **Choose the Bone tool in the Tools panel.**

9. **Click the first Fish symbol instance, hold down the mouse button, and drag to the middle of the second Fish instance.**

   When you use the Bone tool, a new Armature layer is added to the timeline. The objects connected to the armature joints — called IK nodes — are moved from their original layer to the Armature layer.

Note:

The process underlying the Bone tool is called **inverse kinematics**.

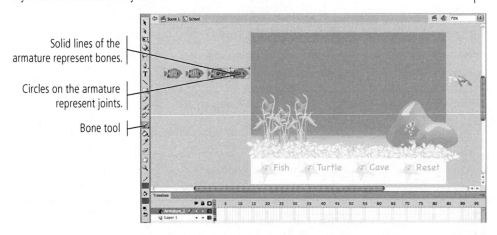

Solid lines of the armature represent bones.

Circles on the armature represent joints.

Bone tool

10. **Click the second Fish instance, hold down the mouse button, and drag to the middle of the third Fish instance.**

11. Click the third Fish instance, hold down the mouse button, and drag to the middle of the fourth Fish instance.

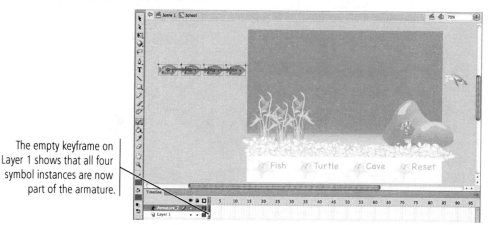

The empty keyframe on Layer 1 shows that all four symbol instances are now part of the armature.

12. Save the file and continue to the next exercise.

ANIMATE THE BONE ARMATURE

Now that you have the armature structure in place, you can use it to animate the instances' movement in both time and space.

1. With **ocean.fla** open, make sure you are editing the School symbol instance in place on the Stage.

2. In the timeline, click Frame 45 of the Armature layer to select it, and then press F5 to insert a new regular frame.

3. Choose the Selection tool in the Tools panel, and then choose Edit>Select All to select all four instances on the armature.

4. Hold down the Option/Alt key, click any of the selected instances, and then drag the selection until the front fish is about halfway across the Stage and approximately one inch down.

You can Option/Alt-drag instances to move them to a new position without rotating the object or bending the armature.

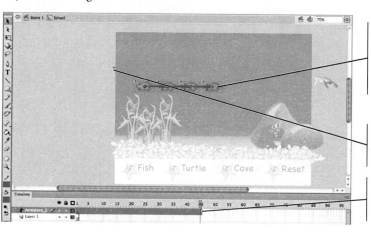

Option/Alt-drag to move the selected objects (and the armature) without bending the armature or rotating the objects.

The registration point shows the symbol's original starting point.

Changing an object on the armature automatically adds a keyframe.

5. **Deselect all instances, click only the back Fish instance on the armature, and then drag up to the top of the Stage.**

   As you drag the Fish instance without pressing Option/Alt, notice how other instances on the armature are affected, and how the different objects (including the one you drag) are rotated around the joints.

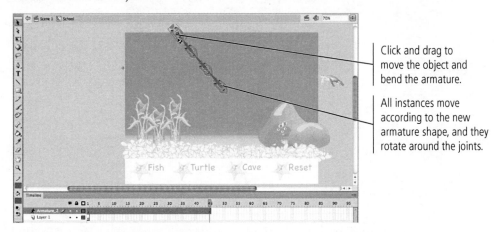

Click and drag to move the object and bend the armature.

All instances move according to the new armature shape, and they rotate around the joints.

6. **Press Option/Alt, click the second Fish instance, and drag down and right until this instance is partially on top of the first Fish instance.**

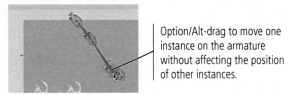

Option/Alt-drag to move one instance on the armature without affecting the position of other instances.

7. **Repeat Step 6 for the other two instances on the armature.**

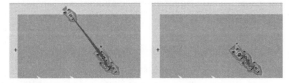

8. **In the timeline, insert a new regular frame at Frame 90 to extend the timeline of the armature tween. Select all four Fish instances on the armature, press Option/Alt, and move all four objects past the right edge of the Stage and up near the top of the Stage.**

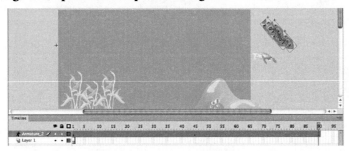

9. **Deselect the four objects, select only the fourth Fish instance, and then Option/Alt-drag down to change the direction of the armature.**

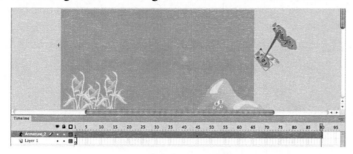

10. **Using the Transform panel, change the rotation of the selected fish as necessary so it appears to point up and away from the Stage.**

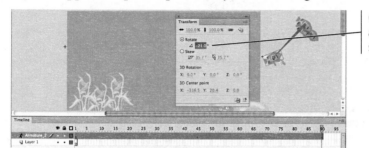

Change the Rotate value to adjust the orientation of the selected symbol instance.

11. **Repeat the process from Steps 9–10 to change the relative position of the fish in the school.**

We spread out the fish so they no longer overlap, and rotated each to point in the same general direction.

> *Note:*
>
> *You can use the Transform panel to precisely control the position and rotation of a specific instance on an armature.*

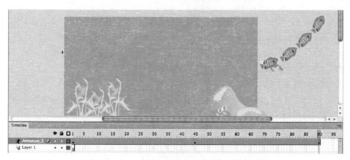

12. **Click Scene 1 on the Edit bar to return to the main Stage.**

13. **Press Command-Return/Control-Enter to test the movie, including the armature animation.**

14. **Close the Player window and return to Flash. Save the file and continue to the next stage of the project.**

Stage 3 Programming Basic Timeline Control

You now have all of the pieces in place for the ocean scene, including a number of animations that play automatically when the movie opens. According to the project specs, however, most of these animations should not play until a user clicks the appropriate button at the bottom of the screen. For everything to work properly, you need to complete several additional steps to accomplish the following goals:

- Play the logo animation only once when the movie first loads.

- Play the school of swimming fish when the Fish button is clicked.

- Play the swimming turtle when the Turtle button is clicked.

- Show the cave with the bubbly fish when the Cave button is clicked.

- Hide the cave, stop the turtle and school of fish, and replay the logo animation when the Reset button is clicked.

CONVERT A MOTION TWEEN TO A MOVIE CLIP

At this point, all but the swimming turtle animations are contained inside of various movie clip symbols. In order to add code that controls the turtle animation independently of the main timeline, you need to move the symbol instance and motion tween into a symbol, and then place an instance of that symbol on the Stage.

1. **With ocean.fla open, double-click anywhere in the Frame 1–94 tween on the Turtle layer.**

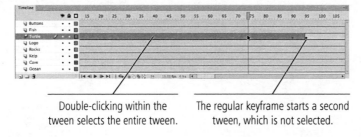

Double-clicking within the tween selects the entire tween.

The regular keyframe starts a second tween, which is not selected.

2. **Press Shift, then click in the Frame 95–184 tween to add it to the selection.**

Because Frame 95 is a regular keyframe and not a property keyframe within the tween, the two tweens are technically treated as separate. You have to manually select both tweens to copy them into a symbol.

3. **Control/right-click inside the selected frames and choose Copy Frames in the contextual menu.**

You are copying both selected tweens.

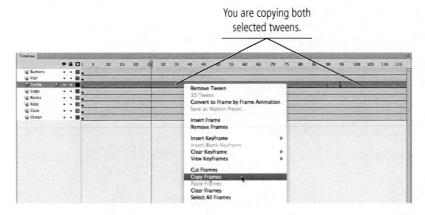

4. **Choose Insert>New Symbol. In the resulting dialog box, type Swimming Turtle in the Name field and choose Movie Clip in the Type menu. Use the Folder link to place the new symbol in the Movie Clips folder, then click OK.**

5. **Control/right-click Frame 1 of the new symbol's timeline and choose Paste Frames from the contextual menu.**

This pastes the full set of contents of the selected frames — including the turtle instance and the motion tweens — inside the symbol.

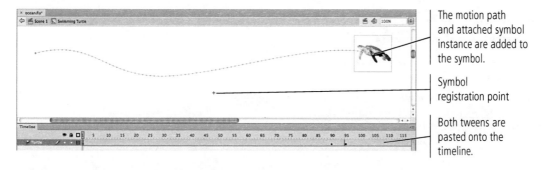

The motion path and attached symbol instance are added to the symbol.

Symbol registration point

Both tweens are pasted onto the timeline.

6. **Click anywhere within the Frame 1–94 tween, then choose Edit>Select All to select the motion path and the turtle symbol instance.**

This command selects both the motion path and the attached instance, so you can drag the entire piece as a single group.

7. **Use the Selection tool to drag the selection until the right end of the motion path aligns to the symbol registration point.**

The existing Swimmer symbol uses the center registration point. You're going to swap symbols, and the registration point in this symbol will align to the position of the previous one. For the tween to work as it does on the main timeline, you need to place the right end of the motion path at the registration point. (This will make more sense shortly).

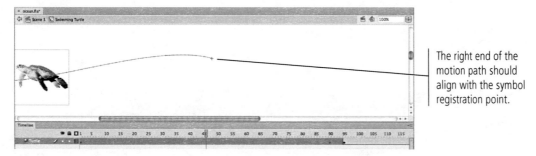

The right end of the motion path should align with the symbol registration point.

8. **Repeat Steps 6–7 for the Frame 95–184 tween.**

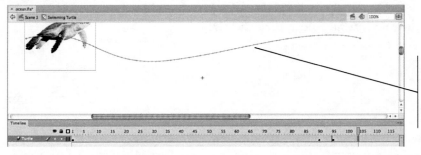

When you select the second tween, you see that the motion path remains where it was first pasted.

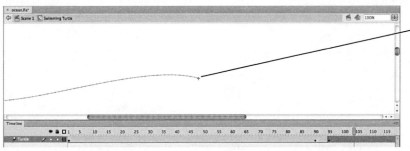

The right end of the second tween motion path must also align to the symbol registration point.

9. **Click Scene 1 in the Edit bar to return to the main Stage.**

10. **Control/right-click the Frame 1–94 tween on the Turtle layer and choose Remove Tween from the contextual menu.**

    The tweens now exist in the new Swimming Turtle movie clip symbol, so they are no longer needed on the main timeline.

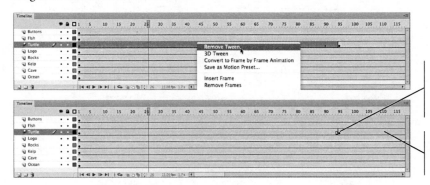

After removing the tween, the frames remain but all property keyframes are removed.

The second tween is still in place after the Frame 95 keyframe.

11. **Repeat Step 10 for the Frame 95–184 tween on the same layer.**

12. **Click Frame 2 of the topmost layer to select it.**

13. **Scroll the Timeline panel as necessary until you see Frame 184. Press Shift, then click the last frame on the bottommost layer to select all frames from 2–184 on all layers.**

Note:

After removing both motion tweens, the Turtle layer is converted back to a regular layer.

Click Frame 2 of the top layer...

...then Shift-click Frame 184 of the bottom layer to select all contiguous frames between the two you click.

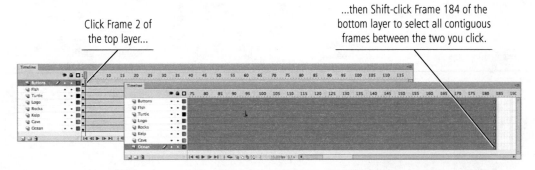

14. **Control/right-click anywhere within the selected frames and choose Remove Frames from the contextual menu.**

   Because all animation in this movie occurs within the timelines of various movie clip symbols, you don't need 184 frames on each layer of the main timeline.

   You can't simply press the Delete key to remove frames. You must use the contextual menu (or the related commands in the Edit>Timeline submenu).

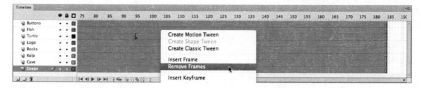

   Because all of the animations are now contained within movie clip symbols, the main timeline now has only a single frame for each layer.

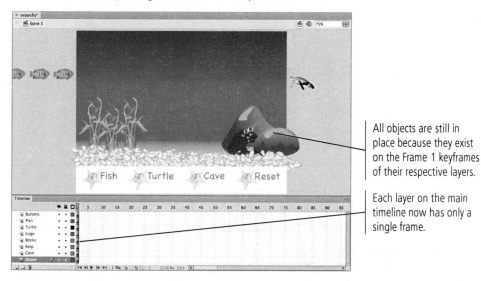

   All objects are still in place because they exist on the Frame 1 keyframes of their respective layers.

   Each layer on the main timeline now has only a single frame.

15. **Click the existing turtle instance on the Stage to select it.**

   As you can see in the Properties panel, this is currently an instance of the Swimmer movie clip. You need to replace it with the Swimming Turtle movie clip.

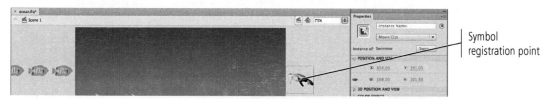

   Symbol registration point

16. **In the Properties panel, click the Swap button. Choose the Swimming Turtle movie clip in the resulting dialog box and click OK.**

When you swap symbols, the registration point of the new symbol is put in exactly the same spot as the registration point of the replacement symbol — which is why you moved the right end of the motion path to align with the symbol's registration point.

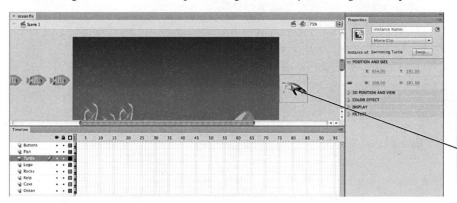

Although you can't see the motion path, you know the center of the turtle was aligned to the right end of the path at Frame 1.

17. **Save the file and continue to the next exercise.**

 PREPARE SYMBOL INSTANCES FOR ACTIONSCRIPT

As you know, when you drag a symbol from the Library panel to the Stage, you create an instance of the symbol. **Named instances** are instances that have been assigned a unique identifier or name, which allows them to be targeted with ActionScript code.

1. **With `ocean.fla` open, make sure you are working on the main Stage.**

2. **Using the Selection tool, click the School instance to the left of the Stage. In the top field of the Properties panel, type `school_mc`.**

Note:

You don't need to name the seaweed instances because those will not be targeted with scripts.

Use the Properties panel to assign instance names.

3. **Define names for the rest of the placed instances as follows:**

Remember, the Cave instance was named cave_mc when you created it during the import process.

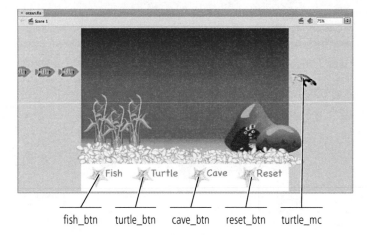

fish_btn   turtle_btn   cave_btn   reset_btn   turtle_mc

Note:

The "_mc" and "_btn" naming convention is common in the world of Flash development. This convention allows programmers to easily recognize the type of a particular instance when they add scripts to the file.

4. **In the Timeline panel, click the Logo layer name to select the layer.**

   Remember, selecting a layer reveals the bounding boxes for all objects on the layer.

5. **Click the symbol registration point to select the logo.**

   Because the logo object has an Alpha value of 0, this is the easiest way to select the instance so you can name it.

6. **In the Properties panel, type** bop_mc **as the instance name.**

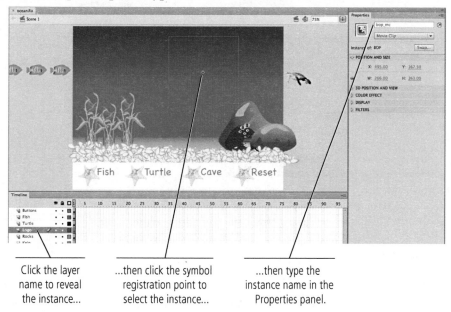

Click the layer name to reveal the instance...

...then click the symbol registration point to select the instance...

...then type the instance name in the Properties panel.

7. **Save the file and continue to the next exercise.**

ADD MOVIE CLIP CONTROLS

If you completed Project 4: Animated Internet Ads, you saw that the Code Snippets panel makes it relatively easy for non-programmers to add basic code to a Flash movie. Items in the panel, written in plain English, automatically add whatever code is necessary to perform the listed function. In this exercise, you will use code snippets to determine what is visible when you first open the movie.

1. **With** ocean.fla **open, open the Code Snippets panel from the Window menu.**

   Different types of common commands are available, grouped into logical sets or folders.

2. **Expand the Actions folder in the Code Snippets panel. Click Stop a Movie Clip to select it, then click the i icon on the right side of the panel to get more information about that snippet.**

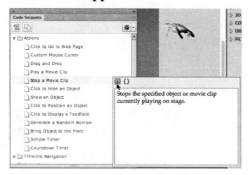

3. Select the Swimming Turtle instance on the stage and then double-click the Stop a Movie Clip item.

Adding the snippet automatically opens the Actions panel, showing the new code.

Code snippets include instructions in the form of comments, which are enclosed by /* and */.

The actual command uses dot syntax, defining what instance is being affected and what will happen to that instance.

The code is added to the selected frame on a new layer named Actions.

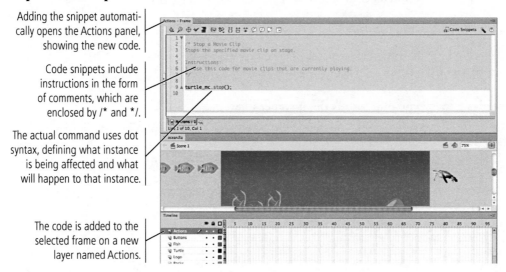

It might seem that by first selecting the object, you are attaching script to that object. Instead, you are telling Flash which object you want the command to address. In ActionScript 3.0, all scripts are placed on the timeline frames rather than attached to specific objects on the Stage. In the Timeline panel, a new layer named Actions is added to the top of the layer stack. (Although not required, this separate layer for the code is a common convention among developers.)

In the Actions panel, which opens automatically when you add the snippet, you can see that the stop command has been added to Frame 1 of the Actions layer. The command references turtle_mc, which is the instance name you defined. In other words, this command stops the turtle_mc instance from playing. The instance is stopped as soon as the main timeline reaches the command; because the command is on Frame 1 of the main timeline, the instance is stopped as soon as the movie opens.

Note:

*The format or syntax of the added code is called **dot syntax**: it first defines the object you are addressing, then adds a dot, then defines what you want to do to that object.*

4. Select the School instance on the Stage, and then double-click the Stop a Movie Clip item in the Code Snippets panel.

When you first select the school instance, the Actions panel warns that code can't be attached directly to objects on the Stage.

The code (including comments) is added to Frame 1 of the Actions layer, after the existing code.

This tab shows where the code is added (Layer:Frame).

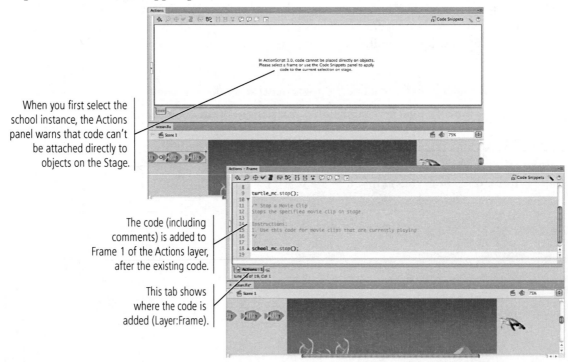

5. Select the Cave instance and then double-click the Stop a Movie Clip item.

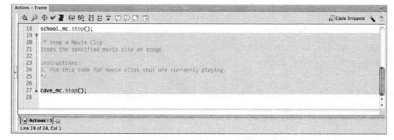

6. Select the Cave instance again and double-click the Show an Object item.

Unfortunately, there is no snippet to simply hide an item without requiring the user to click something. (The Click to Hide an Object item is not appropriate because you want to hide the instance as soon as the movie opens, and not as a reaction to the user's click.)

However, the added Show an Object statement shows that the value "true" is attached to the visible property of the instance. To make the instance *not* visible, you simply have to change the property's value in the code.

7. In the Actions panel, change the word true to false on Line 36.

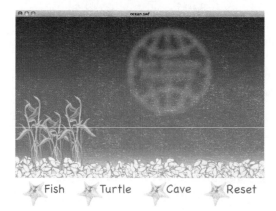

8. Press Command-Return/Control-Enter to test the movie.

The three movie clips are stopped, and the cave is hidden. However, the logo animation still plays continuously and you want it to play only once when the movie opens.

9. Close the Player window and return to Flash.

10. **In the Library panel, double-click the BOP movie clip symbol icon to enter into the symbol's Stage.**

You can't stop the BOP instance on the main Stage because you want the animation to play one time when the movie first opens. To accomplish this goal, you need to add a stop command to the end of the movie clip timeline.

11. **Move the playhead to the last frame in the timeline, then click the logo instance on the Stage to select it.**

12. **Expand the Timeline Navigation folder in the Code Snippets panel, then double-click the Stop at this Frame item to add the necessary code.**

Timeline Navigation snippets can be used to control the timeline (and thus, the playback) of specific symbols. The Stop at this Frame command affects the active timeline at the selected frame, so a specific instance is not referenced in the resulting code.

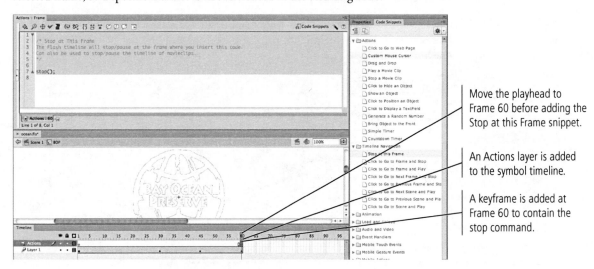

Move the playhead to Frame 60 before adding the Stop at this Frame snippet.

An Actions layer is added to the symbol timeline.

A keyframe is added at Frame 60 to contain the stop command.

13. **Click Scene 1 in the Edit bar to return to the main Stage, then press Command-Return/Control-Enter to test the movie.**

The logo animation now plays only once and then stops.

14. **Close the Player window and return to Flash, then save the file and continue to the next exercise.**

 ## ADD EVENT HANDLERS TO BUTTONS

As you saw in the previous exercise, ActionScript 3.0 requires code to be attached to a frame on the timeline. To affect a specific object on the Stage, you have to use the defined instance names as reference in the code. Programming a button requires more complex code called an **event handler**, with (at least) two referenced objects — the event that triggers the action, and the name of the function that is affected by the event.

The Code Snippets panel includes options for creating event handlers with the proper syntax, although defining what occurs as a result of the event might require a few workaround steps. Even using code snippets, it is helpful if you are familiar with the basics of ActionScript code.

1. **With ocean.fla open, expand the Timeline Navigation folder in the Code Snippets panel.**

2. **Select the Fish button instance on the Stage, then double-click the Click to Go to Frame and Play item in the Code Snippets panel.**

The added code is not attached to the selected instance; it is added to Frame 1 of the existing Actions layer, after all code that you already added.

The selected instance becomes the object that can trigger the function.

The specific trigger (CLICK) is defined inside the event listener.

This is the event listener statement.

This is the function that is called when the defined event occurs.

The function name is the same in the event listener and the defined function.

Although you do not need to know every detail of ActionScript code to use Code Snippets, there are a few important points that you should understand:

- The first line of added code defines what will happen to trigger the function (the **event listener**). Inside the parentheses, the MouseEvent.CLICK statement says that the following function will be called when the fish_btn instance is *clicked*.

- The first line of code includes a **function name** immediately before the closing parenthesis. That same name is defined at the beginning of the following function so the file knows which function to play when the defined button is clicked.

- The **function body** — between the two braces — defines what occurs when the event is triggered.

3. **Place the insertion point before the gotoAndPlay command inside the function body and click the Insert Target Path button at the top of the Actions panel.**

The statement inside this function currently says "go to Frame 5 and play the timeline". Because the statement does not address a specific instance, the code will be interpreted to mean the timeline on which the code is placed (in this case, the main Stage timeline). You want the function to play the School movie clip instance, so you have to add the appropriate reference.

Insert Target Path button

Click here to place the insertion point.

4. **Choose school_mc in the Insert Target Path dialog box and click OK.**

This dialog box lists every nameable instance on the Stage, so you can choose from the list instead of trying to remember the exact name you defined for a specific object.

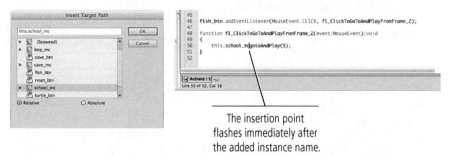

The insertion point flashes immediately after the added instance name.

Note:

If an item in the Insert Target Path dialog box appears in parentheses, the instance is not yet named; selecting it will prompt you to define an instance name.

Note:

The word "this" is automatically included when you use the Insert Target Path dialog box. It is not strictly necessary in this case because the instances are all on the main timeline of the file you are building, but you do not need to remove it from the code.

The word "this" in the instance name refers to the timeline where the code is written. The overall statement is essentially saying, "On *this* timeline, you will find something called school_mc. Tell school_mc to execute its gotoAndPlay() method."

5. **Type a period (dot) immediately after the instance name to separate it from the gotoAndPlay command.**

Remember, dot syntax requires a period separating the different parts of code — in this case, the instance that will be affected by the gotoAndPlay command.

6. **Change the number inside the parentheses to 1.**

This number defines the frame number of the instance that will be called when a user clicks the button. You want the instance to start at the beginning, so you are changing the frame reference to 1.

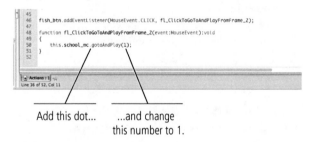

Add this dot...   ...and change this number to 1.

7. **Repeat Steps 2–6 to create an event handler for the Turtle button that plays the turtle_mc movie clip instance from Frame 1.**

Notice that a sequential number is added to the function name, both in the event listener statement and in the first line of the function. Every function in a file must have a unique name so it can be called when necessary.

8. **Repeat Steps 2–6 to create an event handler for the Cave button that plays the cave_mc movie clip instance from Frame 1.**

```
60
61  turtle_btn.addEventListener(MouseEvent.CLICK, fl_ClickToGoToAndPlayFromFrame_3);
62
63  function fl_ClickToGoToAndPlayFromFrame_3(event:MouseEvent):void
64  {
65      this.turtle_mc.gotoAndPlay(1);
66  }
67
68  /* Click to Go to Frame and Play
69  Clicking on the specified symbol instance moves the playhead to the specified frame in the timeline and conti
70  Can be used on the main timeline or on movie clip timelines.
71
72  Instructions:
73  1. Replace the number 5 in the code below with the frame number you would like the playhead to move to when t
74  */
75
76  cave_btn.addEventListener(MouseEvent.CLICK, fl_ClickToGoToAndPlayFromFrame_4);
77
78  function fl_ClickToGoToAndPlayFromFrame_4(event:MouseEvent):void
79  {
80      this.cave_mc.gotoAndPlay(1);
81  }
82
```

9. **Select the cave_mc instance on the Stage (not the Cave button) and double-click the Show an Object item in the Actions folder of the Code Snippets panel.**

The Cave button needs to show the instance before it plays, so this button function needs two lines of code. However, the Code Snippets panel was not designed to add code inside of an existing function. The Show an Object snippet is added at the end of the existing code, *after* the function that is called when a user clicks the cave_btn instance. As a work-around, you have to add the necessary command and then paste it into the function body.

The "show" command is added outside of the existing function.

10. **Select the line of code that makes the cave_mc instance visible (Line 90 in the above example) and press Command/Control-X to cut the selected code.**

You have to use the keyboard shortcuts to copy (Command/Control-C), cut (Command/Control-X), or paste (Command/Control-V) code in the Actions panel. The menu commands do not work while you are active in the Actions panel.

11. **Place the insertion point immediately after the opening brace in the function (Line 79 in our example) and press Return/Enter to add a new line in the function body. Press Command/Control-V to paste the code that you cut in Step 10 to the function body.**

12. **Delete the extra lines of comments at the end of the code.**

Note:

The comments are the gray lines that are surrounded by /* and */. After you moved the actual code into the function body (Steps 10–11), the comments from the original code are unnecessary. Deleting them helps keep the code pane as clean as possible.

13. **Press Command-Return/Control-Enter to test the movie.**

Test the buttons that you just programmed. Each should play the relevant movie clip.

14. **Close the Player window and return to Flash, then save the file and continue to the next exercise.**

COMBINE MULTIPLE EVENT HANDLERS IN A BUTTON

The final element of this project is the Reset button, which needs to accomplish a number of things. As the name suggests, clicking this button should restore the movie to exactly what happens when it first opens. Because the symbols in this movie are controlled with code, you need to add more code that defines what happens when this button is clicked.

1. With `ocean.fla` open, select the Reset button on the Stage.

2. Double-click the Click to Go To Frame and Stop item in the Timeline Navigation folder of the Code Snippets panel.

3. Inside the function body, add a reference to the school_mc instance before the gotoAndStop command, and change the referenced frame inside the parentheses to `1`.

4. Select the line inside the function body (Line 96 in our example) and copy it.

5. Place the insertion point at the beginning of the existing function body (Line 96) and paste the copied code three times.

6. Change the second and third lines to reference the turtle_mc and cave_mc instances, respectively.

7. Change the fourth line to reference the bop_mc instance, and change the command to `gotoAndPlay`.

   When a user clicks the Reset button, the logo animation should replay from the first frame. It will replay only once because you already added the stop command inside the movie clip's timeline.

These lines will stop the first three animations and effectively hide the first two on the Stage.

This command will cause the logo animation to play once.

8. Select the Reset button on the Stage again, and double-click the Click to Hide an Object item in the Actions folder of the Code Snippets panel.

9. In the resulting function, change the referenced instance to `cave_mc`.

   By default, this snippet hides the object that triggers the function. Because you want to hide the cave and not the Reset button, you need to change the instance name inside of the function body.

10. Cut the function body (Line 113 in our example) from the code and then paste it inside the body of the previous function.

In this case, it is not necessary to have two separate event handlers for the same button.

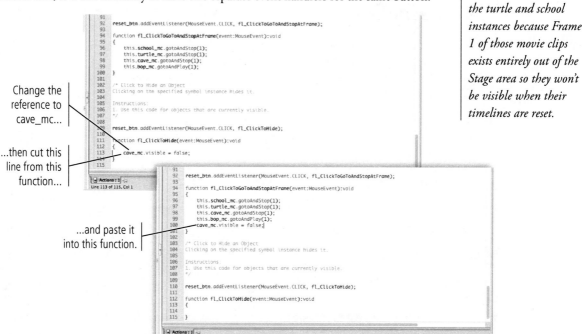

Change the reference to cave_mc...

...then cut this line from this function...

...and paste it into this function.

11. Delete all code related to the second reset_btn event handler (Lines 103–115 in our example above).

Because you combined this function body with the other event handler for the same button, this code is no longer necessary.

12. Press Command-Return/Control-Enter to test the movie.

Test the buttons that you just programmed. The Reset button should stop and hide all animations except for the swaying seaweed.

13. Close the Player window and return to Flash, then save the file and close it.

Project Review

fill in the blank

1. Objects from a Photoshop file should be created on _____ if they need to be managed separately when imported into Flash.

2. The _____ tool places multiple instances of a selected symbol; you can use the Properties panel to randomize the instances that are placed.

3. The _____ defines the point around which object transformations are made.

4. The X and Y position of a symbol instance is based on the _____.

5. You can use the _____ panel to define numeric scale, skew, and rotation values for the selected object.

6. Animation in a _____ requires the same number of frames on the timeline where the instance is placed.

7. Animation in a _____ plays regardless of the number of frames in the timeline where instances are placed.

8. _____ is the format required by ActionScript 3 code.

9. Using ActionScript 3, code is attached to a specific _____, and uses instance names to address specific objects.

10. In ActionScript, a(n) _____ includes a statement defining the instance that triggers an event and the function that is called when the defined event occurs.

short answer

1. Briefly explain the concept of "tweening."

2. Briefly explain the difference between a graphic symbol and a movie clip symbol.

3. Briefly define an event handler.

286 Project 5: Ocean Animation

Use what you learned in this project to complete the following freeform exercise.

Carefully read the art director and client comments, then create your own design to meet the needs of the project.

Use the space below to sketch ideas; when finished, write a brief explanation of your reasoning behind your final design.

art director comments

The media director for the Chicago Wild Animal Park is re-branding the facility from the "City Zoo" image it has had for the past twenty years. He has hired you to create a series of animated icons for the park's new interactive Web site.

To complete this project, you should:

❑ Create each icon in the same shape and size, and use the same general style for each.

❑ Add some kind of animation to each icon. Use any combination of frame animations, shape tweens, and/or motion tweens.

client comments

We've gotten rid of the cages and created realistic natural habitats for the animals. Our main goals now are rehabilitation, preservation, and education. We're going to have educational programs and exhibits throughout the facility, but we don't want people to be scared off by the idea of learning!

We have many international visitors, so most of our collateral — including our new Web site — is based on images that can be understood in any language. Although there will be text as well, the icons should very clearly indicate what users will find when they click on any specific one (even if they can't read the words).

We need a series of six animated icons that will label the different areas of the facility. The six main sections are: the tropics, the desert, the Arctic, the forest, the ocean, and the sky. There will also be a special children's section that needs its own icon.

project justification

_____

_____

_____

_____

_____

_____

_____

_____

_____

_____

_____

_____

_____

This project incorporated artwork that was created in Adobe Photoshop, which is a common development workflow. You also worked with symbols that were created in another Flash file, which is also a common collaborative process.

The second stage of this project focused on different methods of creating animation — frame-by-frame to move something in jumps, motion tweening to move objects smoothly, tweening to change only certain properties over time, and even tweening to rotate an object in three-dimensional space. To create these animations, you have also learned a number of techniques for transforming objects on the Stage; the Transform panel, the Free Transform tool, the Properties panel, and the Motion Editor panel all play valuable roles in Flash development.

Finally, you were introduced to the object-oriented model of ActionScript 3 when you added button controls using the Code Snippets panel. With very little (if any) knowledge of coding or programming, you were able to use the built-in functionality to meet the project's interactive requirements.

Import artwork from an Adobe Photoshop file

Import symbols from an external Flash library

Create frame animations to move objects over time

Animate Alpha properties, graphic filters, and 3D attributes

Animate multiple symbols on an armature

Define movie clip symbols to create tween animations

Define a graphic symbol and spray multiple instances

Add code to control the playback of various movie clip instances.

Adobe Dreamweaver is an industry-standard application for building Web sites. Typical work ranges from static HTML pages with hyperlinks to complex, dynamic sites, where pages are generated on-the-fly based on individual user requests. Mastering the tools and techniques of the application can significantly improve your potential career options.

EXPLORE THE DREAMWEAVER INTERFACE

Much of the Dreamweaver interface functions in the same way as the Photoshop and Flash user interface. Panels can be opened, moved, and grouped in the same manner, and you can save custom workspaces to call specific sets of panels. Dreamweaver also has a number of different options specific to Web-page design; this interface was designed to introduce you to those options.

1. **Download the WC6_RF_InterfaceDW.zip archive from the Student Files Web page.**

2. **Expand the ZIP archive in your WIP folder (Macintosh) or copy the archive contents into your WIP folder (Windows).**

   This results in a folder named **Interface_DW**, which contains all of the files you need for this project.

3. **With nothing open in Dreamweaver, open the Window menu and choose Workspace Layout>Designer.**

4. **Open the Window menu again and choose Workspace Layout>Reset 'Designer'.**

   The default workspace includes the Properties panel at the bottom of the screen, and a set of panels attached to the right side of the screen in the **panel dock**.

   If the Welcome Screen is not visible, you can open the General pane of the Preferences dialog box (in the Dreamweaver menu on Macintosh or the Edit menu on Windows). Check the Show Welcome Screen box and click OK. After you quit and then relaunch the application, the Welcome Screen will be visible.

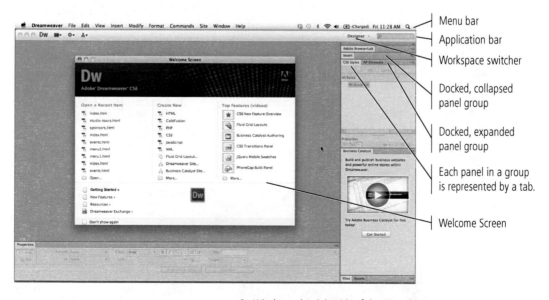

On Windows, the right side of the Menu bar provides access to the same options that are available in the Macintosh Application bar.

5. **In Dreamweaver, click the Manage Sites link in the Files panel.**
If you don't see the Manage Sites link, open the Directory menu and choose
Manage Sites from the bottom of the list.

If no sites are currently open in Dreamweaver, you can click the hot-text link to open the Manage Sites dialog box.

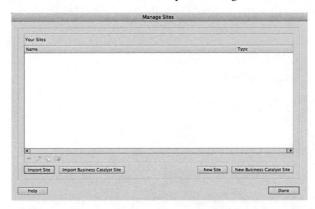

When sites are already open, the Manage Sites link is not available.

You have to open the Directory menu and choose Manage Sites from the bottom of the list.

Although Dreamweaver can be used to build individual HTML pages with no links to external files, the application is more commonly used to build entire sites. The Manage Sites dialog box is used to create new sites or import existing ones into Dreamweaver.

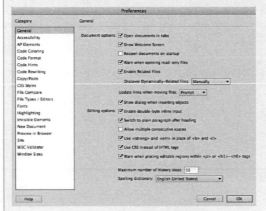

Note:

You can also open the Manage Sites dialog box by choosing Site>Manage Sites.

Customizing Dreamweaver Behavior

In addition to customizing the workspace, you can customize the way many of the program's options function. The left side of the Preferences dialog box (Dreamweaver>Preferences on Macintosh or Edit>Preferences on Windows) allows you to display the various sets of preferences available in Dreamweaver. As you work your way through the projects in this book, you will learn not only what you can do with these collections of Preferences, but also *why* and *when* you might want to use them.

You can also customize the various keyboard shortcuts used to access Dreamweaver commands (Dreamweaver>Keyboard Shortcuts on Macintosh or Edit>Keyboard Shortcuts on Windows). Once you have defined custom shortcuts, you can save your choices as a set so you can access the same custom choices again without having to redo the work.

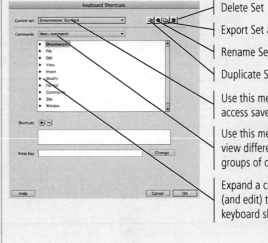

Delete Set

Export Set as HTML

Rename Set

Duplicate Set

Use this menu to access saved sets.

Use this menu to view different groups of commands.

Expand a category to see (and edit) the related keyboard shortcuts.

290   The Dreamweaver User Interface

6. **Click the Import Site button in the Manage Sites dialog box. Navigate to your WIP>Interface_DW folder, select sf-arts.ste in the list of available files, and click Open.**

The ".ste" extension identifies a Dreamweaver site file, which stores information about the site such as URL, FTP login information, etc. By importing this file into Dreamweaver, you can work with an existing site.

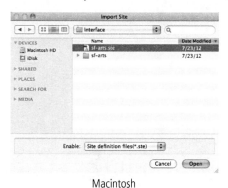 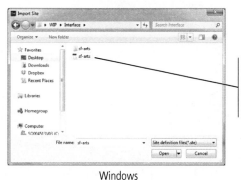

Depending on your system settings, the extension might not appear in your file list.

Macintosh   Windows

7. **When asked to select the local root folder of the site:**

   Macintosh users: Select the sf-arts folder (in your WIP>Interface folder) and click Open.

   Windows users: Navigate to and open the sf-arts folder (in your WIP>Interface folder), then click Select.

Note:

*The **root folder** is simply the base folder that contains the files of your site. This is referred to as the "local" root folder because it is the folder on your computer system. When you upload site files to a Web server, you place the files in the remote root folder.*

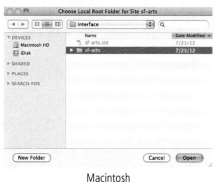 

Macintosh   Windows

8. **When asked to select the local images folder for the imported site:**

   Macintosh users: Select the images folder in the sf-arts folder and click Open.

   Windows users: Navigate to and open the sf-arts>images folder, then click Select.

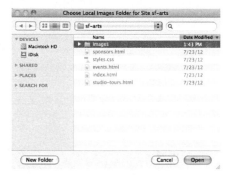 

Macintosh   Windows

After you identify the local images folder, files in the site are processed and then the site is listed in the Manage Sites dialog box. The name of the site (in this case, "sf-arts") is used for internal purposes only; it has no relation to the file names in the live HTML files.

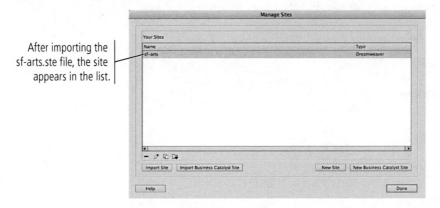

After importing the sf-arts.ste file, the site appears in the list.

9. Click Done to close the Manage Sites dialog box.

A Dreamweaver site typically includes links — from HTML pages to images, from one HTML page to another, and so on — which are the heart of interactive Web sites. When you import a site into Dreamweaver, the application processes the files in the site to identify links and other information required to maintain the integrity of the overall site.

When the import process is complete, the site appears in the Files panel.

Note:

Depending on the number of files in a site, you might see a progress bar indicating that Dreamweaver is processing the files and creating a site cache, which helps the application manage the links between various files in the site.

10. In the Files panel, click the arrow/plus sign (+) to expand the imported site folder.

The Files panel provides access to all the elements that make up a Web site, including page files (whether HTML, PHP, or some other format), images, downloadable PDFs, and anything else required for the site to display properly.

On Macintosh, expanded folders show a down-facing arrow; clicking that arrow collapses the folder and changes the arrow to face to the right. You can click a right-facing arrow to expand a folder and show its contents.

On Windows, expanded folders show a "–" symbol; clicking that symbol collapses the folder and changes the "–" to a "+" symbol. You can click a "+" symbol to expand a folder and show its contents.

Click and drag the line between columns to make a column wider or narrower in the panel.

Click any column heading in the panel to sort the files by that category.

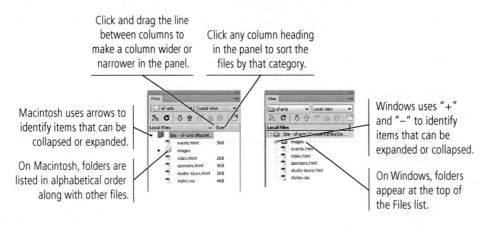

Macintosh uses arrows to identify items that can be collapsed or expanded.

On Macintosh, folders are listed in alphabetical order along with other files.

Windows uses "+" and "–" to identify items that can be expanded or collapsed.

On Windows, folders appear at the top of the Files list.

11. In the Files panel, double-click the **index.html** file.

Double-clicking a file in the Files panel opens that file in the document window.

For Dreamweaver to effectively monitor and manage the various links to required supporting files (images, scripts, etc.), you should only open and change site files from within the Files panel. If you open and change a file outside the context of the Files panel, Dreamweaver can't keep track of those changes, which can result in broken links.

All open files are represented by document tabs.

Related Files bar

Document toolbar

The Files panel provides access to all the files that make up the site.

The Properties panel presents different options depending on what is selected in the document.

12. If you don't see the Code, Split, and Design buttons above the document window, choose View>Toolbars>Document to toggle on the Document toolbar.

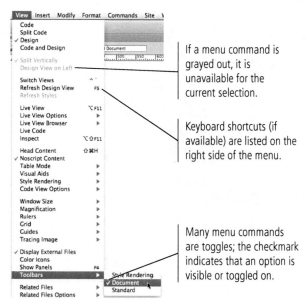

If a menu command is grayed out, it is unavailable for the current selection.

Keyboard shortcuts (if available) are listed on the right side of the menu.

Many menu commands are toggles; the checkmark indicates that an option is visible or toggled on.

Note:

If the Application frame is not active on Macintosh, the first open file will not have a document tab. Instead, a title bar appears at the top of the one open document. When you open more than one file at a time, each open document is represented by a tab at the top of the document window.

13. If you see more than one pane in the document window, click the Design button in the Document toolbar.

Design view is useful for visually-oriented site design, providing a visual preview of the file similar to the way it will appear in a browser window.

14. **If necessary, scroll down to show the bottom of the page. Click the "Art&Architechture" logo to select it, then review the Properties panel.**

At this point, it isn't necessary to understand what the various properties do; you learn about all these options in later projects. For now, you should simply understand that the Properties panel is context sensitive, which means the available options depend on what is currently selected.

Note:

The design for this site is based on the "Barren Savannah" template by Bryant Smith. The original template was found at www.free-templates.me, one of many online sources for Web design templates that are free to use and modify to meet your specific needs.

The selected object is an image.

The Properties panel shows options and information specific to the active selection.

15. **Double-click the word "Francisco" (in the first line of text below the logo) to select the entire word, and then review the Properties panel.**

Unlike many design applications, in Dreamweaver you don't have to choose a specific tool to select objects in a document.

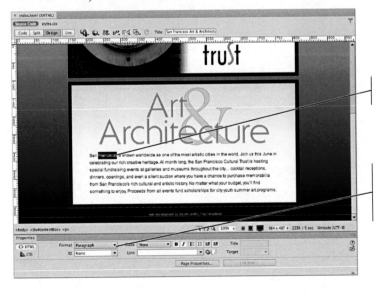

The selected word is editable text.

The Properties panel shows options and information related to the selected text.

16. With the text still selected, click the Split button in the Document toolbar.

Split view shows both the Code and Design view windows. When working in Split view, selecting an object in the Design view highlights the related code in the Code view.

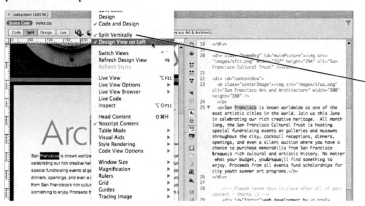

Click to show the Split view.

Code related to the selected text is highlighted in the Code view.

Note:

You can also choose Split Code view in the View menu, which shows the page code in two windows at the same time. This view can be useful if you need to write code in one area that specifically relates or refers to code at another point in the page.

17. Choose View>Design View on Left.

The Split Vertically option is toggled on by default to take advantage of the available space on widescreen monitors. By default, the Split view shows the Code view on the left and the Design view on the right; you can reverse this orientation to suit your personal work preferences.

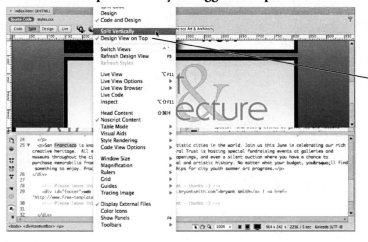

When Split Vertically is active, you can toggle the Design View on Left command to reverse the views in the document window.

18. Choose View>Split Vertically to toggle this option off.

When Split Vertically is not active, you can toggle the Design View on Top command to reverse the views in the document window.

19. Click the Code button in the Document toolbar.

The Code view is useful for people who are familiar with writing code; this mode allows you to (temporarily) ignore the visual design and work solely on the code.

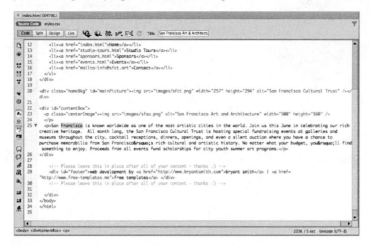

20. Click the Design button in the Document toolbar to return to Design view.

21. Continue to the next exercise.

 ## PREVIEW FILES IN DREAMWEAVER LIVE VIEW

Dreamweaver's Design view does a reasonably good job of allowing you to design Web pages visually, but some common design elements, such as rollovers and multimedia files, are not enabled in the Design view. The Live view provides an internal method for checking many of these elements without leaving the Dreamweaver environment.

You can't edit pages directly in Live view. However, if you are working in Split view, you can make changes to the code and then refresh the Live view to see the effect of those changes.

1. With the **sf-arts** site open in the Files panel, make sure **index.html** is open.

2. In the Files panel, double-click **studio-tours.html** to open that page.

Each open file is represented by a tab at the top of the document window. You can click any tab to make the associated file active in the document window.

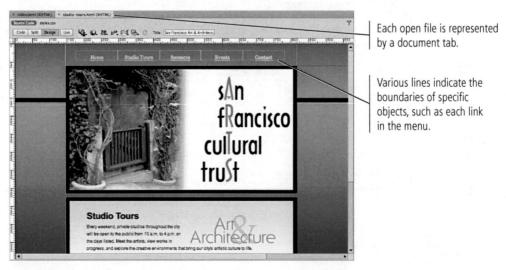

Each open file is represented by a document tab.

Various lines indicate the boundaries of specific objects, such as each link in the menu.

3. **Click the Visual Aids button in the document toolbar (above the document window) and choose Hide All Visual Aids.**

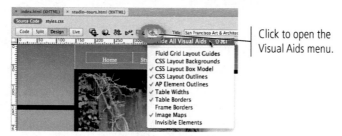

Click to open the Visual Aids menu.

Visual aids make it easier to identify the various elements (such as page divisions) used to create structure but which do not necessarily have a tangible physical appearance. While certainly useful, these visual aids interfere with the physical layout of the site so what you see in the document window is *not* what you get in the browser window.

Turning off visual aids is a good first step in previewing the page as it will actually appear to users.

4. **Click the Live button in the document toolbar, and then move your mouse cursor over the Sponsors link at the top of the page.**

Rollover elements do not function properly in Dreamweaver's Design view. The Live view provides a way to test interactive elements (such as rollovers) within the Dreamweaver environment.

Note:

*The **Live Code** button splits the document window to show the live design view and a non-editable view of the page code.*

In Live view, the rollover button displays as it would in a browser.

5. Press Command/Control and click the Studio Tours link.

One final reminder: throughout this book, we list differing commands in the Macintosh/Windows format. On Macintosh, you need to press the Command key; on Windows, press the Control key. (We will not repeat this explanation every time different commands are required for the different operating systems.)

In Live view, pressing the Command/Control key lets you preview linked files in the local site folder directly in the Dreamweaver document window. If you click a link to an external file, you will see a "File Not Found" error message.

When working in Live view, the Browser Navigation buttons in the Document toolbar function in the same way that standard browser navigation buttons work: Back, Forward, Stop/Refresh (reload), and Home (the site's index file).

Use these buttons to navigate back and forward, just as you would in a browser.

6. Command/Control-click the Contact link.

This button is set to open a new message in an email client. The Live view does not support non-HTML links, so an error message appears at the top of the document window.

The error message shows that Live view does not support non-HTML links.

This rollover is a link that opens a new email message.

7. In the Document toolbar, click the Live button to return to the normal Design view.

Navigating in the Live view does not technically open the linked pages. When you return to the regular Design view, the previously active page — in this case, studio-tours.html — is still the active one.

8. Click the Close button on the studio-tours.html tab to close that file.

Each document has its
own Close button.

9. Click the Close button on the index.html document tab to close that file.

10. Continue to the next exercise.

Note:

*On Macintosh systems,
clicking the Close button
on the document window
closes all open files,
but does not quit the
application.*

*On Windows systems,
clicking the Close (X)
button on the Applica-
tion frame closes all open
files and quits the
application.*

PREVIEW A FILE IN A BROWSER

As you saw in the previous exercise, the Live view can be used to verify the appearance of many common Web design objects. Of course, site users will not be using Dreamweaver to view your pages, so it is always a good idea to test pages using the same method that will actually be used to display your pages — namely, the various browsers that are in common use.

Although there are some standards that govern the way browsers display Web page code, the various browsers do have some different capabilities. Different operating systems also introduce display variables, so what you see in Mozilla Firefox on a Macintosh might appear different than what you see in Firefox on Windows. As a general rule, you should test your pages on as many browsers as possible — on both Macintosh and Windows operating systems.

**1. Macintosh: Choose Dreamweaver>Preferences.
   Windows: Choose Edit>Preferences.**

   On the left side of the Preferences dialog box, click Preview in Browser to display the related options.

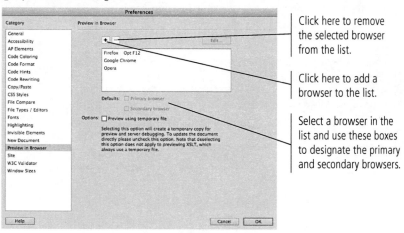

Click here to remove
the selected browser
from the list.

Click here to add a
browser to the list.

Select a browser in the
list and use these boxes
to designate the primary
and secondary browsers.

Note:

*It's a good idea to test
files at regular intervals
throughout the design
process, rather than
waiting until the end to
check your work.*

Note:

*Choosing File>Preview
in Browser>Edit Browser
List opens this pane
directly.*

2. Review the list of browsers that are identified by Dreamweaver.

   When installed, Dreamweaver scans your computer for available browser applications. You likely have at least one browser in this list, and probably even more than one.

3. If a browser is available on your system but not in Dreamweaver, click the "+" button above the list of browsers.

4. **In the resulting Add Browser dialog box, click the Browse button and identify the location of the browser you want to add.**

5. **Click OK to return to the Preferences dialog box.**

The list of browsers shows the defined primary and secondary browsers, which you can invoke using the associated keyboard shortcuts. To change the defaults, you can simply select a browser in the list and check the related Defaults options.

6. **Repeat Steps 3–5 as necessary to add all available browsers to Dreamweaver, then click OK to close the Preferences dialog box.**

7. **In the Files panel, double-click the index.html file to open it.**

8. **Click the Preview/Debug in Browser button in the Document toolbar and choose one of the listed browsers.**

9. **In the resulting browser window, click the Contact link on the right side of the menu.**

Because you are previewing the page in an actual browser, you can now test non-html links such as this one, which opens a new mail message in an email application.

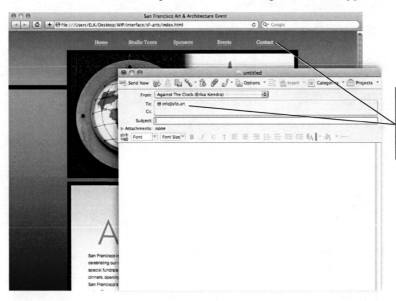

Clicking the link in a browser window correctly opens a new email message in your default email application.

10. **Close the mail message without sending.**

11. **Close the browser window and return to Dreamweaver.**

12. **Close index.html, then continue to the next exercise.**

Note:

Choosing Edit Browser List in this menu opens the Preview in Browser pane of the Preferences dialog box.

Note:

Press Option-F12/F12 to preview a page in your primary browser. Press Command/Control-F12 to preview the page in your secondary browser.

If you are using a Macintosh laptop, you also have to press the Function (FN) key to use the F key shortcuts.

Note:

A mailto: link opens a new mail message in the user's default email application. If a user does not have an email client, or has not specified one as the default option, clicking a mailto: link might open a message asking which application to use to send the email.

REMOVE A SITE FROM DREAMWEAVER

As you gain experience designing and developing Web sites, your site definition list will continue to grow. To keep your list under control, you can export site definitions and remove certain sites from the list. When you remove a site from Dreamweaver, you are not deleting the actual files and folders from your computer; you are simply removing them from Dreamweaver's view.

1. **In the Files panel, open the Directory menu and choose Manage Sites at the bottom of the list.**

2. **In the resulting Manage Sites dialog box, select the sf-arts site in the list and click the "–" button below the list of available sites.**

   In this case, you made no changes to the site definitions or files. Because you already have an STE file with the correct information, it is not necessary to re-export the site definition.

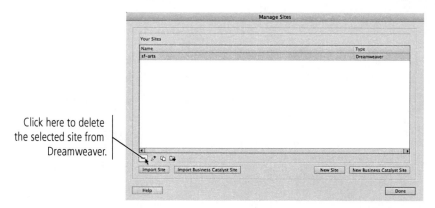

Click here to delete the selected site from Dreamweaver.

3. **Click Yes in the Warning dialog box, and then click Done to close the Manage Sites dialog box.**

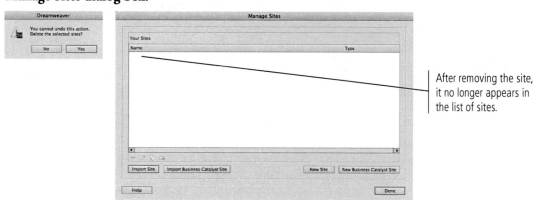

After removing the site, it no longer appears in the list of sites.

Bistro Site Organization

Your client has opened a new restaurant in a fast-growing community in Southern California. He has already designed the pages for his site, but has hired you to make sure everything works properly and then make the site available to the browsing public.

This project incorporates the following skills:

❏ Creating, exporting, and removing site definitions in Dreamweaver

❏ Moving files around in a site root folder

❏ Creating relative links between pages in a site

❏ Defining absolute links to external sites and email addresses

❏ Improving search engine optimization (SEO) with file names and titles

❏ Cloaking site files from a Web server

❏ Uploading files to a Web server

client comments

I already created the pages for our site, but I don't know what links to use, and I'm not sure how to create them. I've also heard that there are certain things you should do to improve a site's search engine rating — which is obviously important for a small business like mine.

art director comments

The more pages you add to a site, the more complex it becomes, until it's almost impossible to make sense of what you have and where it is located. Web sites — even those with only a few pages — should be designed with a good organizational plan, making it easier to modify pages later.

Once you have a handle on the organization, make sure the pages link to each other properly. Visitors get frustrated very quickly when they're forced to return to the home page every time they want to jump to a different set of pages.

The last thing you should do is add page titles and change file names to give a better indication of what's on each page. Doing so will make the site more accessible to people with screen-reader software, and it will also improve the site's ratings on search engines.

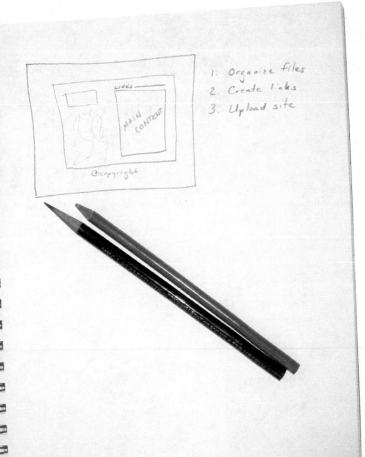

project objectives

To complete this project, you will:

❏ Create a Dreamweaver site definition

❏ Create new folders within the site root folder

❏ Use various methods to move files from one place to another within the site

❏ Create links between pages using several techniques available in Dreamweaver

❏ Differentiate between relative and absolute links

❏ Copy and paste links from one page to another

❏ Improve searchability and usability using page names and titles

❏ Cloak site files to hide them from the Web server

❏ Upload the site files to a server so they can be viewed online

Stage 1 **Exploring Site Structure**

When you start a new project that involves updating an existing site, your first task is to assess the file and folder structure. Doing so gives you a good idea of what the site contains.

A small site with only a few pages requires very little organization; in fact, you *can* place all of the files — Web pages and image files — in one folder (although even a small site benefits from a dedicated folder for images). Larger sites, however, require careful organization of file names, pages, and image files. A good site design with excellent organization speeds development now, and makes it much easier to update the site later.

CREATE A NEW SITE DEFINITION

Web sites are designed so all of the Web pages, image files, style sheets, and other resources are stored on your local drive in a base folder called the **root folder**. Other folders can be placed inside (below) the root folder to make it easier to manage and organize files.

1. Download **WC6_RF_Project6.zip** from the Student Files Web page.

2. Expand the ZIP archive in your WIP folder (Macintosh) or copy the archive contents into your WIP folder (Windows).

   This results in a folder named **Kinetic**, which contains all the files you need to complete this project.

3. In Dreamweaver, set up your workspace so the Files, Insert, and Properties panels are visible.

   It doesn't matter which saved workspace you start with. The primary tools you need for this project are the Files, Insert, and Properties panels. We have closed all other panels to maximize the available space in our screen shots.

4. In the Files panel, click the Manage Sites link or open the Directory menu and choose Manage Sites from the bottom of the list.

This option performs the same function as clicking the blue Manage Sites link to the right of the Directory menu.

If available, clicking Manage Sites opens the Manage Sites dialog box.

Note:

When a site is defined in Dreamweaver, the Manage Sites link at the top of the Files panel is replaced by a menu that defaults to Local view.

5. Click the New Site button in the Manage Sites dialog box.

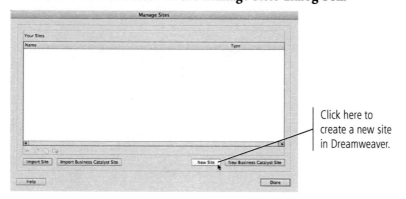

Click here to create a new site in Dreamweaver.

Note:

Ellipses in a menu or button name indicate that clicking will open a dialog box. We do not include the ellipses in our instructions.

6. **In the Site Setup dialog box, make sure Site is selected in the category list.**

7. **Type `Kinetic Site` in the Site Name field.**

   The site name can be anything that will allow you to easily recognize the project; it is only for identification within Dreamweaver. For example, you could use "Eve's site" as the site name within Dreamweaver to describe the Web site (www.evelynsmith.biz) that you are creating for your friend.

8. **Click the Browse for Folder button to the right of the Local Site Folder field. Navigate to the `WIP>Kinetic` folder and click Choose/Select to return to the Site Setup dialog box.**

   Part of the process of defining a site within Dreamweaver is to specify a particular folder as the site root folder of the Web site. Clicking the Local Site Folder button opens a navigation dialog box where you can find the folder you want to use.

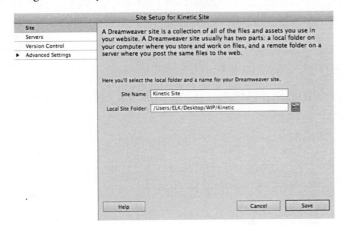

Note:

You will learn about other options in the Site Setup dialog box later in this book.

9. **Click Save to close the Site Setup dialog box.**

10. **In the Manage Sites dialog box, make sure the Kinetic Site item appears in the list of sites, and then click Done.**

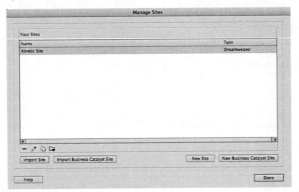

11. **Continue to the next exercise.**

EXAMINE THE SITE FILES

There are many files in the Kinetic Site folder. The first step in organizing the files is to examine the Web page files and understand what they contain.

1. **With Kinetic Site showing in the Directory menu of the Files panel, expand the site folder (if necessary) and examine the files in the site.**

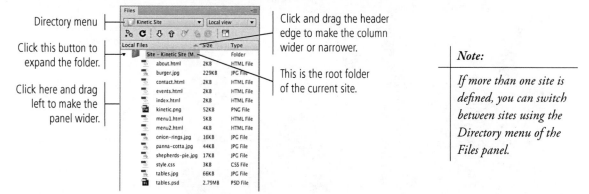

Directory menu

Click this button to expand the folder.

Click here and drag left to make the panel wider.

Click and drag the header edge to make the column wider or narrower.

This is the root folder of the current site.

2. **Double-click index.html in the Files panel to open the file in Dreamweaver.**

   If you see code in addition to the page design, click the Design button in the Document toolbar (above the document window).

   All of the pages in this site use the same basic design. The links at the top of each page need to navigate between the pages. The copyright information at the bottom (in the footer area) needs to navigate to the copyright owner's Web site, which is external to your client's site.

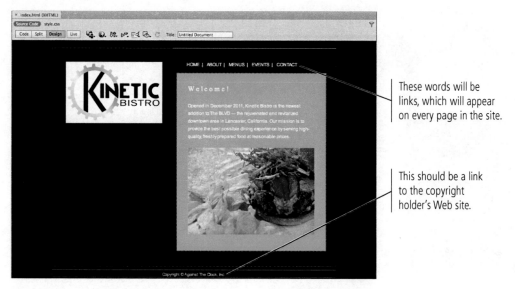

These words will be links, which will appear on every page in the site.

This should be a link to the copyright holder's Web site.

3. Close index.html, then open `contact.html`.

As you can see, this page uses the same basic design as the index page. The specific page content also includes an email link, which you need to define so that users can click the link to send your client an email message.

These links should be the same on every page in the site.

This should be an email link to your client's email address.

4. Close contact.html, then open `menu1.html`.

Again, the page uses the same basic layout as the other pages in the site. The top area of this page's primary content indicates that there are actually two menus — Dinner and Lunch. As you can see in the Files panel, two separate menu files exist. You will use the two headings at the top of the page to create links to each menu.

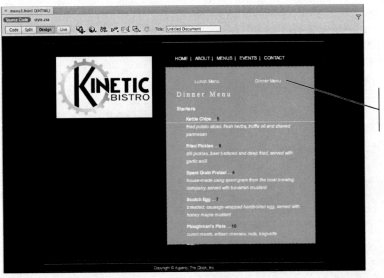

Each of these words should link to the relevant menu page.

5. Close menu1.html, then continue to the next exercise.

PLAN FOLDER ORGANIZATION

When all files are dumped into the main site folder, it can be challenging to manage your work. A well-organized site is an easy-to-manage site. Ideally, organization occurs before the site is constructed, but Dreamweaver makes it easy to reorganize files and folders at any point in the process.

There are no absolute rules to follow for organizing files and folders — other than the general principle of keeping related components together so you know where to find certain files when you need them.

1. **With Kinetic Site open in the Files panel, scroll to the top of the Files panel (if necessary) and click to select the site name at the top of the list.**

   The basic pages (home, about, contact, etc.) form the root of the site, and they should therefore appear within the root folder of the site. Other pages are better kept in folders that are named based on what they contain.

2. **Control/right-click the site name and choose New Folder from the contextual menu.**

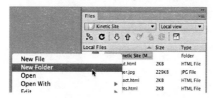

3. **Type resources and press Return/Enter to apply the new folder name.**

   When folders are first created, they appear at the bottom of their containing folders.

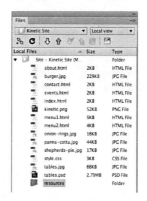

   Note:

   If after pressing Return/Enter, the folder name remains untitled, Control/right-click the untitled folder, choose Edit>Rename (or press F2), and correct the name.

4. **In the Files panel, click the Refresh button.**

   After refreshing the file list, folders on Macintosh are alphabetized along with all other files and folders; on Windows, folders are moved to and alphabetized at the top of the list, above individual files.

   Note:

   Press F5 to refresh the file list in the Files panel.

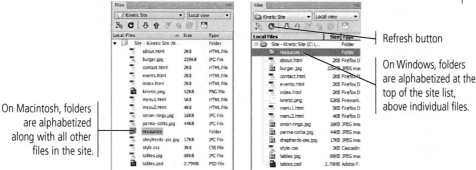

On Macintosh, folders are alphabetized along with all other files in the site.

 Refresh button

On Windows, folders are alphabetized at the top of the site list, above individual files.

5. **Click to again select the site folder at the top of the Files panel. Control/right-click the site folder and choose New Folder from the contextual menu.**

If you don't select the site folder first, the new folder would be created inside of the resources folder that you just created. You want another folder at the same level as the resources folder — in the main level of the site root folder — so you first have to select the site folder as the target location for the second new folder.

6. **Type images and press Return/Enter to apply the new folder name.**

Web design convention dictates image files be placed in a folder named "images" for easier organization. If you have many photos in various categories, you might want to create additional nested folders inside the main images folder.

7. **Repeat Steps 5–6 to create another new folder named menus in the site root folder.**

8. **Refresh the list in the Files panel.**

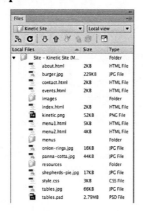

Note:

You can create a new folder inside an existing folder (called nesting) by Control/right-clicking the existing folder — instead of the root folder — and choosing New Folder from the contextual menu.

9. **Continue to the next exercise.**

The Files Panel in Depth

DREAMWEAVER FOUNDATIONS

By default, the Files panel displays the files on your local computer. You can also view the files on the remote or testing servers by choosing the appropriate option from the View menu.

The top of the Files panel also includes buttons that allow you to manage the files in your site:

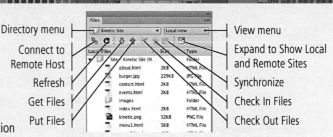

- **Connect to Remote Host** establishes a connection with the remote server (if you defined one). Otherwise, clicking this button opens the Site Definition dialog box.
- **Refresh** refreshes the file list that displays in the panel.
- **Get Files** copies the selected files from a remote server to the local folder. If the Enable File Check In and Check Out option is active, the copied files are available on the local site in read-only mode, which means you can't modify them. You must click the Check Out Files button to edit the files.
- **Put Files** copies the selected files from the local folder to the remote server. If a new file is added to the server, and if the Enable File Check In and Check Out option is active, the file's status is Checked Out.

- **Check Out Files** copies the selected files from the remote server to the local folder and locks the files so only the user who checked out those files can edit them.
- **Check In Files** copies the selected files from the local folder to the remote server and makes the copied files read-only in the local folder. To edit these files, you need to select them and click the Check Out Files button.
- **Synchronize** synchronizes the files between the local folder and the remote server so the same version of the files appears in both places.
- **Expand** shows both local files and the remote site (if one has been defined). The expanded Files panel has two panes; one displays the files on the remote or test server and one displays the local site files.

SORT AND MOVE IMAGE FILES

When you define a site in Dreamweaver, the application reads all of the pages in the site (a process that can take a few minutes in a large site), notes the links between pages, and identifies which images are used in which pages. These associations between files are stored in a cache that Dreamweaver creates when a new site is defined.

When files are moved or renamed within the site, Dreamweaver recognizes that other files are related to the moved or renamed files, and prompts you to update the links in all of the affected files.

1. **With Kinetic Site open in the Files panel, click and drag burger.jpg into the images folder.**

    Make sure you drag the file directly over the name of the folder or folder icon; if you drag the file too far to the left or right, Dreamweaver will not move the file.

    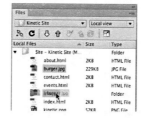

2. **When prompted, click Update to update the affected pages with the new location for the burger.jpg image file.**

    When a browser downloads a Web page, it reads the page code, requests the image files from the defined locations, and displays the images within the page. You should understand that images in Web pages are not embedded into Web pages; they are merged into the page by the browser.

    Files being updated do not need to be open for Dreamweaver to change the required link information. If pages *are* open, links in those pages are updated, but the changes are not automatically saved; you have to manually save each open file to make the updates permanent.

    If you choose Don't Update in the Update Links dialog box, the image will not appear in the page that calls for that file. If you had moved the image file using Windows Explorer or the Macintosh Finder, Dreamweaver would not have been aware of the movement, and you would not have had the opportunity to adjust the path to the image file in pages that link to that image.

> *Note:*
>
> *To avoid potential problems if you accidentally close a file without saving, you might want to close open files before moving or renaming files in the Files panel.*

    The burger.jpg file is now stored in the main images folder. When you move files into a folder, that folder automatically expands in the Files panel.

3. **In the Files panel, click the Type column heading to sort the site files by type.**

By default, site files are sorted by name. You can sort by another criteria by clicking the column headings in the Files panel. Sorting by type allows you to easily find all of the images that are used in this site.

4. **Click the first JPG file in the list (onion-rings.jpg) to select that file. Press Shift and click kinetic.png to select all consecutive files between the first and the last ones you selected.**

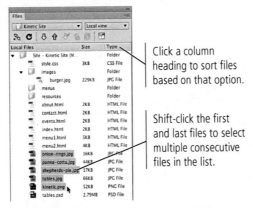

Click a column heading to sort files based on that option.

Shift-click the first and last files to select multiple consecutive files in the list.

Note:

You can change the columns that appear in the Files panel — and the order of those columns — in the File View Columns pane of the Site Setup dialog box.

5. **Click the icon of any of the selected files, and drag the selected files into the images folder. When asked, click Update to update all links to all of the moved files.**

Note:

Press Shift to select multiple consecutive files in the panel.

Press Command/Control and click to select multiple, nonconsecutive files.

You can also Command/Control-click to deselect a selected file. For example, if you select a file by accident, you can deselect it by Command/Control-clicking the file name again.

6. **Click the down-facing arrow (Macintosh) or the "–" symbol (Windows) to the left of the images folder name to collapse the folder.**

7. **Click the Local Files column header to re-sort the files by name.**

8. **Select menu1.html and menu2.html, and move them into the menus folder. Update the links when asked.**

This is a relatively small site, so nesting files into subfolders isn't strictly necessary. However, when you work with larger files, clearly organized subfolders can be extremely helpful in maintaining a site that is easy to update as often as necessary.

Note:

Images in Web sites typically have a GIF, JPG, or PNG extension.

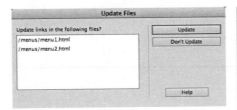

9. **Collapse the menus folder.**

10. **Select and move the file tables.psd into the resources folder.**

In this case, you are not asked to update links. This is a layered Photoshop file that was used to create the background image behind the page content. It is not part of the actual Web site, but it's a good idea to keep this type of file in the site folder in case you need to make changes later. Later in this project, you will learn how to prevent this file from being uploaded as part of the site.

Note:

You can also copy and paste files into a folder using the Edit options in the contextual menus, or using the standard keyboard shortcuts:

Cut:
Command/Control-X

Copy:
Command/Control-C

Paste:
Command/Control-V

11. **Collapse the resources folder.**

From the folder structure alone, the Web site appears to be better organized. You now know what to expect when you open each folder.

12. **Continue to the next stage of the project.**

Changing the Update Preferences

DREAMWEAVER FOUNDATIONS

As you have seen, Dreamweaver automatically asks you to update links when you move a file in the Files panel. You can change this behavior in the General pane of the Preferences dialog box.

If you choose Always in the Update Links... menu, the affected links are automatically updated without user intervention. In other words, you do not see the Update Files dialog box during the process.

If you choose Never, links are not automatically updated when you move files in the Files panel. If you do not manually correct links, they will result in an error when clicked by a user.

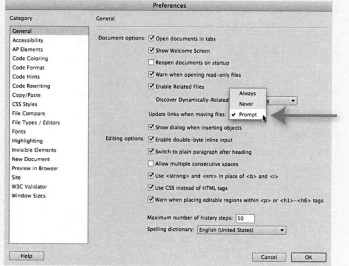

Stage 2 **Organizing the Site Navigation**

Hyperlinks (the official term for links) can be created to link pages on a site to other pages within the same site, or to pages on other sites. A well-designed site includes links that make it easy to get to any part of a site from any other part of a site. You should carefully plan the flow of links and connections between pages — always keeping the reader's usability in mind.

Organizing links is a simple application of a science called **information architecture**, which is the organization of a Web site to support both usability and "findability." As you organize site links, remember that your goal is to enable visitors to see a pattern in your links, which will assist them in navigating through your site. Keep the following points in mind when you plan a site's link structure:

- You can't know how visitors will enter your site. The primary site pages (home, about us, etc.) should be accessible from every page on the site.

- When linking secondary pages such as different menus for different mealtimes, don't make users constantly click the browser's Back button. Links should allow users to navigate all sibling pages (at the same level) as easily as navigating the primary structure. For example, users should be able to access the dinner menu or lunch menu in the restaurant's site without first going back to a main "Menu" page.

Using the terms "parent," "child," and "sibling" is simply a way of describing relationships between pages. A large Web site cannot provide links to all of the pages from its home page. By grouping pages, grouping groups of pages, and so on, you create relationships of equality between pages that are grouped together, as well as between groups that are grouped together.

When you plan a new site, you should create this type of flowchart to make sure you create all the necessary links that make the site as user-friendly as possible. A flowchart of the required Kinetic Site link structure is shown below.

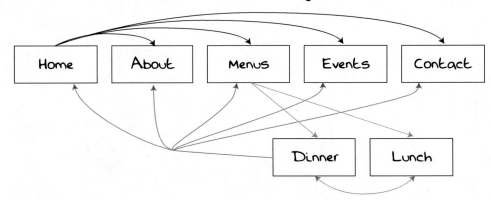

Kinetic Bistro Site Navigation

In this stage of the project, you will learn various techniques to create the necessary links on the Kinetic Site pages.

CREATE HYPERLINKS WITHIN THE SITE

Dreamweaver offers a number of options for creating the necessary links for any Web site structure.

- **Hyperlink Button in the Common Insert Panel.** Clicking the Hyperlink button in the Common Insert panel opens the Hyperlink dialog box, where you define the specific parameters of the link.

- **Insert>Hyperlink menu.** This menu command opens the same dialog box that you see when you click the Hyperlink button in the Insert panel.

- **Properties Panel Fields.** You can also simply define the specifics of a hyperlink in the Properties panel. This method offers the same options as those in the Hyperlink dialog box, but does not require the dialog box interface.

- **Point to File button in the Properties panel.** To create a link using this method, simply click the Point to File button, hold down the mouse button, and drag to a file in the Files panel; Dreamweaver automatically creates a link.

- **Browse for File button in the Properties panel.** The Browse for File button opens a navigation dialog box, where you can select the file that will open when a user clicks on the link.

- **Shift-Drag Method.** You can create a link directly from the document window by pressing Shift and then clicking and dragging from the link source to the destination page in the Files panel. (This method only works for text; you can't Shift-drag to create a link for an image.)

Note:

Dreamweaver often includes several different ways to achieve the same result. You should use the method that is most efficient at the time.

1. With **Kinetic Site** open in the Files panel, open **index.html.**

2. At the top of the page, double-click the word "HOME" to select it.

3. If your Insert panel is docked above the document window, click the Common tab at the top of the panel.

    If your Insert panel is docked on the right side of the screen, or if it is floating as a separate panel, choose Common in the menu at the top of the panel.

If docked in standard mode, use the menu at the top of the panel to access different categories of options.

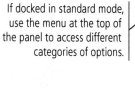

If docked in tabbed mode, use the tabs at the top of the panel to access different categories of options.

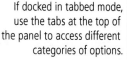
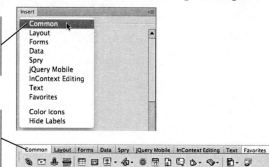

The Common Insert panel contains buttons for frequently used items. For example, to insert a hyperlink, simply click the corresponding button. (Some of the terms and functions in the following descriptions will make more sense as you use those tools to complete later projects.)

- The **Hyperlink** button opens a dialog box where you can create text or image links to another file, either in the same Web site or in an external Web site.

- The **Email Link** button opens a dialog box where you can create links to email addresses. When a user clicks an email link, it opens the user's default email application with the email address in the To line.

- The **Named Anchor** button marks locations within a page. Links can be provided to these locations from within the same page or from other pages of the same Web site or other Web sites.

- The **Horizontal Rule** button inserts a solid line across the width of the page. This can be useful for visually separating sections of text.

- The **Table** button inserts a table into the page.

- The **Insert Div Tag** button inserts new sections (divisions) in a page. Each division in a page is marked by a dotted line in Dreamweaver; these dotted lines do not appear when the page is viewed in a browser. Divisions are useful for inserting blocks of content you want to format independently from other blocks.

- The **Images** button inserts various types of graphics. If you click the arrow on the button icon, a menu shows the available types of objects (basic images, rollover images, etc.). You can also insert an image placeholder, which reserves a portion of the page for inserting an object later.

- The **Media** button inserts audio-visual files. These files could be in any format, but Dreamweaver also has functionality specific to inserting Flash, QuickTime, and Shockwave files; Java applets; and ActiveX controls.

- The **Widget** is used to insert Spry widgets. Dreamweaver ships with a number of built-in Spry widgets. You can download other widgets through the online Widget Browser, which is a separate free download. To access this functionality, you can open the Extend Dreamweaver menu in the Application/Menu bar and choose Widget Browser. (If the Widget Browser extension is not yet installed on your system, you will be prompted to download and install the application.)

- The **Date** button inserts the date and time. An option is provided for updating the date and time whenever the file is saved.

- The **Server-Side Include** button inserts a file within a page by creating a link to the external file.

- The **Comment** button inserts comments in the code that describe something about its use. These comments display in Code view only; they do not appear in Design view or in the browser.

- The **Head** button adds information about the page that will be used by browsers. This information is included in the properties of the page. Click the arrow to select the type of information you want to add.

- The **Script** button enables you to add code that will be used by the browser to perform an action when the page is accessed. Click the arrow and click Script from the menu to add the code. Some older versions of browsers might have the script-reading feature disabled; to display alternate content when browsers fail to read the script, click No Script from the menu. You need to know programming languages to use this feature properly.

- The **Templates** button creates a template based on the current document, which is useful when you need to create multiple documents from the same layout.

- The **Tag Chooser** button inserts tags in the code. Tags are elements in the code that define the kind of content that is included. Tags are included automatically when you edit pages in Design view.

4. Click the Hyperlink button in the Common Insert panel.

The Common Insert panel contains many of the common functions you use to create Web pages. If a different Insert panel is showing, you can return to the Common Insert panel by choosing Common in the panel menu.

Note:

From this point on, we will leave our Insert panel docked on the right side of the workspace, immediately below the Files panel. Feel free to organize your workspace however you prefer.

If docked in standard mode, buttons in the panel are identified by icon and name.

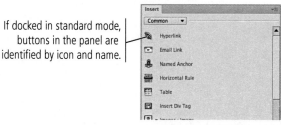

If docked in tabbed mode, hover your mouse over a button to find its name.

This word is selected.

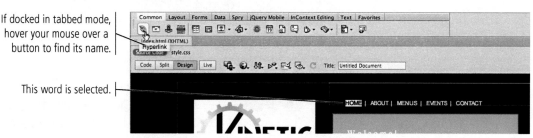

5. In the Hyperlink dialog box, click the Browse button to the right of the Link field.

The text selected in the document appears in the Text field by default. (If an image is selected, this field defaults to be blank.)

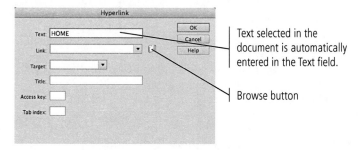

Text selected in the document is automatically entered in the Text field.

Browse button

6. Navigate to your WIP>Kinetic folder, select index.html, and click Open/OK.

In the Link field, you can either type the URL of a location outside the site you're building, or you can click the Browse button to select a file within the current site.

7. **Open the Target menu and choose _self.**

This option determines where the linked file will open:

- **_blank** opens every linked file in a new, unnamed browser window.
- **new** creates a new browser window with the name "_new". Every link assigned the _new target will open in that same _new browser window.
- **_parent** is relevant if a page includes nested frames; this option opens the link in the frame or window that contains the frame with the link.
- **_self** opens the link in the same frame or browser window as the link. This is the default behavior if you do not choose an option in the Target menu.
- **_top** opens the link in the same browser window, regardless of frames.

8. **In the Title field, type `Kinetic Bistro home page`.**

The Title field defines text that appears when the cursor is placed over the link text. Defining a descriptive title for links can help a page achieve better search engine results.

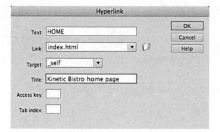

9. **Click OK in the Hyperlink dialog box to create the link.**

10. **Click the Split button in the Document toolbar to review both the design and code views at one time.**

A Web page is basically a page full of code. A browser reads the code to determine how to treat various elements of the page. HTML code largely revolves around tags, which tell a browser how to interpret specific objects on the page.

A hyperlink is identified by the **a** element, which starts with the opening **<a>** tag; the link destination and target are defined as attributes of that tag (**href="index.html" target="_self"**). After the actual link text, the closing tag (**</a>**) identifies the end of the link.

Note:

You can change the destination of a link by selecting the linked text or object in the document and choosing Modify>Change Link. This menu command opens the same dialog box as the Browse for File button, where you can navigate to and select the new link destination.

Note:

You can use the Access Key field to define a keyboard shortcut for the link, and use the Tab Index field to specify the number of times a user needs to press the Tab key to select the link.

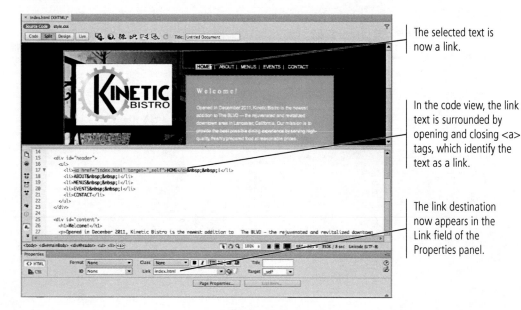

The selected text is now a link.

In the code view, the link text is surrounded by opening and closing <a> tags, which identify the text as a link.

The link destination now appears in the Link field of the Properties panel.

11. **Click the Design button in the Document toolbar to close the Code pane.**

12. **Select the word "ABOUT" at the top of the page.**

Note:

When a link to another page in the site is selected in the document, you can open the related page in Dreamweaver by choosing Modify>Open Linked Page.

13. **Click the Browse for File button to the right of the Link field in the Properties panel.**

    If you don't see the Properties panel, choose Window>Properties. The Properties panel's primary purpose is to review and change the properties of the selected HTML element (such as a heading, paragraph, or table cell).

The word ABOUT is selected.

Browse for File button

14. **In the resulting dialog box, select about.html, and then click Open/OK.**

The link destination now appears in the Link field of the Properties panel.

15. **Select the word "MENUS" at the top of the page.**

16. **Expand the menus folder in the Files panel.**

    You should expand and collapse Files panel folders as necessary, depending on your available screen space. We will not repeat instructions to collapse or expand folders unless it is necessary to perform a specific function.

Note:

You can remove a link by selecting the linked text or object in the document and choosing Modify>Remove Link, or by simply deleting the text from the Link field in the Properties panel.

17. **Click the Point to File button in the Properties panel, hold down the mouse button, and drag to menus/menu1.html in the Files panel.**

The word MENUS is selected.

Point to File button

18. **Select the word "EVENTS" at the top of the page.**

19. **Press the Shift key, then click the selected text and drag to events.html in the Files panel.**

    You have to press the Shift key, and then click and drag to the link destination. If you try to click and drag before pressing the Shift key, this technique will fail.

20. **Use any method you just learned to create a link from the word "CONTACT" to the contact.html file.**

21. **Select the words "Against The Clock, Inc." at the bottom of the page.**

22. **In the Link field of the Properties panel, type http://www.againsttheclock.com and press Return/Enter.**

    Dreamweaver can't help you create an external URL link because it's outside the site definition. You have to simply type or paste the address into the Link field.

    An external **URL link** must begin with the "http://" protocol, followed by the domain name and, if relevant, the folder path and file name of the page to which you are linking.

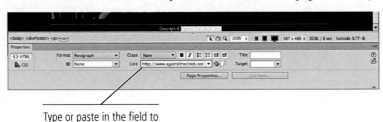

Type or paste in the field to define an external URL link.

Note:

To minimize the repetitive work required, we already defined this link for you on the other pages in the site. In a professional environment, you would need to add this link to every page in the site.

23. **Choose File>Save to save your changes in the file, then continue to the next exercise.**

COPY AND PASTE LINKS

Rather than manually creating the same links on every page, you can now simply copy and paste them from one page to another.

1. **With index.html open (from the Kinetic Site), click in any of the text links to place the insertion point.**

2. **Review the Tag Selector below the document window.**

   The Tag Selector, located in the status bar of the document window, shows the nesting order of HTML tags (the "path of tags") based on the current selection or the current location of the insertion point.

Insertion point

Active tag

Tag Selector

3. **Click the <ul> tag in the Tag Selector.**

   The **<ul>** tag identifies an unordered list, which is how this navigation structure was created; each link is a separate list item (using the **<li>** tag).

   Clicking a tag in the Tag Selector selects that HTML element and all of its content. In the document window, the associated content is highlighted.

   > *Note:*
   >
   > *You will work more extensively with tags beginning in Project 7: Digital Book Chapter.*

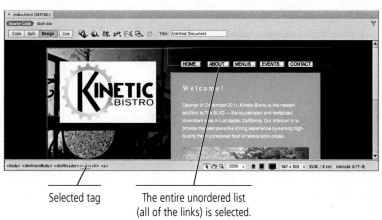

Selected tag

The entire unordered list (all of the links) is selected.

4. **Choose Edit>Copy (or press Command/Control-C) to copy the selected content to the Clipboard.**

5. **Close index.html and open about.html.**

6. **Click to place the insertion point anywhere in the list of links at the top of the page, and then click the <ul> tag in the Tag Selector to select the entire unlinked list.**

The selected list does not yet include links.

7. **Choose Edit>Paste (or press Command/Control-V) to paste the copied content from the Clipboard.**

8. **Place the insertion point in any of the links and review the Tag Selector.**

   The Tag Selector now shows the **<a>** tag for the current insertion point (in our example, the CONTACT link). The Properties panel also shows the destination of the active link.

The pasted content includes the links.

9. **Save the changes to about.html and close the file.**

10. **Repeat Steps 6–9 to paste the copied content (the links) into all HTML pages in the site root level, as well as the two HTML pages in the menus folder.**

11. **Save and close any open files, and then continue to the next exercise.**

ADJUST RELATIVE LINK PATHS

A **path** is the route taken through the folder structure to link one page to another. By default, Dreamweaver uses **relative paths** when creating links (the application refers to this as "relative to the document"). The alternative is to create **absolute paths** ("relative to the site"); but unless your site is running on a Web server, you can't test links that use absolute paths.

As an example, consider creating a link from index.html to about.html, both of which reside in the root folder (as shown in the figure to the right). In this case, the source and destination pages are in the same folder; the relative-path link simply states the file name of the destination page:

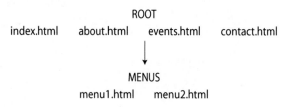

<a href="menu2.html">Link Text</a>

When you drill down into nested levels of folders, the source folder is not identified in the path; the link automatically works starting from the location of the link. To link from index.html to menu1.html, for example, you have to include the nested menus folder in the path:

<a href="menus/menu1.html">Link Text</a>

When the link is in an upward direction, the ../ notation says "go up one folder." To link from menu1.html to index.html in the site root folder means that the link needs to take the visitor up one folder level:

<a href="../index.html">Link Text</a>

Each step up in the folder structure requires another command to "go one step up" in the folder structure. If you had another level of nesting inside the menus folder, for example, a link would have to take the visitor up two folder levels to return to the main index page:

<a href="../../index.html">Link Text</a>

In the next exercise, you are going to adjust the menu links in the menu files so they work properly.

1. **With the Kinetic Site open in the Files panel, open menu1.html.**

2. **Double-click the word HOME at the top of the page to select it.**

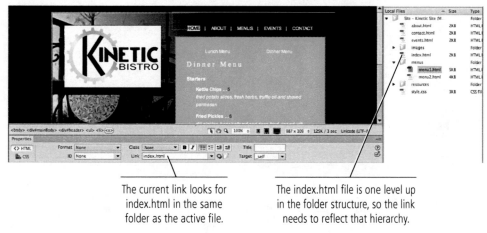

The current link looks for index.html in the same folder as the active file.

The index.html file is one level up in the folder structure, so the link needs to reflect that hierarchy.

3. **In the Properties panel, place the insertion point at the beginning of the Link field and type ../ before the existing link.**

4. **Press Return/Enter to finalize the change.**

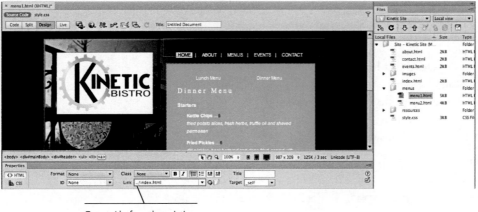

Type ../ before the existing
link to move up one folder
from the active file.

5. **Repeat Steps 2–4 for the ABOUT, EVENTS, and CONTACT links.**

6. **Select the word MENUS at the top of the page.**

   In this case, the link is still a problem because it directs the browser to look for a folder named "menus" inside the same folder as the active page. You need to remove the folder part of the path to prevent an error if a user clicks this link from the menu1.html page.

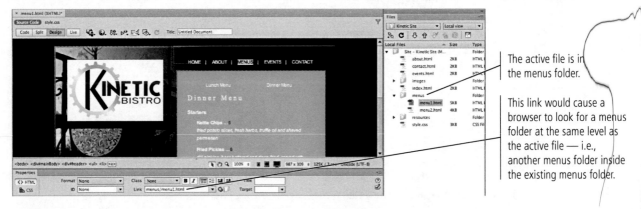

The active file is in
the menus folder.

This link would cause a
browser to look for a menus
folder at the same level as
the active file — i.e.,
another menus folder inside
the existing menus folder.

7. **In the Properties panel, delete menus/ (including the forward slash) from the existing link.**

Delete the folder path
from the existing link.

8. Using any method you already have learned, link "Lunch Menu" to menu2.html and link "Dinner Menu" to menu1.html.

Link this to menu2.html.   Link this to menu1.html.

9. Repeat the process from Steps 1–8 to adjust the top links and add the necessary secondary links in the menu2.html file.

10. Save and close any open files, then continue to the next exercise.

Accessing Page Content in the Menu Pages

The files for this project were created using divs (using the opening and closing <div> tags), which are simply a way to identify and format parts or sections of a page.

(You will begin working with the idea of divs in Project 7: Digital Book Chapter, and then extensively throughout the rest of the book.) Although you don't need to worry about the underlying page structure for now, you might see some unusual behavior when you first try to select content in the main section of each menu page.

The area that holds the actual menu content has a fixed height, but both menus have more content than will fit into the defined size. When the page is viewed in a browser, the area includes a scroll bar for users to access the content that doesn't fit.

In Dreamweaver's Design view, however, this scrollbar doesn't appear. Instead, the first time you click, the entire div is selected and all of the contained text is highlighted.

Clicking inside the area again causes the page to jump down, showing some of the overflow content.

If you click a third time, you can place the insertion point inside the actual text, scroll up as necessary, and then select the link text at the top of the area.

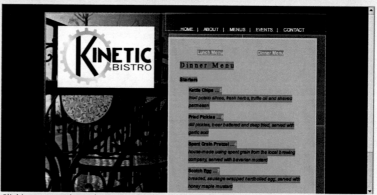

Clicking once selects the entire div that contains the menu content.

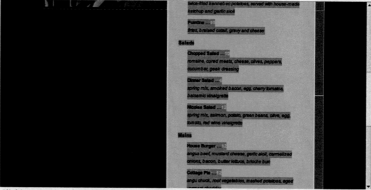

Clicking a second time jumps the page down to show the overflow content.

Clicking a third time places the insertion point so you can select specific text in the menu.

CREATE AN EMAIL LINK

Most Web sites include one or more external links (including email links), which require the appropriate protocol to tell the browser what type of link is present.

An **email link** requires the "mailto:" protocol, followed by the appropriate email address. This instructs the browser to open a new mail message with the defined address already in the To line.

1. **With Kinetic Site open in the Files panel, open contact.html.**

2. **Select the words "info@kineticbistro.atc" in the main content area.**

3. **In the Common Insert panel, click the Email Link button.**

Selected text

4. **Review the resulting dialog box, then click OK.**

   If you select text before clicking the Email Link icon, the Text field is completed for you. Dreamweaver also recognizes that the selected text is an email address, so the Email field is filled in for you.

   If the selected text is not recognized as an email address, the Email field defaults to the last address that was defined in the field.

5. **Click OK to create the email link.**

6. **Review the link field in the Properties panel.**

   An email link must begin with "mailto:" followed by the address. When you use the Email Link dialog box, Dreamweaver automatically inserts the mailto: protocol.

7. **Save the file and close it, then continue to the next stage of the project.**

Note:

You can access the same Email Link dialog box by choosing Insert>Email Link.

Note:

In many cases throughout this book, we use "[company].atc" as the domain of a site.

Although at the time of writing, none of the domain names we use are real, new domains are registered every day. We use the fictitious ".atc" domain to avoid inadvertently using the domain name of a real company.

When you upload files to a server, you should use the accurate domain (.com, .gov, .edu, etc.) for the site you are building.

Stage 3 Naming and Titling Documents

When a **Web server** (special computers that store and deliver Web pages) receives a request for a folder but not a specific page, the Web server delivers the default page for that folder — usually named index.html or index.htm. There is no practical difference between the two extensions; most Web servers can serve files with either extension.

To create links to the default page in a specific folder, you do not need to include the file name if you use the index naming convention. Both **www.kineticbistro.com/** and **www.kineticbistro.com/index.html** refer to the same page.

Note:

If a link does not specify a specific file in a nested folder, the Web server will look for a file named index.html or index.htm inside the defined folder. If you do not have an index file in that folder, the link will result in an error.

RENAME PAGES FOR SEARCH ENGINE OPTIMIZATION

SEO (search engine optimization) is the process of improving the ranking of a Web site and its pages within **SERPs** (search engine results pages, or the pages that list the results of a search). Search engines certainly use the content of a page for ranking purposes, but the names of folders and files also affect search engine rankings. Descriptive folder and file names also improve usability; you can use **m/menu1.html** for the path to the dinner menu page, for example, but **/menus/dinner-menu.html** is much easier for human visitors to understand — and will also improve your search engine ranking.

In this exercise, you rename the menu pages to more accurately describe what is contained in the files. As with moving files, the application recognizes when a file name has been changed and knows that links to the page must be adjusted.

1. **With Kinetic Site open, click menus/menu1.html in the Files panel to select that file.**

2. **Click the selected filename again to highlight it.**

   This highlights the existing filename, exluding the extension.

Note:

You can also Control/ right-click a file in the Files panel and choose Edit>Rename to rename a specific file.

3. **Type dinner-menu, then press Return/Enter. In the resulting dialog box, click Update to update all pages that link to this page.**

   Typing when the filename is highlighted replaces the previous file name. Pressing Return/Enter finalizes the change.

   As with moving files, Dreamweaver recognizes that all links to the renamed page need to point to the new file name.

4. **Repeat Steps 1–3 to rename menu2.html as lunch-menu.html.**

5. **Continue to the next exercise.**

Understanding Web File Naming Conventions

The file names of pages should make the content or purpose of each page clear.

Because different servers run on different operating systems, the safest way to name pages is to use only characters that are guaranteed to work perfectly:

- a through z (use only lowercase letters)
- 0 through 9
- Hyphen (great-site.html)
- Underscore (great_site.html)

Consider everything else to be "illegal," including:

- Spaces
- Brackets of all kinds, including ( ), [ ], { }, and < >
- Symbols, including #, @, %, ~, |, *, and &
- Quotation marks, both double (" ") and single (' ')
- Slashes, both back slashes (\) and forward slashes (/)
- Commas, periods, question marks, and exclamation points
- Uppercase characters

Some designers use **CamelCase** — uppercase letters at the beginning of each word within a file name, such as UniversalStudios.html — file names instead of using hyphen or underscore characters to separate words. The problem with mixing the lettercase is that some Web server software is case-sensitive and some is not.

Most Windows-based Web server software is not case-sensitive; but UNIX- and Linux-based Web server software is case-sensitive. Considering that many Web servers run on UNIX- or Linux-based computers, it's best to use only lowercase file and folder names.

CREATE DOCUMENT TITLES FOR INDIVIDUAL PAGES

Appropriate document titles are an important concern for both search engines and site visitors. While the document title does not appear within the body of a Web page, it does appear in the title bar of the browser, as the default name of the page in the Bookmarks or Favorites list, and as the page name in search-engine results pages.

Page titles should be relatively short, around 70 characters or so to avoid their being truncated in various locations (such as a user's Bookmarks/Favorites list). You should separate the components of the title with some type of divider, such as a colon (:) or pipe (|) character.

In this exercise, you add document titles to the new pages to increase the pages' search engine rankings and improve usability for visitors who find the pages in search engines and bookmarks. You also learn to use the Find and Replace function, which can greatly reduce the amount of effort required to create all of the document titles.

1. **With Kinetic Site open in the Files panel, open index.html.**

2. **Make sure the Document toolbar is showing (View>Toolbars>Document).**

3. **Click the Split button in the Document toolbar to show both the Code and Design views at one time.**

4. **Examine the Title field above the document window.**

   When you create a new page in Dreamweaver, the default title is "Untitled Document". That text appears in the Title field of the Document toolbar, and in the title element in the Code pane (wrapped in the opening and closing **<title>** tags).

Document title ⊢

5. **Choose Edit>Find and Replace.**

6. **Change the Find In menu to Folder, then click the Browse button to the right of the attached field. In the resulting dialog box, navigate to your WIP>Kinetic folder and click Open/Select.**

   You want to affect all files in the site, so you are selecting the defined site root folder in this dialog box.

7. **Choose Source Code in the Search menu.**

   The document title does not appear in the body of the page, so when you use Find and Replace, you must apply the change to the source code rather than the document text.

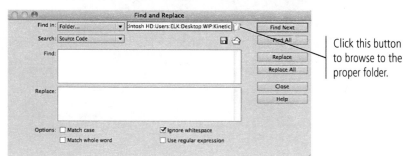

Click this button to browse to the proper folder.

Note:

When you use the Split view, feel free to arrange the pane however you prefer. We arrange them as necessary to best suit what we are trying to show in our screen captures.

8. **In the Find field, type** `Untitled Document`.

9. **In the Replace field, type** `Kinetic Bistro | Lancaster, California |`. **(Include a space after the final pipe character.)**

    All pages in the site will include this block of text at the beginning of the document title. Further detail about individual pages will be added to the right of this information.

Note:

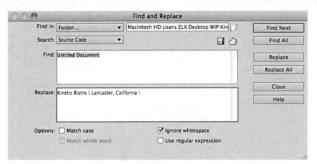

Some experts disagree whether the company name should come before or after the specific page information in a title. However, putting the company name at the beginning of the page title can help with search engine results because the company name is an important keyword.

10. **Click Replace All. When prompted to confirm whether you want to proceed with this function, click Yes.**

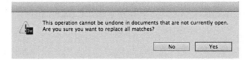

    Like most applications, Dreamweaver has an Undo function that allows you to undo the most recently completed actions; however, this function only works if the document is open. Since you are using the Find and Replace function on the entire folder and not only on an open page, you are making changes in closed documents — which means you cannot use the Undo command.

    After completing the Find and Replace function, Dreamweaver displays the results in the Search panel.

11. **Examine the title in the Document toolbar and the Code pane again for the open file (index.html).**

    As a result of the Find and Replace function, the document title has been changed. The same change has been made in all pages in the site.

12. **Close the Search panel group.**

13. **Click in the Code pane to make it active.**

14. **Click at the end of the existing page title to place the insertion point immediately before the closing `</title>` tag.**

15. **Type Gourmet Casual Dining.**

   You can edit the page title in the Document toolbar or in the Code pane. Changes in either place are automatically applied to the other.

Type the new information immediately before the closing `</title>` tag.

16. **Save index.html and close it.**

17. **Open about.html. Using either the Title field in the Document toolbar or the Code pane, add Hours of Operation to the end of the existing page title.**

18. **Save about.html and close it.**

19. **Repeat this process (Steps 14–18) to change the page titles of the remaining pages as follows:**

File	Title
contact.html	Address and Contact Information
events.html	Special Event Facilities
menus/dinner-menu.html	Dinner Menu
menus/lunch-menu.html	Lunch Menu

20. **Continue to the final stage of the project.**

Note:

Making a specific pane active is called "bringing it into focus".

Note:

Unlike file names, document titles can use mixed lettercase and include spaces and other characters. However, you should avoid both single and double quotation marks.

Stage 4 Making Files Public

To complete the final stage of this project — making your files accessible to the browsing public — you need to have access to some type of server.

On the inside back cover of this book, you have a code that you need to gain access to the required resource files. The same code also provides access to a six-month, free trial Web hosting account at Pair Networks (www.pair.com).

If you don't already have access to an online server, go to **www.pair.com/atc/** to sign up for your hosting account before you complete the final stage of this project. You must enter your contact information, and the code from the inside back cover of your book. You should then define a user name in the last field; this will become part of the server name for your hosting account.

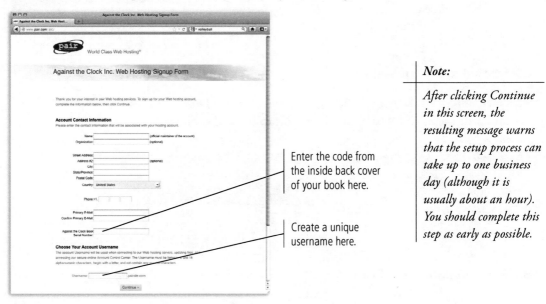

Enter the code from the inside back cover of your book here.

Create a unique username here.

Note:

After clicking Continue in this screen, the resulting message warns that the setup process can take up to one business day (although it is usually about an hour). You should complete this step as early as possible.

After you click Continue, you will receive an acknowledgement that your request is being processed. You will receive a confirmation email (sent to the email you defined in the Signup Form) with your username and password information. Once you receive the confirmation email, you are ready to complete the final stage of this project.

HIDE FILES FROM THE WEB SERVER

As you saw when you created the folders for the new site, not all of the new files are meant to be uploaded to the Web server — specifically, the Photoshop file in the resources folder. (You should, however, store such files locally as source files or documentation for the work you completed.)

Dreamweaver provides a very useful function — called **cloaking** — that allows you to prevent certain files from uploading. You can cloak an individual file; cloak all files with the same extension (for example, all native Photoshop files with the PSD extension); or cloak a folder, which also cloaks all files in that folder.

1. **With Kinetic Site open in the Files panel, double-click the Kinetic Site name in the Directory menu.**

    This opens the Site Setup dialog box for the selected site. You do not need to go through the Manage Sites dialog box to edit the settings for the active site.

Double-click the existing site name to open the Site Setup dialog box for that site.

2. **In the Site Setup dialog box, expand the Advanced Settings menu on the left side and click Cloaking to show the related options.**

3. **Make sure the Enable Cloaking check box is active.**

   When Enable Cloaking is checked, you can hide selected files and folders from a Web server. You can also use the Cloak Files Ending With option to hide all files with the extensions that are listed in the field.

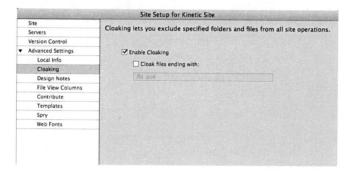

4. **Click Save to close the Site Setup dialog box.**

5. **In the Files panel, collapse all open folders and expand only the resources folder.**

6. **Control/right-click the resources folder and choose Cloaking>Cloak.**

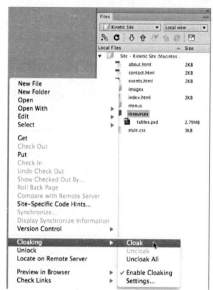

Note:

You can also cloak a specific file by Control/right clicking that file in the Files panel and choosing Cloaking>Cloak.

   Notice the red slash through the resources folder icon and the icon for the file in the resources folder. The red slash refers to the cloaking function only; it does not prevent you from working with the files, adding more files, or deleting any of the existing files.

7. **Continue to the next exercise.**

DEFINE REMOTE CONNECTION INFO FOR THE SITE

For Dreamweaver to manage file uploading, you first have to define the hosting server connection settings as part of the site setup information.

1. **With Kinetic Site open in the Dreamweaver Files panel, double-click the site name in the Directory menu to open the Site Setup dialog box.**

2. **In the Site Setup dialog box, click Servers in the list of categories, then click the + button near the bottom of the dialog box to define a new server.**

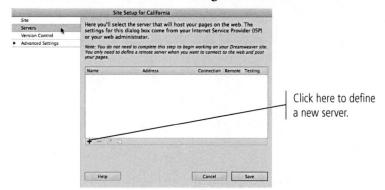

Click here to define a new server.

3. **In the Basic options, type a name for the server you are using.**

   This name is simply for you to identify it in Dreamweaver.

4. **Assuming you are working with a remote server, choose FTP in the Connect Using menu.**

   If you are using a local server, consult your network administrator for the settings to use.

5. **In the FTP Address field, type the hostname for your server.**

   Using our example hosting account at Pair Networks, the FTP host is the same as the server name. (If you signed up for this service, your server name was in the confirmation email that you received after signing up.) Check your hosting account documentation for your FTP hostname and account information.

6. **Type your FTP login (username) and password in the related fields.**

   These are the username and password for your hosting account. Again, this information was probably sent to you via email when you first set up the hosting account; consult your server documentation for the correct information to use.

7. **In the Root Directory field, type the location of the folder where you want the files to be placed.**

   Some hosting providers require you to place public files inside a specific folder, such as public_html or www. When users navigate to your URL, they see the index page located in the designated folder.

   Using a hosting account at Pair Networks, as in our example, public files must be placed in the public_html folder.

8. **In the Web URL field, type the URL at which users will access the site.**

   Dreamweaver automatically defines this URL based on your other choices in this dialog box; the default value will be "http://" plus the FTP Address plus the Root Directory. In our example, the default was http://ekendra.pairserver.com/public_html/

   You need to change the URL to the path a user would type in a browser to access your site. In our example, the address is http://ekendra.pairserver.com/.

   Note that we removed the public_html/ folder path from the URL; it is only required when you upload files for viewing over the Internet.

   Make sure you enter the correct information for your domain name.

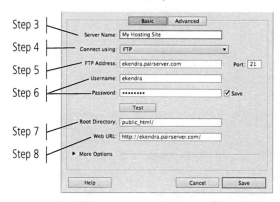

9. **Make sure the Save check box (next to the Password field) is checked, and then click Test.**

   You must receive a message stating that Dreamweaver successfully connected to the Web server. If a connection with the Web server cannot be established, check your entries to make sure your Internet connection is active, and then try again.

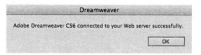

   (If you are working on a shared computer, you might want to uncheck the Save option. However, you will have to retype your username and password every time you upload files to your hosting account.)

10. **Click Save to return to the Site Setup dialog box.**

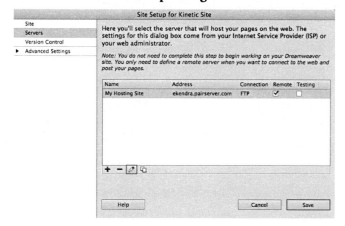

11. **Click Save to close the Site Setup dialog box, then continue to the next exercise.**

UPLOAD FILES TO A REMOTE SITE

Dreamweaver's FTP functionality makes it easy to put files into the remote site folder (defined in the Site Setup dialog box). You can even synchronize all files on the remote and local sites — which is useful when you are ready to publish the site for public Internet access.

1. **With Kinetic Site open in the Files panel, click the Expand button in the Files panel to show both the local and remote sites.**

Click here to connect to the remote site.

Click this button to toggle the panel between expanded and regular modes.

Click this button to synchronize the remote and local site folders.

2. **Above the Remote Server pane, click the Connection button to link to and show the remote site.**

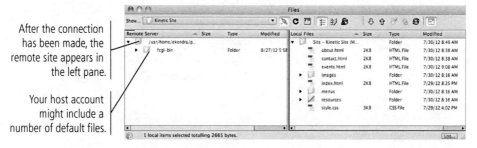

After the connection has been made, the remote site appears in the left pane.

Your host account might include a number of default files.

3. **Click the Synchronize button at the top of the expanded Files panel.**

4. **In the Synchronize Files dialog box, choose Entire 'Kinetic Site' Site in the Synchronize menu, and choose Put Newer Files to Remote in the Direction menu.**

   This utility enables you to synchronize an entire site or only selected files. You can also determine which version (local or remote) to synchronize from. For example, if you accidentally delete files from your local site folder, you can choose to synchronize files from the remote site to the local site to restore the missing files.

5. **Click the Preview button.**

   After a few seconds, the Synchronize dialog box shows a list of all files that will be affected by the process. In this case, this is the first time you are uploading to the remote site, so all site files need to be put onto the remote site.

Click these buttons to change the options for selected files in the list.

6. **Click OK to put the files onto the remote site.**

7. **In the Background File Activity dialog box, click the arrow button to the left of the word "Details."**

When you upload files to the remote server, Dreamweaver keeps a log of affected files. The Background File Activity dialog box shows a list of each file, including any potential problems encountered during the transfer process. Clicking the Details button expands the dialog box and shows the progression of the synchronization.

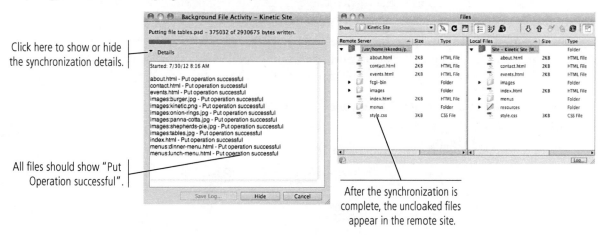

Click here to show or hide the synchronization details.

All files should show "Put Operation successful".

After the synchronization is complete, the uncloaked files appear in the remote site.

8. **Open a browser window. In the navigation bar, type the URL of the Kinetic home page at your domain name.**

Type the same Web URL you defined in the Servers section of the Site Setup dialog box (see Page 335, Step 8). In our example, the complete URL is http://ekendra.pairserver.com/.

9. **Test the various links in the site.**

10. **Close the browser and return to Dreamweaver, then continue to the next exercise.**

EXPORT AND REMOVE THE SITE DEFINITION

To reduce the potential for confusion, it's a good idea to remove the defined sites of completed projects, leaving only the defined sites of current projects.

As stated in the Interface chapter, removing a site from Dreamweaver does not delete the actual files and folders from your computer; it simply removes them from Dreamweaver. Rather than removing a site, however, you can export a site definition file — which you can later import to restore the same settings and options you already defined (as you did in the Interface chapter when you imported the sf-arts site).

As you work through the projects in this book, you will export and remove site definitions for completed projects so your site list remains manageable. You should get into this habit so you can quickly reinstate site definitions if necessary.

1. **With Kinetic Site open in the Files panel, choose Manage Sites at the bottom of the Directory menu.**

   You can access this menu even when the Files panel is in expanded mode.

2. **In the Manage Sites dialog box, choose the Kinetic Site name, and then click the Export button.**

   This function creates a ".ste" file that stores the Dreamweaver site definition settings.

   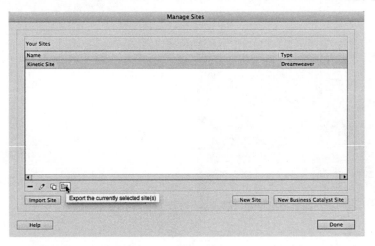

3. **Read the resulting warning. Choose the option you prefer, then click OK.**

   If you are sharing site files with other users, you might want to exclude login and password information in the site setup. Each user should have his or her own password and login information.

4. **Navigate to WIP>Kinetic and click Save.**

The Export Site dialog box defaults to the current site's root folder. You can restore the site settings by importing the site definition file from this location.

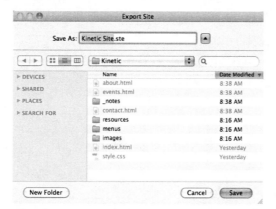

5. **In the Manage Sites dialog box, make sure Kinetic Site is selected and click the "–" button to remove the site from the list.**

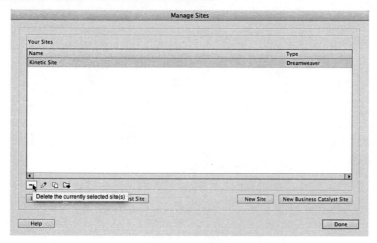

6. **Click Yes to the warning to confirm the removal of the Kinetic Site definition.**

Remember, you are not deleting the files from the site; you are simply removing the site definition from Dreamweaver.

7. **At the bottom of the Manage Sites dialog box, click Done.**

fill in the blank

1. The _____ extension identifies a Dreamweaver site definition file.

2. The _____ is the primary folder that contains all files and subfolders of a Web site.

3. The _____ is used to view and manage files that make up a site in Dreamweaver.

4. _____ is the process of improving a page's ranking in search engine results pages.

5. A(n) _____ is a path from one file to another, beginning from the current location and moving up or down through folder paths to the target image.

6. The notation _____ tells Dreamweaver to move up one folder from the current location.

7. The _____ shows the nested order of HTML tags to the currently selected object.

8. The _____ protocol is used to define an email link.

9. _____ is the process of hiding certain files in the site so they are not uploaded to the Web server.

10. The _____ pane of the Site Setup dialog box defines the settings you need to upload site files through Dreamweaver's Files panel.

short answer

1. Briefly explain why it is important to define a Dreamweaver site file.

2. Briefly explain the importance of creating a site flowchart.

3. Explain three different methods for creating a link to a page in the current site.

Portfolio Builder Project

Use what you learned in this project to complete the following freeform exercise.
Carefully read the art director and client comments, then create your own design to meet the needs of the project.
Use the space below to sketch ideas; when finished, write a brief explanation of your reasoning behind your final design.

Romana Place Town Homes is adding a photo tour to its Web site. The owner is fairly competent at building Web pages, but is having trouble finalizing the new site. Your job is to finish what he started in a professional, organized manner.

To complete this project, you should:

❏ Import the site files into Dreamweaver (from the **WC6_PB_Project6.zip** archive on the Student Files Web page).

❏ Analyze the content of the different pages. Create a flowchart to map the direction of links from one page to another in the site.

❏ Organize the site folder into a clear, understandable structure.

❏ Create the links from one page to another throughout the entire site.

When I started working with our site files I noticed that none of the links exist anymore. I might have worked from an earlier version of the site files, but I'm not sure. Can you fix this for me? Other than the navigation in the middle of the pages, there are a number of other places where links are necessary:

• Users should be able to navigate between the different property pages without going back to the main Properties page.

• There should be a link to our main information email address (info@romanaplace.atc) on every page.

• The original design company's name in the footer should link to its Web site.

This project focused on two of the foundational elements of Web site design — organizing files and creating links. A well-organized site structure includes links that make it easy for users to navigate throughout the entire site. Dreamweaver makes it easy to manage the files in a site — renaming and moving them while maintaining the links between pages within the site. You also learned a number of ways to create links, whether to other pages in the site, to an external URL, or to an email address. The skills you used in this project will be required to complete virtually any site you create in Dreamweaver.

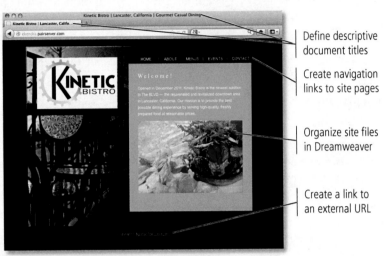

Define descriptive document titles

Create navigation links to site pages

Organize site files in Dreamweaver

Create a link to an external URL

Copy and paste a list of links

Create an email link

Adjust relative link paths to work on nested pages

Digital Book Chapter

Against The Clock Inc. (ATC) publishes textbooks for the graphic communications education market. In addition to application-specific books, the company also has a series of "companion" titles that discuss the concepts underlying the use of digital software — basic design principles, type, color, and so on. You were hired to build an "excerpt" booklet of the companion titles, which ATC will use on its corporate Web site. Visitors will be able to download and read the booklet free of charge. ATC believes this offering will increase sales of the full line of ATC titles. Your task is to structure the content appropriately using HTML code.

This project incorporates the following skills:

❏ Adding text from external sources

❏ Working in both Design view and Code view to add appropriate HTML tags semantically

❏ Organizing content with appropriate heading tags

❏ Properly formatting block quotes and citations

❏ Adding special characters that work in HTML code

❏ Creating lists and tables within text-based content

❏ Attaching a CSS file to new pages

Project Meeting

client comments

We publish a series of books, designed as companion titles to our application-specific training books (which is why it's called *The Companion Series*). The companion titles cover general topics that are important to graphic designers — basic design principles, color, writing, typography, and Web design concepts — but don't quite fit into an application-specific book.

These books have been available for several years, but we haven't done any serious marketing of the titles. When we talk to people about *The Companion Series*, they ask, "Why haven't I heard about these books before?" We're hoping the sample chapters will help get the word out about these books and dramatically improve sales.

We want to be sure of two things: first, this Web page needs to be instantly recognizable as part of our existing site, with the same layout and formatting. Second, the page must include searchable text.

art director comments

The publisher sent the text she wants to offer on the site. When you have this much text on a Web page — which isn't uncommon — it's very important to format it with the proper structural tags. If you use Heading 2 because you think Heading 1 is too big, for example, you're causing problems for search engines and anyone with screen-reader software.

As you know, the client already has a corporate Web site. To create the new page, you can use the existing CSS file that defines the appearance of the various structural elements. Once you apply the correct structural tags to the text in the new pages, you can attach the existing CSS file. This will ensure that the existing format maps to the structural tags in your new page.

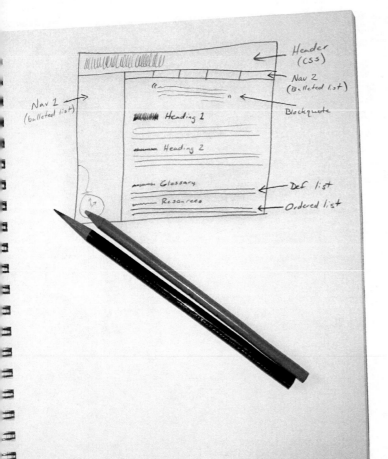

project objectives

To complete this project, you will:

- ❏ Paste text content from a text-only email
- ❏ Apply the appropriate heading and paragraph tags throughout the text
- ❏ Create block quotes and define quote citations
- ❏ Mark up abbreviations for improved usability and accessibility
- ❏ Use the correct HTML tags to show emphasis
- ❏ Add special HTML characters throughout the text
- ❏ Use a table to present well organized content
- ❏ Create ordered, unordered, and definition lists
- ❏ Attach an existing CSS file to the new page

Stage 1 **Preparing the Workspace**

In many Web design jobs, you need to create new HTML files in addition to working with existing files. The first step in any new project, however, is to define the Dreamweaver site so the application can accurately manage the various files and folders that make up the site. Once the site is defined, it's relatively easy to create as many new files as necessary to complete the job.

DEFINE THE ATC SITE

The procedure for defining the ATC site is essentially the same as it was for the Kinetic Site in Project 6: Bistro Site Organization.

1. Download **WC6_RF_Project7.zip** from the Student Files Web page.

2. Expand the ZIP archive in your WIP folder (Macintosh) or copy the archive contents into your WIP folder (Windows).

   This results in a folder named **ATC**, which contains the files you need for this project.

3. In Dreamweaver, revert the workspace to the default Designer option.

4. From the Files panel, choose Manage Sites at the bottom of the Directory menu (or click the link if it is available).

5. In the Manage Sites dialog box, click the New Site button.

6. In the resulting Site Setup dialog box, type **ATC** in the Site Name field.

7. Click the Browse icon to the right of the Local Site Folder field, navigate to your **WIP>ATC** folder, and click Choose/Select.

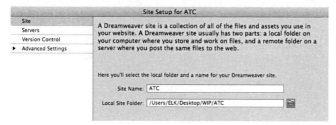

Note:

You can also choose Site>New Site to open the Site Setup dialog box.

8. Click Save to accept the Site Setup definition.

9. In the Manage Sites dialog box, make sure the ATC site appears in the list of sites, and then click Done.

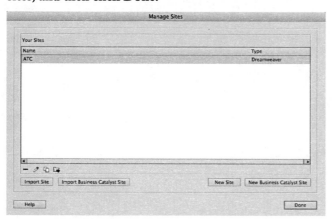

10. Continue to the next exercise.

CREATE A NEW HTML DOCUMENT

The content for the excerpt page was sent to you by the client in an email. You need to create a new HTML page and then move the supplied text into the page so you can apply the necessary HTML structure.

HTML was created as a coding language used to apply structure (paragraphs, headings, and lists) to online documents. By 1996, the modern methods of document markup had outgrown the inflexible HTML, so the extensibility concept from XML (eXtensible Markup Language, a language similar to HTML but primarily used for data instead of documents) was added to HTML 4.01, making it better suited to the evolving needs of Web designers.

Extensibility means that the language can incorporate structures that don't exist in HTML. For example, HTML supports six heading levels, from 1 to 6; the extensibility principle in XHTML allows designers to create heading level 7 if necessary.

Note:

HTML5 is the newest revision of the HTML standard. Although it is already in use by many developers and is supported (to varying degrees) by most current browsers, HTML 5 is still under development by the World Wide Web Consortium (W3C) and the Web Hypertext Application Technology Working Group (WHATWG). It is expected to become the working standard by 2014.

1. **With the ATC site open in the Files panel, choose File>New.**

2. **In the New Document dialog box, choose Blank Page in the left pane. Choose HTML in the Page Type list, and choose <none> in the Layout list.**

   You can use this dialog box to create new files based on existing templates, or use the <none> option to create a new blank page.

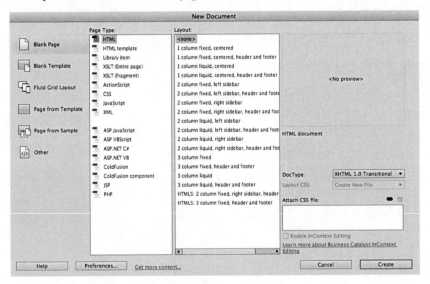

Note:

We use the vertical split in our screen shots. Feel free to use whichever Split mode you prefer in your workspace.

3. **Click Create to create the new blank file.**

4. **If only the Design pane is visible, click the Split button in the Document toolbar.**

   Even though the document appears to be blank in Design view, it contains some XHTML code in the background, which you can see in Code view.

5. Examine the code in the document window.

Content within the **head** element — between the opening **<head>** and closing **</head>** tags — is not visible to the user (except for the content enclosed in the **<title>** tags, which appears in the title bar of a browser, as the title of a bookmark, and as the text in search engine results). Visible Web page content is created within the body section, between the opening **<html><body>** and closing **</body></html>** tags.

Note:

The DTD (document type definition) tells the browser what version of HTML is being used.

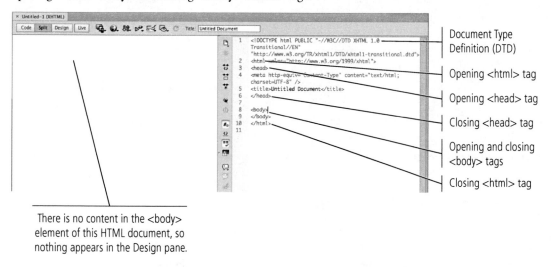

Document Type Definition (DTD)

Opening <html> tag

Opening <head> tag

Closing <head> tag

Opening and closing <body> tags

Closing <html> tag

There is no content in the <body> element of this HTML document, so nothing appears in the Design pane.

6. Select the words "Untitled Document" between the opening and closing <title> tags, then type Against The Clock | Special Characters in Typography.

7. Click the Refresh Design View button in the Document toolbar.

Any time you make changes in the Code pane, you have to refresh the Design view to reflect those changes.

Note:

You can also refresh the Design view by clicking the Refresh button in the Properties panel, or by pressing F5.

Refresh Design View button

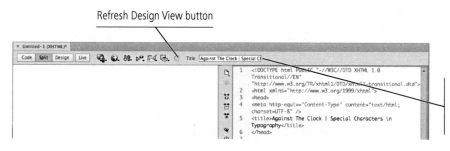

After refreshing the Design view, the new document title appears in the Title field of the Document toolbar.

8. Choose File>Save As. Navigate to your WIP>ATC folder (the root of the ATC site) as the target location and save the document as an HTML file named typography.html.

After the file is saved, it automatically appears in the Files panel.

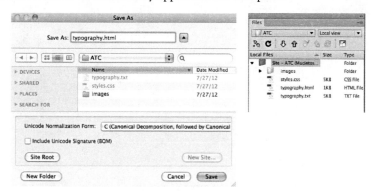

9. Continue to the next stage of the project.

Stage 2 Working with Semantic Markup

Many people have difficulty structuring documents — including word-processing files such as those created in Microsoft Word. Consider creating a heading; the user enters text, and then applies bold styling, increases the font size, and changes the text color. While this **local formatting** makes the text appear to be a heading, it is actually just a styled paragraph. Whether it is a Web page, a PDF file, or a word-processing document, a digital document should make use of available structures to enhance the document's usability. This is where HTML comes into play.

Properly structured HTML documents use tags semantically, to reinforce the meaning of the content, and provide a wide range of benefits to users: they are more accessible, they load quickly in a browser, they reduce bandwidth costs for high-traffic Web sites, they achieve high search-engine rankings, and they are easy to style. As a Web designer, you should take full advantage of these benefits by converting the unstructured or poorly structured documents you receive from clients into properly structured HTML documents. Dreamweaver makes it easy to do this, even if you don't understand a great deal of coding and code syntax.

PASTE TEXT CONTENT IN DESIGN VIEW

HTML is a coding language that defines the structure of the elements in a page; without HTML, the content between the opening and closing **<body>** tags would be completely unstructured. Web browsers depend on the structural markup of HTML to properly display a Web page, so headings stand out from regular text and paragraphs are separated from one another. Without structure, all text on a page would appear as a single, large block of text.

Clients often supply content as plain text without structural markup (paragraph returns do not qualify as structure). When humans read text that doesn't have structural markup, they are able to make logical inferences about the intended structure — for example, they can assume that a short block of text is a heading and a long block is a paragraph. Browsers, however, can't make assumptions; they require structure to correctly display content.

Although not all lines in a text document are paragraphs (some are headings and some are list items), marking each line as a paragraph provides a starting point that you can modify later.

Note:

Web browsers (and Dreamweaver) ignore extra spaces between words and paragraph returns between lines of text. Properly displaying Web page text requires structural markup.

1. **With typography.html (from the ATC site) open in Split view, click in the Design pane to place the insertion point.**

2. **Double-click typography.txt in the Files panel to open that file.**

   Text (.txt) files only appear in Code view because there is no "design".

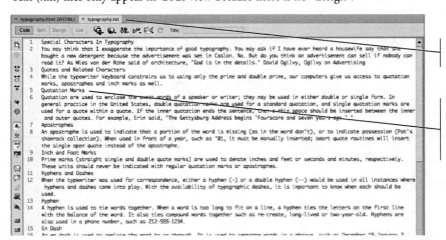

Each open file is accessible in a separate tab.

Although there are smaller and larger blocks of text, there are no codes or styles to separate headings from paragraphs.

3. **Choose Edit>Select All, and then copy the selected content to the Clipboard.**

   Choose Edit>Copy or press Command/Control-C to copy the selected text.

Note:

Press Command/Control-A to select all content in an open file or document.

4. **Close typography.txt.**

5. **In typography.html, paste the copied text into the Design pane.**

   If you pasted the text into the Code pane, the line-break characters would not be included. You will use those bits of codes in the next few steps to apply the proper structure to the paragraphs of text.

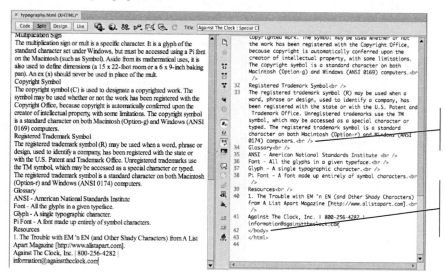

Each paragraph in the pasted text ends with the code for a line break (<br />).

Text pasted into the Design pane automatically appears between the opening and closing <body> tags in the Code pane.

6. **Press Command/Control-A to select all the text in the Design pane, then choose Paragraph in the Format menu of the Properties panel.**

   An HTML paragraph is surrounded by opening **<p>** and closing **</p>** paragraph tags. Because the paragraphs of pasted text are separated by the code for a forced line break (**
**), the entire block of copy is treated as a single paragraph.

   When you apply the paragraph structure to the selected text, the entire block is surrounded by a single set of paragraph tags in the Code pane.

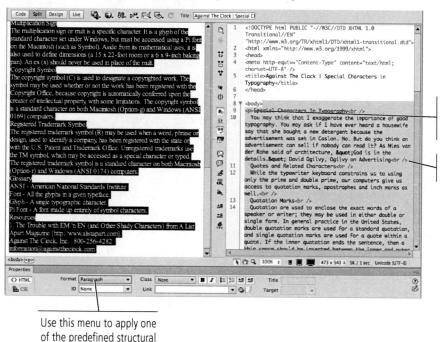

The entire selection is surrounded by a single paragraph tag.

The <br /> tags are not removed or replaced.

Use this menu to apply one of the predefined structural tags to the selected text.

7. **Choose Edit>Find and Replace.**

   As you just saw, the line-break code only appears in the Code pane, so you want to search only the source code of the open document.

8. **Choose Open Documents in the Find In menu and choose Source Code in the Search menu.**

9. **In the Find field, type `<br />`. In the Replace field, type `</p><p>`.**

   Do not press Return/Enter when typing in the Replace field, because the dialog box will prematurely run the Find and Replace operation.

   Each line in the text currently ends with the line-break code (**`<br />`**) when it should end with a closing paragraph tag (**`</p>`**). Each line should also begin with the opening paragraph tag (**`<p>`**), where nothing currently exists.

   Using the search and replace function, you can remove all of the line-break codes and place the necessary closing and opening paragraph tags in a single click.

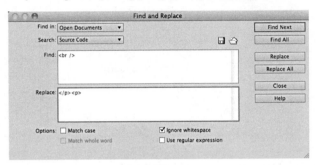

Note:

You cannot undo a Find and Replace in documents that are not open. When doing a Find and Replace that includes files that aren't currently open, you might want to back up the site's root folder outside of Dreamweaver before continuing.

10. **Click Replace All.**

Element Names, Tags, and Attributes

The **element name** is the text that identifies the tag, such as meta, title, head, or body.

A **tag** consists of the element name surrounded by angle brackets, such as <html>, <head>, or <body>.

An **element** is the tag plus its containing content, such as the title element <title>Untitled Document</title>.

Container tags consist of an opening tag (<title>) and a closing tag (</title>). The closing tag is the same as the opening tag, with the addition of the initial forward slash. For example:

   <title>"Weather Forecast"</title>

Empty tags (<meta />) do not have a separate closing tag. In an empty tag, the closing forward slash appears with the closing angle bracket of the tag. For example:

   <img src="sun.gif" alt="sunny day" />

Attributes add properties to HTML elements. For example, the cite attribute of the <blockquote> tag allows you to identify the URL of a quotation. Attributes appear in the opening tag only; they consist of the attribute name and the attribute value (for example, attribute="attribute value").

When marking up a short quotation, you would type:

   <q cite="http://www.useit.com/alertbox/9710a.html">
   People rarely read Web pages word by word.</q>

In this example, the attribute name is cite and the attribute value is http://www.useit.com/alertbox/9710a.html.

Most attributes are optional, such as the cite attribute of the <blockquote> tag. Some attributes are required, such as the alt attribute of the <img> tag, which describes an image for visually impaired visitors. Some attributes are unique to certain elements, such as the src attribute of the <img> tag, which identifies the location (source) of the image.

In HTML, some attributes do not require an attribute value, such as the checked attribute that allows you to preselect a check box option. In XHTML, however, each attribute must have an attribute value (e.g., checked="checked").

Finally, attribute values in XHTML and HTML must be placed within quotes (e.g., width="130").

11. Review the Search panel, and then close the panel group.

12. Refresh the Design view, then review the results in both panes of the document window.

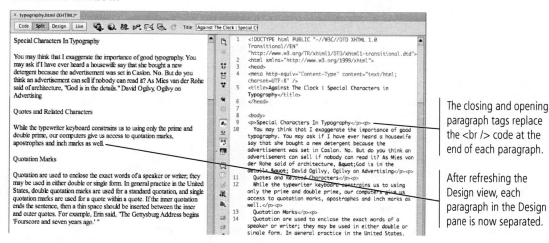

The closing and opening paragraph tags replace the <br /> code at the end of each paragraph.

After refreshing the Design view, each paragraph in the Design pane is now separated.

13. Click the Format Source Code button to the left of the Code pane and choose Apply Source Formatting from the menu.

If you split your screen horizontally, you might not be able to see all of the Code pane buttons (depending on the size of your screen). In that case, you have to click the Show More button to access the Format Source Code button.

This command cleans up the code, moving the opening **<p>** tags to the beginning of each line of copy. Nothing changes in the Design pane when the tags are moved to the appropriate lines.

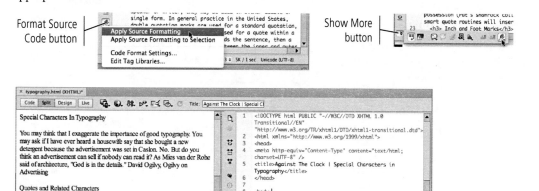

Format Source Code button

Show More button

After applying source formatting, the opening paragraph tags are moved to the beginning of the lines.

14. Save the file and continue to the next exercise.

Headings help readers find the information they need. For visual users, a heading is effective as long as it looks like a heading. This is not the case for visually impaired users who use screen-reading software; screen-reading software and some browsers enable users to skip forward and backward through headings. Also, when reviewing the content of a page and its relevance to a particular topic, search engine software uses headings and heading levels (among other criteria) to make evaluations. For these reasons, it is important to use properly structured headings rather than styled paragraphs.

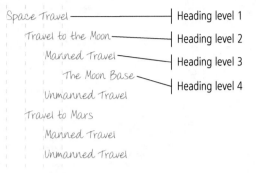

There are six predefined heading levels, **<h1>**, **<h2>**, **<h3>**, and so on to **<h6>**. Heading level 1 is the largest and most important; it should be used only once per page to describe the purpose or title of the Web page. The rest of the headings can be used multiple times, but they should be used in a branch-like pattern or hierarchy.

Many new Web designers complain that heading level 1 appears too large, so they apply heading level 2 or 3 instead. This is a mistake. In a later project, you will learn to use cascading style sheets (CSS) to define the appearance of different elements on a Web page — including different levels of headings.

The special characters described in the text in this project are divided into related groups and subgroups. Your task is to determine which heading level is appropriate for each section. In professional situations, some client-supplied copy will be well-written and well-structured, enabling you to quickly determine appropriate heading levels (called **editorial hierarchy** or **editorial priority**). Other copy will be poorly structured and difficult to decipher; in such a case, you will need to contact the author for clarification or make a best-guess assessment yourself.

1. **With `typography.html` (from your ATC site) open in Split view, click in the Design pane to place the insertion point in the first paragraph.**

   You should be working with the paragraph "Special Characters In Typography".

2. **In the Properties panel, open the Format menu and choose Heading 1.**

   In the Code pane, the opening and closing **<p>** tags automatically change to the **<h1>** tags that identify the paragraph as heading level 1.

Note:

While you should always use properly structured headings, don't overuse them. Some Web pages mark all content as heading level 1, but the various elements are styled differently using CSS. Known as "spamdexing," this method attempts to fool a search engine into ranking the page higher than others with similar content — a technique that generally results in the page being banned from search engines.

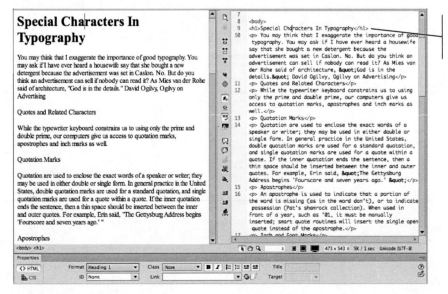

The <p> tags are replaced by the appropriate heading tags (<h1> and </h1>).

Note:

If you use a mouse with a scroll wheel, move the mouse cursor away from the Format menu before you try to scroll through the document window. If the cursor is over the Formatting menu, scrolling with the mouse wheel changes the menu selection.

3. **Move the insertion point to the "Quotes and Related Characters" paragraph and use the Properties panel Format menu to apply the Heading 2 tag.**

After choosing a format in the Properties panel, the Code pane shows that the **<p>** and **</p>** tags have been replaced with **<h2>** and **</h2>** tags, respectively.

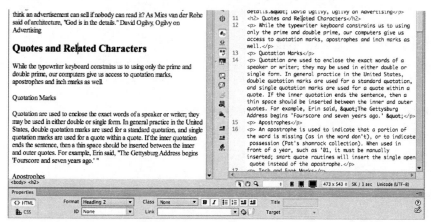

Note:

When you're working in Design view, you can apply paragraph structure and heading levels by choosing from the Format>Paragraph Format menu.

4. **Using the same technique from Step 3, format "Quotation Marks", "Apostrophes", and "Inch and Foot Marks" as Heading 3.**

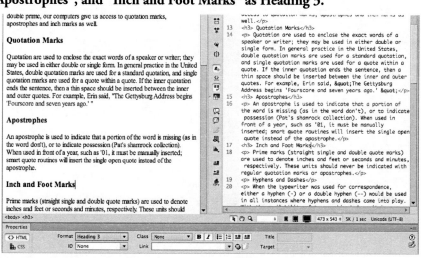

Note:

You can also use keyboard shortcuts to apply common tags:

Paragraph
Command/Control-Shift-p

Heading 1
Command/Control-1

Heading 2
Command/Control-2

Heading 3
Command/Control-3

Heading 4
Command/Control-4

Heading 5
Command/Control-5

Heading 6
Command/Control-6

5. **Apply heading levels to the rest of the document as follows:**

Line Number in the Code pane	Content	Heading Level
19	Hyphens and Dashes	2
21	Hyphen	3
23	En Dash	3
25	Em Dash	3
27	Special Characters	2
28	Multiplication Sign	3
30	Copyright Symbol	3
32	Registered Trademark Symbol	3
34	Glossary	2
39	Resources	2

Note:

The organized content is easier to understand and would enable users (sighted or otherwise) to scan headings and determine whether the page content meets their needs.

6. **Save the file and continue to the next exercise.**

FORMAT A BLOCK QUOTE AND CITATION

The blockquote element formats a quotation as a block of text that is indented from the left and right margins, with extra white space above and below it. The blockquote element requires at least one paragraph element to be nested within it, such as **<blockquote><p>quotation goes here</p></blockquote>**.

The blockquote element has an optional cite attribute designed to identify the URL of the quote source. The URL is not clickable or visible (although in Firefox, you can view the cite URL via the properties of a blockquote or q element).

1. With typography.html open in Split view, click in the paragraph immediately below the heading 1 text (at the top of the page).

2. Click the Blockquote button in the Properties panel to apply the blockquote element to the selected paragraph.

In the Design pane, the blockquote has been indented from the left and right margins. In the Tag Selector, the **<p>** tag appears to the right of the **<blockquote>** tag, indicating that the **<p>** tag has been nested within a **<blockquote>** tag. In the Code pane, you can see the opening and closing blockquote tags before and after the paragraph tags.

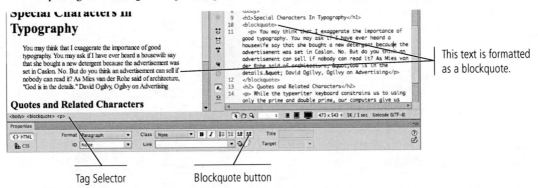

This text is formatted as a blockquote.

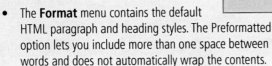

Tag Selector

Blockquote button

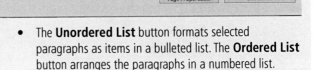

3. **Select "David Ogilvy, Ogilvy on Advertising" at the end of the block quote.**

4. **Control/right-click the selected text and choose Wrap Tag from the contextual menu.**

   The Wrap Tag command opens the Quick Tag Editor, which allows you to temporarily work with code, while still working in Design view.

Note:

You can also open the Quick Tag Editor by choosing Modify>Quick Tag Editor or pressing Command/Control-T.

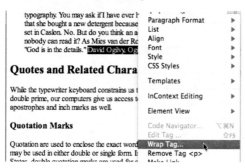

5. **Type `ci`.**

   As you type the code in the Quick Tag Editor, Dreamweaver provides Code Hints (a list of HTML tags) to assist you. As you type, the Code Hint list scrolls to the first HTML tag beginning with the letter "ci" — cite, which is the tag you want.

Note:

If the source of a quotation is a URL, you can add the URL as the cite attribute of either the blockquote or q element.

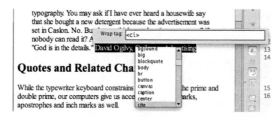

6. **Press Return/Enter to choose cite from the list of tags.**

   When a Code Hint menu is visible, pressing Return/Enter applies the item that is highlighted in the list.

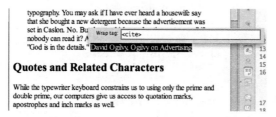

7. **Press Return/Enter again to apply the cite tag to the selected text.**

   The default appearance of the cite element text is italic. As you can see in the Code pane, using the Quick Tag Editor automatically adds the appropriate opening and closing tags.

8. **Save your changes and continue to the next exercise.**

Code hints display by default when you type code in Dreamweaver. You can use the Code Hints pane of the Preferences dialog box to control which code hints display and how.

The Close Tags options can be used to close tags automatically:

- If you select After Typing "**</**", the nearest open tag closes when you type the forward slash after the opening carat. This option is selected by default.

- If you select After Typing the Open Tag's "**>**", Dreamweaver automatically closes a tag as soon as it opens.

- Select Never if you don't want tags to close automatically.

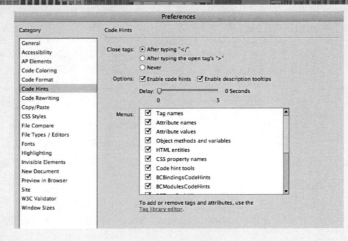

You can disable code hints by deselecting the Enable Code Hints check box. The Delay bar determines how soon code hints display when you open a tag. The Menus options list code categories for which hints can display.

FORMAT AN INLINE QUOTE

The q element is used for marking quotations that are part of a sentence or paragraph, rather than separate paragraphs. (Like the blockquote element, you can also define an optional cite attribute for q element text.)

The current versions of Firefox, Safari, Opera, Chrome, and Internet Explorer automatically place quotation marks around q element text, eliminating the need to insert them as characters in the page content.

In this exercise you will use the Tag Chooser to insert the **<q>** tag. The Tag Chooser provides access for all elements — including the less common ones, for which there are no one-click buttons in the Properties panel or Insert panel.

1. **With typography.html open in Split view, in the Design pane, select the words "God is in the details." (including the period and the quotation marks) at the end of the block quote.**

2. **With the Insert panel in Common mode, click the Tag Chooser button.**

Select this quote inside the blockquote.

3. **In the resulting Tag Chooser dialog box, expand the HTML Tags folder and choose the Formatting and Layout set.**

   In the Tag Chooser dialog box, you can select a specific category of tags in the left pane, and then choose a specific tag from the selected category in the right pane.

4. **In the right side of the dialog box, scroll to find the q element and select it in the list of available tags.**

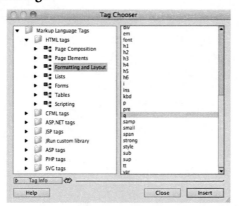

Note:

You can also open the Tag Chooser by choosing Insert > Tag.

5. **Click Insert. In the resulting Tag Editor dialog box, click the arrow to the left of Tag Info to expand the dialog box.**

The Tag Editor automatically presents additional options related to the selected tag. For the q tag, you can define the cite attribute (other options are also available by clicking a different category in the left pane). The browse button to the right of the Cite field allows you to define a page from your current site as the source of the quotation. If the source of your quotation is a page from another site, you must type the URL into the Cite field. (If the source of your quotation is not a URL, enter nothing in the Cite field.)

In the Tag Editor dialog box, you can click the Tag Info arrow to show usage information about the selected tag.

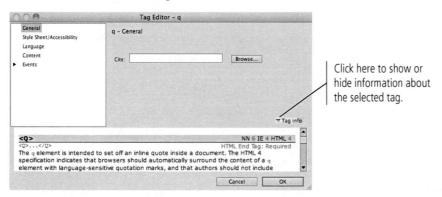

Click here to show or hide information about the selected tag.

6. **Click OK to add the tag to the selected text, and then click Close to close the Tag Chooser dialog box.**

Clicking OK in the Tag Editor dialog box returns you to the Tag Chooser. Clicking Close in the Tag Chooser dialog box returns you to the document window; the q tag is added to the selected text, which you can see in the Code view:

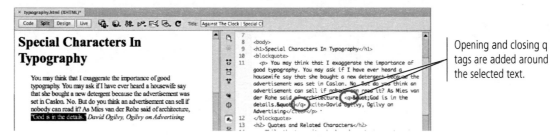

Opening and closing q tags are added around the selected text.

7. **Save the file, then preview the page in one or more browsers, saving when prompted.**

   Safari, Opera, and Chrome apply straight quotes to the q element, while Firefox and Internet Explorer apply curly quotes.

Safari   Opera   Chrome

Firefox   Internet Explorer

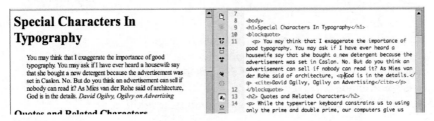

Note:

Older versions of Internet Explorer (7 or earlier) do not add the quotation marks to the tagged text.

8. **Close the browser window and return to Dreamweaver.**

9. **In the Design pane, delete the quote characters from around the "God is in the details." text.**

   ### Special Characters In Typography

   You may think that I exaggerate the importance of good typography. You may ask if I have ever heard a housewife say that she bought a new detergent because the advertisement was set in Caslon. No. But do you think an advertisement can sell if nobody can read it? As Mies van der Rohe said of architecture, God is in the details. *David Ogilvy, Ogilvy on Advertising*

   Quotes and Related Characters

   ```
   7
   8    <body>
   9    <h1>Special Characters In Typography</h1>
   10   <blockquote>
   11       <p> You may think that I exaggerate the importance of
        good typography. You may ask if I have ever heard a
        housewife say that she bought a new detergent because the
        advertisement was set in Caslon. No. But do you think an
        advertisement can sell if nobody can read it? As Mies van
        der Rohe said of architecture, <q>God is in the details.</
        q> <cite>David Ogilvy, Ogilvy on Advertising</cite></p>
   12   </blockquote>
   13   <h2> Quotes and Related Characters</h2>
   14       <p> While the typewriter keyboard constrains us to using
        only the prime and double prime, our computers give us
   ```

10. **Repeat this process to add the q element tags around the quote in the paragraph after the "Quotation Marks" level 3 heading.**

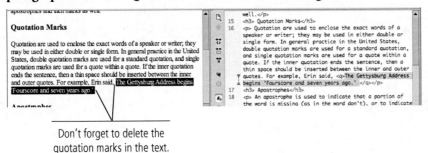

Don't forget to delete the quotation marks in the text.

11. **Save the file and continue to the next exercise.**

MARK UP ABBREVIATIONS IN CODE VIEW

Both abbreviations and acronyms are shortened forms of words or phrases. If you spell out the short form (such as HTML), it is an abbreviation. If you pronounce it like a word (such as NATO), it is an acronym. Some abbreviations are read both ways; SQL, for example, is sometimes spelled out and sometimes spoken as "sequel."

HTML 4 includes two separate elements for these words — the **abbr** element identifies an abbreviation, and the **acronym** element identifies an acronym — but the acronym element has been deprecated (removed) in HTML5, so you should get into the habit of using the abbr element for both types of words.

The title attribute plays a useful role in the **abbr** element. Any text you insert into the title attribute — for example, the full text of the abbreviation or acronym — appears as a tool tip when you hover the mouse over the titled element. People who use screen-reader software also benefit from the title attribute because the software can be set up to read the title text in place of the abbreviation.

In this exercise, you will type directly in the Code pane, using Dreamweaver's code hints to add the necessary tags and attributes.

Note:

Except for the specific tag being used, the basic process for marking up acronyms is the same as for marking up abbreviations. In both cases, the title attribute is used for the long form of the word or phrase.

1. **With typography.html open in Split view, select "ANSI" (in the Design pane) in the paragraph following the Copyright Symbol heading.**

   The text selected in the Design pane is also selected in the Code pane. This is a useful way to locate specific text in code (or vice versa).

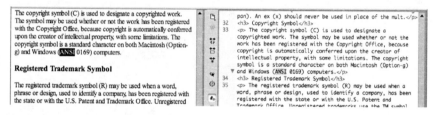

2. **Click in the Code pane to make it the active pane.**

   When working in either pane of Split view, you have to click a pane to bring it into focus (make it active) before you can make changes there.

   When you click the Code pane to bring it into focus, the highlighted text is no longer highlighted.

3. **Place the insertion point before the previously highlighted text, and then type `<ab`.**

   The abbr tag is selected in the code hint list.

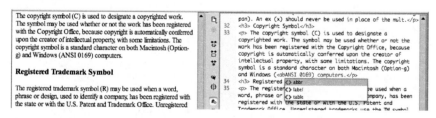

4. **Press Return/Enter to accept abbr.**

   By pressing Return/Enter, you select the **<abbr>** tag. Once you add the tag, the insertion point flashes after the tag, where you can enter attributes of the new tag.

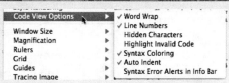

Code View Options

Code View options, which can be toggled on or off in the View menu, determine how code displays.

- **Word Wrap** ensures that code does not extend beyond the available width of the window. This option only affects the appearance of code in the Code pane; it does not insert actual line breaks in the code or content.

- **Line Numbers** shows numbers to the left of each line.

- **Hidden Characters** displays characters such as line-break markers, which would not otherwise display.

- **Highlight Invalid Code** displays incorrect code (such as a tag that has not been closed) in yellow.

- **Syntax Coloring** displays the code in defined colors.

- **Auto Indent** indents every new line of code to the same position as the previous line. A new line is inserted each time you press Return/Enter.

- **Syntax Error Alerts in Info Bar** displays a yellow message bar at the top of the document window if there is a problem in your code.

Code Coloring Preferences

By default, HTML tags appear in blue. You can use the Code Coloring pane of the Preferences dialog box to change the color of specific tags (or other pieces of code).

The Document Type window lists the various types of code that Dreamweaver supports. (The code type in the active document is selected by default.) If you click the Edit Coloring Scheme button, a secondary dialog box displays a list of all possible parts of the selected code type; you can change the text and background color of any individual part.

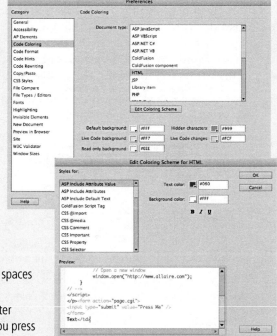

Code Format Preferences

Code Format preferences allow you to specify rules that determine how the code is structured; the sole purpose of these rules is to make it easier for you to read code.

- **Indent With** indents the text within each tag so you can easily identify each block of code. You can indent by character spaces or by tabs.

- **Tab Size** specifies the number of spaces that each tab character contains. For example, if you type "4" in this box, each time you press the Tab key, four space characters are inserted.

- **Line Break Type** ensures the line breaks inserted by Dreamweaver are compatible with the operating system of the remote server on which your site will be hosted.

- **Default Tag Case** changes the case of tags, and **Default Attribute Case** changes the case of attributes. We highly recommend lowercase tags and attributes because XHTML does not support uppercase tags. (HTML supports both cases.)

- **Override Case of Tags** and **Override Case of Attributes** change the case of tags and attributes to the options selected in this pane, even if a different case is defined in Tag Libraries.

- The **TD Tag** option prevents a line break or white space from being inserted directly after a <td> (table cell) tag or directly before a </td> tag. Line breaks and white spaces within the tag cause problems in older browsers.

- The **CSS** button allows you to change code formatting definitions in a cascading style sheet file.

- The **Tag Libraries** button opens a dialog box where you can define formatting options such as line breaks and indents for each tag and its associated attributes.

5. Press the Spacebar, and then type t.

Inserting a space after the abbr element name within the tag prompts Dreamweaver to open code hints and present a list of valid attributes for the current tag.

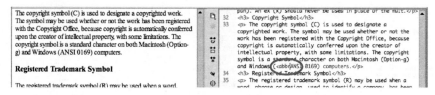

6. Press Return/Enter to accept the title attribute.

When you select the attribute in the code hint list, Dreamweaver follows the attribute with =" " and places the insertion point between the two quotation marks, so you can immediately type a value for the attribute.

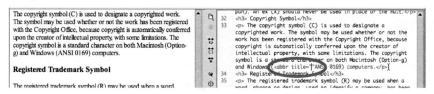

7. Type American National Standards Institute between the quotation marks.

Attribute values must always be surrounded by quotation marks.

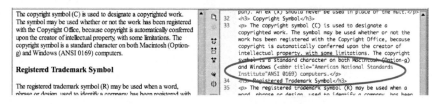

8. Move the insertion point to the right of the closing quotation mark and type > to close the tag.

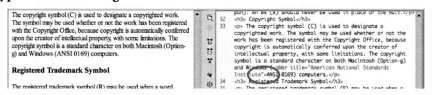

9. Move the insertion point to the right of the text "ANSI," then type </.

In opening tags, the HTML element name is specified between opening and closing angle brackets. In closing tags, the forward slash precedes the element name.

This step shows you another of Dreamweaver's code assistance functions, which is to automatically close the nearest unclosed tag when you type "</". In this case, Dreamweaver closes the abbr tag for you.

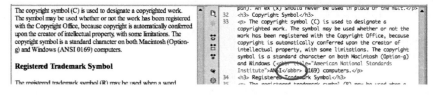

10. **Select all of the code related to the ANSI abbreviation, then choose Edit>Copy to copy the highlighted code to the Clipboard.**

11. **Highlight the instance of "ANSI" near the end of line 35, and choose Edit>Paste to replace the highlighted text with the copied code (including the abbr tags and title attribute).**

Note:

You can also add an abbreviation tag — and a number of other options — using the Insert>HTML>Text Objects submenu.

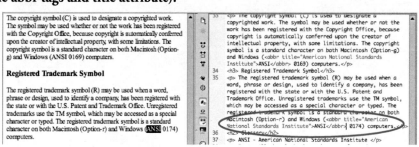

12. **Save the file and then preview the page in one or more browsers. Look for any differences in appearance between abbr elements and regular paragraph text.**

The Firefox and Opera browsers display a dotted line under elements with a defined title attribute. In Internet Explorer, Chrome, and Safari, you will see no obvious difference in the tagged abbreviation. All browsers display title text as a tool tip when the mouse hovers over the element text.

Safari   Chrome   Internet Explorer

Firefox   Opera

13. **Close the browser window(s) and return to Dreamweaver. Continue to the next exercise.**

FORMAT WITH STRONG AND EM ELEMENTS

Two HTML elements can be used to show emphasis — em and strong. The em element is used when light emphasis is needed, such as "you should go to your brother's game to support him." For stronger emphasis, use the strong element, such as "Don't touch the stove top, it is hot!"

Text marked up with the em element appears in italics; text marked up with the strong element appears in bold. Visually, it is the same as using the **<i>** and **<b>** tags (italic and bold, respectively), but the i and b elements are presentational — not structural — HTML. Screen-reader software changes the tone of voice when it finds em and strong element text, but not when it finds i and b element text.

By default, Dreamweaver inserts a strong or em element when you apply bold or italic styling (respectively) through format menus or other means. Don't assume, however, that there is a direct relationship between b and strong elements and i and em elements. Remember: b and i elements are for presentational purposes only, and strong and em elements are for structural purposes.

1. With **typography.html** open, open the Preferences dialog box (Dreamweaver menu on Macintosh or Edit menu on Windows) and show the General category.

2. In the Editing Options group, make sure the "Use <strong> and <em>" option is checked.

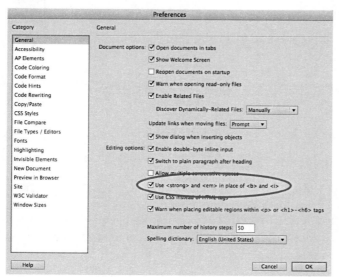

Note:

As you work through this book, remember that preferences are accessed in the Dreamweaver menu on Macintosh and the Edit menu on Windows.

3. Click OK to close the Preferences dialog box.

4. In the Design pane, scroll to the paragraph following the En Dash heading and select "not" in the fourth sentence.

5. Click the Bold button in the Properties panel.

There are no special attributes for the strong and em elements, so you can insert these elements with a single click.

6. With the text still selected, examine the Tag Selector.

The selected text is formatted with the **<strong>** tag, not the **<b>** tag.

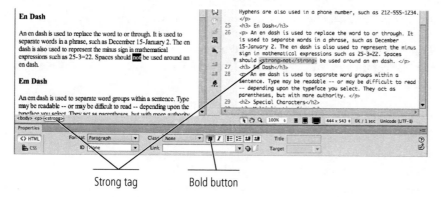

Strong tag   Bold button

7. In the paragraph after the Em Dash heading, select "more authority" in the third sentence and click the Italic button in the Properties panel.

The selected text is now formatted with the **<em>** tag.

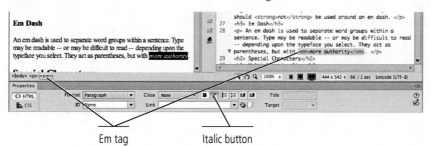

Em tag   Italic button

Note:

You can also click the Bold or Strong buttons in the Text Insert panel to apply the strong tags to selected text.

Click the Emphasis or Italic buttons in the Text Insert panel to apply the em tags to selected text.

8. Save your changes and continue to the next stage of the project.

Stage 3 Working with Special Characters

HTML character entities are characters not directly available from your keyboard. HTML character entities can be specified in code either by name or by number. Using either method, the code begins with an ampersand (&) and ends with a semicolon (;).

- A named character entity uses a specific name for that character such as "©" for the © symbol and "™" for the ™ symbol. Some character names (such as "™") are not supported by all browsers; visitors using these browsers would see "™" in their browser window instead of the ™ symbol.

- Alternatively, you can specify a character using its numeric code, such as "¢" for ¢. (When using the numeric code, be sure to insert a "#" between the ampersand and the number.) All browsers support the numeric codes.

INSERT SPECIAL CHARACTERS

In most cases, you don't need to worry about inserting the codes (named or numbered) for HTML character entities because you can select some of the most common characters from a list in the Text Insert panel; Dreamweaver inserts the code for you.

1. With **typography.html** open in Split view, make the Design pane active. Select the hyphen between "December 15" and "January 2" in the paragraph below the En Dash heading.

2. With the Insert panel in Text mode, click the arrow button to the right of the Characters button icon.

Your button icon might appear different than the one shown in our screen shot because the button reflects the last character inserted from this list. Simply clicking the button (label or icon) — not the arrow — inserts whatever character appears on the button.

Use the menu to show Text options in the Insert panel.

Click the arrow to open the Characters menu.

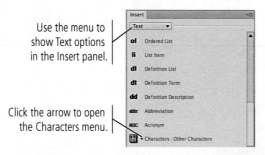

3. **Choose En Dash from the pop-up menu.**

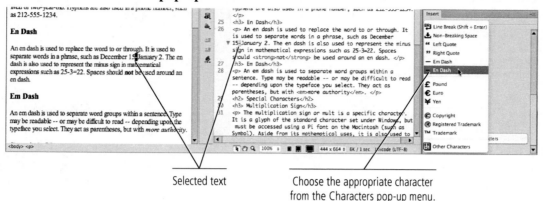

Selected text

Choose the appropriate character from the Characters pop-up menu.

4. **Select the hyphen between "25" and "3" in the same paragraph.**

En dashes are as wide as half an em dash. As you might have read in the text of this project page, en dashes are used to replace the word "to" or "through" or in mathematical expressions of subtraction.

Note:

These same characters can be inserted using the Insert>HTML>Special Characters menu.

5. **In the Text Insert panel, click the Characters:En Dash button.**

Because the button defaults to the last-used character, you can simply click the button to apply another en dash.

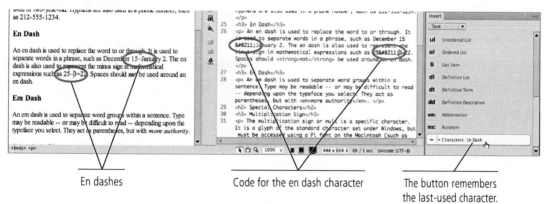

En dashes

Code for the en dash character

The button remembers the last-used character.

6. **Use the same techniques from Steps 2–5 to replace both sets of double hyphens with em dashes in the paragraph after the Em Dash heading.**

The em dash is as wide as the defined type size. This dash can be used to separate part of a sentence — an aside — from the rest of a sentence. Many authors do not know how to insert an em dash; instead, they use a regular hyphen or a pair of hyphens. As there are strict grammatical rules about when to use a hyphen, an en dash, and an em dash, you should consult a professional copy editor for the proper application of these characters.

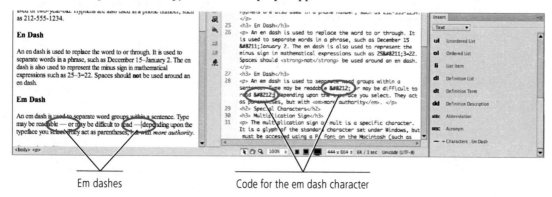

Em dashes

Code for the em dash character

7. **Select the capital C in the first line after the Copyright Symbol heading. Use the Characters menu in the Text Insert panel to replace the letter with the Copyright character.**

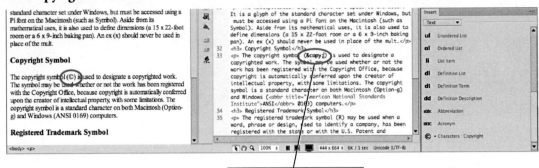

Code for the copyright character

8. **Select the capital R in the first line after the Registered Trademark Symbol heading. Use the Characters menu to replace the selected letter with the Registered Trademark character.**

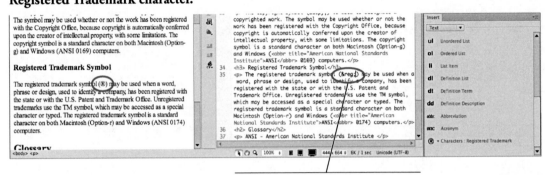

Code for the registered trademark character

9. **Select the capital TM in the same paragraph and use the Characters menu to replace the selected letters with the Trademark character.**

In the Code pane, you can see that Dreamweaver creates this character using the numeric code because some browsers do not support the name for this character.

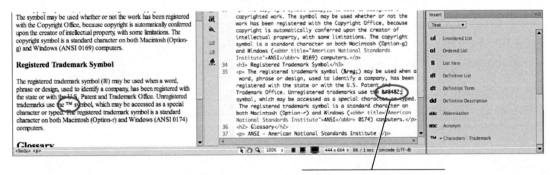

Code for the trademark character

10. **Save the changes to typography.html and continue to the next exercise.**

CREATE A TABLE OF QUOTE CHARACTERS

Common HTML tables that are used to present data or text information consist of only three components: a caption, table header cells, and table data cells.

A caption can be used to briefly describe the contents or purpose of a table. It generally appears at the top of the table. (You can use CSS to move the caption to another position, but many browsers offer poor support for these properties.)

Table data cells make up the majority of the cells in a table. The **<td>** tag is used to mark up the table data cells.

Table header cells, using the **<th>** tag, appear at the top or left (or both) of the table; they label the contents in the regular table cells. Think about a table of the days of the week across the top and the hours of the day down the left side. If the cell at the intersection of the second row and second column contained the text "Staff Meeting," you would know that the staff meeting was scheduled for Tuesday at 10:00 a.m.

The information in table header cells is very important for people using screen-reader software. For example, when they reach the Staff Meeting cell, they can prompt the software to read the headers associated with the cell. The screen-reader would report "Tuesday" and "10:00 a.m." Without proper cell markup, the software would not be able to report the day and time of the meeting.

Note:

When tables are used for layout components of a Web page, they can become very complicated in structure, with tables within table cells (nested tables) and cells that have been merged with other cells. Tables should only be used to present tabular data.

1. **With typography.html open in Design view, switch the Insert panel to show the Layout options.**

2. **Place the insertion point at the end of the paragraph after the Inch and Foot Marks heading. Press Return/Enter to create a new empty paragraph.**

3. **Click the Table button in the Layout Insert panel.**

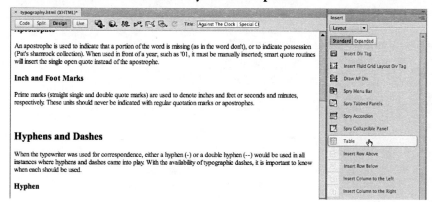

4. **In the Table dialog box:**

   - **Set both the number of rows and number of columns to 2.**

   - **Delete any values in the Table Width, Border Thickness, Cell Padding, and Cell Spacing fields.**

   - **Choose the Top Header option.**

   - **Type Quotation Characters in the Caption field.**

   Many Dreamweaver dialog boxes remember the last-used settings. If you or someone else used the Table dialog box before now, some of these fields might default to other values.

5. **Click OK to create the table.**

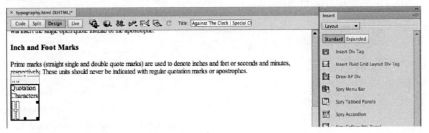

6. **Click the Expanded button in the Layout Insert panel.**

   When empty, the four table cells are small and difficult to work with. The Expanded Tables mode enlarges the cells, making them much easier to work with. This is a temporary change that Dreamweaver provides to help designers work with empty table cells; the expanded appearance does not appear in the Web page.

7. **Read the warning message and click OK.**

   This message only appears the first time you choose Expanded Tables mode after launching the application; if you quit and restart Dreamweaver, this message will appear again the first time you choose Expanded Tables mode. If you are sharing your computer with other users, someone might have checked the Don't Show Me This Message Again option; in that case, you might not see the warning shown here.

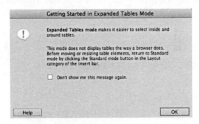

Note:

Expanded Tables mode is really only necessary when a table is completely empty; once content has been entered in at least one cell per column, you can exit Expanded Tables mode.

8. **Examine the page while Expanded Tables mode is active.**

   Notice the enlarged cells in the table and the blue Exit link at the top of the document window. You can click that link to exit or disable Expanded Tables mode.

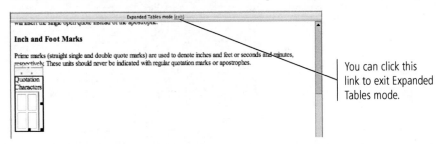

You can click this link to exit Expanded Tables mode.

9. **Click in the top-left table cell to place the insertion point, and then type** `Character Description`**. Press Tab to move the insertion point into the top-right cell, and type** `Character`**.**

   As you type the first heading (Character Description), it will wrap to two lines. When you move the insertion point to the top-right cell, the table adjusts to fit the entire first heading on a single line.

Table cells automatically expand to fit the content you type.

10. **Switch to the Split view and review the code for the table you just created.**

- All content that makes up the table is enclosed in opening and closing **<table>** tags.

- The caption that you defined when you created the table is enclosed in opening and closing **<caption>** tags.

- Each row in the table is enclosed in opening and closing **<tr>** tags.

- Each header cell is identified with opening and closing **<th>** tags. The **scope="col"** attribute identifies that column as information with the heading defined in the related cell.

- Each regular cell in the table is enclosed in opening and closing **<td>** tags. As you can see, each table row includes two <td> tags — one for each column in the row.

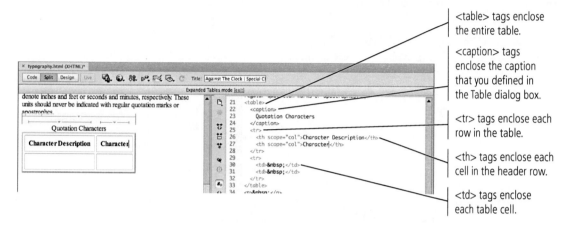

<table> tags enclose the entire table.

<caption> tags enclose the caption that you defined in the Table dialog box.

<tr> tags enclose each row in the table.

<th> tags enclose each cell in the header row.

<td> tags enclose each table cell.

11. **Save the file and continue to the next exercise.**

 ## USE THE INSERT OTHER CHARACTER DIALOG BOX

Although a few special characters are available directly in the Characters menu of the Text Insert panel, there are many more characters available than those in the list. A number of common special characters are available in the Insert Other Character dialog box, which is accessed at the bottom of the Characters menu. Still others (many, in fact) are only available by typing the necessary code in the Code pane.

1. **With typography.html open, click in the lower-left empty cell of the table that you created in the previous exercise. Type Double Curly Quotes.**

2. **Press Tab to move to the right cell, and then choose Left Quote from the Characters menu in the Text Insert panel.**

3. **Press Space, and then choose Right Quote from the Text Insert panel Characters menu.**

4. **Press Tab to insert a new table row.**

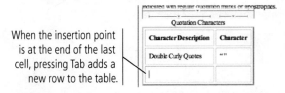

When the insertion point is at the end of the last cell, pressing Tab adds a new row to the table.

5. **In the left cell, type `Single Curly Quotes`, then press Tab to move the insertion point into the right cell.**

6. **Using the Text Insert panel, open the Characters menu and choose Other Characters from the bottom of the list.**

You can use the Other Characters option to find special characters that aren't included in the default list. This option opens the Insert Other Character dialog box, where you can select a specific character, or type the appropriate code in the field at the top of the dialog box.

7. **In the resulting dialog box, click the Single Left Curly Quote character and then click OK to insert that character into the active table cell.**

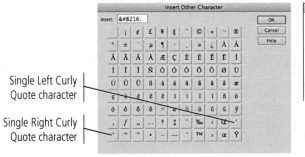

Single Left Curly Quote character

Single Right Curly Quote character

8. **With the insertion point after the quote, press Space and then click the Characters:Other Characters button to reopen the dialog box.**

In this case, the button remembers the last-used option — opening the dialog box — but not the last-used character. Clicking the button opens the Insert Other Character dialog box.

9. **Click the Single Right Curly Quote character and then click OK to insert that character into the table cell.**

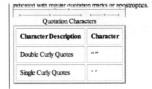

10. **Press Tab to insert another table row. Type** `Double Prime (Inches or Seconds)` **in the left cell of the new row.**

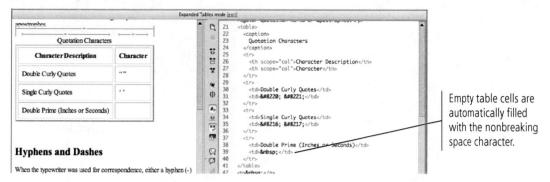

Empty table cells are automatically filled with the nonbreaking space character.

11. **Move the insertion point to the right cell of the new row. Click the Code pane to make it active and type** `&Prime;` **(with a capital P) and then refresh the Design view.**

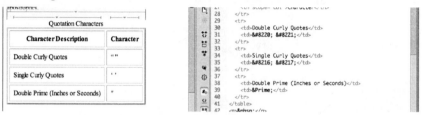

12. **Click in the Design pane to bring it into focus. Place the insertion point after the prime character, then press Tab to insert another table row.**

13. **Type** `Single Prime (Feet or Minutes)` **in the left column, then move the insertion point to the right cell.**

14. **Click the Code pane to make it active and type** `&prime;` **(with a lowercase p) and then refresh the Design view.**

The single- and double-prime codes are almost the same; capitalization makes the difference between the two characters.

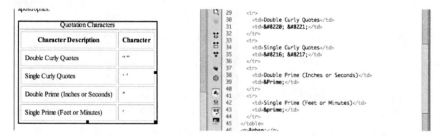

15. **Click the link at the top of the document window to exit Expanded Tables mode.**

16. **Save the file and continue to the next exercise.**

When HTML tables were first conceived, they were intended to allow Web content developers to more clearly present tabular text — primarily charts of data — in a Web page. It wasn't long, however, before visually oriented designers figured out how to use HTML tables to combine graphic elements on a Web page just as they assemble graphics on the printed page. As a result, a significant number of Web pages were (and still are) designed with tables.

HTML tables were never intended as a graphic design tool. The overall page code that results from this method is extremely long and complex, which results in longer download times (still a significant problem for many users). The complexity of table-based page code also makes it more time consuming to make changes.

Another problem with table-based design is that the resulting code mixes content with purely presentational elements. This makes it very difficult (if not impossible) for accessibility software and search engines to separate the content from the structure, which means that table-based pages might not rank as high as a similar page designed without tables.

To solve the problems with table-based design, cascading style sheets (CSS) provide a way to separate content from presentation. CSS-based layout, which you will see in action at the end of this project, is the recommended method of standards organizations such as the World Wide Web Consortium (www.w3c.org). HTML tables should only be used to present tables of data.

Tables in Design View

When you do work with HTML tables, you have a number of options in the Properties panel, depending on whether the entire table or only specific cells are selected. Keep in mind that all table properties are better defined using CSS, which is why we are not explaining all of these options here.

(In Project 9: Yosemite CSS Layout, you will work extensively with CSS to control the appearance of individual page elements, as well as the entire page.)

If a table or column has a defined width, the number appears to the left of the column or table menu.

Use these menus to access column-specific options.

Use this menu to access table-specific options.

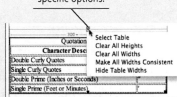

When specific cells are selected, you can change properties of the selected cells.

When the entire table is selected, you can change properties of the overall table.

The Modify>Table Menu

- **Merge Cells** combines selected adjacent cells so they are treated as a single cell.
- **Split Cell** creates multiple cells in a single cell, without affecting other cells in the same row or column.
- **Insert Row** adds a row above the current selection.
- **Insert Column** adds a column left of the selection.
- **Insert Rows or Columns** opens a dialog box where you can add a specific number of rows or columns. You can also choose where to add the new cells relative to the current selection.
- **Delete Row** removes the row of the active cell.
- **Delete Column** removes the column of the active cell.
- **Increase Row Span** merges the current cell with the cell below it.
- **Increase Column Span** merges the current cell with the cell next to it on the right side.

- **Decrease Row Span** splits two or more previously merged or spanned cells into two cells from the bottom.
- **Decrease Column Span** splits previously merged or spanned cells into two cells from the right.
- **Clear Cell Heights** removes all defined numeric row height values from the selected table.
- **Clear Cell Widths** removes all defined numeric column width values from the selected table.
- **Convert Widths to Pixels** and **Convert Widths to Percent** allow you to change defined widths from a percentage of the available space to a specific number of pixels, and vice versa.
- **Convert Heights to Pixels** and **Convert Heights to Percent** allow you to change defined heights from a percentage of the available browser space to a specific number of pixels, and vice versa.

INSERT SPECIAL CHARACTERS IN CODE

The multiplication sign is a seldom-used character; it doesn't even appear in the Insert Other Character dialog box. To insert this character, you can type code directly in the Code pane, or you can use the Insert field in the Insert Other Character dialog box.

There are many lists of HTML character entities on the Internet. Use your favorite search engine to search for "HTML characters." Some Web pages have more characters than others; for very unusual characters, you might need to check a few sites until you find the code you need. Also, make note of both the name and the numeric code because some browsers support one but not the other (test both in your browser).

Note:

To find the necessary code for special characters, look for online sources such as http://www.w3schools.com/html/html_entities.asp.

1. **With typography.html open in Split view, use the Design pane to scroll to the paragraph following the Multiplication Sign heading.**

2. **Select the letter "x" between 15 and 22.**

3. **Click the Code pane to bring it into focus, and then delete the selected letter "x".**

4. **Type &tim and press Return/Enter to choose × from the code hint list.**

   The code hints help you insert named character entities, but not numeric character codes.

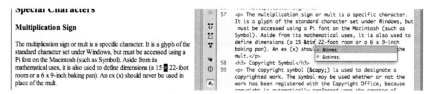

5. **Click the Refresh Design View button in the Document toolbar.**

6. **In the Design pane, compare the appearance of the mult (multiply) character and the letter "x".**

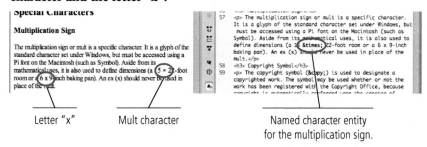

Letter "x"   Mult character   Named character entity
                                       for the multiplication sign

7. **Select the letter "x" between 6 and 9 in the same sentence.**

8. **In the Code pane, replace the selected character with × and then refresh the Design view.**

   This is the numeric code for the mult character. Dreamweaver's code hints for character entities in Code view do not support numeric codes for characters.

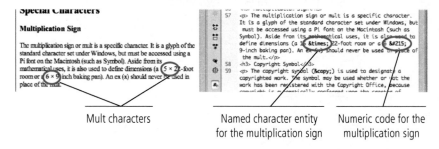

Mult characters   Named character entity   Numeric code for the
                     for the multiplication sign multiplication sign

9. **Preview the page in your browser.**

The current versions of Firefox, Safari, Opera, Chrome, and Internet Explorer all support both the named and numeric character codes. Older versions, however, might show the characters "**×**" instead of the actual mult character.

10. **Close your browser and return to Dreamweaver.**

11. **Continue to the next stage of the project.**

Stage 4 Creating Lists

There are three common types of lists: definition lists, ordered lists, and unordered lists. Ordered and unordered lists (numbered and bulleted, respectively) are very similar. Definition lists, which include a term and a definition, have a different type of structure.

In this stage of the project, you will create a definition list, an ordered list of references, and an unordered list that becomes navigation links in the final Web page.

CREATE A DEFINITION LIST

Definition lists are designed to match a term with its definition or description. The definition or description doesn't necessarily need to come from a dictionary or thesaurus; it might simply be an explanation of the term.

Three tags are part of a definition list. The **<dl>** tag defines the beginning and end of the entire list of terms and definitions. The **<dt>** and **<dd>** tags within the dl element wrap the definition terms and definition descriptions (respectively).

1. **With typography.html open, scroll to the Glossary heading near the bottom of the page.**

2. **Drag to select the four lines of terms and descriptions in the Glossary section.**

3. **In the Text Insert panel, click the Definition List button to wrap the selected text in a <dl> tag.**

The entire selection is enclosed in **<dl>** tags, identifying it as a definition list. A definition list automatically tags every other paragraph in the selection with **<dt>** tags to identify a definition term, and alternating lines with **<dd>** tags to identify definition descriptions (in other words, the meaning of the preceding term).

Note:

By default, content in the <dd> tags is indented. This is a presentation property, and can be changed using CSS.

<dl> tags identify a definition list.

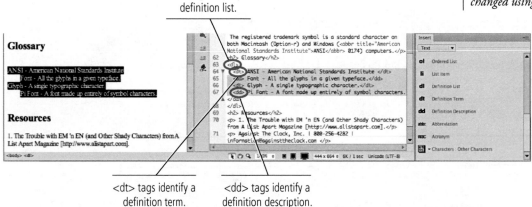

<dt> tags identify a definition term.

<dd> tags identify a definition description.

4. **In the Design pane, click to place the insertion point to the left of "American" in the first line.**

5. **Press Delete/Backspace until the spaces and hyphen have been deleted, and then press Return/Enter.**

The description is now formatted as a definition description. However, the "Font" term is indented at the same level as the ANSI definition, which is incorrect.

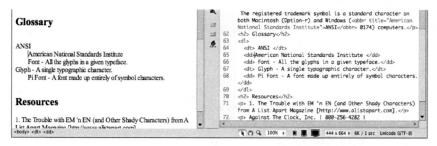

6. **Move the insertion point to the left of "Font," press Backspace, and then press Return/Enter.**

The line beginning with Font is now formatted as a definition term.

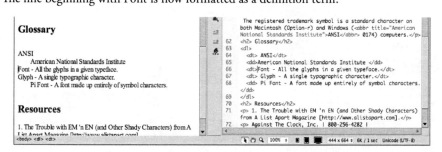

7. **Repeat Steps 5–6 for the rest of the terms and descriptions.**

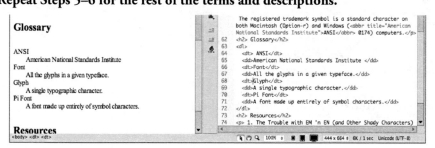

8. **Save the file and continue to the next exercise.**

CREATE AN ORDERED LIST OF WEB RESOURCES

Ordered lists are commonly called numbered lists, although they are not always numbered. You can use Roman numerals (i, ii, iii or I, II, III) or letters (a, b, c or A, B, C).

The purpose of ordered lists is to show a sequence of steps or hierarchical order. If these purposes do not apply to the content of a list, you should use an unordered (bulleted) list instead.

1. **With typography.html open, select the numbered paragraph at the bottom of the page.**

2. **Click the Ordered List button in the Properties panel.**

   The **<ol>** tags surround the entire ordered list, identifying where the list starts and ends. Each list item within the list is surrounded by **<li>** tags.

   In the Design pane, the list as a whole is indented from the left edge of the page, and the space between list items is reduced. These presentation properties clearly identify that the text is part of a list, and not part of a regular paragraph.

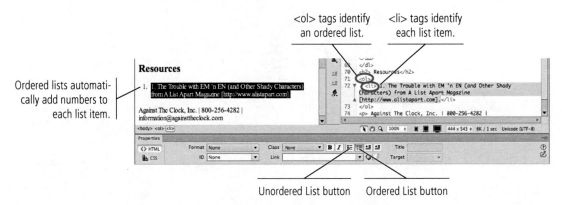

One of the presentation properties of an ordered list is that each list item is automatically numbered. If you receive content from an outside source, the number might already be typed at the beginning of each list item (as is the case in this project); you should remove the original number from the text of each list item.

3. **In the Design pane, delete the redundant number from the beginning of the list item.**

4. **Click at the end of the text in the numbered list item and press Return/Enter.**

   When you press Return/Enter at the end of a list item in the Design pane, Dreamweaver automatically creates a new numbered list item for you.

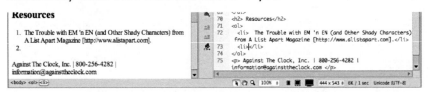

5. **Type HTML entities and other resources at W3schools.com. as the new list item, but do not press Return/Enter.**

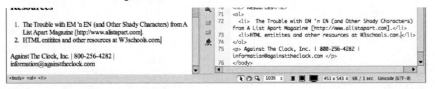

Note:

You have to work in the Design pane to automatically add the new list item. Pressing Return/Enter in the Code pane simply adds white space in the code.

6. **In the first list item, select the URL in the square brackets and cut it to the Clipboard (Edit>Cut or Command/Control-X).**

7. **Delete the two square brackets and the space before them.**

8. **Select "A List Apart Magazine", click in the Link field of the Properties panel, paste the copied URL, and press Return/Enter.**

   As you learned in Project 6: Bistro Site Organization, a link is identified by **<a>** tags. The **href** attribute defines the link destination, or the page that will open when a user clicks the link text.

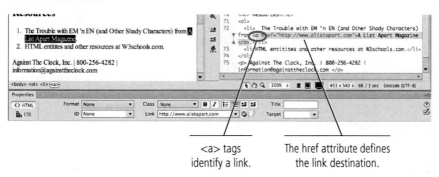

<a> tags
identify a link.

The href attribute defines
the link destination.

9. **Click to place the insertion point in the link.**

   Placing the insertion point removes the highlighting that was applied to the text in the previous step. You can now see the default presentational properties of the <a> tag — blue, underlined text.

Links default to blue,
underlined text.

10. **In the second list item, make "W3schools.com" a link to http://www.w3schools.com.**

11. **Save the file and continue to the next exercise.**

CREATE AN UNORDERED LIST OF NAVIGATION LINKS

A navigation bar is simply a list of links. It is common practice among Web design professionals to mark up a navigation bar as a list of links; after CSS has been applied, however, the list takes on an all-new appearance. In this exercise, you use the unordered list format to create a navigation bar.

1. **With typography.html open, place the insertion point at the end of the last list item in the Resources section in the Design pane.**

2. **Press Return/Enter twice.**

   Pressing Return/Enter once creates the next list item — in this case, #3.

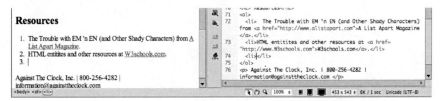

   If you press Return/Enter again (before typing anything else), Dreamweaver recognizes that you want to escape from the ordered list, deletes the last empty list item, and moves the insertion point into an empty paragraph below the ordered list.

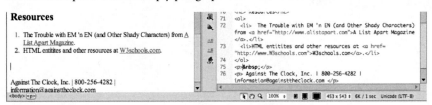

3. **Click the Unordered List button in the Properties panel.**

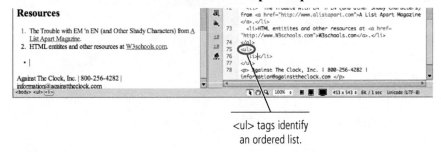

   <ul> tags identify
   an ordered list.

Note:

You will work in depth with CSS in Project 9: Yosemite CSS Layout, including defining your own selectors for both object and layout formatting.

4. **Add six list items: Home, Store, Tools, Downloads, About, and Contact. Press Return/Enter after each item, but not after the final list item.**

5. **Highlight the word "Home" in the Design pane. In the Properties panel, type # in the Link field, the press Return/Enter to finalize the new link.**

   Using the # character in the Link field turns the selected text into a link without defining a specific destination. For the purposes of this project, the important thing is that the text of each list item be tagged as a link.

6. **Repeat Step 5 for each item in the list.**

7. **Save the changes and continue to the next stage of the project.**

Stage 5 Attaching an External CSS File

As you might have noticed, we paid particular attention to the tags that were applied to various structural elements through this project. Rather than simply accepting the default presentational properties, you can use cascading style sheets (CSS), which contain instructions that tell a browser how to format those various elements.

As you complete the rest of the projects in this book, you will work extensively with CSS to format both pages and specific page content. In this project, you are going to attach the client's existing CSS file to your page, so the appearance of your page matches the rest of the client's Web site.

Although we will not discuss the finer details of CSS at this point, the following exercises will make more sense if you understand several key issues:

- A CSS file includes **selectors** (rules) that define the appearance of different tags.

- A **<div>** tag identifies a section, or division, of a page.

- An **ID** attribute is a name that uniquely identifies a specific element.

ADD DIV TAGS AND ELEMENT IDS

A div element (using opening and closing **<div>** tags) has no structural meaning; it simply separates one block of content from another on a page. Each div element on a page must have a unique ID to clearly distinguish it from other divs. The ID has no effect on the structure of content, but simply identifies it for the purposes of CSS styling. This allows you to define different appearances for the same elements in different sections. For example, **<p>** tags in a div named "content" can have a different appearance than **<p>** tags in a div named "sidebar".

You can also assign IDs to other tags, such as individual paragraphs, so those identified objects can be controlled separately. In short, if it's named, it can be visually separated using CSS.

1. **With typography.html open in Split view, click in the level 1 heading in the Design pane to place the insertion point.**

2. **In the Design pane, click the <h1> tag in the Tag Selector to select the entire level 1 heading (including the related tags).**

3. **With the Insert panel in Layout mode, click the Insert Div Tag button.**

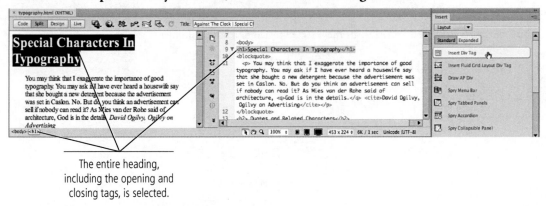

The entire heading,
including the opening and
closing tags, is selected.

4. **In the resulting dialog box, choose Wrap Around Selection in the Insert menu.**

You want the div to include the heading tags, so you are wrapping the div tag *around* the current selection.

5. **Type header in the ID field and click OK.**

The ID you are assigning (header) has defined formatting in the CSS for this site. When you later attach the CSS file to this page, the appropriate header formats will be applied to page content identified (through the ID attribute) as a header.

6. **Click once in the level 1 heading to place the insertion point but deselect the paragraph.**

The ID attribute sets this heading apart from the rest of the text. The boundaries of the div tag (section) are marked by a gray or dotted line in the Design pane. (If you don't see this border, you can turn on CSS Layout Outlines in the Visual Aids menu in the Document toolbar.)

The gray border identifies   Use this menu to turn
the div boundaries.   on CSS Layout Outlines.

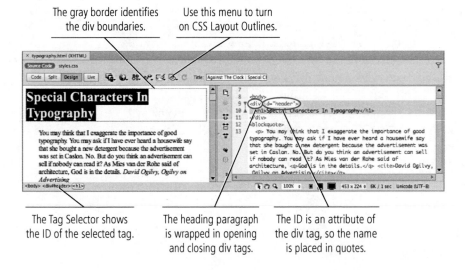

The Tag Selector shows   The heading paragraph   The ID is an attribute of
the ID of the selected tag.   is wrapped in opening   the div tag, so the name
                              and closing div tags.   is placed in quotes.

7. In the Design pane, select "information@againsttheclock.com" in the last paragraph on the page. In the Link field of the Properties panel, type **mailto:information@againsttheclock.com** and press Return/Enter.

8. Click the <p> tag in the Tag Selector to select the entire last paragraph.

9. Type **footer** in the ID field of the Properties panel, and press Return/Enter to apply the ID to the active paragraph.

In this case, no border surrounds the paragraph because you didn't add a new div tag around the selection. Rather, you defined the ID of the active paragraph tag, as you can see in the Tag Selector.

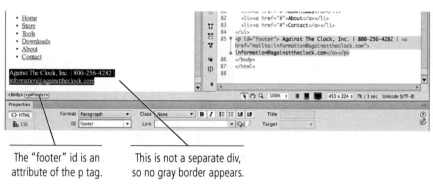

The "footer" id is an attribute of the p tag.

This is not a separate div, so no gray border appears.

10. Switch to Design view and select all the text from the blockquote (at the top of the page) to the last numbered list item under the "Resources" heading.

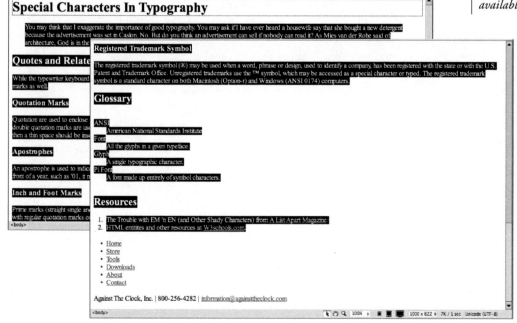

Note:

The most important issue is to use the exact same ID for an element as the ID defined in the CSS file that will format the appearance of the different elements. In this case, we are telling you what IDs to use based on the IDs that exist in the CSS file that you will attach to the HTML file; in a professional environment, you would have to examine the CSS styles yourself to determine which IDs are available.

11. **Use the process from Steps 3–5 to wrap the active selection with a new div tag with an ID of content.**

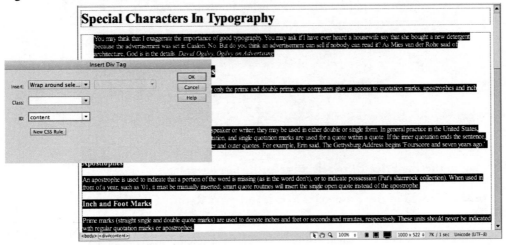

12. **Save the file and continue to the next exercise.**

 ## ATTACH THE CSS FILE

To make this page more visually pleasing to ATC site visitors — and to be consistent with the rest of the ATC site — you need to attach the CSS file already used for other pages in the client's site.

The CSS file, which is a set of instructions on how to display the Web page, is separate from the HTML document. When a browser downloads an HTML file, it examines the code for external files required to display it, such as images and CSS files. The browser then downloads the external files and merges them into the display of the Web page. In the case of a CSS file, the browser reads the instructions, and then applies the styles to the page.

After attaching the style sheet to the page, and depending on what the CSS file defines, you might see a dramatic difference in the appearance of the page. Not only will text styling change, but the layout will change too — even to the point of moving some page components to new locations.

1. **With typography.html open in Design view, open the CSS Styles panel.**

    Remember, all panels can be opened from the Window menu. If a panel is already available in the dock, you can click the relevant panel tab or button to show that panel.

Attach Style Sheet button

2. **Click the Attach Style Sheet button at the bottom of the panel.**

3. **In the Attach External Style Sheet dialog box, click the Browse button.**

4. **In the resulting Select Style Sheet File dialog box, navigate to styles.css in the root folder of the ATC site (WIP>ATC). Click Open/OK to return to the Attach External Style Sheet dialog box.**

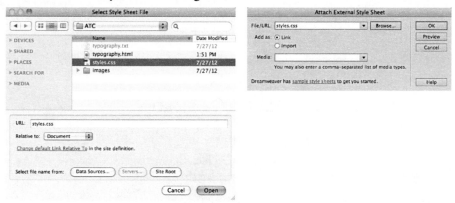

5. **Click OK in the Attach External Style Sheet dialog box to apply the CSS file.**

   The navigation unordered list now appears at the top of the page instead of below the header. It is not formatted properly because you did not yet define an ID for the unordered list. (It is difficult to see because it overlaps the black background.)

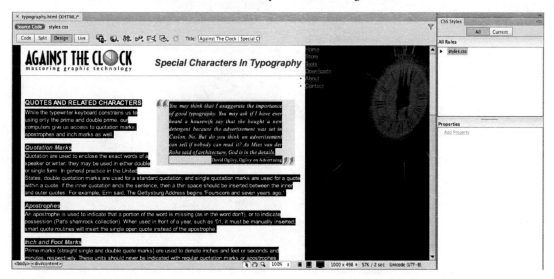

6. **Save the file and continue to the next exercise.**

IDENTIFY THE LIST AS A NAVIGATION BAR

Note:

An ID can only be assigned once in a particular page or section; you have already used header, footer, and content, so those are not included in this menu.

As you can see in Design view, the unordered list is clearly not formatted properly within the context of the rest of the formatted page. We intentionally omitted this element ID in the earlier exercise to show that you don't need to identify every section before attaching the external style sheet. In fact, it can be easier to wait until the CSS file is attached, because the application can help apply the correct IDs.

1. **With typography.html open in Design view, click in any element of the navigation unordered list to place the insertion point.**

2. **Using the Tag Selector, click the <ul> tag to select the entire unordered list.**

3. **In the Properties panel, open the ID menu and choose topnav.**

   This menu shows all available IDs that are defined in the attached CSS file. This method is an easy way to make sure that the ID you apply already exists in the attached CSS file.

   You will work extensively with CSS in later projects. For now, you should simply understand that the attached CSS file includes an ID selector named "topnav", which defines the appearance of the unordered list items as a horizontal navigation bar.

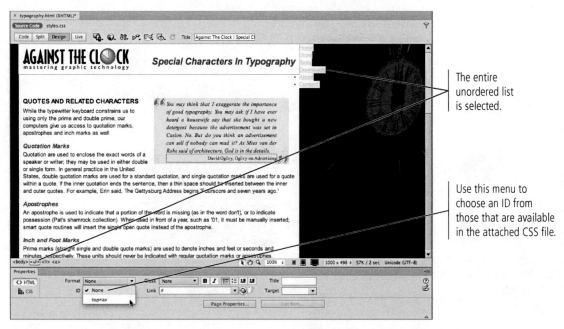

The entire unordered list is selected.

Use this menu to choose an ID from those that are available in the attached CSS file.

Even without the CSS, the text content in this page was very readable. By attaching a CSS file that defines the appearance of various tags and IDs, the page is now visually attractive in addition to being properly structured.

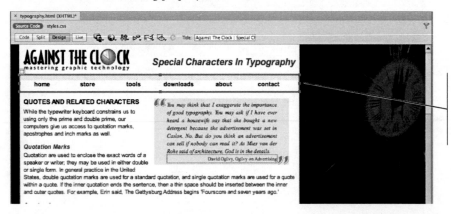

The definition of topnav in the attached CSS file converts the unordered list into a horizontal navigation bar below the header div.

4. Switch to the Live view and review the page.

The Live view is a very good tool for reviewing most design elements. However, you should remember that Dreamweaver is not a browser; site visitors will not use the Dreamweaver Live view to view your pages, so you should also review your work in at least one actual browser application.

Note:

Don't depend solely on Dreamweaver Design view or even Live view when you design pages, and don't depend on a single browser to test your pages. Every browser has its own bugs and weaknesses; to be sure of your design, test your pages in multiple browsers.

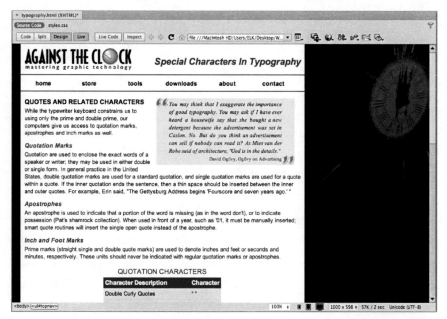

5. Turn off the Live view and then preview the page in at least one browser.

Scroll through the document and review the appearance of different elements (including special characters). If possible, review the document in multiple browsers and on different operating systems.

6. Close any open browsers and return to Dreamweaver.

7. Close typography.html.

8. Choose Manage Sites from the bottom of the Directory menu in the Files panel.

9. In the Manage Sites dialog box, choose the ATC site name, and then click the Export button. Navigate to your WIP>ATC folder and click Save to create the ATC.ste file.

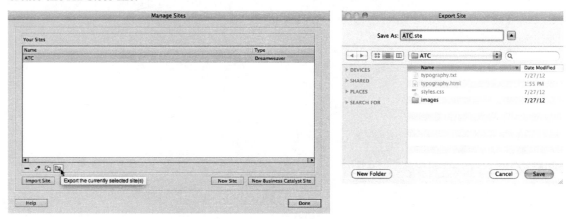

10. In the Manage Sites dialog box, remove the ATC site from the list.

1. The _____ tag marks up individual paragraphs in a story.

2. Each HTML page should have only one _____ element.

3. All visible content of a Web page is contained within the opening and closing _____ tags.

4. _____ appear when you begin typing in the Code pane, showing a list of tags or elements that can be added at the current insertion point.

5. A(n) _____ tag includes both opening and closing tags, such as <title>text</title>.

6. A(n) _____ adds properties to HTML elements, such as the citation of a quote.

7. The _____ element is used to mark up text that is indented on the right and left, with extra white space above and below the affected text.

8. The _____ element is best used to mark up the short form of a phrase that is spoken as letters, such as HTML.

9. The _____ element identifies an individual item in an ordered or unordered list.

10. The _____ allows you to work temporarily with code, while still working in Design view.

1. Briefly explain the importance of properly structuring an HTML document.

2. Briefly explain the difference between an ordered list and an unordered list.

3. Briefly explain the importance of div tags for formatting an HTML page.

Portfolio Builder Project

Use what you learned in this project to complete the following freeform exercise.
Carefully read the art director and client comments, then create your own design to meet the needs of the project.
Use the space below to sketch ideas; when finished, write a brief explanation of your reasoning behind your final design.

art director comments

The owner of Against The Clock has received a number of positive comments — and new sales — because of the *Typography Companion* sample chapter that you created for her to post on her Web site. She would like to add another page with a sample from the *Color Companion* from the same series.

To complete this project, you should:

❑ Use the ATC site folder that you already created for the new page.

❑ Create a new HTML page and copy the text from **ColorCh3.txt** into the file. (The file is in the **WC6_PB_Project7.zip** archive on the Student Files Web page.)

❑ Mark up the page text with proper structural tags.

❑ Create header and footer elements, and attach the same CSS file that you used in the type chapter.

client comments

We've had such a positive response from the type chapter that we also want to include a sample from the *Color Companion*. If we get the same increase in sales leads from this chapter, we'll probably go ahead and do online samples for all of our books.

In addition to the text file for the *Color Companion* chapter, we've sent you a PDF file of the printed chapter so you can more easily see the different text elements — headings, lists, italics, special characters, and so on. You can just ignore the images and sidebars in the printed chapter; we don't need those in the online sample. There is, however, a table near the end of the file that we would like you to include in the online version.

At the end of the text file, we added in the glossary terms that we think are important for this chapter. There aren't any resources, so you can leave out that section.

project justification

_____

_____

_____

_____

_____

_____

_____

_____

_____

_____

_____

_____

_____

_____

No matter how you receive content for a Web page, you will likely need to correct the formatting with the appropriate HTML tags. In this project, you learned how to use HTML tags and elements to semantically structure and mark up a document so all visitors can successfully access and use a Web page. You also learned that by applying ID attributes, <div> tags, and using CSS, you can turn a plain HTML document into a visually pleasing and highly structured Web page.

The Web pages that you create for clients will seldom be as text-intensive as this page, but now that you have a solid understanding of how to work with HTML structures, from both Design view and Code view, you are ready to format any content you receive from a client — regardless of its condition.

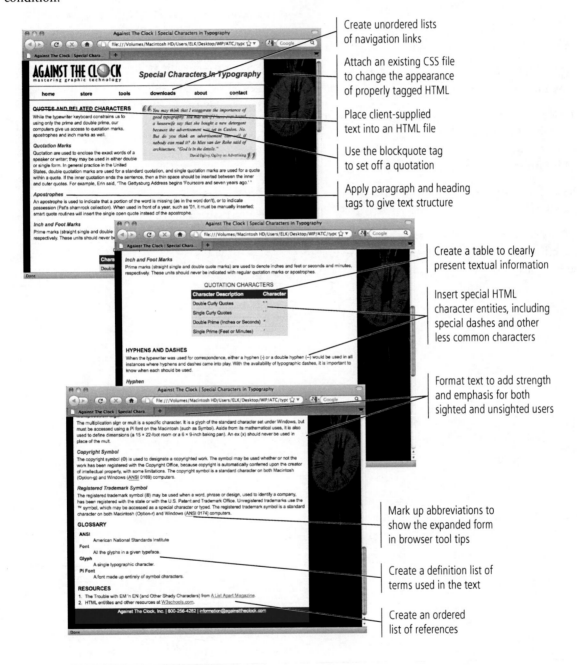

Create unordered lists of navigation links

Attach an existing CSS file to change the appearance of properly tagged HTML

Place client-supplied text into an HTML file

Use the blockquote tag to set off a quotation

Apply paragraph and heading tags to give text structure

Create a table to clearly present textual information

Insert special HTML character entities, including special dashes and other less common characters

Format text to add strength and emphasis for both sighted and unsighted users

Mark up abbreviations to show the expanded form in browser tool tips

Create a definition list of terms used in the text

Create an ordered list of references

Photographer's Web Site

Your client is the owner of Crowe Photography, an art studio in central California near San Francisco. You have been hired to add a number of visual elements to her Web site, including static images, animation, and video.

This project incorporates the following skills:

❑ Using various methods to add static images into a Web page

❑ Assigning alt tags to images for improved usability

❑ Manipulating images in a Web page

❑ Defining background colors and images

❑ Working with multimedia files

❑ Defining a page favicon

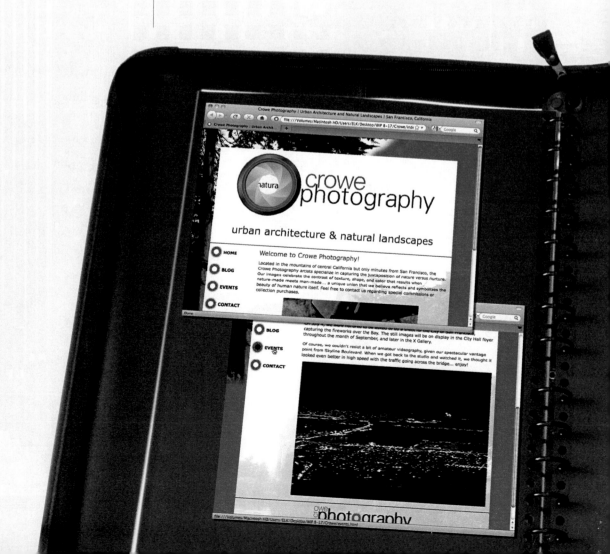

Our site is very basic — only three pages. We don't need to be complicated, we just need to get the information out there.

At the same time, we're a photography studio, so we want to include images!

I just created a new logo that I also want to incorporate; there's a regular version and an animated one that I'd like to place on every page.

We're probably going to add a gallery page down the road, but I'm not organized enough to get all the files together. A rotating slideshow on the home page with a few samples should be fine for now.

I just updated the blog page, and I'd like you to place the video that we mention.

Dreamweaver makes it very easy to incorporate visual elements into a Web page. You can work directly in the Design view to place the basic images and multimedia objects.

For the background images, CSS makes it relatively easy to define different backgrounds as long as you understand the concepts of HTML elements and selectors.

I chose two of the images the client provided and manipulated them in Photoshop to work well as background images in different sections of the page.

I also think the aperture part of the logo will be a good "hover" image for the navigation links. Again, you can use CSS to make this happen rather than inserting actual rollover images.

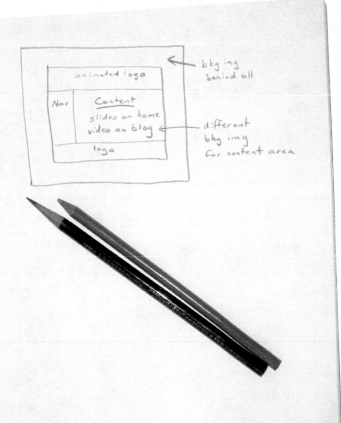

To complete this project, you will:

❏ Use multiple techniques to add images to Web pages

❏ Resize images to fit page areas

❏ Resample images to reduce download time

❏ Use CSS to control background colors and images for specific page elements

❏ Insert a Flash animation file, a slideshow, and a video file

❏ Add a page favicon

Stage 1 **Working with Static Images**

Images serve two primary purposes in Web pages: informing and decorating. Examples of informative images include an illustration of how to fasten a seat belt, or a graphic that serves as a link in a navigation bar. Decorative images are supporting images that could be removed from the site without affecting its content or message, such as the background behind the content of a page.

 DEFINE THE CROWE PHOTOGRAPHY SITE

As in the previous project, the first step to working in Dreamweaver is to prepare the site definition. To ensure that links between documents and paths to images are created properly, the site must be defined in Dreamweaver.

1. **Download WC6_RF_Project8.zip from the Student Files Web page.**

2. **Expand the ZIP archive in your WIP folder (Macintosh) or copy the archive contents into your WIP folder (Windows).**

   This results in a folder named **Crowe**, which contains the files you need for this project.

3. **Create a new site named Photography, using the WIP>Crowe folder as the site root folder.**

   The procedure for defining this site is the same as for the sites you created in previous projects (except for the path, which is unique for every project). If necessary, refer to the first exercises in Project 6: Bistro Site Organization for more detailed instructions.

4. **Continue to the next exercise.**

 INSERT AN IMAGE ONTO A PAGE

In this exercise, you will learn how to place an image in a Web page — a fairly basic process once you understand what types of images you should use. Four primary formats are used for images and graphics on the Web:

- **JPEG** (Joint Photographic Experts Group), which supports 24-bit color, is used primarily for continuous-tone images with subtle changes in color, such as photographs or other images that are created in Adobe Photoshop.

- **GIF** (Graphics Interchange Format), which supports only 8-bit color or 256 possible values, is best used for graphics with areas of solid color, such as logos or other illustrations created in an application such as Adobe Illustrator. This format also supports simple frame-by-frame animation.

- **PNG** (Portable Network Graphics), which supports both 8- and 24-bit color, as well as a special 32-bit format allowing for partial transparency, can be used for both illustrations and continuous-tone images.

- **SVG** (Scalable Vector Graphics) images are made up of mathematically defined lines called **vectors** (unlike **raster images**, which are made up entirely of pixels). Vector graphics are completely **scalable** without affecting their quality.

Note:

Although current browsers support all four file formats, support in older browsers' versions can be problematic or nonexistent (especially for PNG and SVG formats).

Image Bit Depth

Bit depth refers to how many bits define the color value of a particular pixel. A **bit** is a unit of information that is either on or off (represented as 1 and 0, respectively). One bit has 2 states or colors, 8 bits have 256 possible colors ($2 \times 2 \times 2 \times 2 \times 2 \times 2 \times 2 \times 2 = 256$), and 24 bits have 16,777,216 (2^{24}) possible colors.

In an RGB photograph, three color channels define how much of each primary color (red, green, and blue) makes up each pixel. Each channel requires 8 bits, resulting in a total of 24 bits for each pixel (called "true color").

Image Compression

The JPEG format incorporates **lossy compression**, which means that pixels are thrown away in order to reduce file size. When areas of flat color are highly compressed, speckles of other colors (called artifacts) often appear, which negatively impacts the quality of the design.

Both GIF and PNG formats employ **lossless compression** to reduce file size and download time, while ensuring that no information is lost during the compression. The lossless compression routine in the PNG format is generally better than that used in GIF images, so you might achieve a slightly smaller file size if you use 8-bit PNG.

Although 24-bit PNG is capable of displaying as many colors as the JPEG format, PNG uses a lossless compression routine. As a result, PNG doesn't compress 24-bit images as small as the JPEG format.

1. **With the Photography site open in the Files panel, double-click index.html to open the file.**

2. **Review the page contents in the Design view.**

   This is a fairly simple site, with several places marked to add various content. As you complete this project, you will use a number of techniques to place and manage images and other media to add visual interest.

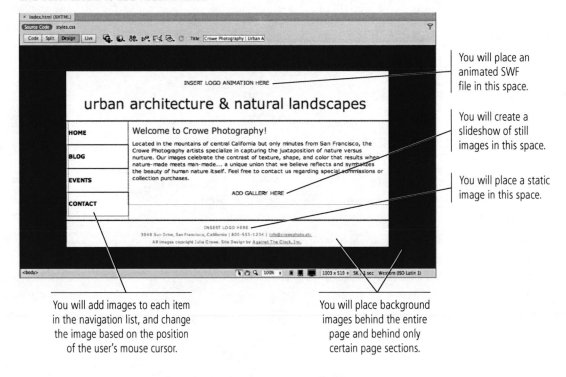

You will place an animated SWF file in this space.

You will create a slideshow of still images in this space.

You will place a static image in this space.

You will add images to each item in the navigation list, and change the image based on the position of the user's mouse cursor.

You will place background images behind the entire page and behind only certain page sections.

3. **Click the Split button in the Document toolbar to show both the Design and Code views.**

   In this project we use the horizontal split view to maximize the line length that is visible in both panes. Feel free to use whichever method you prefer.

4. **In the Design pane, select the words "Insert Logo Here" near the bottom of the page.**

5. **Delete the selected text from the Design pane.**

   When you delete the footer text, the code for a nonbreaking space (** **) is automatically added as a placeholder inside the **<p>** tags within the footer div.

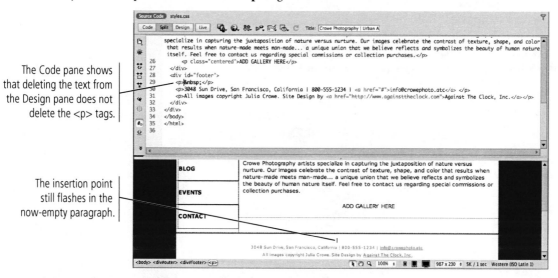

The Code pane shows that deleting the text from the Design pane does not delete the <p> tags.

The insertion point still flashes in the now-empty paragraph.

6. **With the insertion point flashing in the empty paragraph (in the Design pane), click the arrow on the Images button icon of the Common Insert panel and choose Image from the pop-up menu.**

   The Images button defaults to the last-used option. If you (or someone else) already used the Images button on the Insert panel, it might say Images: Image or some other type. To be sure you are inserting the correct type of image in this step, click the button icon to open the menu and choose Image from the menu.

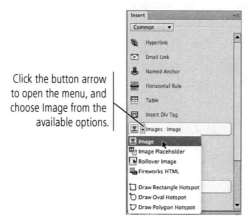

Click the button arrow to open the menu, and choose Image from the available options.

Note:

You can also choose Insert>Image.

7. **In the Select Image Source dialog box, open the site images folder, select the crowe-photography.png file, and click Open/OK.**

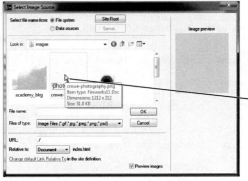

If file extensions are hidden on Windows, move your cursor over a file and wait a second to see the file name and extension in a pop-up window.

8. **In the resulting Image Tag Accessibility Attributes dialog box, type `Crowe Photography` in the Alternate Text field and click OK.**

Text you enter in the Alternate Text field of this dialog box becomes the **alt** attribute of the **<img>** (image) tag.

The **alt** attribute provides a text alternative to the image, so visitors who use screen readers (or who have disabled image display in their browsers) will be able to understand the content of the image. The alt text is also indexed by search engines, which allows them to show your site's images in the search engine image gallery and make a more qualified determination of your site's rank.

Although most tag attributes are optional, the **alt** attribute of the **<img>** tag is required. If an image is simply decorative and does not merit alternate text, you use an empty alt attribute (**alt=""**), which satisfies the requirement. (Using **alt=""** is considered better than **alt=" "** because some screen readers pronounce the space.)

You can choose <empty> in the dialog box menu to add the empty **alt** attribute. If you simply don't type in the field, no alt attribute is added to the **<img>** tag.

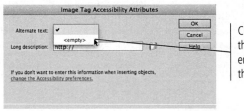

Choose <empty> in the menu to add an empty alt attribute to the selected image.

Note:

The alt attribute is commonly misnamed the alt tag; it is not an HTML tag but an attribute of a tag.

Note:

If you replace one image with another, the original alt text still applies to the new image. Basically, you are only changing the src attribute without affecting the alt attribute.

Note:

The Long Description field completes the longdesc attribute of an image. Its purpose is to allow the designer to offer a link to a longer description of an image on a separate Web page.

9. **With the image selected in the Design pane, examine the Tag Selector and the Code pane.**

The **<img>** tag appears inside the opening and closing **<p>** tags.

Some attributes of the **<img>** tag are automatically populated based on information saved in the image file:

- The **src** attribute defines the file name and location of the image.

- The **width** and **height** attributes are automatically populated based on the file's physical dimensions.

- The **alt** attribute is the alternate text, which you defined in the Image Tag Accessibility Attributes dialog box.

Note:

You can simply type in the Alt field of the Properties panel to assign or change the alt text for a specific image.

Code related to the selected image is selected in the Code pane.

Handles (on the right and bottom sides and the bottom-right corner) indicate that the image is selected.

The <img> tag represents the selected image.

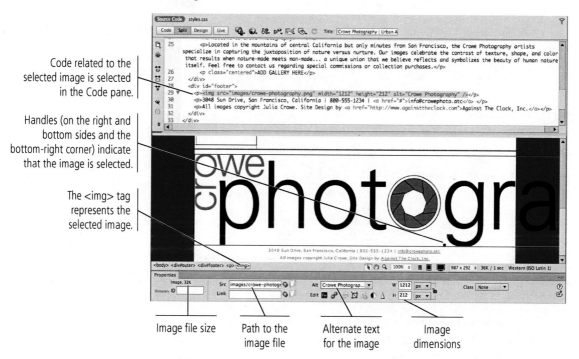

Image file size

Path to the image file

Alternate text for the image

Image dimensions

10. **Save the file (File>Save) and then continue to the next exercise.**

Note:

WebAIM (Web Accessibility In Mind, www.webaim.org/) is an organization that promotes Web accessibility and offers instructions and tutorials on how to meet accessibility guidelines.

RESIZE AND RESAMPLE AN IMAGE

As you can see in the Design pane, the placed logo is much too large to fit in the footer area of the page. In this exercise, you will adjust the image to better fit the space.

As with most tasks, there is more than one way to resize an image. You can enter new dimensions in the Properties panel, or simply drag the handles of the selected image in the Design view.

1. **With index.html open, click the placed logo to select the image (if necessary).**

The bottom center of the image shows a control handle, which you can drag to resize the height of the placed image. Because this image is so large, you might not be able to see the right edge of the image (depending on the size and arrangement of your workspace).

Since you might not be able to see all of the handles, it is better to use the Properties panel to change the image's dimensions.

2. **In the Properties panel, make sure the lock icon to the right of the W and H fields is locked. If the icon is unlocked, click it to make it locked.**

When the icon is locked, changing one dimension applies a proportional change to the other dimension; in other words, changes to the image dimensions maintain the original width-to-height aspect ratio.

If the icon is locked, changing one
dimension affects the other proportionally.

If the icon is unlocked, changing one dimension
has no effect on the other dimension.

3. **Highlight the current value in the W field. Type 400, then press Return/ Enter to finalize the change.**

After the image has been resized, you should be able to see all three resizing handles.

In the Properties panel, the image dimensions appear in bold, indicating that the image has been resized.

Two additional buttons are now available to the right of the W and H fields. Clicking the **Reset to Original Size button** restores the original image dimensions, regardless of how many times you have changed the image size in the page or in the Properties panel.

Clicking the **Commit Image Size button** changes the placed image file to match the current image dimensions on the page.

Note:

You can usually reduce an image without losing quality, but enlarging an image beyond its original size can result in a significant loss of image quality.

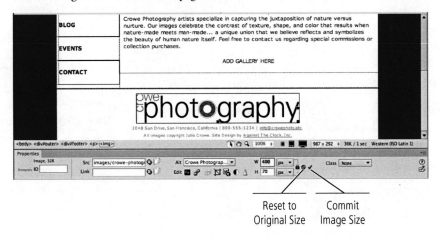

Reset to   Commit
Original Size   Image Size

4. **Click the bottom-right image handle, press Shift, and drag up and left. When the W field shows the width of 300, release the mouse button.**

You can drag any of the handles to resize the image in only one direction (by dragging the side handles) or in both directions at once (by dragging the corner handle).

Keep in mind that manually resizing the image using these handles does not honor the Lock icon in the Properties panel. If you drag either of the side handles, or the corner handle without pressing Shift, the lock icon in the Properties panel is automatically unlocked. By pressing Shift while dragging the corner handle, you constrain the resizing process and maintain the image's original aspect ratio.

Note:

Pressing Shift while dragging a side handle does not maintain the image's aspect ratio. You have to Shift-drag the corner handle to resize the image proportionally.

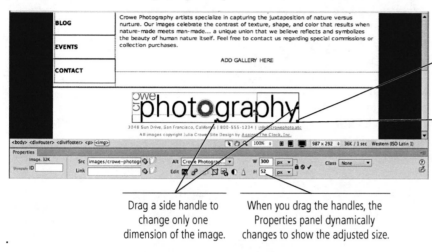

Drag the corner handle to change both dimensions at one time.

Shift-drag the corner handle to change both dimensions proportionally.

Drag a side handle to change only one dimension of the image.

When you drag the handles, the Properties panel dynamically changes to show the adjusted size.

5. **In the Files panel, expand the images folder.**

6. **Control/right-click the `crowe-photography.png` file, and choose Edit>Duplicate from the contextual menu.**

It's a common mistake to insert a large image into a Web page, and then simply resize the image to take up less space on the page. The problem with resizing is that, while the image will *appear* smaller, the file size ("weight") remains the same. Users might need to wait a considerable length of time to download the large image file.

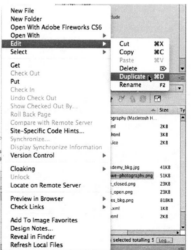

Instead of simply resizing, you should also resample any resized images to include only the necessary data. **Resampling** discards pixels (while downsizing) so the specified dimensions of the image are the actual dimensions of the image. This reduces the weight of the image, which reduces the download time for your visitors.

In the next few steps, you are going to resample the image that you placed into the index.html page. However, you should understand that resampling in Dreamweaver permanently changes the image file. Before you make this type of change permanent, it is a good idea to create a copy of the image file so you can still access the original file if necessary.

7. **In the Files panel, click the original `crowe-photography.png` file once to highlight the file name.**

Make sure you don't rename the one that has "Copy" in the file name; that file is the original-size logo. You want to rename the image file that you placed into the footer and decreased to a smaller physical size.

8. **At the end of the current file name, type -small, then press Return/Enter to finalize the new file name.**

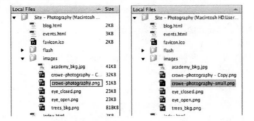

9. **In the resulting dialog box, click Update to update the link in index.html to the new file name.**

10. **With the image selected on the page, click the Commit Image Size button to the right of the W and H fields.**

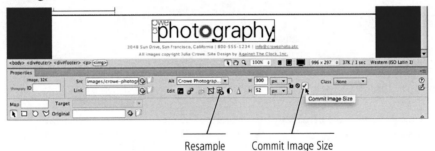

Resample   Commit Image Size

Note:

You could also click the Resample button to accomplish the same effect.

11. **Click OK to acknowledge the warning.**

As we explained earlier, resampling in Dreamweaver permanently changes the image file; the resized dimensions become its (new) actual size. After resampling, the Reset Size button is no longer visible, and the Resample button is grayed out (not available).

Also note the file size of the resampled image; it was originally 32 KB, and now (after resizing and resampling) it's around 10 KB.

Note:

If another user clicked the "Don't show me this message again" option, you won't see this warning.

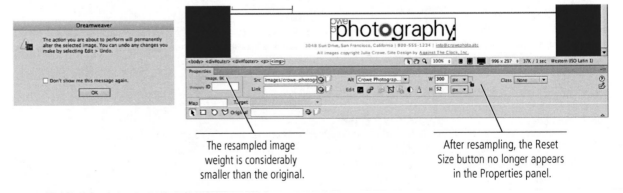

The resampled image weight is considerably smaller than the original.

After resampling, the Reset Size button no longer appears in the Properties panel.

12. **Save the file and continue to the next exercise.**

INSERT AN IMAGE FROM THE FILES PANEL

Dreamweaver provides many ways to insert images into Web pages, one of which is using the Images button on the Common Insert panel. Another way is to simply drag a file from the Files panel and place it onto a Web page.

1. **Open the `blog.html` file from the Files panel.**

2. **In the Design pane, select and delete the words "INSERT LOGO HERE" at the bottom of the page.**

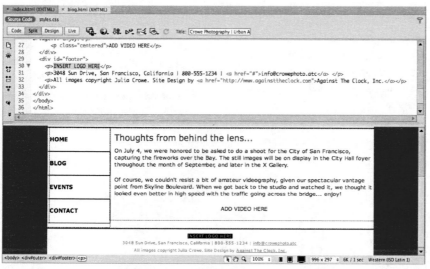

3. **In the Files panel, expand the images folder (if necessary).**

4. **From the Files panel, drag `crowe-photography-small.png` to the location of the insertion point (where you deleted the text in Step 2).**

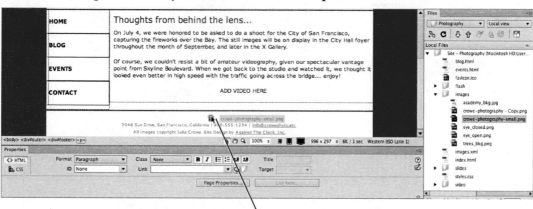

Drag the file from the Files panel to the location where you want to place the image.

5. **In the resulting Image Tag Accessibility Attributes dialog box, type `Crowe Photography` in the Alternate Text field.**

Note:

Do not double-click the image in the Files panel to insert it. Double-clicking an image in the Files panel prompts Dreamweaver to open the file in an image-editing application.

The Image Properties Panel in Depth

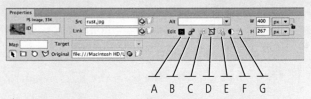

A B C D E F G

When an image is selected in the document window, the Properties panel not only displays properties (attributes) of the image, but also provides access to a number of image-related functions.

A. **Edit** opens the image file in its native application. GIF and JPG files open in Photoshop; PNG files open in Fireworks (assuming you have those applications).

B. **Edit Image Settings** opens a dialog box where you can change a variety of options for the selected file format. You can also use the Format menu to change the format of the selected image; if you change the format, you will be asked where you want to save the new file.

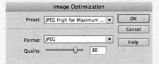

C. **Update From Original** can be used to make sure an inserted Photoshop image in the HTML file is the most recently saved version of the image.

If you insert a native Photoshop (PSD) file into a page, Dreamweaver converts it to a file that is appropriate for Web browsers. The original link to the PSD file is maintained; if the PSD file is changed, Dreamweaver notifies you that the image must be updated to the most recent version.

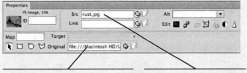

When you place a native Photoshop file, Dreamweaver stores a link to the original file.

The actual image in the page is converted to a Web-friendly format.

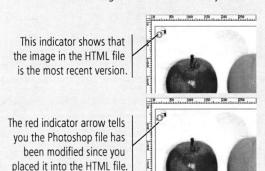

This indicator shows that the image in the HTML file is the most recent version.

The red indicator arrow tells you the Photoshop file has been modified since you placed it into the HTML file.

Although Dreamweaver is not an image-editing application, you can use it to perform some basic image-editing functions. These tools can't replace Adobe Photoshop, but they are well suited for making quick adjustments to an image from directly within the Dreamweaver application.

D. The **Crop tool** can be used to remove unwanted areas of an image. When you click the Crop tool, the lighter area shows the area that will be included in the cropped image; you can drag any of the eight handles around the edge of the crop area to change the area. Pressing Return/Enter finalizes the crop; pressing ESC cancels the crop and restores the original image.

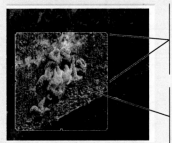

Drag any of the handles to change the area that will be included in the cropped version.

The lighter area shows what will remain after the crop has been applied.

E. The **Resample tool** changes the number of pixels in an image to exactly match the size of the selected instance in the page. This has the same effect as clicking the Commit Image Size button after resizing an image in the Design pane.

F. **Brightness and Contrast** can be used to change those properties in a selected image.

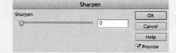

G. The **Sharpen** option can be useful for restoring some detail after resizing/resampling (especially upsizing). Keep in mind, however, that oversharpening can often produce worse results than what you start with.

Remember: All of the Dreamweaver image-editing tools permanently modify the edited file. If you use any of the image-editing buttons, you see a warning that the changes permanently affect the file (unless someone has checked the Don't Show ... option in the dialog box). Always keep a backup image so if you over-edit, you can replace the backup image and start over.

6. Click OK to return to the document.

Dragging an image from the Files panel has the same result as clicking the Images:Image button in the Common Insert panel.

Because you resampled this image in the previous exercise, it is already the appropriate smaller size.

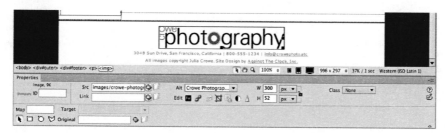

7. Save the file and close it, then continue to the next exercise.

 ## INSERT AN IMAGE FROM THE ASSETS PANEL

The Assets panel, which is part of the Files panel group, offers another way to insert images. The Assets panel allows you to sort the various assets in a site by type rather than by their location within the site.

1. Open the `events.html` file from the Files panel.

2. In the Design pane, select and delete the words "INSERT LOGO HERE" at the bottom of the page.

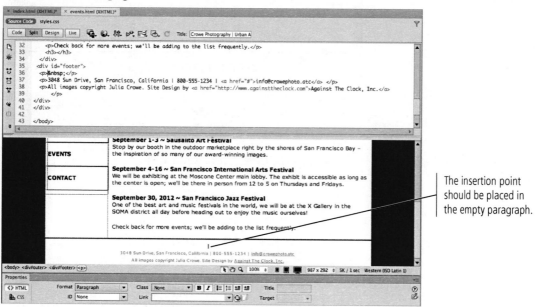

The insertion point should be placed in the empty paragraph.

3. Open the Assets panel (Window>Assets).

4. **On the left side of the Assets panel, click the Images button to show all images in the site.**

The Assets panel displays a thumbnail of the selected image at the top of the panel.

5. **Click the Refresh Site List button to make sure all images are visible.**

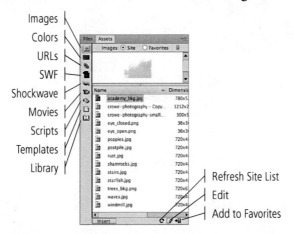

6. **Select crowe-photography-small.png in the panel. With the insertion point flashing where you deleted the text in Step 2, click the Insert button at the bottom of the Assets panel.**

Note:

You can also simply drag images from the Assets panel to place them on a page.

7. **Define Crowe Photography as the alternate text and click OK.**

8. **Save your changes and close the file, then continue to the next stage of the project.**

Creating an Image Map

Although not as common as they once were, you can still use Dreamweaver to create an **image map**, which is an image with certain areas identified as **hotspots** that link to different pages.

When an image is selected on the page, you can use the tools in the bottom-left corner of the Properties panel to define hotspot areas for that image.

In the Design view, Dreamweaver applies a semi-transparent colored shape to represent the location, shape, and size of each hotspot area.

When the page is opened in a browser, there is no immediate visual cue to identify the defined hotspots. The cursor changes to the pointing-hand (link) cursor when the mouse enters the hotspot area. If you want the link to be identified in a tool tip, you should add the title attribute to the <area> tag (in the Code pane).

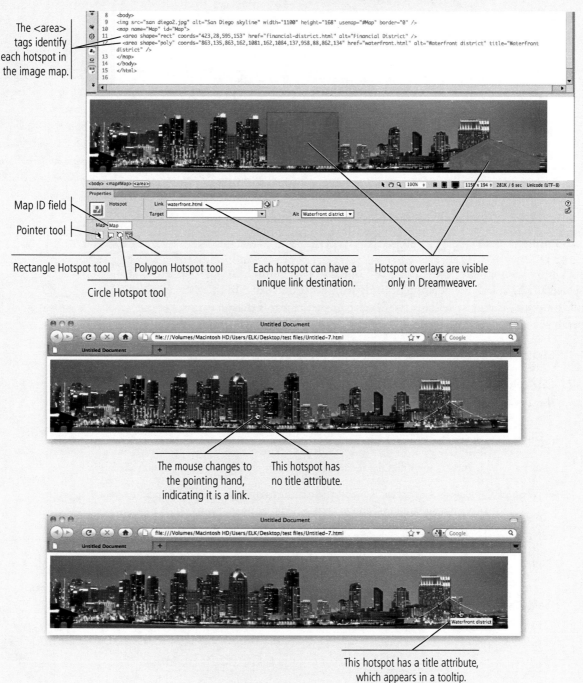

The <area> tags identify each hotspot in the image map.

Map ID field

Pointer tool

Rectangle Hotspot tool

Polygon Hotspot tool

Circle Hotspot tool

Each hotspot can have a unique link destination.

Hotspot overlays are visible only in Dreamweaver.

The mouse changes to the pointing hand, indicating it is a link.

This hotspot has no title attribute.

This hotspot has a title attribute, which appears in a tooltip.

Stage 2 Controlling Backgrounds with CSS

Knowing how to use and apply CSS is especially helpful when you need to work with background images. Without CSS, a background image can only be placed behind the whole page. With CSS, a background image can be placed behind any HTML element, it can repeat, it can scroll with the element or remain locked in position, and it can be positioned anywhere within the element.

The files in the Crowe Photography site were created with a number of sections or divisions. Each division has been assigned a unique **ID** or name (using the **<div>** tag) so different CSS styles can be applied to different sections of the page, thus applying different backgrounds and formatting options for elements within each division.

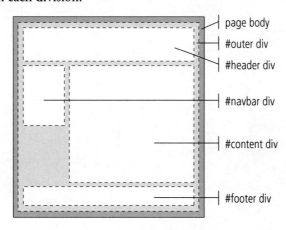

page body
#outer div
#header div
#navbar div
#content div
#footer div

Note:

Background images are properties of CSS styles and do not have the alt attribute option, so you should not put an informative image in the background.

DEFINE A PAGE BACKGROUND IMAGE

The Crowe Photography site requires two different background images — one for the overall page, and one that appears only within the outer div. In this exercise, you will edit the cascading style sheet (CSS) selector that controls the appearance of the overall page.

1. **Make sure the index.html file (in the Photography site) is open.**

2. **Click the Crowe Photography logo near the bottom of the page, then review the Tag Selector.**

   As we explained in Project 7: Digital Book Chapter, the Tag Selector shows the "path of tags", or the nested order of tags to the active selection.

   <body>   This tag identifies the basic page, where all visible content is contained.

   <div#outer> identifies a div that is used to center the overall page content inside the document window. "#outer" is the ID or name of the div.

   <div#footer> identifies the specific div that contains footer information for the page. "#footer" is the ID of the div.

   <p>   identifies the specific paragraph that contains the image.

   <img>   identifies the placed image.

Note:

In the Design pane, divisions are identified by dotted lines.

The Tag Selector shows that this element is in the footer div, which is itself inside the outer div.

3. Open the CSS Styles panel, and click the All button.

Remember, you can open all panels from the Window menu, or by clicking the relevant tab if the panel is open in the panel dock.

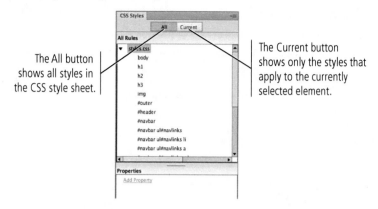

The All button shows all styles in the CSS style sheet.

The Current button shows only the styles that apply to the currently selected element.

4. Click body at the top of the list to select it. At the bottom of the panel, click the Show Only Set Properties button.

In the context of the CSS panel, items that define properties of a specific element (such as "body" in this example) are called **selectors** or **rules**.

Using CSS, **tag selectors** assign properties to specific HTML tags. The body selector defines the appearance of the <body> tag — or the overall visible page area.

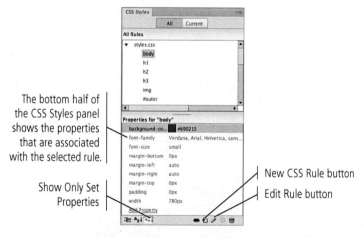

The bottom half of the CSS Styles panel shows the properties that are associated with the selected rule.

Show Only Set Properties

New CSS Rule button

Edit Rule button

Note:

You might need to expand the panel to see the Properties section.

5. Click the Edit Rule button at the bottom of the panel to open the CSS Rule Definition dialog box.

6. In the resulting CSS Rule Definition dialog box, click Background in the Category list (on the left side of the dialog box).

Note:

You can also Control/ right-click a selector name in the panel and choose Edit from the contextual menu.

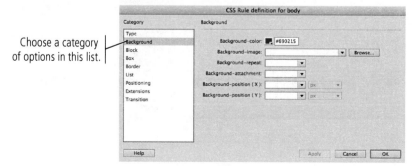

Choose a category of options in this list.

7. **To the right of the Background-image field, click the Browse button. Navigate to the Photography site images folder, select trees-bkg.png, and click Open/OK.**

8. **Choose no-repeat in the Background-repeat menu.**

   Unless you specify otherwise, a background image will repeat (tile) across and down until the background of the element is completely filled with the background image.

   The CSS **background-repeat** property has four options: repeat (the default), repeat-x (horizontally only), repeat-y (vertically only), and no-repeat (the background image appears only once in the top-left corner of the element).

9. **Choose fixed in the Background-attachment menu.**

   By choosing fixed, the image stays attached to the top-left corner of the body element; when a user scrolls the page, the image remains in place while the page scrolls on top of the background image.

   If you choose Scroll in this menu, the image will scroll along with the rest of the page.

10. **Choose left in the Background-position (X) menu, and choose top in the Background-position (Y) menu.**

    The CSS **background-position** property requires two values: horizontal positioning (left, right, or center) and vertical positioning (top, bottom, or center). You can also use measurements such as "5 pixels" to position a background image.

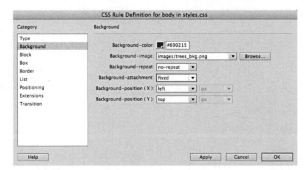

Note:

These fields define the horizontal (X) and vertical (Y) positions of the background image relative to the containing element.

11. **Click OK to close the CSS Rule Definition dialog box and apply the background image to the body element.**

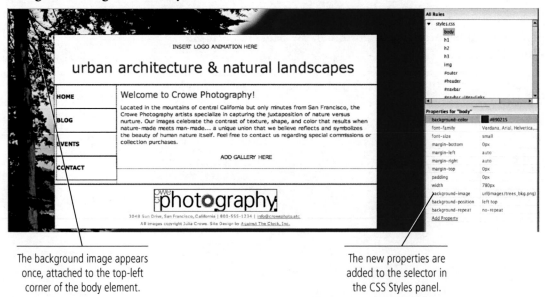

The background image appears once, attached to the top-left corner of the body element.

The new properties are added to the selector in the CSS Styles panel.

12. In the CSS Styles panel, click the color swatch for the background-color property to open the color picker.

After placing the background image, you can see that the dark red background color is not appropriate for the overall site content. You can use CSS to edit the background color of any element in the page.

13. Move the mouse cursor over the blue area in the placed logo image, then click to sample the logo color as the body element background color.

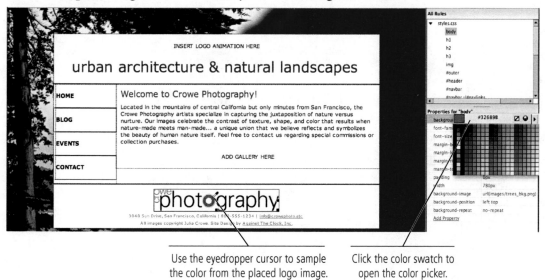

Use the eyedropper cursor to sample the color from the placed logo image.

Click the color swatch to open the color picker.

14. Look at the document bar at the top of the document window.

Although you made changes that affect the appearance of the index.html file, the document tab does not show an asterisk — in other words, the HTML document has not been changed. You do not need to save it before continuing.

All changes in this exercise were made to the CSS file that is linked to the open HTML file. The Related Files bar below the document tab shows an asterisk next to styles.css, indicating that the CSS file has been changed and so should be saved.

The index.html file has not been changed in this exercise.

The styles.css file has been changed in this exercise.

15. Click styles.css in the Related Files bar, then choose File>Save.

When you click one of the related files in the bar, the document window automatically switches to Split view and the file you clicked is displayed in the Code pane.

Clicking one of the related files opens the relevant code in the Code pane of the document window.

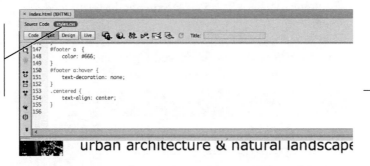

Note:

Although Dreamweaver offers Undo and Redo functions, they don't apply to changes to CSS unless you are working directly on the code of the CSS file (in Code view). If you want to undo a change in the CSS file, you must switch to the CSS file (in the Code pane) and use the Undo command.

16. Click Source Code in the Related Files bar to return to the main HTML file, and then click the Design button to return to Design view.

Clicking the Source Code button restores the active page's HTML code to the Code pane.

Clicking Source Code reverts the Code pane to the HTML file's code.

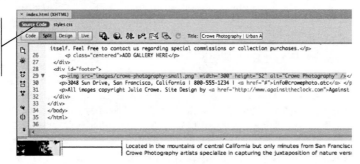

17. Continue to the next exercise.

Hexadecimal Color Codes

DREAMWEAVER FOUNDATIONS

The RGB color model describes colors using values for red, green, and blue respectively. Each color can be assigned a value from 0 (none of that color) to 255 (full strength of that color), for a range of 256 values.

Black has zero values for all three colors, so it is represented as 0, 0, 0. White has full values for all three colors, so it is represented as 255, 255, 255. The hexadecimal system is a numeric system that uses 16 numerals from 0–9 plus A–F (11 is represented by A, 12 by B, up to 15 by F). Since 256 = 16 × 16, in hexadecimal code, 256 = F × F.

The range of 256 values for each color is from 0 to FF (by convention, the first 16 values from 0 to F are given a leading zero: 00 to 0F). Since RGB requires a value for each of the three colors, you will see hexadecimal color values such as #EE04F3, #40896C, and #E843A0.

When both digits for a particular color value are the same, you can abbreviate the code to only three digits. For example, the full code for black is #000000, but it can be abbreviated to #000.

In Web design, the hexadecimal color code must be preceded by the "#" sign (called the hash, pound, or octothorpe character). By convention, the letters should be uppercase, but neither Dreamweaver nor browsers differentiate between #EE04F3, #ee04f3, or #eE04f3.

DEFINE A BACKGROUND IMAGE FOR THE OUTER DIV

Many Web pages use different background properties — colors and/or images — to separate different areas of the page. In this exercise, you are going to define a separate background image that appears behind all of the main content (**div#outer**).

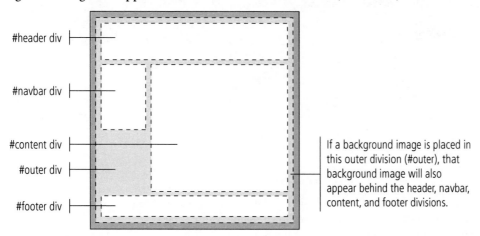

If a background image is placed in this outer division (#outer), that background image will also appear behind the header, navbar, content, and footer divisions.

1. **With index.html open, locate and select #outer in the CSS Styles panel.**

   ID selectors, which begin with the # symbol, assign specific properties to the element that is named with that ID.

2. **In the CSS Styles panel, click the Edit Rule button.**

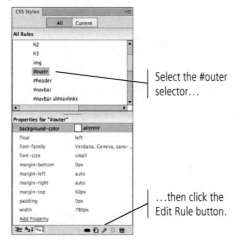

Select the #outer selector...

...then click the Edit Rule button.

3. **In the CSS Rule Definition dialog box, select the Background category.**

4. **Click the Browse button for the Background-image property. Select academy-bkg.jpg (in the site images folder), then click Open/OK.**

5. **Choose no-repeat in the Background-repeat menu.**

6. **Choose right in the Background-position (X) menu, and choose bottom in the Background-position (Y) menu.**

Remember, these properties define the horizontal (X) and vertical (Y) positions of the background image *relative to the containing element*.

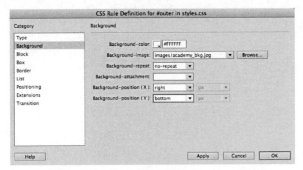

7. **Click OK to apply the change and return to the document window.**

The new background image appears inside the #outer div — behind all of the actual page content area. (If any of the nested divs had a defined background color or image, the background image in the #outer div would be obscured in those areas.)

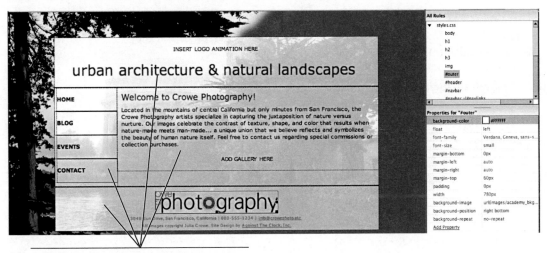

The background image in the #outer div appears behind the header, navbar, content, and footer divs.

8. **Preview the page in your browser. Read the resulting warning message.**

When you make changes to CSS rules that are stored in an external CSS file (as they are in this project), Dreamweaver makes the necessary changes in the related CSS file. The styles.css file is tagged with an asterisk in the bar at the top of the document window, indicating that it has been changed but not yet saved.

The styles.css file has been changed and not yet saved.

9. **Click Yes to save the styles.css file and open the page in your browser.**

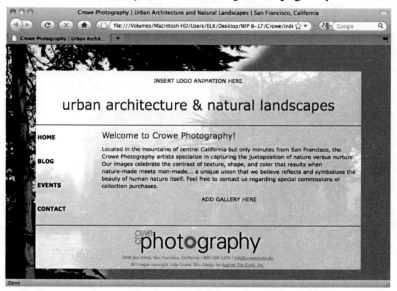

10. **Close the browser window.**

11. **Return to Dreamweaver and continue to the next exercise.**

DEFINE BACKGROUND IMAGES FOR NAVIGATION LINK STATES

One advantage of CSS is that you can define different background properties for every identified element. In this exercise, you will use those capabilities to create a custom background behind every list item in the left navigation bar.

1. **In the open index.html file, place the insertion point in any of the links in the navigation bar.**

2. **Review the Tag Selector below the Design pane.**

Each navigation link is actually an item in an unordered list, which you can see from the **<ul>** and **<li>** tags in the Tag Selector. The list has been named with the **#navlinks** ID. Because each item is also a link, the final tag in the list is the **<a>** tag.

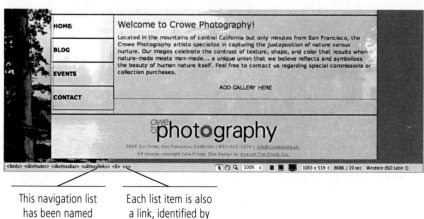

This navigation list has been named with the #navlinks ID.

Each list item is also a link, identified by the <a> tag.

3. **In the CSS Styles panel, locate and select #navbar ul#navlinks a, and then click the Edit Rule button at the bottom of the panel.**

This type of rule is called a **compound** or **descendant selector**, which defines a very specific element that will be affected. The name of this selector tells you where it will apply.

In this case, the "a" at the end of the selector name means that this rule will apply to all links within the unordered list named "navlinks" (ul#navlinks), which is in turn inside the division named "navbar" (#navbar).

Note:

For the sake of readability, we identify compound selector names in red.

Properties in this compound selector apply only to links in the unordered navlink list in the navbar div.

4. **In the Background category, define eye-open.png (from the main site images folder) as the background image.**

5. **Choose no-repeat in the Background-repeat menu.**

6. **Choose left in the Background-position (X) menu, and choose center in the Background-position (Y) menu.**

7. **Click Apply (don't click OK).**

The Apply button allows you to view the changes without exiting the dialog box.

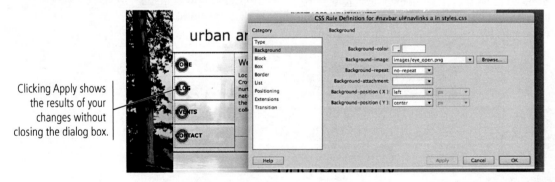

Clicking Apply shows the results of your changes without closing the dialog box.

8. **Switch to the Box category on the left. Type 40 in the Left Padding field and click Apply.**

   Padding is the extra space between the element content and the element border. Background colors and images extend into the padding.

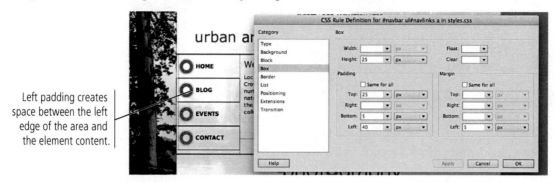

   Left padding creates space between the left edge of the area and the element content.

9. **Click OK to close the CSS Rule Definition dialog box.**

10. **Select the #navbar ul#navlinks a:hover selector in the CSS Styles panel and click the Edit Rule button.**

    The "hover" selector defines the **mouseover state** for a particular link, which determines what happens when the user moves the mouse cursor over the link.

11. **In the Background category, browse to select eye-closed.png from the main site images folder. Set the Background-repeat property to no-repeat, choose left in the in the Background-position (X) field, and choose center from the Background-position (Y) menu. Click OK.**

    The **:hover** pseudo-class only applies when the mouse cursor hovers over a link; it does not apply when the mouse cursor is away from the link.

12. **Click the Live button in the Document toolbar and move your mouse cursor over the navigation links to test the hover effect.**

    The **:hover** pseudo-class is a dynamic effect that Dreamweaver's Design pane cannot display. To see the effect, you must view the page in a browser or switch to Live view.

    Live view is active.

    As you move your mouse cursor over a link, the :hover pseudo-class is activated and swaps the "open eye" icon with the "closed eye" icon.

13. **Click the styles.css button in the Related Files bar. Save the changes in the CSS file.**

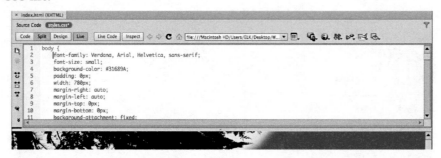

14. **Click the Design button to close the Code pane, then click the Live button to toggle that feature off and return to the regular Design view.**

15. **Continue to the next stage of the project.**

Creating a Rollover Image

In the last exercise you used CSS to create an element that changes based on the position of the user's mouse cursor.

You can also use Dreamweaver to insert a rollover image directly into an HTML page.

To create a rollover image, open the Image menu in the Insert panel and choose Rollover image (or choose Insert>Image Objects>Rollover Image).

In the resulting dialog box, you can define the two images to use — the original or default image, and the rollover image that appears when a user's mouse enters the image area.

If the Preload Rollover Image option is checked, the Web server will automatically download the rollover image when the page is first opened. This prevents a delay when a user triggers the rollover.

A number of JavaScript functions are required in the page head to make rollover images function properly.

Code related to the rollover image on the page.

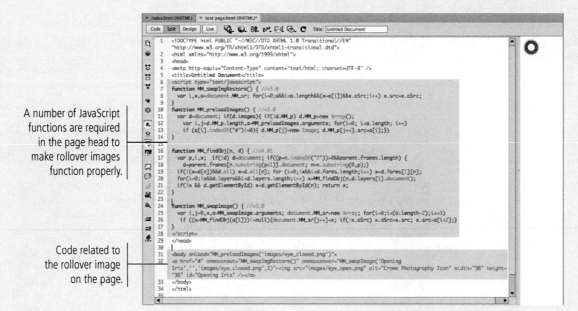

Stage 3 Working with Other Image Types

In addition to static images such as photos, logos, and graphic text, two other forms of images are commonly incorporated into Web designs — Flash animations and video files, collectively known as **multimedia**.

Depending on the configuration of a Web page, video and audio files might need to completely download to your computer before playing, or they might be embedded within a Web page so they can play as they download — known as **streaming**. The purpose of streaming is to allow the video or audio to play before the entire file has been downloaded; streaming can also provide some protection because the video and audio files aren't stored on the user's computer.

Adobe Flash can be used to create simple animations such as moving text, as well as more complex animations such as online games. Flash can also be used to display and control video. Although most desktop computers have the required Flash Player plug-in installed, many mobile devices — specifically, those running the iOS operating system — do not support Flash-based animations or video.

Note:

To view Flash objects in your browser, the Flash plug-in must be installed on your computer. In the past, you had to manually download and install the plug-in; today, however, most browsers have the Flash plug-in installed (or it is automatically installed the first time you need the plug-in to view a Flash movie).

INSERT A FLASH ANIMATION

Inserting Flash objects into a Web page requires a complicated mix of HTML tags, including the **<object>** and **<param>** tags. Furthermore, to comply with an ongoing patent dispute regarding embedding plug-ins within a Web page, Flash objects (among others) must be loaded into a browser using JavaScript. Fortunately, Dreamweaver embeds Flash objects within Web pages and properly writes the **<object>** and **<param>** tags for you, surrounding them with the appropriate JavaScript code to comply with the patent.

1. **Make sure index.html in the Photography site is open.**

2. **In Design view, select and delete the words "INSERT LOGO ANIMATION HERE" at the top of the page. Leave the insertion point in the now-empty paragraph.**

3. **With the Insert panel in Common mode, click the arrow on the Media button and choose SWF from the menu.**

   Like the Images button, the Media button remembers the last-used option. To be sure you are inserting the correct type of object in this step, open the menu and choose SWF.

Note:

You can also choose Insert>Media>SWF.

The insertion point should be in this empty paragraph.

Click the arrow on the button icon to open the menu.

4. **Open the flash folder in the Photography site root folder, select `logo-animated.swf`, and click Open/OK.**

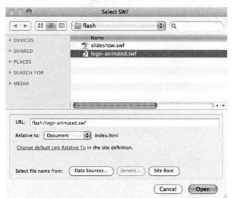

Note:

SWF is the final, compressed, uneditable format of an Adobe Flash file.

5. **Type `Crowe Photography` in the Title field of the Object Tag Accessibility Attributes dialog box, and then click OK.**

The title attribute provides some measure of accessibility to SWF files. This animation is simple, containing the text "Crowe Photography," as well as an animated camera aperture. In this case, the text of the animation is sufficient for accessibility purposes.

Note:

Interactive files that change with user interaction and include a large amount of text require accessibility to be built into the Flash object.

6. **With the placed SWF object selected in the Design pane, examine the Properties panel.**

When a placed SWF file is selected on the page, a blue tag (above the placeholder) displays the type and ID of the asset. You can click the eye icon to toggle between the SWF file and the information users see if they don't have the correct version of Flash Player.

When the mouse cursor is over the SWF object, this tag identifies the type and ID of the asset.

The Flash object appears as a gray box in the Design view.

These options control the animation playback.

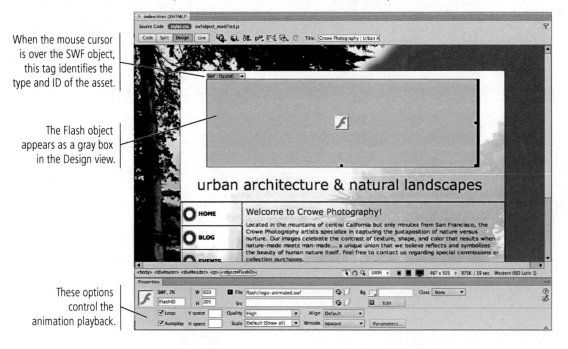

7. Click the Live view button in the document toolbar and watch the animation.

You have to use the Live view to preview a SWF animation in Dreamweaver.

Note:

If you preview the page in Live view, the SWF file plays just as if it were in a browser window.

The background of the Flash object window obscures the underlying background image.

8. Turn off the Live view, then select the Flash object on the page.

Remember, you can't select and modify page content when the Live view is active.

9. In the Properties panel, choose Transparent in the WMode menu.

The WMode property defines the background color of the window in which the Flash object is placed. By choosing Transparent in the menu, you allow the background image to be visible behind the animation.

Choose Transparent in this menu.

10. Turn the Live view back on and review the animation.

The now-transparent window allows the background image to show behind the animation.

11. Turn off the Live view, then save the file (File>Save). Read the message in the resulting dialog box.

Some placed assets — including SWF files — require specific scripts to work properly in the final page. When you save a page after placing one of these objects, Dreamweaver identifies the necessary files and alerts you that they will be copied into your site folder. For the SWF file to work properly in the live Web site, these files should be uploaded along with the rest of your site files.

Copy Dependent Files

This page uses an object or behavior that requires supporting files. The following files have been copied to your local site. You must upload them to your server in order for the object or behavior to function correctly.

Scripts/expressInstall.swf
Scripts/swfobject_modified.js

OK

12. Click OK in the Copy Dependent Files dialog box.

13. **Repeat this process to insert the animated logo at the top of the blog.html and events.html files.**

Don't forget to change the WMode property for the SWF object in each file.

14. **Continue to the next exercise.**

 ## INSERT AND CONFIGURE A FLASH SLIDESHOW

Todd Dominey (www.todddominey.org) created a Flash-based slideshow object that you can easily configure to include your own photos. The slideshow reads the content of an XML file called images.xml, which contains the file names (and paths if necessary) of the photos to be shown in the slideshow. By changing the file names, you can use the same Flash object to show different photos. You must save the images in JPEG format, and you must resize the images to fit within the dimensions of the Flash object. Once those tasks are done, you have access to an easily customizable slideshow animation — without using the full Flash application.

1. **With index.html open (from the Photography site), select and delete the words "ADD GALLERY HERE" from the content div.**

2. **In the Common Insert panel, click the Media:SWF button.**

If you did not continue directly from the previous exercise, and your button does not say "Media:SWF", click the arrow on the button and choose SWF from the top of the list.

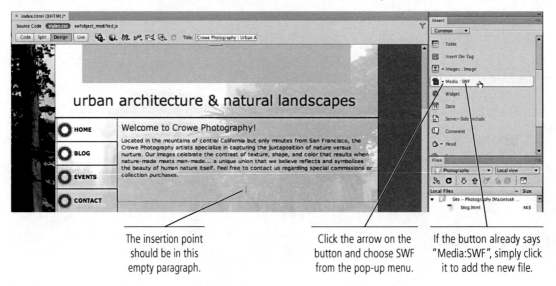

The insertion point should be in this empty paragraph.

Click the arrow on the button and choose SWF from the pop-up menu.

If the button already says "Media:SWF", simply click it to add the new file.

3. **Navigate to the flash folder in the Photography site (if necessary), select slideshow.swf, and click Open/OK.**

4. **In the Title field of the Object Tag Accessibility Attributes dialog box, type Photos from the Crowe collection, and then click OK.**

5. Turn on the Live view and review the placed object.

The slideshow is black because the images identified in the XML file don't exist in this site. You need to edit the images.xml file and replace the image file names with those found on this site.

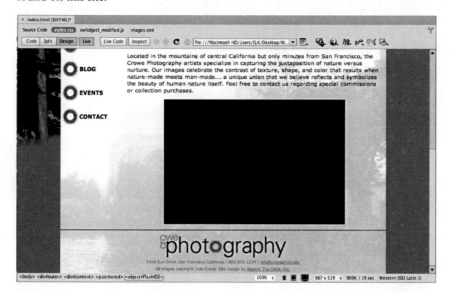

Note:

The slideshow used in this exercise is available at no cost. You can purchase the full SlideShowPro (www.slideshowpro.net), which contains a wide range of options and features.

6. Using the Files panel, double-click images.xml (in the site root folder) to open the XML file.

Some options for the slideshow are described in the comments at the top of the XML file; they are inserted as attributes of the opening <gallery> tag.

Use as many images as you like by listing them here.

7. In the Files panel, expand the slides folder.

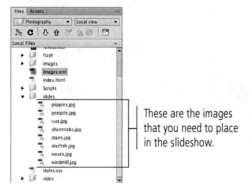

These are the images that you need to place in the slideshow.

8. **Select the first image path in the XML file code (images/calliandra.jpg) and replace it with `slides/poppies.jpg`.**

Leave the quotes from the original image path in place, and simply type the new path name.

Change the first image path to match the path of the image you want to show.

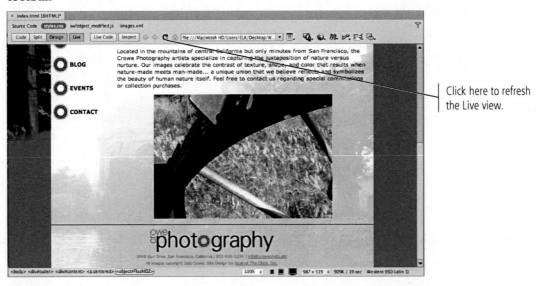

9. **Replace the image paths for the remaining images in the code, using the correct names from the site's slides folder.**

For this slideshow to work properly, the file slideshow.swf can be placed in any folder within your site, but images.xml must be placed in the same folder as the page calling the file. Because of code in the slideshow.swf file, images.xml cannot be renamed; if you want to use it for two different slideshows in the same folder, you must move one of the slideshows to another folder. Finally, the paths to the images must be relative to the location of the images.xml file. (You can also use absolute paths, but you won't be able to preview the slideshow from your local computer.)

10. **Save the changes to images.xml and close the file.**

11. **With the Live view active, click the Refresh button in the Document toolbar.**

Click here to refresh the Live view.

12. **Turn off the Live view, save the file and close it, and then continue to the next exercise.**

INSERT A FLASH VIDEO

The FLV format is the native Flash video format. Using Adobe Media Encoder (a separate application that is included with Flash), you can import videos in a variety of formats and save them in the Flash video format (.flv or .f4v). You can wrap video inside a Flash video player, and then use Dreamweaver to embed the video in a Web page. This way, your visitors can view the video from directly within the Web page.

As with the SWF format, support for the FLV format is not available on some mobile devices. You will learn different options for working with video files in Project 6: Kayaking HTML5 Site.

1. **Open blog.html from the Photography site root folder.**

2. **Select and delete the text "ADD VIDEO HERE" from the bottom of the content div.**

3. **In the Common Insert panel, click the arrow on the Media button and choose FLV from the menu.**

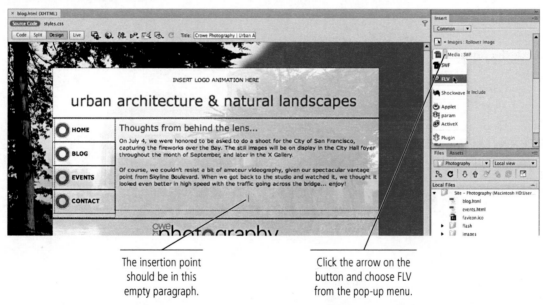

The insertion point should be in this empty paragraph.

Click the arrow on the button and choose FLV from the pop-up menu.

4. **In the resulting Insert FLV dialog box, make sure the Video Type menu is set to Progressive Download Video.**

   The other option, Streaming Video, is used when the video is very large, the copyright owner doesn't want visitors to have a copy of the video on their systems, or there is a continuous feed from the source.

5. **Click the Browse button to the right of the URL field. In the resulting navigation dialog box, choose fireworks.flv from the Photography site's video folder and click Open/OK.**

6. **Click the Detect Size button.**

   The width and height of the video are detected and the fields are filled. The dimensions of the video affect the skin options (which we explain in the next step).

7. Open the Skin menu and choose Clear Skin 3.

The **skin** is the appearance of the video contols that are added to the video object. There are three basic skin appearances — Clear, Corona, and Halo. Each skin appearance has three Width options. The Width options affect the number and appearance of video controls. Video controls include play, pause, stop, skip to anywhere within the video, mute the sound, and increase/decrease the volume. A narrow-width video has less room for video controls. This video is wider than any of the minimum widths, so any Skin option will work.

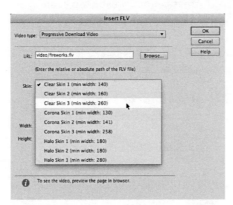

8. Uncheck the Auto Play option below the Height field.

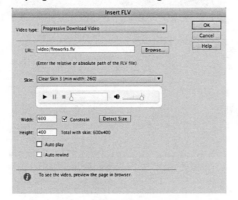

9. Click OK to insert the video into the open HTML file.

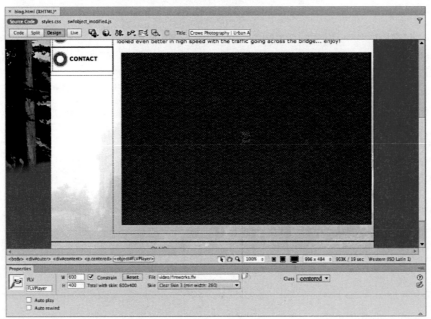

10. Turn on the Live view and watch the video.

After the video starts playing, the controls fade out. If you move your mouse over the video, the controls reappear.

11. Save the file and close it, then continue to the final exercise.

 ## ADD A PAGE FAVICON

Favicon is a word created by combining "favorite" and "icon." It refers to the icon that represents a site in your Favorites or Bookmarks list (beside the site name). A favicon is not randomly generated; it is downloaded from the bookmarked site. In addition to the Favorites or Bookmarks list, the favicon also appears at the left end of the browser's address bar or tab (if your browser supports tabs).

A favicon is an image in the icon format, which supports a limited number of colors and is generally restricted to 16×16 and 32×32 pixels. (The format supports both resolutions within the same file, which is one reason why it is unique.)

Although some desktop graphics applications can create icons, some graphic and Web design applications (such as Adobe Photoshop and Fireworks) do not support the icon format. There are a number of free online applications for converting GIF, PNG, JPEG, or BMP images to the icon format; we used the converter at www.favicon.cc to create the icon file for this project.

Because the icon is commonly used as a representation of an entire Web site, the favicon.ico file is commonly stored in the root folder of the Web site. The file must be named "favicon.ico".

The following code block is supported by most browsers:

```
<link rel="shortcut icon" type="image/x-icon" href="favicon.ico" />
```

Dreamweaver does not provide code hints for most of the attribute values of the **<link />** tag, so it is easiest to simply type the code in the appropriate location.

1. **Open index.html from the root folder of the Photography site.**

2. **Click the Code button to switch to Code view.**

3. **Click to the left of the closing </head> tag on line 8, press Return/Enter three times, and move the insertion point into the middle empty line.**

   In general, the **<link />** tag should be used to insert the favicon as the last tag in the head section of the document.

Note:

In an actual site, you would likely use an absolute path to the favicon file, so the browser will always look for the favicon.ico file in the root folder of the Web site. Since you can't use absolute paths when previewing pages on your local computer, however, you must use a relative path.

4. **Type the code required to insert the favicon:**

   ```
   <link rel="shortcut icon" type="image/x-icon" href="favicon.ico" />
   ```

   As you type, code hints appear when Dreamweaver recognizes a specific tag. In this case, it is easier to simply ignore these hints and type the required code.

5. **Save the file, and then preview the page in your browser.**

   If possible, preview in a browser other than Safari or Internet Explorer; these browsers require the site to be online, not local.

There's the favicon in Firefox.

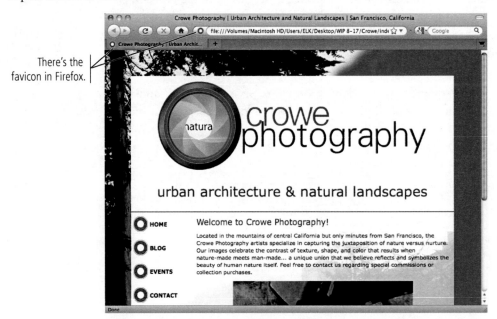

6. **Return to Dreamweaver and close index.html.**

7. **Export a site definition named Photography.ste into your WIP>Crowe folder, and then remove the Photography site from Dreamweaver.**

   If necessary, refer back to Project 6: Bistro Site Organization for complete instructions on exporting a site definition or removing a site from Dreamweaver.

Project Review

fill in the blank

1. The _____ attribute of the <img> tag is required to make images accessible for all Web users.

2. The _____ attribute defines the specific file that will appear in the <img> tag location.

3. The _____ property of CSS can be used to tile a single background image horizontally, vertically, or both throughout the entire document window.

4. _____ is the process of cutting out/ off portions of an image.

5. The _____ format supports continuous-tone color but not transparency; it is best used for photographs.

6. The _____ format supports transparency but not a large gamut of color; it is best used for graphics and artwork.

7. A(n) _____ replaces one image with another when the mouse cursor enters the image area.

8. The _____ extension identifies an animation file that was exported from Adobe Flash.

9. The _____ extension identifies a Flash video file.

10. A _____ is a graphic that appears to the left of the site URL in the browser's navigation bar.

short answer

1. Briefly describe three image file formats that might be used on the Web, including advantages and disadvantages of each.

2. Briefly explain the importance of resampling, relative to resizing images in Dreamweaver.

3. Briefly explain the advantages to using CSS to define background colors and images.

Use what you learned in this project to complete the following freeform exercise.
Carefully read the art director and client comments, then create your own design to meet the needs of the project.
Use the space below to sketch ideas; when finished, write a brief explanation of your reasoning behind your final design.

art director comments

Everything Green Flowers wants to include a digital portfolio in the company's new Web site. As part of the team that is building the new site, your job is to create and implement pages for a Flash version and an HTML version of the portfolio.

To complete this project, you should:

❑ Create a new site in Dreamweaver using the files that have already been created (in the **WC6_PB_Project8.zip** archive on the Student Files Web page).

❑ Place the client's logo on every page.

❑ Add background images to the header and footer sections of the page.

❑ Add a background image to the navigation links in the header section.

❑ Add a photo gallery to the Sample Designs page, using the techniques you used to complete the Crowe Photography site.

client comments

The page structure has already been defined, but the images need to be put into place.

Our logo should appear on every page, at the top of the main content area.

The header and footer sections need background images placed.

We want our pink icon to appear to the left of each navigation item in the header section. It should change to white when users move the mouse over the links.

On the Sample Designs page, add the Flash-based slideshow. All of the images we want to show are in the images>flowers folder. You will need to modify the size of the placed Flash object on the page to fit the images that we've provided.

project justification

_____

_____

_____

_____

_____

_____

_____

_____

_____

_____

_____

_____

_____

When you prepare the design for a site, you need to determine which images will carry content (they must be placed in the foreground using the **<img>** tag), and which images will appear in the background. Appropriate alt text — which enables visually impaired visitors, users who have disabled the display of images, and search engines to use the content of your pages — is required for all foreground images. By editing various CSS properties, you have virtually unlimited options for controlling the background images in different sections of a page.

Dreamweaver also provides image-editing tools that enable you to crop, resize, resample, and sharpen images. Although these tools do not replace full-featured image-editing applications such as Photoshop, the Dreamweaver tools enable you to complete simple editing tasks quickly and easily, without requiring another application.

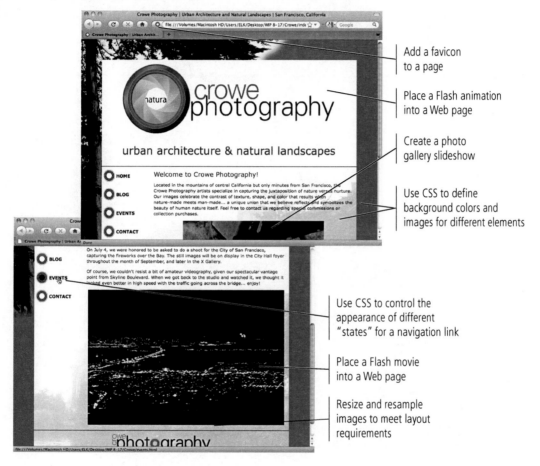

Add a favicon to a page

Place a Flash animation into a Web page

Create a photo gallery slideshow

Use CSS to define background colors and images for different elements

Use CSS to control the appearance of different "states" for a navigation link

Place a Flash movie into a Web page

Resize and resample images to meet layout requirements

Yosemite CSS Layout

The Yosemite Valley Visitor's Bureau hired you to build a new Web site to provide area visitors with as much information as possible about the activities and opportunities that are available in and around the national park. The client wants a Web site that can be quickly and easily updated and modified. In addition, the site should project a consistent look and style across all pages. To fulfill these requirements, you will create and apply a cascading style sheet for the Web site.

This project incorporates the following skills:

❏ Working with tracing images to replicate a site designed in an image-editing application

❏ Creating and linking an external CSS file

❏ Understanding the CSS box model

❏ Creating a layout with div elements

❏ Editing CSS rules to adjust the layout

❏ Defining HTML tag selectors and compound tag selectors

❏ Creating pseudo-class selectors

client comments

We've been getting a lot of inquiries now that spring is coming, and we want to create a new Web site to help answer some of the preliminary questions so our administrative time can focus on conservation efforts.

We have a site already but we can't figure out how it was built, so it's extremely difficult to change even a comma. We called the site designer, but he can't work us into his schedule for more than a month — and we don't have the time to wait.

The new site should be very easy to manage and, more importantly, easy to change — whether it's a comma or the entire site layout.

art director comments

I asked the graphic designer to put together the look and feel of the new site. She created a comp image that shows the overall layout, which you should review carefully to see what elements of the new site you need to implement in Dreamweaver.

The client wants to be able to make his own changes to the actual page content, but we don't want him to be able to destroy the integrity of the page layout. Cascading style sheets are the best way to accomplish this goal because the actual HTML pages will be almost entirely text. The layout will be defined in the CSS file, so the client can edit the text all he wants without touching the layout.

CSS separates the page content from the presentational issues like containers and backgrounds, so search engines can more easily scan and rank the actual page content.

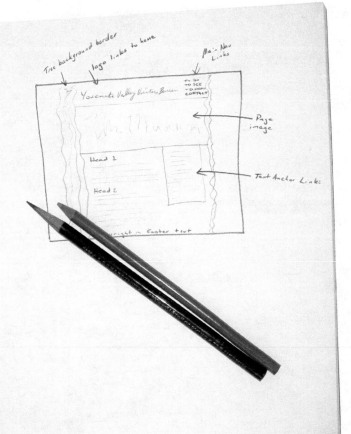

project objectives

To complete this project, you will:

- [ ] Define a tracing image
- [ ] Create and link an external CSS file
- [ ] Create ID selectors
- [ ] Create a layout with div elements
- [ ] Edit CSS rules to adjust the layout
- [ ] Use the float property to control nested divs
- [ ] Use margins and padding to affect element placement
- [ ] Define properties for the body tag
- [ ] Create a template file
- [ ] Define HTML tag selectors
- [ ] Create compound tag selectors
- [ ] Create pseudo-class selectors

Stage 1 Creating Layouts with Style Sheets

A **cascading style sheet** (CSS) is a collection of formatting rules that control the appearance of different elements in a Web page. By attaching a style sheet file to an HTML page and applying the styles to the content of the page, you can control every aspect of the page layout. A CSS file includes formatting instructions in **rules**. A rule consists of two parts: a **selector** (basically, naming the element to be formatted) and **attributes** (such as font, color, width, height, etc.) that will be applied to the selected element.

A style sheet offers a great deal of flexibility in applying styles. Different types of styles can automatically target HTML tags, target HTML tags only in certain places in a page, control specific elements, control multiple elements at once, and control links.

When using a style sheet, you are separating the formatting of a page (CSS) from the structure and content (HTML). To make changes with the CSS formatting, you are usually just editing the style sheet itself rather than the HTML in individual pages. If all pages in a site use the same style sheet, the task of providing control and consistency will be far easier.

DEFINE A TRACING IMAGE

Before creating CSS rules, you should have a clear idea about how the page or site should look. Understanding the appearance (and other requirements) of a site helps you determine what rules you need to create.

In many workflows, the look of a site is designed in a graphics application such as Adobe Photoshop, Fireworks, or Illustrator. In this case, you can import the final image file of the design into Dreamweaver and use it as a map when defining CSS rules to replicate the image as an HTML page. Using the Tracing Image feature, the image you select appears in the background in Design view; you can change the opacity and position of the image as necessary. When you have finished the layout design, you can hide or remove the tracing image.

Note:

A tracing image can be a JPEG, GIF, BMP, or PNG file.

Note:

A tracing image is a Dreamweaver Design view-only feature, it will not appear in Live view or in a Web browser.

1. Download **WC6_RF_Project9.zip** from the **Student Files Web page**.

2. **Expand the ZIP archive in your WIP folder (Macintosh) or copy the archive contents into your WIP folder (Windows).**

   This results in a folder named **Yosemite**, which contains the files you need for this project.

3. **Create a new site named Yosemite, using the WIP>Yosemite folder as the site root folder.**

   If necessary, refer to the first exercises in Project 6: Bistro Site Organization for more detailed instructions.

4. **With the Yosemite site open in the Files panel, choose New in the File menu. Using the New Document dialog box, create a new, blank HTML page using the XHTML 1.0 Transitional DocType.**

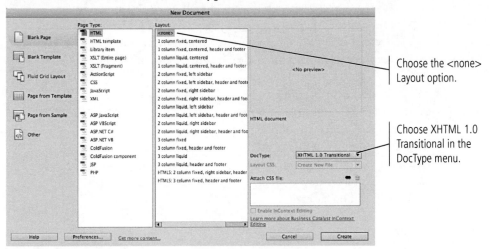

Choose the <none> Layout option.

Choose XHTML 1.0 Transitional in the DocType menu.

5. **Choose File>Save. Save the new page as an HTML file named `design.html` in the root folder of the Yosemite site.**

Note:

You can also create a new blank HTML page by Control/right-clicking the site name in the Files panel and choosing New File in the contextual menu. The resulting file is automatically placed in the site root folder.

6. **With `design.html` open in Design view, Click the Page Properties button in the Properties panel.**

7. **Click Tracing Image in the left side of the dialog box to display those options, then click the Browse button to the right of the Tracing Image field.**

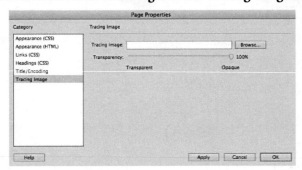

8. **In the Select Image Source dialog box, navigate to the file `tracing.jpg` in the site root folder (WIP>Yosemite) and click Open/OK.**

When you load a tracing image, the Page Properties dialog box automatically appears. You can use the Tracing Image options to change the transparency of the tracing image, as well as browse to select a different image.

Note:

To show or hide the tracing image, use the Show/Hide toggle control in the View>Tracing Image menu.

Note:

If you hide the tracing image, then close the HTML file and reopen it, the tracing image will again be visible; you can rehide it as necessary.

9. **Click OK to close the resulting Page Properties dialog box.**

You can use this dialog box to define a different tracing image (with the Browse button), or reduce the opacity of the image in the file.

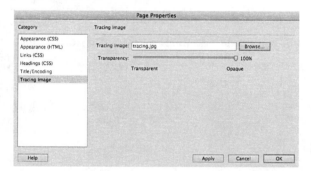

Note:

The other options in the Page Properties dialog box create CSS properties as internal or embedded styles, which means they cannot be reused in other files. It is better to set those properties in an external CSS file, which can be attached to multiple HTML files.

The tracing image appears in design.html. If you have a small screen, you might not be able to see the entire image at 100% magnification.

The tracing image is aligned by default at the insertion point, which is slightly inset from the document edges.

You can't scroll to see the rest of the tracing image.

10. **Choose View>Tracing Image>Reset Position.**

This command moves the tracing image to the actual document edges.

11. **Change your view percentage as necessary to see the entire tracing image.**

12. **Analyze the image to determine what you need to do to create this site layout.**

Use this menu to change the view percentage in the Design view.

- The layout is attached to the left side of the window.
- The background image should repeat over the entire height of the window.
- The left border area is 200 pixels wide.
- The white space in between the borders is 700 pixels wide.
- The right border area is 50 pixels wide.
- The layout is broken into four rows: header, image, page content, and footer.
- The first and third rows each have two separate areas of content.

Note:

When rulers are visible (View>Rulers>Show), guides can be dragged out from them to mark specific places on the page. This can make it easier to measure elements in a tracing image.

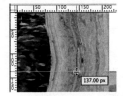

When rulers are visible, you can press Command/Control to show measurements between guides, as well as between guides and page edges.

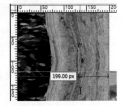

To remove individual guides, click a guide and drag it back to the ruler. To remove all guides, choose View>Guides>Clear Guides.

Note:

You can also change the viewing percentage in the View>Magnification menu.

13. **Take note of the following information, which was provided by the designer who developed the look of the site:**

- The site should have a green background color that fills in the browser window space behind the background image.

- Each page will have the same layout; only the image in the second row and the text in the third row will differ from page to page.

- The images for the second row are all the same size: 700 px × 280 px.

- A sans-serif font should be applied to all text in the site. The client wants to use gray text instead of plain black text.

- First-level headings and the navigation links in the header should be a dark orange color from the bark in the border image.

- Second-level headings should be a bit smaller than first-level headings, italicized, and use the same color as the main text.

- Link text should not be underlined. In the header navigation area and the main body text, link text should be a dark orange color from the background image. In the sidebar navigation (at the right of the third row), link text should use a green color from the background.

- Links in the two navigation areas should be bold. Links in the side navigation area should be centered within the sidebar space.

- Link text should switch to a lighter color when the mouse rolls over the links.

14. **Reset the view percentage to 100%, save the file, and continue to the next exercise.**

CREATE AN EXTERNAL CSS FILE

There are three types of style sheets: external, embedded (also known as internal), and inline. To make the best use of styles, you should have a clear understanding of these different types — including when each is best suited to a specific goal.

An **external style sheet** is saved as a separate CSS file (with the extension ".css"), which is uploaded to the Web server along with the Web site pages. This file can be attached to multiple HTML pages at one time, applying the same rules to similar elements in the different pages. When a user calls a specific URL, the Web browser reads the HTML, finds the directions to the attached CSS file, and reads the rules in the CSS file to present the HTML content exactly as intended.

An **embedded or internal style sheet** is added directly in an HTML page, within style tags; this type of style affects only the particular HTML page in which it is placed. The following code for an embedded style sheet includes a style that defines the formatting of all H1 elements:

```
<style type="text/css"
<!--
h1 {
    font-size: 24px;
}
-->
</style>
```

An **inline style** applies directly and instantly to an individual element within a tag, affecting only that single element of the HTML page. For example, if you apply a font size and color to a paragraph, the inline style looks like this:

```
<p style="font-size: 10px; color: blue">Paragraph content goes here.</p>
```

Note:

All three types of style sheets can be applied to the same HTML page at the same time.

Note:

The set of **<!--** and **-->** tags prevents a few older browsers from displaying the style rules.

Note:

Because inline styles are not reusable even within the same page and don't appear in Dreamweaver's CSS Styles panel, it is better to use external or internal style sheets.

1. **With design.html open, choose File>New.**

2. **In the New Document dialog box, choose Blank Page in the left column. Choose CSS from the Page Type list and click Create.**

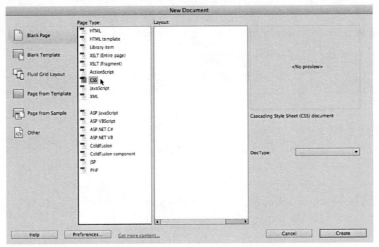

3. **Choose File>Save. Name the file master.css, and then click Save to save the file in the site root folder.**

   This file will contain all the selectors you define to format the Yosemite Valley Web site.

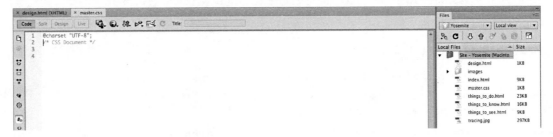

4. **Click the design.html tab to make that file active, then choose Window> CSS Styles to show the CSS Styles panel.**

master.css is open in a separate file.
It is not yet related to design.html.

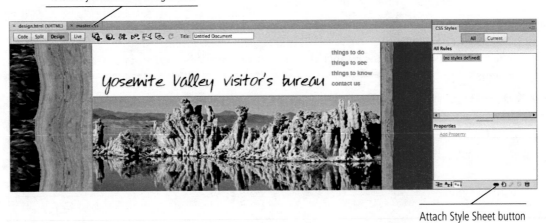

Attach Style Sheet button

5. **Click the Attach Style Sheet button at the bottom of the CSS Styles panel.**

   The resulting dialog box allows you to select an external style sheet for the active HTML file.

6. **In the resulting Attach External Style Sheet dialog box, select the Link option in the Add As area.**

Using the Link option, the style sheet file is connected to the HTML page using the **<link>** tag in the HTML page's header information. When a user opens the HTML page, the browser merges the instructions in the linked CSS file with the information in the HTML file to present the final page design.

The CSS Styles Panel in Depth

The CSS Styles panel has two modes, which are accessed using the buttons at the top of the panel.

All mode displays style rules from external and embedded style sheets, but does not display inline styles defined within the HTML content. The top half of the panel shows a list of existing selectors. The lower half shows the properties associated with the active selector.

This pane shows all properties that apply to the tag that is selected in the document window.

Click to show information about the property that is selected in the top pane.

Click to show all rules that affect the tag that is selected in the document window.

Current mode displays all styles that relate to the current selection in the document window.

This pane shows all properties of the rule that is selected in the middle pane.

- The Summary for Selection pane shows all properties (and values) that apply to the active selection in the document window.

- The Rules pane shows either the rules that apply to the selection, or information about the property that is selected in the Summary for Selection pane.

- The Properties pane shows the properties of the rule that is selected in the Rules pane; the appearance of properties depends on the active option in the bottom-left corner of the panel. You can use the Properties pane to add new properties or modify the values of existing properties. If a property shows a black line through it, that property has been applied by an enclosing tag rather than by the active selection.

You can view the properties and values in the Properties pane in Show Category view, Show List view, or Show Only Set Properties (the default).

- **Show Category view** categorizes properties in the same groups that are available in the CSS Rule Definition dialog box. Every available property is listed; properties with defined values appear in blue. You can add new properties by clicking the white space to the right of a property and typing a new value or choosing from a menu.

- **Show List view** lists all CSS properties in alphabetical order; the groups from Category view are not included.

- **Show Only Set Properties** shows only the properties that have defined values in the lower half of the panel. You can add new properties by clicking the Add Property link at the bottom of the list.

Show Only Set Properties

Show List View

Show Category View

Attach Style Sheet

New CSS Rule

Edit Rule

Disable/Enable CSS Property

Delete CSS Rule

Five buttons in the bottom-right corner of the CSS Styles panel provide additional functionality. From left to right:

- The **Attach Style Sheet** button attaches an external style sheet to the active HTML page. You can browse to locate an existing file, and attach the saved style sheet to the HTML page by using the import or link method.

- The **New CSS Rule** button creates a new rule for ID selectors, tag selectors, compound selectors, and class selectors.

- The **Edit Rule** button opens the CSS Rule Definition dialog box for the selected style (in the list at the top of the panel).

- The **Disable/Enable CSS Property** button turns a selected property on and off by temporarily commenting out the property in the CSS code, so you can view the effects of specific properties in the open file.

- The **Delete CSS Rule** (or Property) button deletes the selected style (selected in the top half of the panel) or property (selected in the bottom half of the panel).

7. **Click the Browse button to the right of the File/URL field. Navigate to the master.css file that you saved in Step 3 and click Choose/OK.**

8. **When you return to the Attach External Style Sheet dialog box, click OK to attach the style sheet file to design.html.**

9. **Click the All button at the top of the CSS Styles panel.**

master.css is now
related to design.html.

10. **Save the file and continue to the next exercise.**

 ## CREATE ID SELECTORS

Using the tracing image and the information you received from the graphic designer, you can now begin to build the overall site layout.

To build a layout with CSS, you need to apply the HTML div element. As you learned in Project 7: Digital Book Chapter and Project 8: Photographer's Web Site, a **<div>** tag marks a division (or section) of a page. A style sheet can define a large number of properties for each div, including height, width, background color, margins, and more.

Each div on a page can have a different identity (defined using the ID attribute), which allows you to define different properties for different areas, as shown here:

```
#header {
    background-color: #999;
}
#footer {
    background-color: #00CCCC;
}
```

Using the code shown above, the header div will have a gray background, and the footer div will have a light aqua background.

You define ID selectors in a style sheet to control the appearance of unique, named HTML div elements. When you insert a div element into a page, you choose a defined ID for that div element; the properties defined in the ID selector (in the style sheet) are then used to format the div in the page.

Note:

If you completed Project 7: Digital Book Chapter and Project 8: Photographer's Web Site, you already know a bit about <div> tags. This project looks more deeply into <div> tags, showing you how to create and control your own divs.

1. **With design.html open, click the New CSS Rule button at the bottom of the CSS Styles panel.**

New CSS Rule

2. **Choose ID in the Selector Type menu.**

   In the New CSS Rule dialog box, you can define the type and name of a selector, as well as where to create the rule (in the attached external CSS file or embedded in the active HTML file).

   As the parenthetical notation suggests, an ID selector can apply to only one element on the page; this type of selector identifies specific sections or divisions of a page, each of which must be unique.

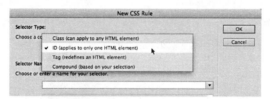

3. **In the Selector Name field, type #header.**

   This ID will be the container for the client's logo and the site's top navigation. The area is 700 pixels wide, so you need the container to be the same width. You also need to move it 200 pixels away from the left edge.

4. **Make sure master.css is selected in the Rule Definition menu (at the bottom of the dialog box).**

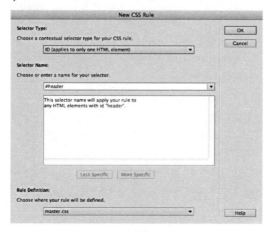

5. **Click OK to open the CSS Rule Definition dialog box.**

   This dialog box includes eight categories of options. All properties that can be saved in a CSS rule are available in the various panes of this dialog box.

Note:

If you have not already created an external CSS file, you can choose New Style Sheet File in the Rule Definition menu. When you click OK, you first name the new style sheet file (which is saved in the active site root folder) before you define the rule properties. The new style sheet file is automatically linked to the active HTML page.

Note:

All ID selector names must begin with the "#" character. If you forget to include the character, Dreamweaver will add it for you.

Note:

ID selector names are case-sensitive. However the rule is named must be exactly how it is used when applied to the appropriate div element.

6. **Click Box in the Category list. Type** `700` **in the Width field, and make sure px (pixels) is selected in the related menu.**

7. **In the Margin area, uncheck the Same for All check box. Type** `200` **in the Left field, and make sure px is selected in the related menu.**

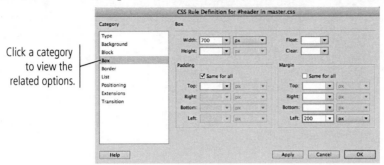

Click a category to view the related options.

Note:

The header of the dialog box includes the name of the selector being edited. For the sake of brevity, we exclude this distinction when we refer to the dialog box.

8. **Click OK to add the rule to the master.css file.**

9. **In the CSS Styles panel, click the arrow/plus sign to expand the master.css item, and then select the #header item in the list.**

   In the Design pane, the design.html file is not affected because the #header div has not yet been placed in the file. The new rule appears only in the CSS Styles panel; specific properties of the rule are listed in the lower half of the panel.

This area shows the two properties you defined for this ID selector.

If you see more than these two properties, click the Show Only Set Properties button.

10. **Click the master.css tab at the top of the document window.**

    You can now see the code for the new rule you defined. Properties and values for the selector are contained within curly brackets; each property is separated by a semicolon.

The asterisk tells you the file has been modified since it was last saved.

11. **Choose File>Save to save the master.css file, then click the Close button on the file's tab to close only that file.**

12. Click the New CSS Rule button in the CSS Styles panel.

13. In the resulting dialog box, choose ID in the Selector Type menu and type **#image** in the Selector Name field. Make sure master.css is selected in the Rule Definition menu and click OK.

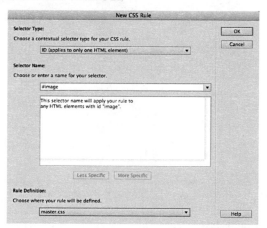

14. In the Box category of options, define a width of **700** pixels, height of **280** pixels, and left margin of **200** pixels.

   All of the images for this Web site are 700 pixels wide by 280 pixels high; you're creating the div to fit those images. (We are telling you the correct dimensions to use in this example. In a professional environment, you would have to determine the correct size for this div by evaluating the supplied images.)

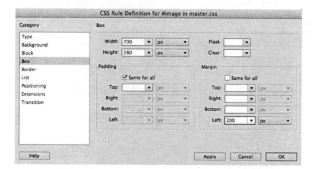

15. In the Border category, uncheck all three Same for All check boxes. Open the menu next to the Top Style field and choose Solid.

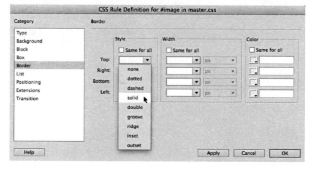

16. Type 3 in the Top Width field and make sure px is selected in the related menu.

17. **Click the color swatch for the Top Color field. Move the cursor over the green color on the right side of the tracing image and click to select that color.**

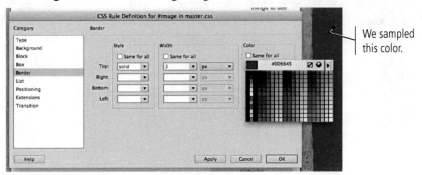

We sampled this color.

18. **Apply the same settings to the Bottom fields, then click OK.**

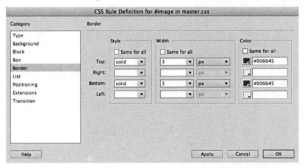

19. **In the Related Files bar above the document window, click the master.css item to show that code in the Code pane.**

Although you intentionally closed the master.css file, it is still open through its relationship to the open HTML file. In the Related Files bar, an asterisk next to the CSS file name shows that the code has been modified since it was last saved. Clicking the CSS file name button automatically switches the document window to Split mode; the CSS file code is displayed in the Code pane.

Clicking master.css in the Related Files bar shows the related code in the Code pane.

20. **Choose File>Save to save your changes to the master.css file.**

The CSS Rule Definition Dialog Box in Depth

The CSS Rule Definition dialog box is the primary tool for defining CSS rules. When you create a new selector, the CSS Rule Definition dialog box for that selector opens so you can set the selector's properties and values. You can access different categories of options by clicking in the list on the left side of the dialog box.

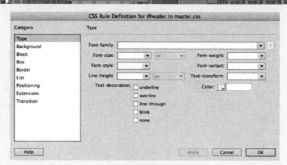

It should be noted that the dialog box capitalizes the first word of each property name. In CSS code, the property names are entirely lowercase, using a hyphen to separate words.

Type options control the appearance of the text.

- font-family defines the font sequence for the text (e.g., Arial, Helvetica, sans-serif); you can also edit the available list.

- font-size sets the size of the font in a variety of measurement units (using pixels for font-size measurements can prevent text distortion).

- font-weight affects the apparent boldness of the text (normal, bold, bolder, lighter, or specific values).

- font-style specifies the font style (normal, italic, or oblique).

- font-variant sets the text as normal or small-caps.

- line-height determines the height of the line (similar to leading, if you are familiar with print design).

- text-transform controls the capitalization of the text. Capitalize changes the first letter of each word, uppercase shows all letters as capitals, and lowercase shows all letters as lowercase.

- text-decoration sets a predefined text style (underline, overline, line-through, blink, or none). This option is particularly useful for removing the default underline of hyperlink text.

- color specifies the font color.

Background options control the background color and images for a specific selector.

- background-color can be set by typing a hexadecimal color code in the field, by clicking the color swatch and choosing a color from the color picker, or by clicking the color swatch and using the eyedropper cursor to sample a color from anywhere on your screen.

- background-image can be set by typing the path or by clicking the Browse button and navigating to the image location.

- background-repeat determines how background images fill the space available in their containers. No-repeat places the image one time, in the top-left corner. Repeat tiles the image horizontally and vertically. Repeat-x tiles the image only horizontally. Repeat-y tiles the image vertically.

- background-attachment controls how a background image moves in relation to the page. Fixed allows the image to stay in place even if the page scrolls. Scroll allows the background image to stay in the same position relative to the page; the background image scrolls along with the page.

- background-position (X) sets the image to the left, center, or right of the page.

- background-position (Y) sets the image to the top, center, or bottom of the page.

If nothing is selected in these menus, background images default to repeat in both directions, scroll with the page, and are positioned at the left and top corners of the element.

Block options define spacing and alignment for content within a container.

- word-spacing controls the spacing between words.

- letter-spacing controls the spacing between individual characters.

- vertical-align aligns the selected element vertically.

- text-align aligns text to the left, right, center, or justified across the full width of the container.

- text-indent specifies where text begins in a line.

- white-space manages extra spaces and tabs. Normal collapses all whitespace (ignoring double spaces and tabs). Pre retains all whitespace. Nowrap prevents lines of text from wrapping, based on the horizontal dimensions of the container (unless a **\<br/\>** tag is used).

- display controls how an element should be displayed. "None" makes an element not visible; "Block" makes an element behave like a div tag, which can be sized and positioned; and "Inline" makes an element behave like simple text content.

Box options control the dimensions of elements such as divs and paragraphs.

- width and height control the dimensions of the selected element.

- float determines where an element will be placed in relation to its containing element. Other content in the same element will float around the affected element on the opposite side.

- clear allows an element to "reset" the vertical position and appear below a preceding element that is floating.

- padding is the amount of space that separates the element border and the content in the element.

- margin is the amount of space that separates the element border and surrounding elements.

(Background colors and images appear behind padding areas, but not behind margin areas.)

Border options control the style, width, and color of the borders around the selected elements. You can specify values individually (top, right, bottom, left) or select the Same for All check box to apply the same border attributes to all four sides of an element.

List options control the appearance and style of lists.

- list-style-type specifies the type of identifier to use (disc, circle, square, decimal, lower- or upper-roman, and lower- or upper-alpha).

- list-style-image defines a custom image to use as a bullet character. None disables the list appearance; no bullets will appear.

- list-style-position defines the list position as inside or outside (i.e., the list either wraps indented from the bullet character or wraps to the left margin).

Positioning options control the position of the CSS elements.

- position determines the position of the element (absolute, fixed, relative, or static). Absolute enables the element to remain stable on the page, regardless of the position of the other elements. Fixed positions the element according to the window size. Relative positions the element based on the position of other elements on the page. Static, the default method, positions the element as it appears in an HTML page.

- width and height are the same as the same-named options in the Box category; values entered in one category automatically reflect in the other.

- visibility displays the element in three states. If no visibility property is selected, the element inherits its visibility from the containing element (the parent). Visible displays the element. Hidden hides the element.

- z-index shows the depth of an element in the layer stacking order. Elements with higher z-index values appear above elements with lower z-index values. Z-index is a valid property only for absolute, fixed, and relative positioning; normal static positioning cannot use this property.

- overflow determines how the element should appear when the element exceeds the allotted space. Visible enables the block to expand, so you can view the content. Hidden only shows content that fits in the block; the remaining content is clipped and not hidden. Auto inserts a scrollbar (horizontal, vertical, or both).

- placement defines the specific location of an absolute-positioned element.

- clip specifies the visible parts of an element.

Extensions options create page breaks and apply visual effects.

- page-break-before sets a page break for printing, before the element.

- page-break-after sets a page break for printing, after the element.

- cursor specifies the pointer style when you place the mouse cursor over the element.

- filter adds artistic effects to change the appearance of an element.

Transition options allow animation of CSS properties with duration, delay, and timing functions.

21. Using the same basic process as outlined for the #header and #image selectors, create two additional ID selectors using the following information:

Selector name	Settings to Apply
#pageContent	Box Width: 700 pixels, Left Margin: 200 pixels
#footer	Box Width: 700 pixels, Left Margin: 200 pixels

Note:

When the master.css code is showing in the Code pane, the Rule Definition menu in the New CSS Rule dialog box defaults to This Document Only, referring to the active CSS file.

22. With the master.css file visible in the Code pane, choose File>Save.

Appropriate code for all selectors has been added to the file.

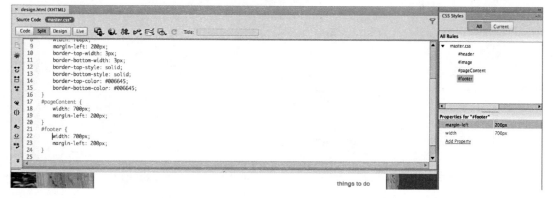

23. Continue to the next exercise.

You don't need to save the design.html file, because you haven't actually changed anything in that file throughout this exercise.

CREATE A LAYOUT WITH DIV ELEMENTS

In the previous exercise, as noted, the design.html file was not affected by the new IDs. This is because you must intentionally place div elements associated with those IDs into the HTML file to create the page layout.

1. With **design.html** open, click Source Code in the Related Files bar to show the page code in the Code pane.

2. Select and delete the code related to the tracing image. Make sure you do not delete the closing > of the body tag.

You no longer need this image, so it is safe to delete it. If you simply hide it, problems could arise later when you save the file as a template.

Note:

You can also remove a tracing image by clearing the Tracing Image field in the Page Properties dialog box.

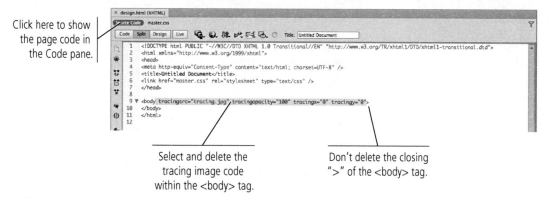

Click here to show the page code in the Code pane.

Select and delete the tracing image code within the <body> tag.

Don't delete the closing ">" of the <body> tag.

3. Click the Refresh button in the Properties panel or the Document toolbar to remove the tracing image.

4. Click in the Design pane to place the insertion point in the file, then choose Insert>Layout Objects>Div Tag.

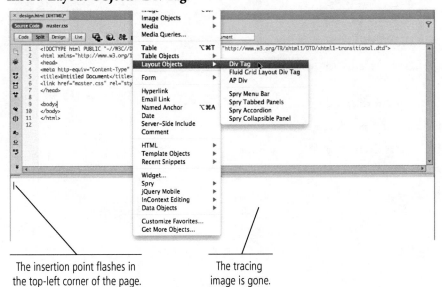

Note:

Other options in the Insert menu will be useful when you start to nest div elements inside each other.

Note:

You can also use the Insert Div Tag button when the Insert bar is in Common or Layout mode.

The insertion point flashes in the top-left corner of the page.

The tracing image is gone.

5. In the Insert Div Tag dialog box, leave the Insert menu set to At Insertion Point.

The div you insert will be placed at the current insertion point, which is by default in the top-left corner of the page. The insertion point is slightly indented because Dreamweaver automatically adds several pixels of padding around the content of a new page. (Some browsers do the same, so Dreamweaver tries to accurately show what you will see when you preview the page in a browser.)

6. Choose header in the ID menu.

All ID selectors that are defined in the CSS file, but have not yet been used in the active HTML file, are available in this menu.

7. Click OK to add the <div> tag to the page.

Because the placeholder text is highlighted in the Design pane, the corresponding text is also highlighted in the Code pane; this allows you to easily identify the code for the placed div element.

In the Design pane, the div element is indented 200 pixels from the left, as defined by the left margin value of the #header ID selector.

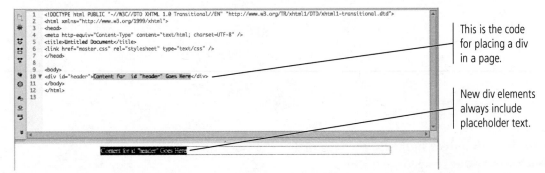

This is the code for placing a div in a page.

New div elements always include placeholder text.

8. In the Design pane, click the edge of the div element to select it.

When a div is selected in the page, you can see various aspects of the CSS Layout Box Model in the design page.

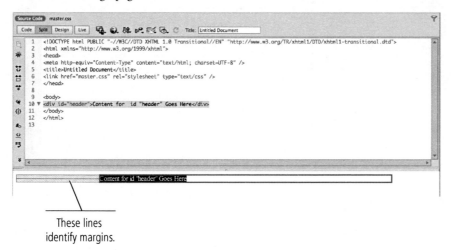

These lines identify margins.

Note:

If you don't see the margin area, make sure CSS Layout Box Model is toggled on in the Visual Aids menu.

9. Choose Insert>Layout Objects>Div Tag again.

Note:

You can use each ID only once on any given page.

10. In the Insert Div Tag dialog box, choose After Tag in the Insert menu. Leave <div id="header"> selected in the secondary menu.

Using the After Tag option, you can place a new div element after any existing div, regardless of the location of the insertion point.

If anything is selected when you insert a div tag, the Insert menu defaults to Wrap Around Selection.

After defining where to add the div tag, choose from the existing named tags in this menu.

Note:

The Wrap Around Selection option is useful if you need to add a new div element around existing content. Because you are creating the layout from scratch, however, this option is not needed at this point.

Understanding the CSS Box Model

DREAMWEAVER FOUNDATIONS

When you design layouts using CSS, think of any block element (such as a div element) as a box made up of four parts: margin, border, padding, and content. The object's overall size — the amount of space it occupies on the page — is the sum of the values for these four properties:

```
6   <style type="text/css">
7   #box {
8       width: 200px;
9       margin: 20px;
10      margin-left: 100px;
11      padding: 20px;
12      padding-right: 100px;
13      border: 10px solid #096;
14  }
15  </style>
```

200-pixel width defines the actual content area.

10-pixel border is on all four sides of the box.

100-pixel right padding is added inside the box edge.

20-pixel padding is applied to the other three edges (the padding-right value overrides the padding value for only the right edge).

Content for id "box" Goes Here

100-pixel left margin is added outside the box edge.

20-pixel margins are applied to the other three edges (the margin-left value overrides the margin value for only the left edge).

- The **margin** is outside the box edges; it is invisible and has no background color. Margin does not affect content within the element.

- The **border** is the edge of the element, based on the specified dimensions.

- The **padding** lies inside the edge of the element, forming a cushion between the box edge and the box content. (If you are familiar with print-design applications such as Adobe InDesign, think of padding as text inset.)

- The **content** lies inside the padding. When you define the width and height for an element, you are defining the content area.

11. **Choose image in the ID menu, then click OK to add the div element to the page.**

The header ID is not available because it is already placed in the page.

You want to place each row, one right after the other. Since the header div is already in place, you are adding the next **\<div>** tag immediately after the existing one.

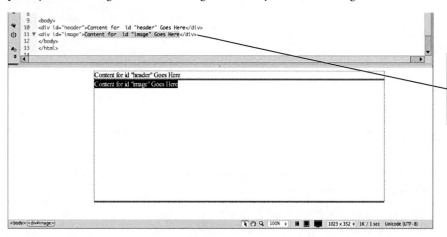

The code shows that the image div is added immediately after the header div (at the same nesting level).

12. **Repeat Steps 9–11 to add the pageContent div after the image div, and then add the footer div after the pageContent div.**

When you add these divs, make sure you choose the correct div in the secondary Insert menu so that the divs are in the correct order from top to bottom (header, image, pageContent, footer).

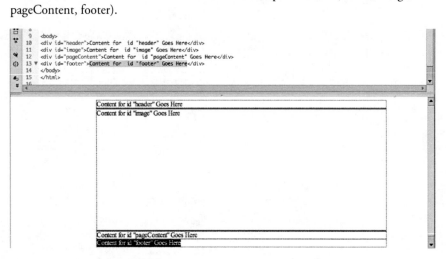

13. **Save the design.html file and continue to the next exercise.**

Note:

Adding div elements adds to the page's HTML code. Those elements, however, are very short — they simply identify each div element and add some placeholder content. In the page code, there is no mention of background images, colors, or other attributes that make up the page layout. Those attributes are controlled by editing the ID selectors applied to each div element within the CSS file.

USE THE FLOAT PROPERTY TO CONTROL NESTED DIVS

In the previous exercises, you created ID selectors and placed div elements using the selectors you had already defined. If you are experimenting with a layout, or if you want to work within the context of an existing layout, you can also insert div tags and create ID selectors at the same time.

1. **With the design.html page active, select and delete the placeholder content in the pageContent div. Make sure the insertion point remains inside the now empty pageContent div.**

   When you remove the div content, the div collapses to the smallest possible height. Because you did not define a specific height in the #pageContent selector rules, the div height will expand as necessary to accommodate whatever you place in the container.

   As you saw in the examination of the tracing image, the pageContent needs to be divided into two separate divs — one to hold the main body of text, and another to contain a series of links. This is accomplished by creating **nested divs**, or div elements that exist entirely within other div elements.

2. **Choose Insert>Layout Objects>Div Tag.**

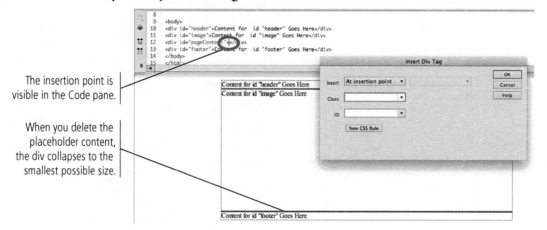

The insertion point is visible in the Code pane.

When you delete the placeholder content, the div collapses to the smallest possible size.

3. **In the Insert Div Tag dialog box, click the New CSS Rule button.**

4. **In the resulting New CSS Rule dialog box, choose ID in the Selector Type menu.**

5. **Type #mainText in the Selector Name field, and make sure master.css is selected in the Rule Definition menu.**

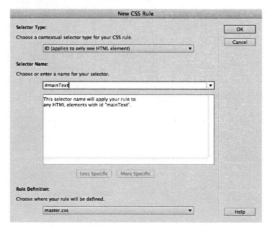

6. **Click OK to define properties for the new selector.**

7. **In the Box options of the CSS Rule Definition dialog box, define the box width as `450` pixels. Choose left in the Float menu.**

Nested div elements automatically align based on the horizontal alignment properties of the containing element. If no specific alignment is defined, the nested div aligns to the left side of the container. The float property allows you to attach a div to the left or right edge of the containing element, and allows other content to sit beside or wrap around that element. This gives you greater flexibility when creating complex layouts such as the one in this project. In this case, the mainText div will attach to the left edge of the pageContent div.

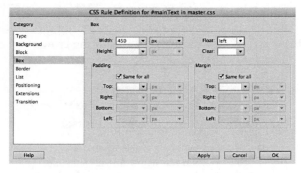

8. **Click OK to return to the Insert Div Tag dialog box, and then click OK again to insert the new div tag into the page at the current insertion point.**

When you work with nested div elements, unexpected things can sometimes happen in the Design pane. In this case, the left edge of the footer div moves to the middle of the page (to the right of the mainText div) because the mainText div is floating left.

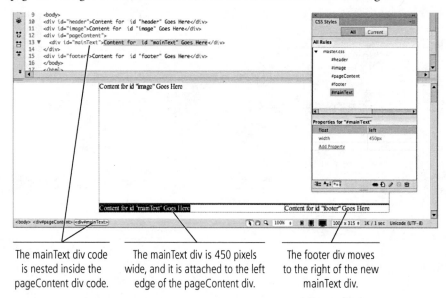

The mainText div code is nested inside the pageContent div code.

The mainText div is 450 pixels wide, and it is attached to the left edge of the pageContent div.

The footer div moves to the right of the new mainText div.

Note:

If you only see "master.css" in the CSS Styles panel, click the arrow/plus sign to expand it and show the selectors in that file.

9. **Select #footer in the CSS Styles panel and click the Edit Rule button at the bottom of the panel.**

10. **In the Box properties, choose left in the Float menu and then click OK.**

You can edit selectors at any time by selecting one in the panel and clicking the Edit Rule button at the bottom of the panel.

Adding the float property to the footer div moves the div to attach to the left edge of its container, which is the page body. It no longer appears to the right of the mainText div.

11. **Choose Insert>Layout Objects>Div Tag again.**

12. **Choose After Tag in the Insert menu, choose <div id="mainText"> in the secondary menu, then click New CSS Rule at the bottom of the dialog box.**

    The New CSS Rule button is useful for adding a div that you have not yet created.

13. **In the resulting New CSS Rule dialog box, choose ID in the Selector Type menu. Type #sidebarNav in the Selector Name field, make sure master.css is selected in the Rule Definition menu, and click OK.**

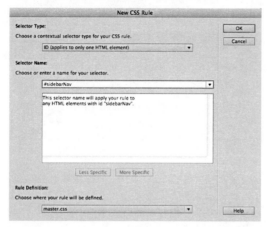

14. **In the Background properties, define the following settings:**

    background-image: back_sidebar.jpg (from the site images folder)

    background-repeat: no-repeat

    background-position (X): center

    background-position (Y): top

15. **In the Box properties, define the following settings:**

    width: 220px

    height: 395px

    float: right

    As with the width of the main content area, you are defining this element to match the size of the provided image. In a professional workflow, you would have to determine the image size yourself so you could create the div element appropriately.

Note:

Repeat *repeats the image vertically and horizontally.*

No-repeat *prevents the image from repeating.*

Repeat-x *repeats the image horizontally.*

Repeat-y *repeats the image vertically.*

16. **Click OK to return to the Insert Div dialog box, then OK again to return to the document.**

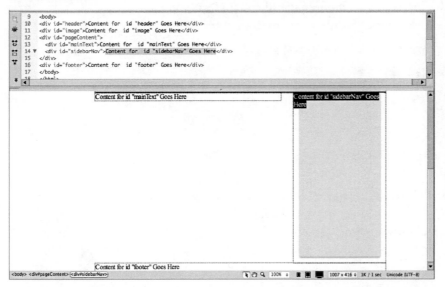

17. **Insert the file yvvb.jpg (from the site images folder) into the header div. Define Yosemite Valley Visitor's Bureau as the alternate text.**

Remember from Project 8: Photographer's Web Site, you can drag an image from the Files panel, use the Common Insert panel, use the Insert>Image command, or use the Assets panel to place an image in a page. Also remember, all images in the foreground require the **alt** attribute.

18. **Delete the placeholder text from the header div.**

If you delete the placeholder text before placing the image, the div collapses to the smallest possible height. It is easier to place the image before you remove the placeholder text.

19. **Place the insertion point before the placed image.**

The insertion point should be in front of the image.

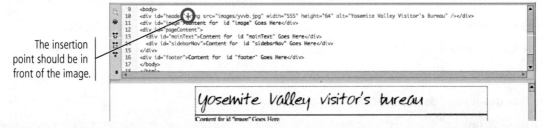

Comparing the <span> and <div> Tags

A **<span>** tag is used for "inline" content (within another piece of text) such as a paragraph. A <span> tag does not create a line break in the text; it applies styles to text (usually a small section) even in the middle of a sentence. For example:

> A span tag can <span style="font:14pt verdana">change font</span> in the middle of a sentence.

results in:

> A span tag can **change font** in the middle of a sentence.

A **<div>** tag is a "block" element that can be sized and positioned, more commonly used to divide a page into different sections. If you apply a <div> tag in the middle of a sentence, a line break is automatically added before the div. For example:

> Using div tags, you can divide a Web page <div style="text-align:center"> into different divisions. </div>

results in:

> Using div tags, you can divide a Web page
> into different divisions.

20. Using the same process as in Steps 11–16, insert a new ID div at the location of the insertion point. Name the div **#topNav**, using the following settings:

width: 110px   float: right

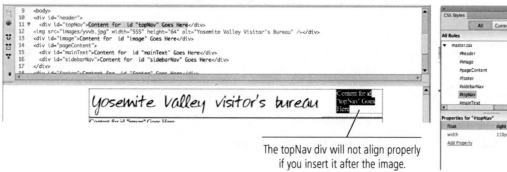

The topNav div will not align properly if you insert it after the image.

Nested divs should appear before other content in the container div. If you place the topNav div after the image, the nested div will not align properly.

21. Save the HTML and CSS files, and then continue to the next exercise.

To save the CSS file, click master.css in the Related Files bar, then choose File>Save. Once the CSS file is saved, click Source Code in the Related Files bar to reshow the actual page code.

DEFINE PROPERTIES FOR THE <BODY> TAG

As you learned in an earlier project, the **<body>** tag surrounds all visible content in a Web page. As with any other HTML tag, you can use a CSS rule to define properties for the **<body>** tag.

1. With **design.html** open, click the New CSS Rule button at the bottom of the CSS Styles panel.

2. In the New CSS Rule dialog box, choose Tag in the Selector Type menu.

<body> is an HTML tag, so you have to create a tag selector to define properties for the body element.

3. Scroll through the Tag menu (under Selector Name) and click body in the list of options.

This menu lists all HTML tags that can be affected by CSS rules. You can choose from the menu, or simply type a specific tag name in the field if you know the exact tag you want to modify.

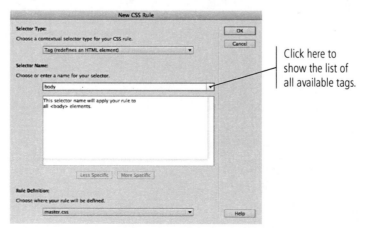

Click here to show the list of all available tags.

Note:

Technically, you do not need to place the insertion point before inserting a div. You could also choose the After Start of Tag option in the Insert menu, then choose <div id="header"> to place the topNav div in the correct location.

Until you are more comfortable creating and placing divs, however, it can be useful to use the insertion point to define exactly where you want a div to be placed.

4. **Make sure master.css is targeted in the Rule Definition menu, and then click OK.**

5. **In the CSS Rule Definition dialog box, change the following settings:**

Type category	**font-family: Arial, Helvetica, sans-serif**
	font-size: 12px
	line-height: 19px
	color: #666
Background category	**background-image: back_yosemite.png**
	background-repeat: repeat-y
Box category	**padding: 0px (all four edges)**
	margin: 0px (all four edges)

6. **Click OK to add the body selector to the master.css file.**

The new body selector is a tag selector, so it does not have the preceding "#" at the beginning of the selector name.

By this point you should understand the concept of nested tags. The <body> tag is the parent of the div tags it contains. Properties of the parent tag are automatically inherited by the child (nested) tags. In this case, the font family, size, line height, and color you defined for the <body> tag are automatically applied to content in the nested divs.

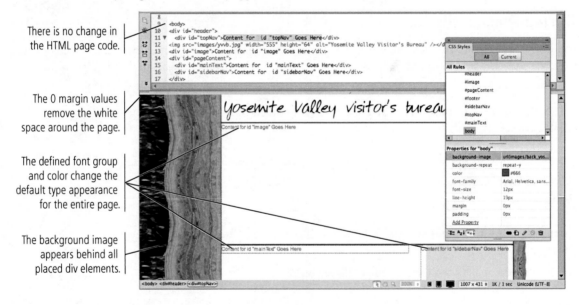

There is no change in the HTML page code.

The 0 margin values remove the white space around the page.

The defined font group and color change the default type appearance for the entire page.

The background image appears behind all placed div elements.

7. **Save the CSS file, and then continue to the next exercise.**

EDIT CSS RULES TO ADJUST THE LAYOUT

Now that the background image is in place, you can see a number of elements that need to be addressed. It's important to realize that layout development is an ongoing evolutionary process; as you continue to work, new issues will pop up. You can always add or remove properties to specific rules, and even add new rules as necessary to meet a project's needs. As long as you work with an external CSS file — as you are in this project — the changes will apply to any HTML file that is linked to the same CSS file.

1. **With design.html open, make sure the body selector is selected in the CSS Styles panel.**

2. **In the lower half of the panel, click the Add Property link at the bottom of the list of current properties.**

3. **Open the resulting menu. Scroll to and select the background-color property.**

   If you know the exact name of the property you want to add, you can also simply type in the resulting field to add that property.

Type the exact property name in this field...   ...or click here to open a list of all available properties.

4. **To the right of the new background-color property, click the color swatch and then sample a dark green from the existing background image.**

   You couldn't do this when you first created the <body> tag selector because the background image was not yet visible.

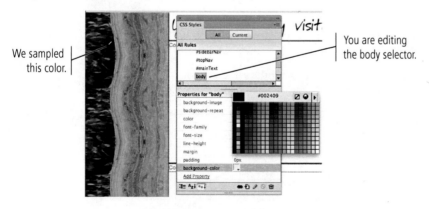

We sampled this color.   You are editing the body selector.

5. **In the CSS Styles panel, click the #mainText selector.**

   As you can see in the page, the text in this div currently begins at the very edge of the area. You need to move the text away from the edge for better readability.

6. **Click the Edit Rule button to open the CSS Rule Definition dialog box.**

Note:

If you don't see the Add Property link, click the Show Only Set Properties button at the bottom of the panel. The Add Property link is not available when the properties are showing in Category or List view.

7. **In the Box category, deselect the Same For All option in the Margin section. Change the Top and Left margins to 10px.**

Unless you're very familiar with CSS property names and coding rules, it is often easier to use the CSS Rule Definition dialog box to make multiple changes like this.

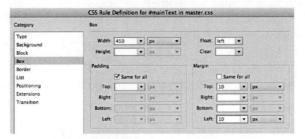

8. **Click OK to add the new properties to the #mainText selector.**

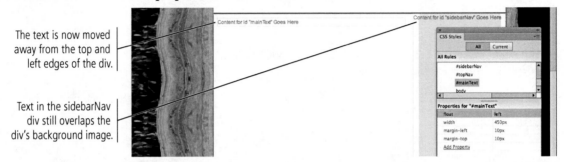

The text is now moved away from the top and left edges of the div.

Text in the sidebarNav div still overlaps the div's background image.

9. **In the CSS Styles panel, select the #sidebarNav selector and then click the Add Property link in the lower half of the panel.**

10. **In the resulting field, type `padding`.**

Rather than scroll through the very long menu of properties, you can simply type the propety if you know the exact name. In this case, the "padding" property defines a single padding value for all four edges of the box.

11. **In the resulting field to the right of the new padding property, type `15px`. Press Return/Enter to finalize the change.**

If you don't type the unit of measurement immediately after the value (with no space character), the property will have no effect.

Note:

In CSS, the unit of measurement must always be specified, unless the value is zero.

Note:

You have to type the "px" in the field when you add the padding property to the selector.

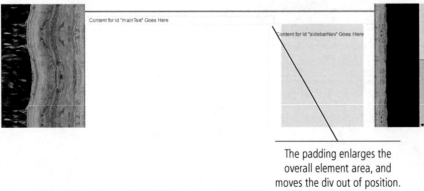

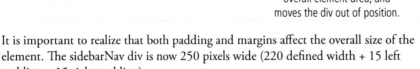

The padding enlarges the overall element area, and moves the div out of position.

It is important to realize that both padding and margins affect the overall size of the element. The sidebarNav div is now 250 pixels wide (220 defined width + 15 left padding + 15 right padding).

When you change the margins and/or padding, you have to make a proportional change to the width/height properties if you want the element to occupy the same overall space.

12. Subtract 30 from both the height and width values of the sidebarNav div.

To change the existing property values, simply click the value to highlight it and then type the new value.

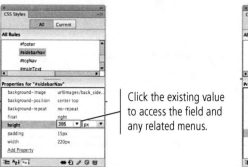

Click the existing value to access the field and any related menus.

Note:

The background image extends into the padding area because the padding is part of the actual element area. Margin values are added outside the element; background images do not extend into the margin area.

After changing the height and width, the sidebarNav div moves back into place.

13. Using the same basic process, edit the #topNav selector to add 10px padding to all four edges.

For this div you are not trying to maintain a certain amount of space, so it is not necessary to remove the extra pixels from the defined width.

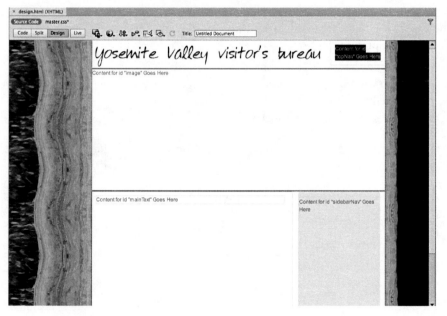

14. Save the CSS file and then continue to the next stage of the project.

Stage 2 Working with a Template

Dreamweaver professionals often use templates (with the ".dwt" extension) to create HTML pages. When you use a template file, you create common page elements only once, rather than recreating them every time you add a new page to a site. A template can contain everything an HTML page requires, including text, graphics, and hyperlinks.

When you create a template, you indicate which elements of a page should remain constant (non-editable; locked) in pages based on that template, and which elements can be changed. While the non-editable regions appear exactly the same from one page to the next, the editable regions enable you to add unique content to each new page.

You can modify a template even after you have created pages based on it. When you modify a template, the locked (non-editable) regions in pages based on the template automatically update to match the changes to the template.

If you open a template file, you can edit everything in it, whether it is marked as editable or locked. If you open a document based on a template file, you can edit only the regions marked as editable. The terms **editable** and **locked** refer to whether a region is editable in a document based on a template, not to whether the region is editable in the template file itself.

CREATE A TEMPLATE

When all pages in a site will have the same basic layout, you can save the common elements as a template, and then apply the template to all pages. This workflow makes it much faster and easier to complete the project.

Following the same logic, keep in mind that the master.css file in this site is attached to the design.html file — which will become the template. Any pages created from the template file will also be attached to the master.css file, so changes made in the master.css file will also affect pages created from the template.

1. **With design.html from the Yosemite site open in Design view, choose File>Save As Template.**

2. **In the Save As Template dialog box, make sure Yosemite is selected in the Site menu.**

3. **In the Description field, type Yosemite Site template.**

   The description is only relevant in Dreamweaver; it will not appear in any page based on the template. You can also modify the template description by choosing Modify>Templates> Description.

Note:

You can also create a template from the active page by choosing Insert>Template Objects>Make Template.

4. **Click Save to save the active file as a template.**

   The extension ".dwt" is automatically added on both Macintosh and Windows.

5. Click Yes in the resulting dialog box.

The template is saved in a Templates folder, which Dreamweaver automatically creates for you when saving the template, in the local root folder of the Yosemite site. To ensure that all images and links function properly, you should allow Dreamweaver to update the link information as necessary.

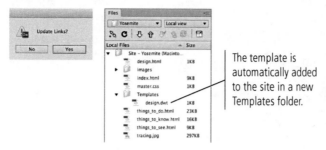

The template is automatically added to the site in a new Templates folder.

Your template contains the layout structure you created in the first stage of this project. However, after converting the document into a template, all parts of the page become non-editable. Until you define an editable region, you won't be able to add page-specific content to any pages based on this template.

Do not move your templates out of the Templates folder or save any non-template files in the Templates folder. Also, do not move the Templates folder out of your local root folder. Doing so causes errors in paths in the templates.

6. In the Document toolbar above the design pane, change the Title field to Yosemite Valley Visitor's Bureau.

When you define a title in a template file, that title is automatically applied to any page attached to the template. You are adding the basic information in the template, so you can then simply add page-specific information in each attached file.

7. In the Design pane, select the placeholder text in the image div.

Make sure you only select the div content, and not the actual div element.

8. Choose Insert>Template Objects>Editable Region.

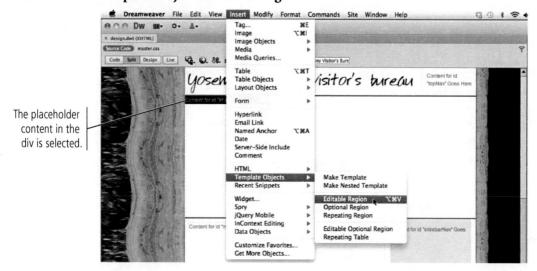

The placeholder content in the div is selected.

9. **Type Page Image in the resulting dialog box and then click OK.**

When pages are created from this template, the editable regions will be the only areas that can be modified (e.g., adding specific page content).

In the Design view, editable areas are identified with a blue tag and border; these are for design purposes, and will not be visible in the resulting HTML pages. If you don't see a blue tag with the Page Image region name, open the Visual Aids menu (in the Document toolbar) and choose Invisible Elements to toggle on that option.

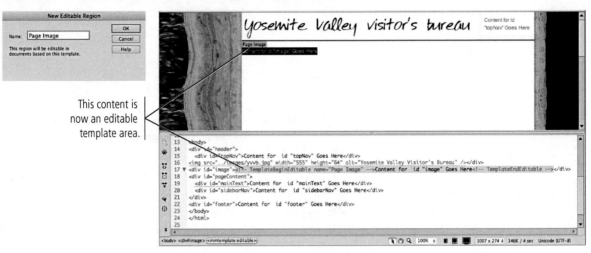

This content is now an editable template area.

10. **Click in the placeholder text of the mainText div, then click div#mainText in the Tag Selector to select the entire element.**

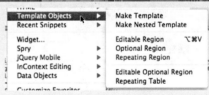

11. Choose Insert>Template Objects>Editable Region.

Place the insertion point in the mainText placeholder content...

...then click the div#mainText tag to select the entire div.

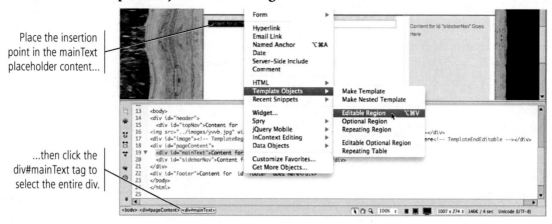

12. Type `Page Content` in the resulting dialog box and then click OK.

The new editable area is added around the selected div. Because you want the mainText *and* sidebarNav divs inside the editable area, you have to edit the page code.

The editable region code surrounds only the mainText div.

13. In the page code, move the closing code of the editable region (**<!--TemplateEndEditable-->**) to be after the closing tag of the sidebarNav div.

When something is selected in the Code pane, you can click the selected code and drag to move that code to a new position. Alternatively, you can cut (Command/Control-X) the relevant code from its original location, move the insertion point to another position, and then paste (Command/Control-V) the cut code into place.

The editable area now contains the two divs (but not the surrounding pageContent div).

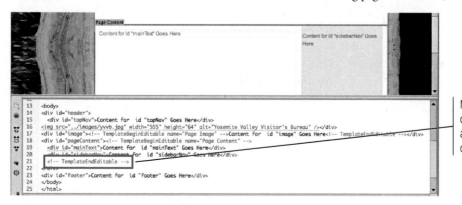

Move the closing code of the editable area after the closing div tag of the sidebarNav div.

14. Save the file (File>Save) and close it, then continue to the next exercise.

Unlike other applications, you do not have to use the Save As command to rewrite a Dreamweaver template. You can simply choose File>Save or press Command/Control-S.

APPLY THE TEMPLATE TO EXISTING PAGES

Templates can be applied to existing HTML pages, basically wrapping the template around the existing content. You can simply map existing page content to editable regions in the template, while adding the non-editable regions to the page design. After the template is applied, you can begin to make whatever changes are necessary based on the actual content in the files.

1. **Open the Manage Sites dialog box and select the Yosemite site, then click the Edit button to open the Site Setup dialog box for the selected site.**

2. **Expand the Advanced Settings options and click Templates in the category list to show the related options.**

Note:

You can also double-click the Yosemite site name in the Sites menu at the top of the Files panel to open the Site Setup dialog box for a specific site. This method bypasses the Manage Sites dialog box.

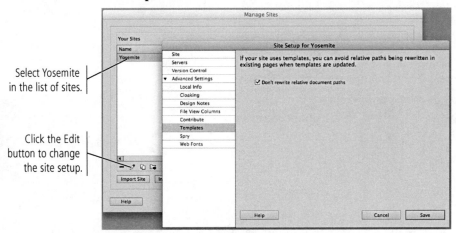

Select Yosemite in the list of sites.

Click the Edit button to change the site setup.

3. **Make sure the Don't Rewrite option is checked.**

   When you saved the template file, it was placed in a folder named Templates. Links from this template file to images or other pages must first go up from the Templates folder to the root folder (e.g., **../images/yvvb.jpg**).

   When this template is attached to a page in the root level of the site, the same link would not be accurate. For example, the path from index.html in the root folder to the same image would simply be **images/yvvb.jpg**. If this check box is not active, the links on pages where the template is attached would not work properly.

4. **Click Save to close the Site Setup dialog box, then click Done to close the Manage Sites dialog box.**

5. **Open the file index.html from the root folder of the Yosemite site.**

   Each file in the site contains two areas of content — the primary page content, and a list of links to help users navigate through the long blocks of text. The two sections are already tagged with div ids (#mainText and #sidebarNav) that match the ones you used in the template file. This will direct the appropriate elements of the index page to appear in the defined areas of the template.

6. Choose Modify>Templates>Apply Template to Page.

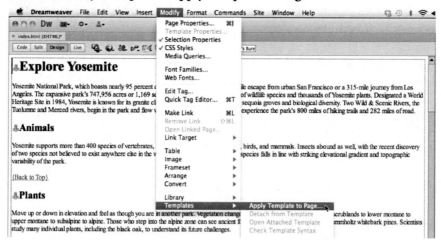

The Modify>Templates Menu in Depth

The commands on the Modify>Templates menu are useful when you want to make changes to a template or to pages based on a template.

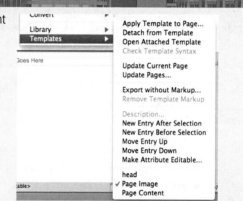

- The **Apply Template to Page** option applies a template to the current HTML page.

- If you don't want a page to be based on a template, **Detach from Template** separates the page from the template. Non-editable regions become editable, but changes in the template do not reflect in the page.

- The **Open Attached Template** option opens the template attached to a page.

- If code is written directly in the code area, there is a chance that the code might contain some errors. The **Check Template Syntax** option enables Dreamweaver to automatically check the code syntax in the template.

- The **Update Current Page** option updates a page if the template on which it is based is modified. Before closing the file, Dreamweaver prompts you to update the page; a dialog box appears, asking if you want to save the changed document.

- If you update only the template and not pages derived from the template, you can use the **Update Pages** option to update all pages based on the template.

- The **Export without Markup** option exports an entire site to a different location by detaching all pages from the templates on which they are based. You can also save the template information in XML by selecting Keep Template Data Files after you choose this command from the menu. If you exported the site earlier, then you can choose to extract only the modified files.

- Use the **Remove Template Markup** option to convert an editable region to a non-editable region.

- The **Description** is simply a textual explanation of the selected file, which does not appear in the body of the page (or any pages created from the template).

- **New Entry After** or **Before Selection.** In template working areas, repeating regions include more than one editable region, which enables you to add repeated page elements such as rows of a table. (Clicking the "+" button of the repeating region's blue tab adds a new entry in the region.)

- Use the **Move Entry Up** or **Down** option to move a repeating element up or down.

- You can use the **Make Attribute Editable** option to make a specific attribute of an HTML tag editable in pages using a template. For example, you can apply Make Attribute Editable to a "class" attribute on a link tag in a navigation bar to have the link appear "on" when you are visiting that page; a CSS class that changes the appearance would be applied to an otherwise locked link tag.

7. **In the Select Template dialog box, make sure Yosemite is selected in the Site menu.**

   Since this is the active site, the menu should default to the correct choice.

8. **Click design in the Templates list to select it, and make sure the Update Page... option is checked at the bottom of the dialog box.**

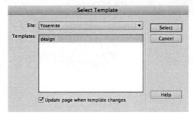

9. **Click Select to apply the template to the open page.**

   In the Inconsistent Region Names dialog box that appears, you have to determine where to place the named regions of the open file, relative to the editable regions in the template you selected.

10. **In the resulting dialog box, click the Document body (in the Name column) to select it. In the Move Content to New Region menu, choose Page Content.**

    Remember, "Page Content" is the name you assigned to the template's editable region. The page body (named "Document body" by default) will be placed into the "Page Content" editable region when the template is applied to the page.

This refers to content within the <body> section of the HTML page to which you are attaching the template.

Use this menu to map file content to an editable region in the template file.

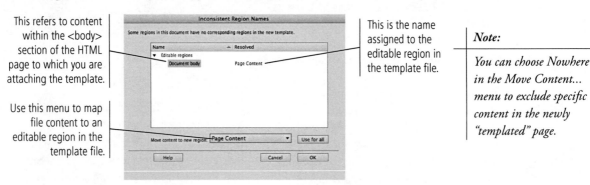

This is the name assigned to the editable region in the template file.

Note:

You can choose Nowhere in the Move Content... menu to exclude specific content in the newly "templated" page.

11. **Click OK to finalize the process.**

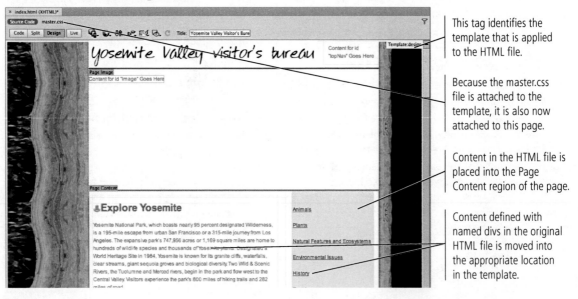

This tag identifies the template that is applied to the HTML file.

Because the master.css file is attached to the template, it is also now attached to this page.

Content in the HTML file is placed into the Page Content region of the page.

Content defined with named divs in the original HTML file is moved into the appropriate location in the template.

12. **Insert the tufas.jpg image (from the site images folder) into the Page Image editable region, and define Tufas at Mono Lake as the alternate text. Delete the placeholder text from the region.**

Because the Page Image area is an editable region, you can place new content (including images) into each page where the template is attached.

Note:

If you move the cursor over areas other than an editable region, an icon indicates that you can't select or modify that area. You can modify only the editable region.

13. **Save the file and close it.**

14. **Repeat this process to attach the design.dwt template to the three remaining pages in the site. Use the following images and alternate text for each page:**

File	Image	Alternate Text
things_to_do.html	flowers.jpg	Wildflowers in bloom
things_to_know.html	trees.jpg	Sequoia grove
things_to_see.html	lake.jpg	Lake overlook

15. **Save and close any open files, and continue to the next exercise.**

Creating a New Page from a Template

In addition to attaching a template to an existing page, you can also create a new HTML page from an existing template.

You can use the Assets panel (Window>Assets) to show all templates that are available in the current site. Control/right-clicking a specific template file opens a contextual menu, where you can choose New from Template.

This results in a new untitled HTML file containing all the content that is defined in the template, with the template already attached to the HTML page. Any changes in the template file will apply to files created from the template.

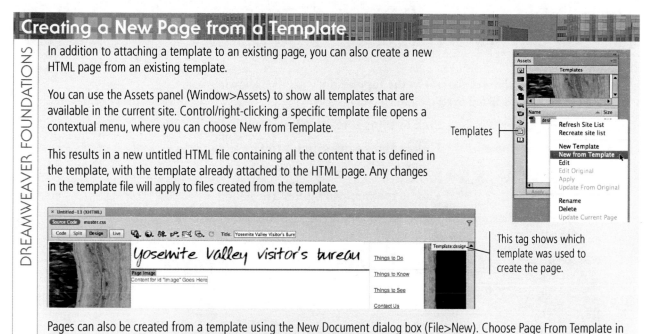

Pages can also be created from a template using the New Document dialog box (File>New). Choose Page From Template in the left column of the New Document dialog box, select your site in the middle column, and then choose the template you want to apply in the right column.

EDIT THE DESIGN TEMPLATE

The header and footer information for this site is common to every page in the site, so you can add the actual content for these areas to the template. When you make changes to the template, those changes automatically apply to any page attached to the template — another advantage of using Dreamweaver template files.

1. **Open design.dwt from the Templates folder.**

2. **Replace the placeholder text in the footer div with the following:**

   Text from the National Park Service Web site is in the public domain. All images copyright Against The Clock, Inc.

3. **In the Properties panel, choose Paragraph in the Format menu.**

4. **Highlight the words "National Park Service Web site". In the Properties panel, type http://www.nps.gov/yose/index.htm in the Link field and choose _blank in the Target menu.**

Note:

Remember, the _blank target causes the link to open in a new browser tab or window.

5. **In the Design pane, highlight the words "Against The Clock, Inc.". In the Properties panel, type http://www.againsttheclock.com in the Link field and choose _blank in the Target menu.**

6. **Select the placed logo in the header and create a link to index.html in the site root folder.**

7. **Replace the placeholder content in the topNav div with the following text, and create links as listed here:**

Things to Do	Link to things-to-do.html
Things to Know	Link to things-to-know.html
Things to See	Link to things-to-see.html
Contact Us	Link to mailto:info@yvvb.atc

   As you can see, the link formatting does not currently fit the space that it should; you will fix that in the next stage of the project.

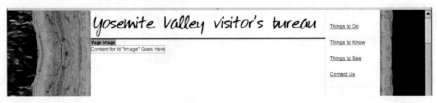

8. **Choose File>Save to save the template file.**

9. **Read the resulting message, then click Update.**

When you save changes to a template file, Dreamweaver recognizes the link from the template to pages where that template is attached. You are automatically asked if you want to update those pages to reflect the new template content.

10. **When the resulting Update Pages dialog box shows "Done", click the Close button.**

This dialog box shows the status of the update process.

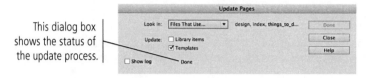

11. **Close the template file, then open things-to-do.html.**

As you can see, the content you added to the template file is automatically added to the page that is attached to the template. This type of workflow makes it much easier to maintain consistency across an entire site — make changes to common content once in the template file, and those changes are automatically applied in any page where the template is attached.

Changes you made in the template appear in all pages where the template is attached.

The image is no longer properly aligned because of the space required by the topNav element.

12. **Using the Title field at the top of the doccument window, add the text | Things to Do to the end of the existing document title.**

13. Click the Split button to show the page code, and scroll to the top of the code.

Although you did not specifically define it as an editable area, the <title> tag of each page is always editable, even when attached to a template file.

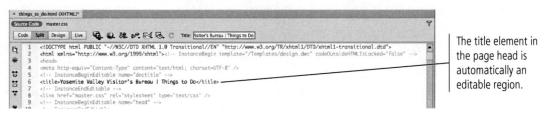

The title element in the page head is automatically an editable region.

14. Save the file and close it.

15. Open things-to-know.html and things-to-see.html, and add appropriate text to each page title.

16. Save and close any open files, then continue to the next stage of the project.

Understanding Named Anchors

Documents with large blocks of copy — like the ones in this site — often benefit from **named anchors**, which mark specific locations on a page that can be linked from other locations within the same page or from other pages. Instead of forcing the reader to search for the information by scrolling or other means, you can create a hyperlink that points to the exact location of the information. Clicking the anchor link moves that anchor to the top-left corner of the frame.

Named anchors can be especially useful on long Web pages. For example, on a page that contains many sections, you can include a table of contents at the top with a link to each section. To help the reader return to the table of contents from any section of the page, it is considered good practice to include a link to the top of the page at the end of each section (such as "Back to Top").

When linking to the named anchor, type the number sign (#) followed by the name of the anchor in the Link field of the dialog box or Properties panel, or choose the appropriate anchor from the Link menu of the Hyperlink dialog box. If you are linking to the anchor from another page, type the name of the file containing the anchor, followed by the number sign and the name of the anchor.

To use named anchors:

1. Place the insertion point where you want to add an anchor, and then click the Named Anchor button in the Common Insert panel (or choose Insert>Named Anchor).

2. Define a name for the anchor; do not use any illegal characters (including spaces).

In Design view, an anchor appears as a small anchor icon.

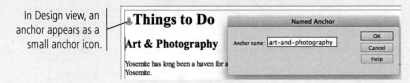

3. Create a list of links. Select the link text, open the Hyperlink dialog box, and choose one of the named anchors from the Link menu. (You can also choose an existing anchor from the Link menu in the Properties panel.)

The selected text automatically appears in the Text field.

Choose an existing anchor from the Link menu.

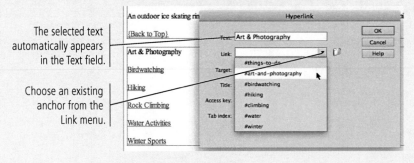

Stage 3 Using CSS to Control Content

The first stage of this project focused on building a layout structure with div tags and ID selectors; in the second stage, you created a template file to more easily apply the defined layout to multiple pages. Although defining structure is a significant part of designing pages, it is only half the story — professional Web design also requires controlling the content in pages.

When you create a complex project such as a complete Web site, it's a good idea to have a solid plan for completing all required work. Consider what you know from the initial project analysis:

- The background image should extend the entire height of the browser window.

- All text in the site should use a sans-serif font.

- Paragraphs of copy in the main text need to be small and dark gray, with large spacing between lines in a single paragraph.

- Heading 1 in the main text area needs to be large, bold, and colored dark orange.

- Heading 2 should be slightly smaller, italic, and should use the same color as main text.

- Text links should appear in orange text in all but the sidebar navigation list. The link text should not be underlined.

- Footer text should be light gray and centered.

- The sidebar links should be centered, and use the same color as the page background.

- Text links should switch to a different color when the mouse rolls over them.

The first three items on this list were accomplished when you defined properties for the **<body>** tag. You now need to complete the remaining items.

 ## DEFINE HTML TAG SELECTORS

In addition to the **<body>** tag that encloses the page content, properly structured pages use HTML tags to identify different types of content. CSS uses tag selectors to format HTML tags such as paragraphs (**<p>**), headings (**<h1>**, **<h2>**, etc.), unordered lists (**<ul>**), and so on.

1. **Open index.html from the Yosemite site root folder.**

2. **Click the New CSS Rule button at the bottom of the CSS Styles panel.**

3. **Choose Tag in the Selector Type menu, type** h1 **in the Selector Name field, and make sure master.css is selected in the Rule Definition menu. Click OK to define the new rule.**

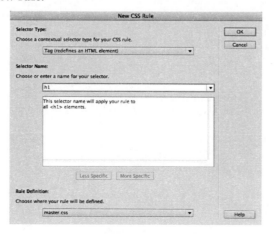

4. **In the Type properties, define the following options:**

   font-size: 22px

   font-weight: bold

   color: sample a dark orange from the bark in the background image

5. **In the Box properties, define the following options:**

   margin-top: 10px

   margin-bottom: 0px

   Content block elements such as headings and paragraphs have default top and bottom margins equivalent to the current text size. When a paragraph is placed below a heading, for example, the larger bottom margin of a heading overrides the smaller top margin of a paragraph. It is common to modify some of these margins with CSS. By defining the bottom margin of 0 for <h1> tags, any subsequent paragraph or heading's top margin will determine the spacing between the elements.

6. **Click OK to return to the document.**

   The first paragraph in the text — which is formatted with the <h1> tag — is affected by the new selector definition.

We sampled this color for the h1 tag selector.

7. **Create another tag selector for the <h2> tag, using the following settings:**

   font-size: 16px

   font-style: italic

   margin: 0px (all four sides)

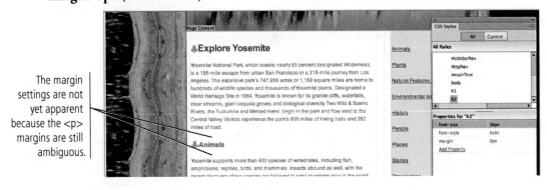

The margin settings are not yet apparent because the <p> margins are still ambiguous.

8. **Create another tag selector for the <p> tag, using the following settings:**

> margin-top: 5px
>
> margin-bottom: 5px

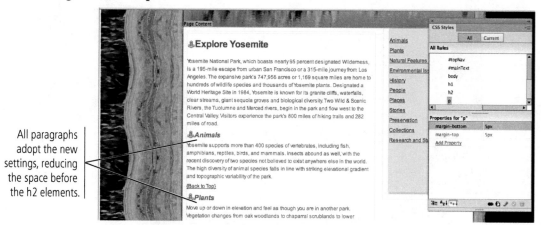

All paragraphs adopt the new settings, reducing the space before the h2 elements.

9. **Edit the h2 selector to add a 10px margin to only the top edge.**

In many cases, editing one tag selector will clarify a need to edit another selector. It is easy to make these adjustments by manipulating the selectors in the attached CSS file.

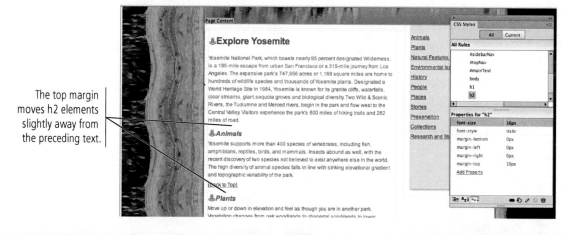

The top margin moves h2 elements slightly away from the preceding text.

CSS Mode of the Properties Panel

You can easily make changes to CSS rules using the options in the CSS mode of the Properties panel:

- Targeted Rule shows the CSS rule applied to the current selection. You can also choose a different target rule in the attached menu, or choose New CSS Rule from the menu to create a new selector.

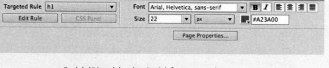

- Edit Rule opens the CSS Rule Definition dialog box for the targeted rule.

- CSS Panel opens the CSS Styles panel and displays properties for the targeted rule in Current view.

- Font, Size, and Color change the associated options in the targeted rule.

- Bold (B) adds the bold font-weight property to the targeted rule.

- Italic (I) adds the italic font-style property to the targeted rule.

- Align Left, Align Center, Align Right, and Justify change the text-align property of the targeted rule.

10. **Add another tag selector for the <a> tag, using the following settings:**

   color: sample an orange color from the background image

   text-decoration: none

All links on the pages are affected.

11. **Close the HTML file. When asked, click Save to save your changes to the master.css file.**

   You did not change the actual HTML file, so you don't need to save it when you close it. However, you did make changes to the related master.css file. Dreamweaver recognizes the changes in this file even though it isn't technically open, so you are asked to save the CSS file changes before you close the open file.

12. **Open things_to_do.html. Scroll and review the document content.**

   This file includes several additional HTML tags that are not included in the index file. You need to define additional selectors for those.

13. **Create new tag selectors as follows:**

h3	font-size: 13px
	font-weight: bold
	margin-top: 10px
	margin-bottom: 0px
ul	margin-top: 5px
	margin-bottom: 5px
li	margin-bottom: 5px

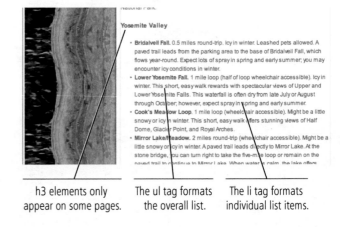

h3 elements only appear on some pages.   The ul tag formats the overall list.   The li tag formats individual list items.

14. **Close things_to_do.html, saving the changes to master.css when asked.**

15. **Open things_to_know.html and review the page content. Create new tag selectors as follows:**

      table   **width: 450px**

      th   **font-weight: bold**

              text-align: left

              border-bottom-color: orange (from the background image)

              border-bottom-style: solid

              border-bottom-width: 1px

      td   **border-bottom-color: use the same color as the th tag**

              border-bottom-style: solid

              border-bottom-width: 1px

Note:

The text-align property is in the Block category of the CSS Rule Definition dialog box.

| The table tag affects the overall table. | The th tag formats table header cells. | The td tag formats regular table cells. |

16. **Close things_to_know.html, saving the changes to master.css when asked.**

17. **Open things_to_see.html and review the page content.**

This file does not include any additional tags that need to be defined. However, it is always a good idea to review each page in a site to see if changes are necessary.

Note:

If you hide visual aids, you will be better able to see the table-cell borders.

18. **Close things_to_see.html, and then continue to the next exercise.**

CREATE DESCENDANT SELECTORS

Three items remain in the list of known formatting requirements:

- Navigation links in the header area should be bold, and should appear entirely above the line that separates the header from the main page image.

- The sidebar links should be centered, and use the same color as the page background.

- Footer text should be light gray and centered.

- All links should switch to a lighter color when the mouse rolls over them.

Each of these items refers to content in a specific area of the page. To meet these requirements without affecting similar tags in other areas, you need to define **descendant selectors**, which are a type of compound selector, to format certain elements only within a specific div tag.

1. **Open design.dwt from the Yosemite site Templates folder.**

Although it isn't necessary to be able to select an object in the layout to define CSS selectors, it can be helpful to be able to select something so you can see what tags affect it. In order to select objects or text in non-editable regions of this site, you need to open the actual template file.

2. Place the insertion point anywhere in the topNav link text, then click the New CSS Rule button at the bottom of the CSS Styles panel.

Although you are using this selector to format content in a specific tag (the **<a>** or link tag), you also have to identify where the specific links are located on the page. If you don't use a compound selector to format this element, you would change the appearance of every link in the site instead of only the links in the top navigation area.

Note:

You can click the More Specific button to add nested IDs into the current selector name.

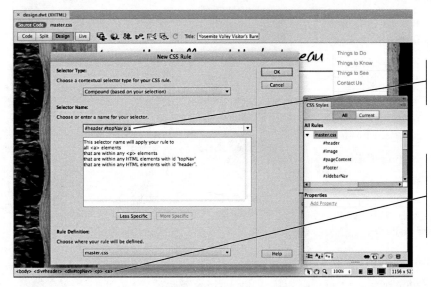

By default, the Selector Name field automatically includes the full path to the active tag.

The insertion point is in the link text <a> that is in a paragraph <p> that is in the topNav div <div#topNav>, which is nested within the header div <div#header>.

3. Click the Less Specific button below the information pane to remove the first part of the selector name.

This button removes elements from the beginning of the path; each click makes the name less specific. To keep the code short and the selector name easy to read, you are making the descendant selector only as specific as necessary to get the job done.

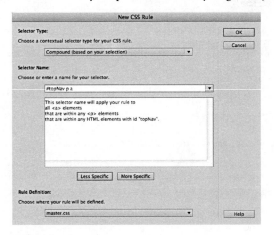

4. Delete the p tag from the selector name.

This tag should format all links in the topNav div, regardless of whether they exist within a paragraph. You can simply remove that character to make the selector less specific.

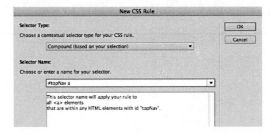

5. **Make sure master.css is selected in the Rule Definition menu, then click OK.**

6. **In the Type category, change the font-weight to bold. Click OK to create the new compound selector.**

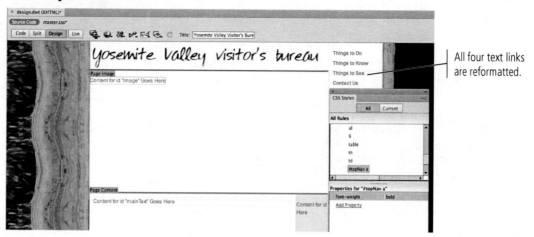

All four text links are reformatted.

7. **Open the index.html file and review the page content.**

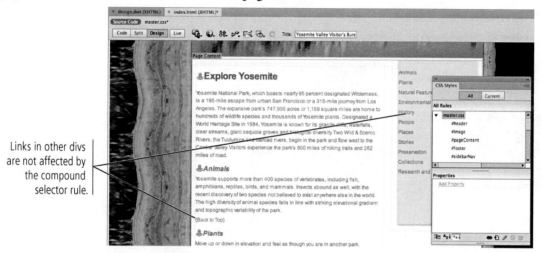

Links in other divs are not affected by the compound selector rule.

8. **With index.html active, click the New CSS Rule button in the CSS Styles panel. In the New CSS Rule dialog box, choose Compound in the Selector Type menu and type #header img in the Selector Name field. Make sure master.css is selected in the Rule Definition menu and click OK.**

If you select an element in the page, the Selector Name field of the New CSS Rule dialog box is already filled with the path to the selected tag. However, it is not necessary to first select the object you want to modify. You can simply type the appropriate compound selector name — in this case, #header img — in the field.

Note:

You are using a descendant selector here because you only want to affect this logo image. Other images in the site, including the main page image, should not have the large top padding applied.

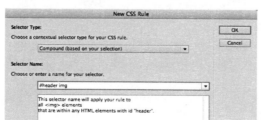

9. **Define the following settings for the new selector:**

> **border-width: 0px**
>
> **margin-top: 55px**

Note:

The border-width property removes the border that is added to image links by default in some browsers.

Increasing the image padding increases the containing div height.

10. **Create another compound selector named #sidebarNav a using the following settings:**

> **font-size: 13px**
>
> **font-weight: bold**
>
> **color: sample the green color from the page background**

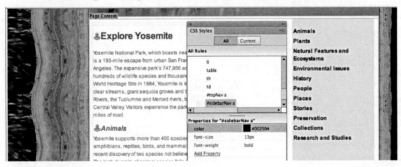

11. **Create another compound selector named #sidebarNav p using the following settings:**

> **margin-bottom: 12px**
>
> **text-align: center**

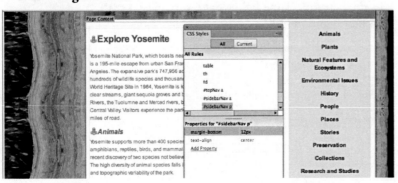

12. Create another compound selector named `#footer p` using the following settings:

> color: #999

> text-align: center

13. Save all HTML and CSS files, then continue to the next exercise.

 ## CREATE PSEUDO-CLASS SELECTORS

One item remains on your list of things to do:

- Text links should switch to a lighter color when the mouse rolls over the link.

A **class selector** is used when the same style needs to be applied to more than one element in a page. Unlike an ID selector, which is used only once per page, a class selector is used to repeat the same style throughout the page.

As you should remember from the previous exercise, controlling the default appearance of link text is accomplished with the <a> tag selector. To affect the rollover behavior, you have to define **pseudo-classes** (or variants) of the <a> selector. The five pseudo-class selectors relevant to different appearances of links are:

- **a:link** refers to a hyperlink that has not yet been visited.

- **a:visited** refers to a hyperlink that has been visited.

- **a:hover** refers to a hyperlink when the mouse pointer is hovering over the link.

- **a:focus** refers to a hyperlink that has been given "focus," such as when a user presses the Tab key to move through links on a page. This pseudo-class does not appear in Dreamweaver's list, but can be typed in manually.

- **a:active** refers to an active hyperlink (in other words: when the link is clicked before the mouse button is released).

1. With **index.html** open, click the New CSS Rule button in the CSS Styles panel.

2. Choose Compound in the Selector Type menu, then open the Selector Name menu and choose a:hover.

For a compound selector, this menu shows the four pseudo-classes that can be defined for the <a> tag, as well as paths to any selected elements. The hover pseudo-class determines what happens when the cursor moves (hovers) over link text.

Note:

For them to work correctly in all Web browsers, these pseudo-class selectors should be ordered as follows in the CSS file:

> *link*

> *visited*

> *hover*

> *focus*

> *active*

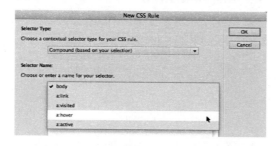

3. **Make sure master.css is selected in the Rule Definition menu and click OK.**

4. **In the Type options, change the color field to a light orange color sampled from the background image.**

5. **Click OK to create the new selector and return to the document.**

6. **With index.html active, switch to Live view, then test the rollover property of the links in the topNav, main, and footer areas.**

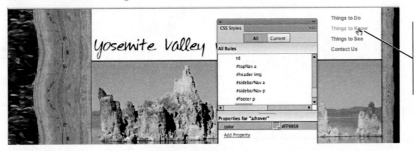

The a:hover selector changes the color of the topNav links, links in the main body, and links in the footer.

7. **Create another new compound selector for the a:hover pseudo-class within the sidebarNav div. Change the type color to a light green sampled from the background image.**

When you choose the a:hover pseudo-class in the menu, the existing selector name is replaced with the pseudo-class name. To change the pseudo-class of links only within a certain div, you have to type the div's ID in front of the pseudo-class name (or type the pseudo-class after an existing compound selector name). The full name of the new selector should be #sidebarNav a:hover.

By adding the ID selector to the pseudo-class, you are defining the behavior for links in the sidebarNav area only. You need to create this selector separately because you have already defined the color of links in this area to be different than the color value defined in the primary **<a>** tag selector.

8. **With Live view active, test the rollover property of the links in the sidebarNav area.**

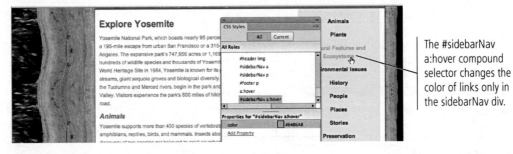

The #sidebarNav a:hover compound selector changes the color of links only in the sidebarNav div.

9. **Save any open files and close them.**

10. **Export a site definition named `Yosemite.ste` into your WIP>Yosemite folder, and then remove the Yosemite site from Dreamweaver.**

If necessary, refer back to Project 6: Bistro Site Organization for complete instructions on exporting a site definition or removing a site from Dreamweaver.

Project Review

fill in the blank

1. A(n) _____ is a flat image placed in the background of a page, used as a guide for reassembling the component pieces of the page.

2. A(n) _____ is the formal name of a CSS rule.

3. Using the _____ mode of the CSS Styles panel simplifies the panel to show only properties and values related to a selection.

4. Click the _____ button in the CSS Styles panel to define an external CSS file that should be used for the active page.

5. A(n) _____ selector type is used to control unique div elements.

6. A(n) _____ selector type is used to format specific HTML tags.

7. A(n) _____ selector type can be used to format specific tags only within a certain div.

8. The _____ property can be used to attach an object to the right or left side of the containing object.

9. The _____ property exists inside the container; background properties of the container extend into this area.

10. The _____ exists around the container; background properties of the container do not extend into this area.

short answer

1. Briefly explain two reasons why CSS is the preferred method for creating a Web page layout.

2. Briefly explain the difference between external, embedded, and inline styles.

3. Briefly explain how padding, margin, and border properties relate to the CSS box model.

Portfolio Builder Project

Use what you learned in this project to complete the following freeform exercise.
Carefully read the art director and client comments, then create your own design to meet the needs of the project.
Use the space below to sketch ideas; when finished, write a brief explanation of your reasoning behind your final design.

art director comments

Every professional Web designer needs a portfolio to display their work to prospective clients. By completing the projects in this book, you have created a number of different examples that showcase your Photoshop, Flash, and Dreamweaver CS6 skills.

The projects in this book were specifically designed to include a wide variety of skills and techniques, as well as different types of projects for different types of clients. Your portfolio should follow the same basic principle, offering a variety of samples of both creative and technical skills.

client comments

For this project, you are your own client. Using the following suggestions, gather your work and create your own portfolio.

❏ If possible, set up your own domain name to host your portfolio site. If you can't set up a personal domain name, use a free subdomain name from an established server company.

❏ Include links to files or sites you have created, whether the pages are kept in folders of your own domain or posted on other public servers.

❏ If you can't include links to certain sites, take screen shots and post those images on your site.

❏ For each sample site you include, add a brief description or explanation of your role in creating the site. (Did you design it? What techniques were used to build the site?)

❏ Be sure to include full contact information in a prominent location on your site.

project justification

_____
_____
_____
_____
_____
_____
_____
_____
_____
_____
_____
_____
_____
_____

Cascading style sheets offer tremendous flexibility when you are designing the look and feel of a Web site. By linking multiple HTML files to a single external CSS file — with or without an HTML page template — you can experiment with options by altering the CSS selectors and immediately seeing the effect on all linked pages. In addition to this flexibility, CSS is also compliant with current Web design standards, which means pages designed with CSS are both search-engine and accessibility-software friendly.

By completing this project, you have worked with different types of selectors to control both the layout of an HTML page and the formatting attributes of different elements on different pages in the site. The site structure is entirely controlled by the selectors in the linked CSS file, so you could change the appearance of the entire site without ever touching the individual HTML pages. And the inverse is also true — you can change the content of individual pages without affecting the site structure.

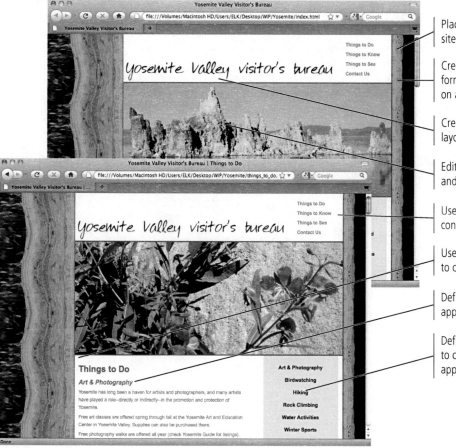

Place a tracing image to review site design requirements

Create an external CSS file to format multiple pages (based on a template file)

Create ID selectors to define layout elements (divs)

Edit CSS rules to adjust layout and content formatting

Use the float property to control nested div positioning

Use margin and padding options to control content positioning

Define tag selectors to control the appearance of specific HTML tags

Define pseudo-class selectors to control the alternate appearance of link text

Use our portfolio to build yours.

The Against The Clock Professional
Portfolio Series walks you step-by-step
through the tools and techniques of
graphic design professionals.

Order online at www.againsttheclock.com
Use code **PFS712** for a 10% discount

Go to **www.againsttheclock.com** to enter our
monthly drawing for a free book of your choice.